Human Rights, Public Values, and Leadership in Healthcare Policy

Augustine Nduka Eneanya
University of Lagos, Nigeria

A volume in the Advances in Healthcare Information Systems and Administration (AHISA) Book Series

IGI Global
DISSEMINATOR OF KNOWLEDGE

Published in the United States of America by
IGI Global
Medical Information Science Reference (an imprint of IGI Global)
701 E. Chocolate Avenue
Hershey PA, USA 17033
Tel: 717-533-8845
Fax: 717-533-8661
E-mail: cust@igi-global.com
Web site: http://www.igi-global.com

Library of Congress Cataloging-in-Publication Data

Names: Eneanya, Augustine Nduka, editor.
Title: Human rights, public values, and leadership in healthcare policy / Augustine Nduka Eneanya, editor.
Description: Hershey PA : Medical Information Science Reference, [2019] | Includes bibliographical references.
Identifiers: LCCN 2018001688| ISBN 9781522561330 (hardcover) | ISBN 9781522561347 (ebook)
Subjects: | MESH: Delivery of Health Care--ethics | Delivery of Health Care--economics | Human Rights Abuses | Health Policy | Leadership | Nigeria | Africa
Classification: LCC RA552.N5 | NLM W 84 HN5 | DDC 362.109669--dc23 LC record available at https://lccn.loc.gov/2018001688

This book is published in the IGI Global book series Advances in Healthcare Information Systems and Administration (AHISA) (ISSN: 2328-1243; eISSN: 2328-126X)

British Cataloguing in Publication Data
A Cataloguing in Publication record for this book is available from the British Library.

Advances in Healthcare Information Systems and Administration (AHISA) Book Series

ISSN:2328-1243
EISSN:2328-126X

Editor-in-Chief: Anastasius Moumtzoglou, Hellenic Society for Quality & Safety in Healthcare and P. & A. Kyriakou Children's Hospital, Greece

MISSION

The **Advances in Healthcare Information Systems and Administration (AHISA) Book Series** aims to provide a channel for international researchers to progress the field of study on technology and its implications on healthcare and health information systems. With the growing focus on healthcare and the importance of enhancing this industry to tend to the expanding population, the book series seeks to accelerate the awareness of technological advancements of health information systems and expand awareness and implementation.

Driven by advancing technologies and their clinical applications, the emerging field of health information systems and informatics is still searching for coherent directing frameworks to advance health care and clinical practices and research. Conducting research in these areas is both promising and challenging due to a host of factors, including rapidly evolving technologies and their application complexity. At the same time, organizational issues, including technology adoption, diffusion and acceptance as well as cost benefits and cost effectiveness of advancing health information systems and informatics applications as innovative forms of investment in healthcare are gaining attention as well. **AHISA** addresses these concepts and critical issues.

COVERAGE

- Role of informatics specialists
- Nursing Expert Systems
- Medical informatics
- Decision Support Systems
- Telemedicine
- IT Applications in Health Organizations and Practices
- IT Applications in Physical Therapeutic Treatments
- Management of Emerging Health Care Technologies
- Rehabilitative Technologies
- Clinical Decision Support Design, Development and Implementation

IGI Global is currently accepting manuscripts for publication within this series. To submit a proposal for a volume in this series, please contact our Acquisition Editors at Acquisitions@igi-global.com or visit: http://www.igi-global.com/publish/.

The Advances in Healthcare Information Systems and Administration (AHISA) Book Series (ISSN 2328-1243) is published by IGI Global, 701 E. Chocolate Avenue, Hershey, PA 17033-1240, USA, www.igi-global.com. This series is composed of titles available for purchase individually; each title is edited to be contextually exclusive from any other title within the series. For pricing and ordering information please visit http://www.igi-global.com/book-series/advances-healthcare-information-systems-administration/37156. Postmaster: Send all address changes to above address.

Titles in this Series

For a list of additional titles in this series, please visit:
https://www.igi-global.com/book-series/advances-healthcare-information-systems-administration/37156

Contemporary Applications of Mobile Computing in Healthcare Settings
R. Rajkumar (VIT University, India)
Medical Information Science Reference • ©2018 • 259pp • H/C (ISBN: 9781522550365) • US $205.00

Handbook of Research on Emerging Perspectives on Healthcare Information Systems ...
Joseph Tan (McMaster University, Canada)
Medical Information Science Reference • ©2018 • 641pp • H/C (ISBN: 9781522554608) • US $355.00

Big Data Analytics in HIV/AIDS Research
Ali Al Mazari (Alfaisal University, Saudi Arabia)
Medical Information Science Reference • ©2018 • 294pp • H/C (ISBN: 9781522532033) • US $215.00

Advanced Systems for Improved Public Healthcare and Disease Prevention...
Thierry Oscar Edoh (Technical University of Munich, Germany)
Medical Information Science Reference • ©2018 • 262pp • H/C (ISBN: 9781522555285) • US $185.00

Global Perspectives on Health Communication in the Age of Social Media
Seif Sekalala (Kean University, USA) and Brandon C. Niezgoda (Drexel University, USA)
Medical Information Science Reference • ©2018 • 348pp • H/C (ISBN: 9781522537168) • US $225.00

Healthcare Administration for Patient Safety and Engagement
Aleksandra Rosiek-Kryszewska (Nicolaus Copernicus University, Poland) and Krzysztof Leksowski (Military Clinical Hospital, Poland & Nicolaus Copernicus University, Poland)
Medical Information Science Reference • ©2018 • 343pp • H/C (ISBN: 9781522539469) • US $235.00

For an entire list of titles in this series, please visit:
https://www.igi-global.com/book-series/advances-healthcare-information-systems-administration/37156

IGI Global
DISSEMINATOR OF KNOWLEDGE

701 East Chocolate Avenue, Hershey, PA 17033, USA
Tel: 717-533-8845 x100 • Fax: 717-533-8661
E-Mail: cust@igi-global.com • www.igi-global.com

Table of Contents

Detailed Table of Contents

The main thrust of the chapter was to explore the discrimination experienced by people living with HIV and AIDS (PLHIV) in the workplace in Lagos State. A purposive sample of 80 PLHIV was selected from two local government areas (LGAs) of Lagos state: Epe, a rural setting, and Lagos Mainland, an urban one. Secondary data were obtained from internet sources while primary data were collected through structured interviews September 2005–April 2006. Data were analyzed using SPSS versions 11 and 13. Data between and within the rural and urban areas were also analyzed comparatively. The results indicate that PLHIV experienced instant dismissal from offices, mandatory HIV tests, alienation, denial of promotion, and exclusion from insurance schemes. This indicates that PLHIV's rights were violated. The study recommends intensive HIV education and enforcement of national HIV policy and international legal instruments in the workplace to protect PLHIV's rights.

Health institution is a typology of formal organization that is designed manifestly to ensure the diagnosis, treatment, and rehabilitation of the sick and the wounded. There are three levels of health institutions in Nigeria: the primary, secondary, and the tertiary/specialist care organizations. Their clienteles range from the infants, very young, adolescents, middle-aged, and the very old afflicted with acute or chronic health conditions, contagious or non-communicable disorders. A number of healthcare workers are involved in the process of patients/clients' care and treatment. The process and the divergent human resources in the healthcare industry tend to throw up "red-tapism" and complex bottlenecks resulting from specialization, hierarchy of authority, and chains of command of bureaucracy. The chapter relying on guided participant observation, desk research, and key informants interrogated this phenomenon. The chapter concludes that if bureaucracy is tamed, there is bound to be better health outcome for health consumers in health institutions in Nigeria.

Section 2
Human Rights, Public Values, and Health Policies

The health of a people is a major social capital to be prioritized and optimized for the growth and development of any country. Therefore, any government desirous of development should make healthcare delivery one of the cornerstones of its policy on development. In pursuance of these goals, the purpose of this chapter is to examine the dominant policy value, particularly the failure to faithfully implement government policies and achieve set goals. The method applied in the study is participant observatory method, using the basic need theory (BNT) as theoretical framework of analysis. The findings revealed that policy values frustrate the attainment of sustainable primary healthcare delivery in Nigeria. Challenges were highlighted such as improper monitoring and evaluation of policies, inadequate funding, program implementation, and lack of skilled professionals. The chapter concludes by suggesting opportunities to open primary healthcare delivery in the rural areas.

Forty-two states have considered a mandatory vaccination for school-age girls, but the proposed legislation is most often met with hostility and it rarely succeeds. Using newspaper articles from Arizona, Colorado, the District of Columbia, Georgia, Texas, and Virginia during these legislative sessions, narrative analysis is used to find common themes in the debate, including a medical/clinical approach, "government to the rescue," individual cost constraint/access issues, logical narrative, sexuality/morality issues, parental rights, vaccination ethics, skepticism, and negative assumptions toward African-American girls. Using Schneider and Ingram's social construction theory, further discussion points to a better understanding of the target populations of this public policy. In reviewing this health policy debate, it is suggested that considerations go beyond the perceived health benefits of the policy and spill over into the civil and social welfare rights of the legislation.

The chapter explores and describes community participation in the National Development Plan through Primary Health Care by using case studies of LGBT organizations in South Africa. Post-Apartheid and democratic South Africa has endorsed community participation as one of the fundamental pillars of the public Primary Health Care approach in its governance structures. This chapter focuses on the current major health issue in South Africa, the HIV epidemic, which is one of the leading causes of death in the country. Particular attention is paid to members of the LGBT community because of their discrimination in public healthcare facilities on grounds of their sexual orientation. The chapter relies on secondary sources of data collection from extant literature, textbooks, journal articles, and internet sources. Challenges to address LGBT community discrimination in HIV testing, prevention, treatment, care, and support were identified and solutions to uphold their human rights were proffered. These solutions are based on the principles of social justice, inclusion, diversity, and equality.

Persisting absence of human rights, widening inequality, and social justice in healthcare delivery systems within and between countries present significant challenges to the focus and practice of contemporary public health. This chapter compares how cases of human rights, equity, and social justice are integrated in America's and Nigeria's healthcare policies. Qualitative research and case study design were adopted. Data were collected from secondary sources, such as reviewed literature, textbooks, journal articles, government reports, and internet. Content and critical case studies analysis methods were utilized to analyze, explain, and compare America's and Nigeria's health policies. Findings reveal absence of human rights, equity, and social justice among sub-groups in healthcare service delivery in America and Nigeria. The chapter concludes by suggesting that human rights, equity, and social justice should be integrated into health policies of America and Nigeria in order to make access to healthcare service delivery a right for citizens.

Section 3
Value-Based Leadership and Health Systems

Foreword

The search for the role of valued-based leadership and ethical policies in public health has gained momentum globally. Studies have focused on attributes of specific national health policies and systems rather than the role of human rights, ethics and social justice in policy development process. Drawing from these previous studies, human rights, ethics and social justice can be viewed as an integral component of health systems development. Crucial in this is knowledge of society which differs from knowledge of diseases or nature and society interactions.

The notion of social justice often plays an important role in public health policy and is usually applied out of a concern for equity. The concern for human rights and equity is to ensure that rights to health are fairly distributed within the population, reducing as much as possible the extent to which people's health status and life-span are determined by morally and arbitrary attributes, such as race, ethnicity or socio-economic status.

The right to the highest attainable standard of health requires a set of social criteria that is conducive to the health of all people, including the availability of health services, safe working conditions, adequate housing and nutritious foods. Achieving the right to health is closely related to that of other human rights, including the right to food, housing, work, education, non-discrimination, access to information and participation. The right to health includes both freedoms and entitlements. Freedoms include the right to control one's health and body and to be free from interference from non-consensual medical treatment and experimentation. Entitlements include the right to a system of health protection that gives everyone an equal opportunity to enjoy the highest attainable level of health. Violations or lack of attention to human rights can have serious health consequences. Overt or implicit discrimination in the delivery of health services violates fundamental human rights.

The goal of leaderships in the development of national health policies and strategies, therefore, is to achieve universal health coverage based on public values, such as: human rights, ethics, social justice and equity. These values are often neglected by leaders when designing health policies and programmes with negative health outcomes consequences. Leaderships in health sectors developing policies and programmes have the ability to either promote or violate human rights, including the right to health, depending on the way the health policies are designed or implemented. It is, therefore, the responsibility of leaderships in governance to design national health policies and programmes that respect and protect human rights, rectify inequalities and discrimination practices, which are often at the heart of inequitable health outcomes in the society.

This book, therefore, is a compendium of well-researched articles on vexing issues on human rights, public values and leadership in health policy-making. It tackles healthcare issues on human rights, its abuses, discrimination, marginalization and inequity in healthcare service delivery. The reading public, researchers, consultants, students, health professionals and practitioners and other general readers will find these narratives, empirical findings and their solutions very attractive to read.

Solomon O. Akinboye
University of Lagos, Nigeria

Preface

The legitimacy of any national health system depends on how best it serves the interest of the poorest and most vulnerable people, for which improvements in their health status gear towards the realization of poverty reduction goals. The world's most disadvantaged people are missing out on even the most basic health services. World Health Organization report in 2015 revealed that more than 400 million people around the world do not have access to essential health services, and many of them are in Sub-Saharan Africa, where the resources are needed. Health policies and programs which are supposed to provide quality health services for the poorest people, women, children, people living in rural areas and those in minority group are non-existent. Gaps in health coverage problems with access to health care and unhealthy lifestyles are thought to contribute to the many disappointingly poor health outcomes recorded in most parts of the world.

The relative high costs and poor health outcomes that characterize the performance of health systems in developed and developing countries are the result of many factors. These factors include poverty, lack of universal health coverage, a general lack of focus on primary care and public health, high rates of accidents, violence and teenage pregnancy and poor health behaviors.

The World Health organization's constitution states that the highest attainable standard of health is a fundamental right of every human being. The right to health includes access to timely, acceptable and affordable health care of appropriate quality. Yet, about 100 million people globally are pushed below the poverty line and discriminated in terms of access to quality healthcare because of healthcare expenditure every year. Overt or implicit discrimination in the delivery of health services violates fundamental human rights. Violations of human rights have serious health consequences.

Current health polices debates or reforms in most countries of the world focus on extending universal health coverage, decreasing the growth of costs through improved efficiency and expanding prevention and wellness of programs. A commitment to equity is at the heart of universal health coverage. Health policies and programs should focus on providing quality health services for the poorest people and minority groups living in rural areas.

Vulnerable and marginalized groups in societies tend to bear an undue proportion of health problems. Within countries – some populations – such as indigenous communities are exposed to greater rates of ill-health and face significant obstacles to accessing quality and affordable healthcare. This population has substantially higher mortality and morbidity rates due to communicable diseases such as – malaria, HIV /AIDs and tuberculosis and non-communicable diseases, such as cancer, cardiovascular and chronic respiratory diseases. People who are particularly vulnerable to HIV infection-including young women, men who have sex with men, and injecting drug users – are often characterized by social and economic disadvantage and discrimination. These vulnerable populations may also be the subject of laws and policies that further compound this marginalization and make it harder to access prevention and care services.

Health policies and programs, therefore, have the ability to violate human rights, including the right to health, depending on the way they are designed or implemented. Leaders in developed and developing countries, therefore, have the responsibilities to address issues of human rights, ethics, equity and social justice in policy-making process.

CHALLENGES

The major challenges faced by most developed and developing countries' health systems focus on three-core public values, namely: universal health coverage, cost (expenditure) and quality. These core values compete for attention in the health care arena for their containment. The last decade has witnessed the emergence of many government initiatives and reform proposals that seek to diminish the oft noted trade-offs among these values. Various leaders of developed and developing countries have sought to enhance access to higher quality care while containing costs. For example, the US health system does not have a uniform health system, and has no universal health care coverage. It operates a hybrid system like Nigeria. In USA, for instance, the Affordable Care Act (ACA) enacted in 2010 was promoted as a way of achieving universal health insurance coverage. In 2014 approximately "32.9 million people in the U.S. had no health insurance" (Smith & Medalia, 2015, p. 5). However, the market-based health insurance system in the United States has caused a human rights crisis that deprives a large number of people of the health care they need. The most visible problem is the 32.9 million people without health insurance and the number of preventable deaths of up to 101,000 per year (National Economic and Social Rights Initiative, 2018) that cannot be avoided due to the way the health care system is organized.

This crisis has persisted despite available resources to protect the right to health, record levels of health care, spending and repeated health reform efforts. Since social determinants, such as race, income and environment, strongly influence who becomes ill and who receives access to quality care, the health crisis disproportionately affects disadvantaged groups and under-resourced communities, such as people living in poverty, people of color, and immigrants. Yet, barriers to accessing care, the burden of medical debt and the shortage of primary care providers affect all people, including those with employer-sponsored insurance.

In Sub-Saharan Africa, despites Abuja declaration of African countries allocating 15 percent of budgets to health sector, cost constitutes another barrier to access to quality health care. Among other African countries, Nigeria lagged behind on expenditure to health sector. With 15 percent of GDP as benchmark showed that (WHO, 2015): Rwanda committed 18 percent, South Africa 18 percent; Botswana 17.8 percent, Niger 17.8 percent Malawi 17.1, Zambia 16. 4 percent and Burkina Faso 15. 8 percent. Since 2012, Nigeria budgetary allocation to healthy sector has been at best 6 percent of GDP to health sector. Even in 2016 budget, 4.12 percent was allocated to health sector. Nigeria's expenditure on health sector is below 15 percent set by Abuja declaration of 2001 benchmark (Edeh, 2016, p. 10). These data point to one issue – under funding in health sector, resulting in poverty and poor health outcomes. For example, WHO (2015) showed that Nigeria's under-five mortality rate still remained very high at 109 per 1000 live births. Preventive infectious disease, "such as malaria, pneumonia, diarrhea, measles and HIV/AIDS account for more than 70 percent of the estimated one million under-five deaths in Nigeria" (Edeh, 2016, p. 10).

On the issue of quality, quality improvement is constrained by the supply and access to primary care providers. In Nigeria, the quality of health services leaves much to be desired.

Nigerians suffer from inadequate numbers of skill health workers. Medical doctor's population ratio per 100,000 as at 2013, rates 38.9 per 100,000 (National Health Policy, 2016). This has led to some people seeking care outside the country, such as: Dubai, India, US, United Kingdom and others. Certain services are not generally available to a large percentage of the population. Many health facilities are situated far away from the people, especially in rural and hard-to-reach areas. The most common barriers to accessing health services by the population are the cost of services, distance to health facilities and inadequate skilled health personnel and professionals. Besides, there is inequality in access to services due to socio-economic status and geographic location.

SEARCHING FOR SOLUTION

In response to these challenges, countries in developed and developing countries should increase government's health expenditure, which is vital to support progress towards universal healthcare coverage, and especially, subsidizing the cost of services for poor population. A commitment to equity is at the heart of universal health coverage. Investment in medical care expenses make a substantial difference in health system's performance and health outcomes. Increase in health expenditure will not only improve health, it will reduce health disparities, subsidize households from impoverishment due to medical cost and respect dignity of patient in terms of human rights.

Health policies and programs should focus on providing quality health services for the poorest people, women and children, people living in rural areas and those from minority groups. Taking steps to respect and protect human rights among these vulnerable and marginalized people in the society would assist the health sectors in developed and developing countries of the world to address the problem of universal health coverage.

A human right – based policy-making approach to healthcare service delivery would provide strategies and solutions to address and rectify inequalities, discriminatory practices and unjust power relations, which are often at the heart of inequitable health outcomes. Such policies and programs would be responsive to the needs of the population in the area of non-discrimination in terms of race, color, sex, language, religion and so on. It would provide sufficient quantity and quality of functioning public healthcare facilities, goods and services; physical, affordability and information accessibility on medical products and services; and universal health coverage, which will make all people everywhere in the world to be entitled to health care. And states and other duty – bearers would be answerable for the observance of human rights contained in the national health policy as World Health Organization (WHO) is strengthening the capacity of its member states to integrate a human-rights-based approach to health at both national and regional levels. Furthermore, there is prospects of advancing the right to health in international law and international policy development processes following different initiatives and reforms being undertaken all over the world. In addition, it is the responsibility of World Health Organization to actively strengthen its role in providing political leadership on the right to health movement.

ORGANIZATION OF THE BOOK

This book is organized into 12 chapters. A brief description of each of the chapters are as follows:

Chapter 1 examines mighty issues with respect to Ebola outbreak in West Africa as they collide with state actions to combat infectious diseases. It concludes that the threats posed by infectious diseases like the Ebola Virus Disease (EVD) are now seen as universally relevant, as the speed and volume of international travel has made the outbreak potential threat to anywhere else.

Chapter 2 explores the discrimination experienced by people living with HIV and AIDS (PLHIV) in the workplace in Lagos State. Findings in the chapter indicates that PLHIV experienced instant dismissal from offices, mandatory HIV tests, alienation, denial of promotion and exclusion from insurance schemes. These findings showed that human rights of PLHIV were violated by their employers and colleagues. The chapter recommends intensive HIV education and enforcement of nation HIV policy.

Chapter 3, using guided participant observation, desk research and key informants, interrogated the phenomenon of "red-tapes" and complex bottlenecks resulting from specialization, hierarchy of authority and chains of command of bureaucracy involved in the process of patient/client's care and health treatment and suggested the bureaucratic bottleneck should be tamed.

Chapter 4 examines the sources of healthcare financing in Zambia used in providing and protecting health facilities that would guarantee people's rights to access quality healthcare that would produce positive health outcomes. The chapter revealed that government expenditure is less than expected target and reliance is on donor financing and out-of-pocket health expenditure by citizens. As such, there is inequality in the health care facilities in Zambia. The chapter recommends that expenditure for health sector should be increased.

Chapter 5 examines how primary healthcare policies affect health system's performance and health outcomes in Nigeria. It concludes that health outcomes remain poor because of weak health system as infant and maternal mortality still remain high and universal access coverage low. The chapter concludes that strong health system would improve health outcomes.

Chapter 6 examines the dominant policy value particularly the failure to faithfully implement government policies and achieve set goals. Though, challenges abound, findings revealed that policy values frustrate the attainment of sustainable primary healthcare delivery in Nigeria. The chapter recommends that local governments should be financially empowered to implement Primary health Centers' affairs.

Chapter 7, using social construction theory and narrative analysis method, examines 42 states' mandatory vaccination of school-age girls. The chapter reviewing this health policy debates concluded that beyond perceived health benefits of the policy, civil and welfare right of the legislation should be considered.

Chapter 8 focuses on the current major health issues in South Africa, especially the HIV epidemic, which is one of the leading causes of death in the country. It explores and describes community participation in the National Development plan through primary healthcare, by using case studies of LGBT organizations in South Africa. Post-apartheid and democratic South Africa has endorsed community participation as one of the fundamental pillars of approach for its governance structure in managing health sector.

Chapter 9 compares US and Nigeria's health systems in an attempt to examine whether human rights, equity and social justice are embedded in their national health policies. It concludes that U.S. and Nigeria's health care systems failed to protect human right to health. The chapter recommended that human right, equity and social justice should be integrated into health policies of America and Nigeria in order to make access to healthcare service delivery a right for citizens.

Chapter 10 provides a discourse on the relevance of occupational health and safety systems in modern day workplaces as well as the nexus between work leadership and occupational health and safety. It concludes by recommending the role work leaders should play to improve safety and health in the workplace.

Chapter 11 analyzes the implementation process of the social organizations in management program. It focuses on the role played by factors, such as administrative and financial autonomy, direction, innovative management practices and efficiency in the management of health facilities.

Chapter 12 addresses the feasibility of Nigeria achieving target 3.1 of sustainable Development Goal 3, which aims at reducing material deaths to less than 70 per 100, 000 live births by 2030. It assesses the materials landscape of Nigeria and measures taken by the government to address material health from the perspective of the feasibility of achieving SDG 3, target 3.1 by 2030.

This book will be very useful to health practitioners/professionals, scholars, researchers, institutions, students, consultants, all stakeholders in health and health-related sectors. The book is also a good resource material for policy Advocates championing the movement on right to health.

Augustine Nduka Eneanya
University of Lagos, Nigeria
July 17, 2018

REFERENCES

Edeh, H. (2016). Sector bleeds on absent Health Act. *Businessday.* Retrieved on May 26, 2016 from www.businessdayonline.com

National Economic & Social Rights Initiative (NESRI). (2018). *Health Care in the United States.* Retrieved on May 24, 2018 from https://www.nesri.org/programs/healt-care-in-the-united-states

National Health Policy Act. (2016). Abuja: Federal Government Printing Press.

Smith, J. C., & Medalia, C. (2014). U.S. Census current population Reports, Health Insurance coverage in the United States. Washington, DC: U.S. Government Printing Office.

World Health Organization (WHO). (2015). Sub-Saharan African Lags other Regions in health care. *Businessday.* Retrieved on September 29, 2015 from www.businessdayonline.com

Acknowledgment

The ideas and approaches inspiring this book arose out of community of scholars in the field of national health policies. I acknowledge these authors and scholars whose studies added value to this book. Furthermore, I acknowledge the contributions of authors and reviewers in this book. The list of contributors and reviewers are:

Professor Fatai Badru, Professors Syed Ali, Professor Sheriff Folarin, Dr. Akhakpe Ighodalo, Dr Franca Attoh, Dr Maryam Quadri, Dr Adisa Waziri, Dr Paulo O. Vasconcelos Filho, Dr. Magdalena Denham, Dr. Leigh Hersey, Dr Idongesit Eshiet, Dr Gabriel Akinbode, Dr B. I. Malomo, Dr Chinwe Nwanna, Dr Johanannes Mampane, Dr Sylvester Dekolo, Mrs Oluwatobi Njoaguani and Professor Urooj Afshan Jabeen.

I am grateful to the Authors and reviewers. I am also grateful to the Dean of Post-graduate School, University of Lagos, Nigeria, Professor Solomon O. Akinboye for writing the forward for this book. I also thank members of Editorial Advisory Board. They include: Professor Solomon O. Akinboye, Professor Fatai Badru, Professor Syed Ali, Dr Magdalena Denham, Dr Francis E. Ndinchuwe, Professor Sheriff Folarin and Dr Vincent M. Mwange.

I equally appreciate Mrs. Amanda Fanton and Mrs Jan Travers Director of Intellectual Property and Contracts for their interventions on issues that needed urgent attention. I am grateful to members of Development teams department, and IGI - Global publishers for giving me the opportunity to serve as the Editor of this book.

Finally, I thank my wife, Mary and children for their understanding, cooperation, encouragement and patience during the development, reviewing and editing process of this book.

I hope that readers will be enriched with the research findings and knowledge revealed in this book.

Augustine Nduka Eneanya
University of Lagos, Nigeria
17th July 2018

Section 1

Human Rights, Equity, Social Justice, and Health Outcomes

Chapter 1

Global Health Governance, Human Rights, and the Control of Infectious Diseases:
A Case of the Ebola Epidemic in West Africa

Sheriff Folarin
Covenant University, Nigeria

Oluwatobi Njoaguani
Covenant University, Nigeria

ABSTRACT

The human right to the highest attainable standard of health has both a legal and normative basis. The legal foundations derive from a range of international agreements and declarations while the normative basis is rooted in humanitarianism. Alongside the rights-based declarations came the growing recognition of emerging and reemerging infectious diseases, as ill effects of globalization and potential risk to peace and development. The threats posed by infectious diseases like the Ebola virus disease (EVD) are now seen as universally relevant, as the speed and volume of international travel has made an outbreak or epidemic anywhere in the world a potential threat anywhere else. The question then arises as to where individual freedom is given up in the protection of the collective interest and national security of states. This chapter examines these right issues, with respect to the Ebola outbreak in West Africa, as they collide with state actions to combat infectious diseases.

DOI: 10.4018/978-1-5225-6133-0.ch001

INTRODUCTION

The human right to the highest attainable standard of health has both a legal and normative basis. The legal foundations derive from a range of international agreements and declarations while the normative basis is rooted in humanitarianism. Alongside the rights-based declarations, came the growing recognition of emerging and reemerging infectious diseases, as ill effects of globalization and potential risk to peace and development. The threats posed by Infectious diseases like the Ebola Virus Disease (EVD), are now seen as universally relevant, as the speed and volume of international travel has made an outbreak or epidemic anywhere in the world a potential threat anywhere else. In effect, stricter border controls and attempts to regulate migration as well as containment have been key features in states' response to the spread of infectious diseases. Historically, measures to combat infectious diseases have served as demarcation by which 'we' protect ourselves from the diseases of 'others'. These issues point to tensions between two separate rights- the right of individuals to free movement and association, and the collective right to health of societies. The latter manifests in those regulations seeking to control trans-border spread of diseases, potentially infringing on individual rights when deemed necessary.

During the Ebola outbreak in West Africa, for instance, the quarantine and isolation measures used were a restriction on the fundamental rights to movement and association of individuals. The Controversy also arose over the ethical allocation of therapies after several Americans and a Spanish national, rather than West Africans, received doses of the scarce ZMapp. More so, State governments like Liberia deployed the military to enforce a cordon sanitaire in West Point, Monrovia, and Sierra Leone declared a 3-day curfew, thereby restricting the right to movement. Moreover, The United States enforced rigorous point of entry screening and several states invoked travel bans and flight suspensions and quarantined health workers returning from the region. The question then arises as to where individual freedom is given up, in the protection of the collective interest and national security of states. Is there an ethical or legal justification for restricting the rights of few to protect the health rights of many? This chapter will be examining these right issues, with respect to the Ebola outbreak in West Africa, as they collide with state actions to combat infectious diseases.

BACKGROUND

Historically, diseases have been conferred the status of threats both to national security and national interest of states. The typhus during the Peloponnesian war, plaque in the Byzantine Roman empire, the bubonic plague of the 14th century and the cholera outbreak of 1800s, the pandemic influenza (amongst others) were responsible not only for the death of many populations across borders but were a threat to the economic and political interests of the state. Infections (especially in the case of epidemics) share features with war and can even be more dangerous as they affect combatants and civilians alike. Hence it is accepted that health outcomes transcend the biological space comprising of the individual and his body (McInnes & Lee, 2012:11). Also, health at the macro level compasses determinants like health services, income, social status, gender, education, cultural factors, working conditions, employment, social and physical environments amongst other factors. Fundamentally, the state of health and the health of the state are mutually inclusive and interdependent and the precincts between the two levels are blurring. Hence health holds an important place in interstate politics and on the international agenda (Lamy & Phua, 2012: 9). Infectious disease and health issues are leaving the confined space of national borders and often ride on the wings of globalization to increase their frequency, speed and effect. Consequently, the distinction between the global sphere and the domestic with regards to health issues (amongst others) is losing utility.

In response to the threats of diseases, especially infectious diseases, states have always attempted to govern its spread and fatality. The international sanitary Conference in Venice in 1851, the establishment of the International Sanitary Bureau in 1903 and the International Office of Public Hygiene, were first amongst the initiatives of states cooperation geared towards curbing infectious disease threats (Fidler, 2001; Fidler, 2005). Through these organizations, states established epidemiological surveillance systems with regulatory capacity for health issues, a form of bio-political arrangement for states to secure their populations from the diseases of others. More progress was said to have been made in the interwar years with the inclusion of nongovernmental agencies like the International Health Division (IHD) of the Rockefellar foundation. however, it was also in this period that the influenza pandemic dealt its greatest blow riding on the early instruments of globalization- sea travel and world trade, killing about 50 to 100 million people across the globe (Jimoh, 2015). By 1946, the World Health Organization (WHO) had been created and remains the most prominent organisation for health governance till date. The organization is at the fore of international health cooperation on a wide range of health issues including infectious and non-communicable diseases. The creation of the WHO was a milestone for global health diplomacy, signifying the institutionalization of sanitary regulations and norms for the control of infectious diseases as well as the establishment of a regulatory framework for global health governance.

Many health concerns today are often laid at the feet of globalization and its attendant deterritorialization, as diseases have no borders. It is important to note, however that while the risk of infection everywhere is multiplied, it also provides opportunities for inclusive action amongst states and non-states actors. Is it safe to say therefore that globalization fuels the fire (in this case infectious diseases) and also quenches the fire? There has been a significant increase in the number and functions of global health actors, some which have no particular health mandate (like the World Bank) and some others with health-related activities. The global health arena has therefore become fluid and diffused (Lamy & Phua, 2012,p. 9). Also, there has been an increase in the microbial traffic, medical tourism, cross border trade and health services and migration. This state in Fidler's (2004;2005) words is a "new world health order".

Brundtland (1999, p. 2) sums up the transition succinctly:

...the world has changed and that furthering national interests in health requires international cooperation. With globalization on which this nation's prosperity so much depends, all of mankind paddle in a single microbial sea- and we have to conclude that there are no health sanctuaries.

Especially with infectious disease, this assertion becomes even more germane, as infectious diseases often rely on the globalization and its attendant deterritorialization to increase their speed and scope.

CONCEPTUAL CLARIFICATION

Global Health Governance

Global Health Governance (GHG) as a concept and a regime has come to be associated with all kinds of interventions that address health issues that have trans-border implications. This web of interventions involves formal and informal activities of states and non-state actors responding to a variety of health issues across borders. The concept lies at the intersection between International Relations and Public Health. (Lamy & Phua, 2012; Yoon, 2015).

Fidler (2010) gave a rather detailed yet defining description of the term. Global health governance, he noted was the:

...use of formal and informal institutions, rules and processes by states, intergovernmental organizations, and non-state actors to deal with changes to health that require cross border collective action to address effectively.

In other words, Global health governance is both a pro-action and a reaction involving not just state actors (as in earlier regimes described as International health) but also a large array of international actors, reacting and responding to changes in health and care. A study puts the number of institutions currently engaged in health governance and financing at the global level at 203 (Hoffman, Cole & Pearcey, 2015). Specifically, Negin, Morgan and Condon (2012) recognizes 40 bilateral donors, 26 UN agencies, 20 global and regional funds and 90 global health initiatives, with many more springing up with every major outbreak.

With this growing community of health enthusiasts, comes the problem of coordination, duplication and high transaction cost. This results in multiplicity of actors and duplicity of actions oftentimes with a disconnect between global priorities and local needs. Consequently, global priorities seemed to have been imposed in an unbalanced way. In this post-Westphalia regime, as Fidler tagged it, there exist a non-hierarchical structure with near to no guidance and leadership, even by the World Health Organisation. Important to note in this chapter is the collision and sometimes confusion that exists in the GHG response to health emergencies. The global health governance regime mirrors the international system in which it is played and this anarchy also impacts on the responses to infectious disease outbreak. How then should global actors react to health emergencies of trans border health crisis? Do they react to protect the individual's right to health or the collective public health or in some cases, the interest of their home governments?

Infectious Diseases

Political attention and more health aid are often directed at infectious diseases, which are considered likely to cause illness (and even death) on a global scale, and therefore have become a matter of high politics (Davies, 2010). Infectious diseases, biologically are caused by a micro-organism which may cause high mortality or disability. However, a disease can be infectious but not communicable (that is passed on from person to person) but all communicable diseases are infectious (Davies, 2010). Ebola for example, is caused by infection with a virus of the family Filoviridae, genus *Ebolavirus* (CDC, 2016).

In 1990, about 16 million people died from infectious diseases. In 2010, the number of deaths had fallen only to 15 million (although offset with a population growth of 47%). Meanwhile, the World Health Organization (WHO) forecasts 13 million deaths attributed to infectious disease in 2050 (Dye, 2014).

The importance given to infectious diseases politically has been attributed to the different ways by which diseases have been framed by policy makers and states, as well as other actors. Amaya, Rollet and Kingah (2015) identify these narratives as security, development and human rights. We will attempt a discussion of these three frames and emphasize the human rights narrative which is a central theme in this chapter.

1. Health as Security

The early conceptualization of health and its relationship with security was narrow as the scope covered infectious diseases and its victims, whom were principally armed forces. The traditional narrative also often focused on the effect of conflict on health in terms of casualties of war, refugee health crisis and the effect on healthcare delivery, as access to hospitals and healthcare workers are often stalled during wars (McInness & Lee, 2012). However, the link between health and security is changing gradually to encompass more perspectives. The WHO takes the lead by conceptualizing the relationship, in what the institution called Public Health Security.

The 2007 WHO World Health Report defines public health security as the proactive and reactive activities needed to reduce vulnerability to acute public health events that threaten the collective health of national populations (Hwenda, Mahlathi & Maphanga, 2011, p. 2; McInness & Lee,2012, p. 130). The UN joined in on this too in her *UN Secretary General's High Level Panel on Threats, Challenges and Change* in 2002, where threats were defined as 'any event or process that leads to large scale death or lessening of life chances' (UN High Level Panel 2004, p. 2; McInness & Lee,2012, p. 131). In January 2000, the UN Security Council chose to open up the new millennium with a discussion on a health issue, HIV/AIDS, as matter for security. The 2014 NATO meeting in Wales marked an important milestone for the security narrative, as health risk were included as factors that could torpedo military planning in their operations around the world. For Davies (2010, p. 27), these various policy documents represent an attempt to abandon traditional notions of sovereignty and the uptight 'inside/outside' distinction between states. The emphasis hence is the identification and containment of transnational risk factors that could cross borders.

Hinged on the relationship of health and security is the concept of Bio-security and bio-terrorism. The concepts are vague and subject to many interpretations. Bio-security may refer to threats from the deliberate use of pathogens (McInness & Lee 2012, p. 135). Or as proposed by Lakoff and Collier (2008) biosecurity is seen in four areas which include the:

...reappearance on new diseases such as SARS; bioterrorism; the ability of fields such as synthetic biology to create new lethal organisms and the inadequacies of existing bio-safety protocols to deal with such developments; and food safety including both the contamination of food supply.

The focus on infectious diseases and bioterrorism in global health security discourse reflects the national concerns of countries actively involved in shaping the global health security agenda which is at best, one sided according to Hwenda, Mahlathi, and T. Maphanga (2011, p. 3).

A more holistic view on health and security embrace the human security perspective. Brundtand (2002 cited in McInness & Lee 2012, p. 145) sums up the relationship between health and human security:

…the levels of ill health in countries constituting the majority of the world's population pose a direct threat to their own national economic and political viability and therefore to global economic and political interests of all countries. So investing in global health is investing in national security.

2. Health as Development

The framing of health as development is based on the idea that policies and practices should improve conditions in the developing countries with the developed countries as the benchmark for measurement. The Millennium Development goals (MDGs) that 'expired' in 2015 had three out its eight goals focused on health (McInnes & Lee,2012, p. 49). It included the specific areas of controlling epidemics infectious disease, reducing child mortality and providing access to safe drinking water and adequate food to combat preventable diseases, and reducing the maternal mortality of women. The Sustainable Development Goals (SDGs) goal three is focused on achieving certain health goals by the year 2030, with such ambitious objectives to end HIV/AIDs, global maternal mortality and end preventable death of newborns.

More so, development assistance for aid is variants in the development frame. The impact of foreign health aid has however been contested

3. Health as Rights

The rights-based approach to health is highlighted in many policy documents. The Alma Ata Declaration in 1978 was a milestone for the 'right' narrative in public health discourse. The declaration stated that "health is a fundamental human right and the attainment of the highest possible level of health is a most important world –wide social goal" (McInness & Lee 2012, p. 66). The Oslo declaration, on other hand, was based on the 'recognition that life is the most fundamental of human rights and that life and health are the most precious assets' (McInness & Lee 2012, p. 66). Davies (2010, p. 67) acknowledges the grand work of Jonathan Mann (and some of his colleagues) in situating the link between Health and Rights. They argued that human rights violations (including torture) always have an impact on health and that health should take a complementary view that understand that health refers to physical, mental and social well-being. Therefore, linking health to human rights was the best mechanisms for individuals to attain their best personal outcomes in these areas. The way an individual is diagnosed, what treatment they have access to and what conditions led to them contracting the disease all have human rights implications. Hence, Health systems are designed to work to improve the health of people as seen in the World Health Organization Report 2000 and the WHO European Region Tallinn Charter. All members of the WHO share a goal to attain the 'highest attainable standard of health as a fundamental right and for health equality (Goran, 2010, p. 6).

However, the reality of the world today is that the most vulnerable have less care owing to accessibility and affordability (Goran, 2010, p. 6). Davies (2010, p. 2) adds that the thirty countries of the Organization for Economic Co-operation and Development (OECD) are home to less than 20% of the world's population but their spending on health account for 90% of the world's total health expenditure. Labonte and Gagnon (2010, p. 11) adds that the right to health is not fully represented in the actual international human rights framework.

It is important to note, however, that of the three narratives of Infectious diseases, the securitization of diseases take the front row in foreign policy decisions more than any other frame. Infectious diseases are included in the black list of threats that can lead to large scale death and lessening of life chances. This information is important as we go through the study of human rights and disease control which may be safely interpreted as threat control thereby leading to certain human right abuses as it will be discussed in the Ebola outbreak.

The Ebola Outbreak (2014-2016)

The Ebola Virus Disease was first identified in Africa in 1976 but it only became widely known during the 2014 outbreak (Fidler, 2015). However, unlike the previous Ebola outbreaks, that of 2014 occurred in West Africa as opposed to Central Africa, and in urban environments as well as rural settings (Fidler, 2015). Specifically, more than 11 000 people (out of 28000 cases) died from Ebola virus disease (EVD) during the 2014–15 West Africa epidemic, which is many times more than the total infected during all previous outbreaks of the disease combined (UNDP,2015; World Bank, 2016). Also, the outbreak in West Africa has been described as the longest, largest, deadliest, and the most complex in its history (UNDP, 2015). In economic terms, the impact of the Ebola crisis on Guinea, Liberia, and Sierra Leone has been estimated at $2.8 billion (World Bank, 2016)

The West African states most affected by the outbreak are developing countries emerging from civil wars that devastated governmental capacity in many sectors, including health care (Fidler, 2015, Gostin and Friedmann,2015). For many years, Guinea, Liberia, and Sierra Leone have been on the agenda of the UN's Peace-building Commission, whose mission is to help post-conflict nations by coordinating assistance, raising resources, and providing advice on peace building strategies. The lack of health-sector capacity, including inadequate medical facilities and insufficient numbers of health care personnel, became a frequent explanation for the Ebola outbreak's severity (Fidler, 2015).

Moreover, the unfamiliarity of Ebola in that region delayed its detection (Gostin & Friedman, 2015). The first case of Ebola occurred In December 2013, but Guinean health officials misdiagnosed initial cases and Ebola was not confirmed in Guinea until March 21, 2014, and in Liberia 2 days later (Gostin & Friedman, 2015). In Sierra Leone, scientists suspected Ebola, but their information did not reach surveillance teams and Ebola remained unconfirmed until late May. By late June 2014, Ebola was confirmed in 60 locations across three countries, with cases rising exponentially, and health workers were dying in large numbers. Yet the international machinery did not move into higher gear until late July, after the medical evacuation of two US aid workers from Liberia (Fidler, 2015; Gostin & Friedman, 2015, p. 1092). The disease spread to Nigerian megacity of Lagos, provoking fears of unmitigated disaster. The polio vaccination infrastructure in Nigeria was re-purposed, rapidly containing the outbreak. In the ensuing months, Ebola spread to Senegal, Mali, the USA, and the UK, but was controlled. It was not until Aug 8, 2014-4·5 months after the first international spread—that the WHO Director-General declared a Public Health Emergency of International Concern (PHEIC) under the 2005 International Health Regulations (IHR), a global treaty (Fidler, 2015; Gostin & Friedman, 2015, p. 1092). International donations finally began to flow, with the largest contributions from the World Bank and the USA. Building on historical ties, US assistance focused on Liberia, British assistance on Sierra Leone and French assistance on Guinea. On Sept 16, 2014, President Obama mobilised military assets—3000 troops to support logistics, train health workers, and build seventeen treatment centers. The UN Security Council passed an unprecedented resolution calling Ebola a threat to international peace and security, urging an escalated response and an end to travel restrictions, which several states had enacted. The next day, the UN Secretary-General announced the UN Mission for Emergency Ebola Response (UNMEER) to lead operations in the region. Fear increased in October when the US Centers for Disease Control and Prevention (CDC) posited a worst-case scenario of 1·4 million infections by mid-January 2015. Travel bans, and flight suspensions harmed fragile economies and hampered the flow of trade and aid. On September 30, public fear intensified in the USA when health workers in Dallas, TX, diagnosed Ebola in a traveler originating in Liberia. Two Dallas nurses contracted the virus. Soon thereafter, a medical worker returning from Guinea to New York City was diagnosed with Ebola. President Obama resisted calls for a travel ban, but erected rigorous entry screening, and several states quarantined health workers.

Disease outbreaks highlight the limitations of the current global health system to address externalities; for example, the WHO and bilateral donor agencies were criticized for moving slowly on the 2014 West Africa Ebola outbreak (Hoffman, Cole & Pearcey, 2015). Slow responses to disease outbreaks suggest a lack of surge capacity at the global level, marred by systems that lack resilience and responsiveness. Moreover, the global health system is still limited in its ability to hold states to account in terms of international laws and regulations when confronted by questions of economic and/or political self-interest (Hoffman, Cole & Pearcey, 2015).

The Impact of the Ebola Epidemic

The relatively free movement of goods and people, as well as the porous and under-governed borders across West Africa was a major factor in the spread of the infectious disease. According to the report of the United Nations Development Group (2015), the 2014 Ebola outbreak was the largest, longest, deadliest and the most complex in the history of the disease. Since the first outbreak in 1976 till the period leading the 2014 outbreak, only about 2,232 cases were detected with about 1,503 deaths. This is a sharp contrast to the about 9,446 cases and 2,758 deaths recorded in Sierra Leone alone in the 2014 attack.

Figure 1. Colorized transmission electron micrograph (TEM) of Ebola virus
Source: Centers of Disease Control and Prevention, 2016

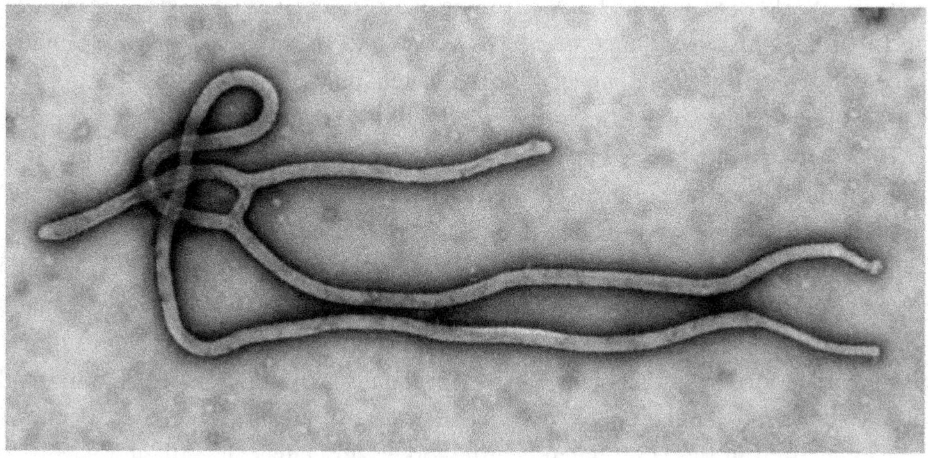

**For a more accurate representation see the electronic version.*

Figure 2 refers to the progression in the case fatality in the Ebola epidemic since its first appearance in 1976 till the year 2014. In contrast with older outbreaks which were predominately in local areas, the 2014 outbreak spread to cities and urban settlement including Freetown, Conakry, Monrovia and Lagos. One of the indicators for failure in the recent outbreak was the poor diagnosis of the outbreak due to its similar symptoms with other endemic diseases in the sub region, including Malaria and Cholera (UNDG, 2015). Culture was also identified as one of the key issues that lengthen the life circle of the epidemic in the region. There existed before the outbreak, cultural practices including some burial practices and communal engagements which exposed more people to the dangers of contacting the disease.

Furthermore, the already weak health system of the Ebola epicenter (sierra- Leone, Guinea and Liberia) were further weakened by the epidemic as access to non-Ebola services were disrupted. There was also loss of jobs and livelihoods due to closed borders and stigmatization of survivors and relative of the dead. The UNDG (2015) accounts for children as 20% of the worst hit demography. About 16,600 children lost a parent or both to the EVD. School hours were also lost, estimated at about 780 hours in Sierra Leone.

Figure 2. Case Fatality in Ebola Outbreaks
Source: CDC 2016

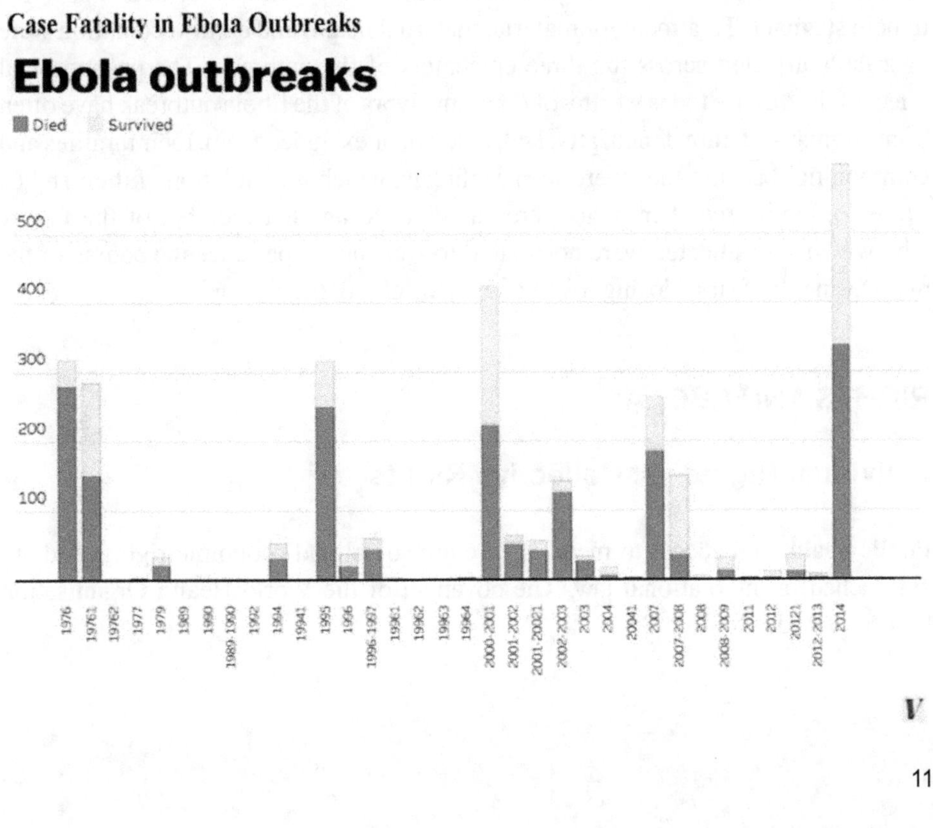

The UNFPA (2014) notes that many expectant women were giving birth at home rather than at the health centres and many without the supervision of a health professional. This was partly due to the limited health facilities and also the fear of contacting Ebola from such facilities. Looking at the gender dimensions of the Ebola outbreak, women were more on the receiving end. First, as the primary caregivers in homes, women were at a high risk of catching the disease. Also, since women, according to the UNDG (2015) were the most employed in the informal sector, they were most affected by closure of borders and stricter quarantine measures. Ebola also had economic implications. The EVD reversed most of the gains made during the MDGs years. The under-five child mortality rate, for instance is a case in point in Liberia, where children were once again vulnerable to death.

The world bank (2016) estimated the overall impact of the Ebola crisis on the three EVD epicenters (Guina, Liberia and Sierra Leone) at $2.8billion; and conclude that the economic impact will outlive the epidemiological impact. The GDP growth in Liberia for instance, slowed to 0.7% in 2014 from 8.7% in 2013. Beyond the economic, Brolin, Saulnier, Eriksson and Von (2016) identified more effects of EVD on the healthcare system in the affected countries. For them, the impact of the EVD stretches beyond the cases and fatality figures of the disease itself as non-Ebola related deaths were significant and reported. They emphasized that the uptake of health services by the population (particularly due to the fear of being infected with the new disease) decreased while the provisions of health services remain stagnant. Treatment for malaria, maternal health and child vaccination were invariably affected across the three epicenters of the outbreak. The psychosocial effect of the disease too is worthy of note. survivors of the Ebola outbreak have often been stigmatized, threatened, attacked, evicted, or excluded from, their families and communities because they were seen as threats, which is a violation of their rights. More so, family members who were caregiver to another member of the family who was sick or infected were not spared too, as they experience the course of the disease and the fear of losing loved ones (Bortel, 2016).

RIGHTS AND EBOLA

Individual Rights vs. Collective Rights

Public health and access to medical care are social and economic rights; and are entrenched in international law. The covenant of the World Health Organisation (1946) provides for the:

...enjoyment of the highest attainable standard of health" as one of the fundamental rights of every human being without discrimination in "race, religion and political belief, economic or social condition.

This establishes the individual right to health. The Article 25 (1) of the Universal Declaration of Human Rights also acknowledges this right. The Article 25 provides that "everyone has the right to a standard of living adequate for the health and well-being of himself and his family...". The Alma Ata declaration also includes a right to primary healthcare. the Oslo declaration recognizes that 'life is the most fundamental of human rights and that life and health are the most precious assets. Davies (2010) acknowledged the grand work of Jonathan Mann in situating the link between health and rights. Human rights violations (including torture) have an impact on health and that health should be more holistic comprising of the physical, mental and social wellbeing. Also, the way an individual is diagnosed, the kind of the treatment they have access to and what conditions exposed them to such infection or disease all have human rights implication. Labonte and Gagnon (2010) adds that the right to health is not fully represented in the actual international human rights framework.

Oftentimes the individual right to well-being as entrenched in all of these treaties/conventions on the one hand, and the demands of public health appear to be mutually inclusive, belonging to the same family of rights. However, in practice, the two domains conflict especially in times of emergencies involving bio-political measures imposed by state authorities which are responsible for containing epidemics (Rollison, 2015). Maintaining rights at the collective or community level sometimes requires the elimination of certain individual rights, in the interest of the greater good of a general population (Leary, 2014). It is often difficult to find a balance, as well as the boundaries between the two domains of health rights. During the influenza pandemic that claimed many lives all over the world, the colonial government in a bid to contain the infection, initiated forceful detention of suspected infectious people in what has been described as the colonisation of the body (Jimoh, 2015). Also, across Africa in this period, the need to eliminate diseases were the justification for racial segregation policies. Eradicating mosquitoes and preventing malaria was an important part of the colonial administration in West Africa too. Malaria was a "recurring lethal threat" to the colonial administration and was met with the segregation of the residences between the governed and the rulers (Jimoh, 2017). A recent example during the Ebola outbreak was the case of a nurse, an official of the Doctors without Borders Kaci Hickox, who had just returned from Sierra Leone. Hickox was quarantined by officials in New Jersey and in Maine for the good of public health but she defied the quarantine on human rights ground. This case amongst others was significant in its impact on the containment of the EVD. Consequently, this deterred some health care workers from traveling to Ebola infected regions to render their expertise in curbing the epidemic. This is one of the many undocumented effects of such extreme and misappropriate measures by states. The issue of rights and heath is also influenced by the determination of who gets what, when and how they get. The politics of naming and sometimes marginalization of certain groups, sometimes from poorer nation or community. Even in the developed world, the prevalence of a certain disease in certain marginalized groups could mean the total evasion of that group by the government. The instance of the AIDs outbreak in the 1980s is a case in point. AID at that time seemed to be the preserve of stigmatized populations of gay men and injection drug user, hence the disease received little attention from the machinery of the state. Rollinson (2005) compared the state response to an outbreak of Legionnaires disease which was happening simultaneously with the AIDS spread and noted that less than a million dollars was spent on AIDS compared to the over $9million spent on the other disease. Pisani (2008) notes that AIDS was then known as GRIDS- Gay Related Immune Deficiency Syndrome tagged to the population with the highest fatality rate.

Human Rights Violations During Ebola

The right to life and health drew the attention of the world to respond to the epidemic in West Africa but with the myriad of responses came more human rights questions. The impact of the outbreak on populations coupled with measures taken by governments to contain it, have led to serious human rights concerns. These human rights issues, according to a United Nations report (2014) range from:

...restrictions on the exercise of the right to information, the right to freedom of movement, and the rights to health and to education, to infringements on the right to life and to physical integrity through the excessive use of force by security forces elements.

Restrictions and bans on public gatherings and places including markets, schools and places of worship were imposed without any alternatives. This impacted greatly on children's right to education and women's right to income generating activities.

In May 2014, a public health state of emergency was declared in Sierra Leone to contain the spread of the disease, which is increased by human mobility and contact. The quarantines imposed involved restricting people's liberties, freedom of movement, and access to healthcare, food and water. Quarantines are also instituted to facilitate contact tracing. Oxfam (2015) reports notes that in November 2014, about 2,075 households had been placed under quarantine in three communities in Sierra Leone. Though these quarantines yielded some success, there were violations of basic rights of the quarantine communities, through delayed or inadequate supplies of food, water and other basic needs. Some communities reported that they only received food on the 14th day of the quarantine. This was a case of poorly managed quarantine. These communities had struggled in the Pre-Ebola period to access resources and were worst off during these quarantine period.

Liberian authorities also imposed 10-day quarantine over West Point, reputed to be the country's largest slum. Soldiers were used to enforce the blockade of about 75000 inhabitants of that region (Oxfam, 2015). This enforced quarantine led to clashes between the soldiers and the community leading to the death of one child, with many more injured. These quarantine measures seem counterproductive, limiting the right of the people rather than limiting the spread of the virus. It resulted in restricting the freedom to movement, limiting the social and economic rights and infringing the right to life and physical integrity.

The right to access to healthcare was also limited. In Monrovia, a UN report noted that, there were instances of individuals being refused access to facilities and treatment due to fear factor, on the part of unprotected and poorly equipped hospital staff. Similarly, people avoided hospitals for fear of being quarantined thereby making the containment method counterproductive as the disease continued to spread uncontained. The fear was in two ways, fear of being quarantine and sometimes fear of being infected by health workers who had been exposed to earlier infected people (Eba, 2014; Gostin, 2014; Oxfam, 2015; Rollinson, 2015).

Figure 3. An Ebola enforcement officer beats a local resident in Liberia
Source: Callan (2014). Retrieved from http://edition.cnn.com/2014/10/06/justice/callan-law-on-quarantine/index.html

The right to life was also threatened in this regard. It was alleged that Liberian armed forces were instructed to shoot down people crossing the borders from neighbouring Sierra Leone in search of better healthcare (UN Report, 2014). In all, health workers needed quality working environments. Cases of escapee quarantined patients who were hunted down, sprayed with disinfectant and violently forced into vehicles to transport them back to the facilities. Following imposed quarantines, security forces were barely non-existent in providing the required protection for the quarantined communities. Even in the pre-Ebola period, the lack of functioning healthcare centers and access to good healthcare generally was a right issue in these countries in the West African sub region, some of which are post conflict countries.

In Sierra Leone, it was reported that names of Ebola suspects were aired on radio and posted on social media platforms and members of the public were encouraged to report to authorities if they suspected anyone of carrying the disease (Kabia, 2014).

The inadequate, and now decimated, health systems, and the rippling effects of the crisis on education, housing, and food, all raise issues of access to - and the enjoyment of - fundamental economic and social rights. These are just as important as the violations of civil rights, including unwarranted restrictions on movement, which might stem from the Ebola epidemic. But it is equally important to realize how massive violations of human rights -- civil and political, as well as economic and social-- drive epidemics such as Ebola (Yamin, 2014)

The rights-based approach sees the affected persons as right holders and not just products of humanitarian intervention. The right to food was affected due to quarantine measures but also due to the restriction on public gathering. In the latter, markets were closed and farmlands were abandoned resulting in possible loss of current and future crops (UN, 2014). The restriction on public gathering was a limitation on the right to assembly, education and freedom of religion. Misinformation had led to angry mobs attacking healthcare workers, who were assumed to be carriers and distributors of the EVD.

More so, while epidemics affects rights in many ways, human rights violations also impact on the spread of epidemic. They tend to facilitate the spread. Such violations as lack of access to education, human trafficking and poor access to healthcare also increase the risk of exposure to epidemics. In another instance, Paul Farmer notes that in Russian prisons which were ridden with human rights abuses, inmates were susceptible to infectious disease like Tuberculosis. Hence it is clear that healthcare and human rights are interdependent and overlapping. How can states and global health actors curtail the impact of public health initiatives on individual freedoms?

International agreements have the answer. Siracusa principles (1948) stipulates that public health may be invoked as a ground for limiting certain rights in order to allow a state to take measures dealing with a serious threat to the health of the population or individual members of the population. The Siracusa principles, however, provides that, laws imposing limitations on the exercise of human rights shall not be arbitrary or unreasonable, shall be clear and accessible to everyone (Siracusa Principles, 1984). Article 29(2) of the Universal Declaration of Human Rights also sets out the terms of limitation of rights. In the exercise of his rights and freedoms, everyone shall be subject only to such limitations as are determined by law solely for the purpose of securing due recognition and respect for the rights and freedoms of others and of meeting the just requirements of morality public order and the general welfare in a democratic society.

However, these agreements remain vague as to what limitations are too much or too little, and leave the responsibility of determining the boundaries of public health initiatives at the mercy of states who are sometimes the defaulters. How do we determine what measures are proportionate, arbitrary and non-discriminatory? Is there a way to monitor the activities of healthcare workers who are often at the forefront of these interventions? Oftentimes these healthcare workers are in a strait between this two contending health rights- the individual's right to health and the collective right to health; and sometimes contending with their own right to health and life.

CONCLUSION

From the foregoing, it is clear that there exists a dispute between the individual rights to health and the state security concerns, often embedded in rights of the collective to health (and of course national security). The Ebola outbreak and the attendant response are no exceptions in this conflict as international agreements and convention, provide for a level of infringement to protect the right of many (rather the right of one individual). Where do we go from here? In protecting the health rights of the collective, it is important that states recognize that the war they wage should not be about the individual or the body but against a virus/ infection. Hence, for quarantine measures and other kinds of biopolitical restrictions should be done in a respectable manner, while also providing for proper and consensual treatment to the afflicted. More so, it is recommended that people who will be subjected to those kinds of treatment should be communicated with on why they are being quarantined and how they are contributing to a public good and security of others. Affected people should know why, when, where and how long they will be quarantined. Furthermore, States and other actors should take advantage of advances in technology and research to reduce quarantine and testing period. Similar advances have successfully reduced test time for HIV/AIDS as opposed to the six-month period which was associated with earlier detection systems. The WHO must enforce evidence-based responses that involve the communities and not alienate them. There is also a need for support services to deal with fearful quarantined people and escaping quarantined patients in a dignified manner. Though some of these restrictions are necessary to protect the right of others but they must be proportionate and necessary, involve timely communication of information to the affected communities so that they can prepare for isolation by stocking up on basic supplies. It is also recommended that to prevent such outbreaks of epidemics in the Africa, the factor of re-emerging diseases should be addressed, and health aid should be targeted towards a more holistic approach to strengthening health systems worldwide.

REFERENCES

Amaya, A., Rollet, V., & Kingah, S. (2015). What's in a word? The framing of health at the regional level: ASEAN, EU, SADC and UNASUR. *Global Social Policy*, *15*(3), 229–260. doi:10.1177/1468018115599816 PMID:26635496

Bortel. (2016). Psychosocial effects of an Ebola outbreak at individual, community and international levels. *Bulletin of the World Health Organization*, *94*(3), 210–214. doi:10.2471/BLT.15.158543 PMID:26966332

Brolin Ribacke, K. J., Saulnier, D. D., Eriksson, A., & von Schreeb, J. (2016). Effects of the West Africa Ebola Virus Disease on Health-Care Utilization – A Systematic Review. *Frontiers in Public Health*, *4*, 222. doi:10.3389/fpubh.2016.00222 PMID:27777926

Brundtland, G. (1999). The Globalization of Disease. *New Perspectives Quarterly*, *16*(5), 17–17. doi:10.1111/j.1540-5842.1999.tb00008.x

Callan, P. (2014). *Ebola quarantine is perfectly legal*. Retrieved from http://edition.cnn.com/2014/10/06/justice/callan-law-on-quarantine/index.html

Centers of Disease Control and Prevention. (2016). *About Ebola Virus Disease*. Retrieved from https://www.cdc.gov/vhf/ebola/about.html

Davies, S. (2010). Global politics of health. *Polity*.

Delamou, A., Delvaux, T., El Ayadi, A. M., Beavogui, A. H., Okumura, J., Van Damme, W., & De Brouwere, V. (2017, March). Public health impact of the 2014–2015 Ebola outbreak in West Africa: Seizing opportunities for the future. *BMJ Global Health*, *2*(2), e000202. doi:10.1136/bmjgh-2016-000202 PMID:28589018

Dye, C. (2014). After 2015: Infectious diseases in a new era of health and development. *Philosophical Transactions of the Royal Society of London. Series B, Biological Sciences*, *369*(1645), 20130426. doi:10.1098/rstb.2013.0426 PMID:24821913

Eba, P. (2014). Ebola and human rights in West Africa. *Lancet*, *384*(9960), 2091–2093. doi:10.1016/S0140-6736(14)61412-4 PMID:25245179

Farmer, P. (1999). Pathologies of power: Rethinking health and human rights. *American Journal of Public Health*, *89*(10), 1486–1496. doi:10.2105/AJPH.89.10.1486 PMID:10511828

Fidler, D. (2001). The globalization of public health: 100 years of international health diplomacy. *Bullentin of the WHO*, *79*, 842–849. PMID:11584732

Fidler, D. (2005). Health, globalization and governance: an introduction to public health's new world order. *Global Change and Health*, 161-177.

Gostin, L. (2014). Ebola: Towards an international health systems fund. *Lancet*, *384*(9951), e49–e51. doi:10.1016/S0140-6736(14)61345-3 PMID:25201591

Gostin, L. O., & Friedman, E. A. (2015). A retrospective and prospective analysis of the west African Ebola virus disease epidemic: Robust national health systems at the foundation and an empowered WHO at the apex. *Lancet*, *385*(9980), 1902–1909. doi:10.1016/S0140-6736(15)60644-4 PMID:25987158

Hoffman, S. J., Cole, C. B., & Pearcey, M. (2015). *Mapping Global Health Architecture to Inform the Future*. Chatham House.

Hwenda, L., Mahlathi, P., & Maphanga, T. (2011). Why African Countries Need to Participate in Global Health Security Discourse. *Global Health Governance*, *4*(2), 1–24. PMID:24729828

Jimoh, O. (2015). Managing epidemic: The british approach to 1918–1919 influenza in Lagos. *Journal of Asian and African Studies*. doi:10.1177/0021909615587367

Kabia, J. (2014). *The human rights dimension of West Africa's Ebola outbreak*. Retrieved from http://globalhumanrights.org/the-human-rights-dimension-of-west-africas-ebola-outbreak

Labonté, R., & Gagnon, M. L. (2010). Framing health and foreign policy: Lessons for global health diplomacy. *Globalization and Health*, *6*(1), 14. doi:10.1186/1744-8603-6-14 PMID:20727211

Lakoff, A., & Collier, S. J. (Eds.). (2008). *Biosecurity interventions: global health & security in question*. Columbia University Press. doi:10.7312/lako14606

Lamy, M., & Phua, K. H. (2012). Southeast Asian cooperation in health: A comparative perspective on regional health governance in ASEAN and the EU. *Asia Europe Journal*, *10*(4), 233–250. doi:10.100710308-012-0335-1

Leary, V. (1994). The right to health in international human rights law. *Health and Human Rights*, *1*(1), 24. doi:10.2307/4065261 PMID:10395710

McInnes, C., & Lee, K. (2012). *Global health and international relations*. Cambridge, UK: Polity.

McInnes, C., & Lee, K. (2012). Global health and international relations. *Polity*.

Negin, J., Morgan, C., & Condon, R. (2012). Regional Health Meetings in the Pacific and their Impact on Health Governance. *Global Health Governance*, *5*(2).

Oxfam. (2015). *Quarantines in Sierra Leone: Putting people first in the Ebola crisis*. Oxfam Report.

Rollinson, R. (2015). *Public health and human rights in an era of epidemics*. Academic Press.

UN. (2014). *A human rights perspective into the Ebola outbreak. UN report*. Geneva: United Nations.

UN High-Level panel. (2004). *Panel on Threats, Challenges, and Change. A more secure world: our shared responsibility*. New York: Author.

UNFPA. (2014). *Liberia's Ebola outbreak leaves pregnant women stranded*. Retrieved from www.unfpa.org/news/liberias-ebola-outbreak-leaves-pregnant-womenstranded#sthash.zdvmnjF2.dpuf

United Nations Development Group. (2015). *Socio-economic impact of Ebola Virus Disease (United Nations Development Programme report). Western and central Africa*. Author.

World Bank. (2016). *2014-2015 West African Ebola crisis: Impact update (World Bank report)*. Geneva, Switzerland: Author.

World Health Organisation. (2007). *Working together for health (World Health Organisation report)*. Geneva, Switzerland: Author.

Yamin, A. (2014). Ebola, human rights, and poverty – making the links. *openDemocracy*. Available at https://www.opendemocracy.net/openglobalrights-blog/alicia-ely-yamin/ebola-human-rights-and-poverty-%E2%80%93-making-links

Yoon, S. (2015). *The Role of Epistemic Communities in the Global Response to Severe Acute Respiratory Syndrome: Implications for Global Health Governance* (Doctoral dissertation). London School of Hygiene & Tropical Medicine.

Youde, J. (2012). *Global health governance*. Cambridge, UK: Polity.

Chapter 2
Discrimination Against People With HIV and AIDS in the Workplace:
A Lagos State Example

Chinwe Rosabelle Nwanna
University of Lagos, Nigeria

ABSTRACT

The main thrust of the chapter was to explore the discrimination experienced by people living with HIV and AIDS (PLHIV) in the workplace in Lagos State. A purposive sample of 80 PLHIV was selected from two local government areas (LGAs) of Lagos state: Epe, a rural setting, and Lagos Mainland, an urban one. Secondary data were obtained from internet sources while primary data were collected through structured interviews September 2005–April 2006. Data were analyzed using SPSS versions 11 and 13. Data between and within the rural and urban areas were also analyzed comparatively. The results indicate that PLHIV experienced instant dismissal from offices, mandatory HIV tests, alienation, denial of promotion, and exclusion from insurance schemes. This indicates that PLHIV's rights were violated. The study recommends intensive HIV education and enforcement of national HIV policy and international legal instruments in the workplace to protect PLHIV's rights.

INTRODUCTION

According to Joint United Nations Programme on HIV/AIDS (UNAIDS) Data (2017), 36.7 million people were living with HIV and AIDS (PLHIV) in 2016. Sub Saharan Africa bears the highest burden of the pandemic with about two-thirds of the global number of PLHIV. Nigeria has the second largest HIV epidemic in the world with

DOI: 10.4018/978-1-5225-6133-0.ch002

3.2 million people and has one of the highest new infection rates in sub-Saharan Africa in 2016 (UNAIDS, 2017). HIV has decimated world population. Globally, many people have died due to AIDS and about one million died of the disease in 2016 alone (UNAIDS, 2017).

HIV attacks and interferes with the immune system. It can progress to AIDS if not diagnosed early. This will make infected people vulnerable to infections. Although HIV cannot be cured, it can be effectively controlled with antiretroviral therapy (ART) so that it may not progress to AIDS. This implies that PLHIV can continue to be productive members of the workforce (Fit for Work Team, 2015). However, its incurability and association with promiscuity and homosexuality has accentuated social discrimination. Furthermore, ignorance of the disease and the phobia it provokes in people have resulted in self-defence mechanisms among the public including employers and colleagues in the workplace and have occasioned the rejection of the PLHIV by segregation, exclusion, or the denial of equal opportunities (Nwanna, 2011).

Discrimination may occur in different forms and in various settings including the workplace, healthcare facilities, local communities and the family. In Nigeria, people care for one another when sick but when one is living with HIV, people tend to run away from that person. HIV-related discrimination has become a powerful tool of social control. It can be used to marginalize, exclude or manipulate PLHIV covertly or openly. Studies have shown that PLHIV were dismissed from their jobs due to their HIV status (Owolabi, Araoye, & Osagbemi, 2011). The study in this chapter would contribute to the formulation of policies that would favour PLHIV and protect their rights.

HIV-discrimination undermines HIV prevention efforts and the ability of people to access and adhere to treatment. Acts of discrimination deny people's rights to information, to services to protect them against HIV infection, and to receive appropriate treatment, care and support when HIV-positive. Although discrimination is not experienced by every PLHIV, it may bring about conditions of stress, low self-esteem, suicide, job losses, unemployment, and dislocation among PLHIV who have experienced it (Nwanna, 2011). Shosanya (2015) reported that there had been cases of employers terminating services of infected persons and there were few or no known employers who were willing to employ identified PLHIV. Most of the employers always hinged on the fact that it was their prerogative to employ whoever befits their organizations. Shosanya (2015) went on to state that the stigmatization of the PLHIV had continued to hang on the necks of PLHIV like an albatross, despite their hues and cries to the society to morally rekindle their survival and support them to live a worthy life. In view of this, Lagos State government enacted a law in 2007, to protect persons living with HIV and affected by AIDS and to prevent discrimination of any type against any PLHIV particularly in matter of employment (Shosanya, 2015). Discrimination against PLHIV continues to be pervasive in Nigeria to the extent that in 2014, the immediate past president, Goodluck Jonathan, signed into law an Antidiscrimination Bill that protects the rights and dignity of PLHIV (Shosanya, 2015). Despite these laws, discrimination continues unabated. Furthermore, there are very few empirical studies on the forms of discrimination against PLHIV in the workplace particularly from the perspective of PLHIV. In the light of the afore-stated, this study set out to investigate the forms of discrimination experienced by PLHIV in the workplace in Epe and Lagos Mainland local government areas (LGAs) of Lagos State.

BACKGROUND

As far back as 1958, the UN International Labour Organization (ILO) Discrimination Convention (No. 111) in Article 1 subsection1 (1a) defines discrimination as "any distinction, exclusion or preference made on the basis of race, colour, sex, religion, political opinion, national extraction or social origin, which has the effect of nullifying or impairing equality of opportunity or treatment in employment or occupation as may be determined". However, in the context of HIV and AIDS, Aggleton and Parker (2002) assert that discrimination occurs when a distinction is made against a person that results in his or her being treated unfairly and unjustly on the basis of belonging or being perceived to belong to a particular group. According to UNAIDS protocol (2000 cited in UNAIDS, 2005) discrimination is defined as any form of arbitrary distinction, exclusion, or restriction affecting a person, usually but not only by virtue of an inherent personal characteristic or perceived belonging to a particular group—in the case of HIV and AIDS, a person's confirmed or suspected HIV-positive status—irrespective of whether or not there is any justification for these measures.

The concept of stigma will help in understanding the concept of discrimination because discrimination is the acting out of stigmatising attitude. Goffman (1963) describes stigma as an attribute that is deeply discrediting within a particular social interaction that reduces the bearer from a whole and usual person to a tainted, discounted one. His explanation of stigma focuses on society's attitude toward people who possess attributes that fall short of public expectations. Contrary to Goffman's description, Weiss and Ramakrishna (2001) define stigma as a social process or related personal experience characterized by exclusion, rejection, blame, or devaluation that result from an adverse social judgment about a person or group.

In this chapter, therefore, discrimination is presented as negative attitudes, beliefs, attributes, behaviours, activities and experiences that occur in social interactions.

Earlier Studies

In this section, earlier researches will be reviewed beginning from studies conducted in other countries before focusing on Nigeria.

Population Council (2002) reported a qualitative research that was carried out to explore the manifestations of stigma and discrimination in the workplace, family, and community; contribute to the development of appropriate quantitative measures for stigma; and inform stigma reduction intervention activities. The study revealed that many workers expressed fear that they would be isolated, avoided, and ridiculed if their co-workers and managers knew about their sero-positive status. The main manifestation of stigma is social isolation and ridicule. A higher proportion of male respondents (73%) than female respondents (65%) reported cases of social isolation. Similarly, a greater percentage of the male workers (49%) than the females (44%) reported rumours and gossips (Population Council, 2002).

UNAIDS (2011) reported a study that used PLHIV Stigma Index as the instrument in 9 countries in Asia and the Pacific Region namely Bangladesh, Cambodia, China, Fiji, Myanmar, Pakistan, Philippines, Sri Lanka and Thailand. According to UNAIDS (2011), between 16% in Fiji and 50% in Cambodia lost their employment or sources of income while 19% in Fiji to 38% in Philippines were denied opportunity to work while 8–52% had promotion denied or the nature of work changed. Furthermore, many respondents decided to stop work due to discrimination or decided not to apply for a job or promotion. UNAIDS (2011) also revealed that discrimination was pervasive in 3 countries where employer and managers (13–55%), colleagues (15–50%) and clients (0–50%) were not likely to be supportive or more likely to change their behaviours. In conclusion, UNAIDS (2011) asserts that stigma and discrimination are key factors responsible for loss of employment among PLHIV.

Corroborating the above findings, another study that applied PLHIV Stigma Index in 9 countries from 4 regions: Kenya, Nigeria and Zambia from sub- Saharan Africa, Estonia and Poland from Eastern Europe, Malaysia and the Philippines from Asia-Pacific, and Argentina and Mexico from South America, was conducted by The Global Network of People Living with HIV (GNP+), ILO, The PLHIV Stigma Index (2012). The research revealed that discrimination was the commonest factor responsible for job loss. The study revealed that many respondents had lost a job or source of income during the preceding 12 months of the study ranging from 13% in Poland to 40% in Kenya and Zambia. It also indicated that many of these PLHIV lost employment as a result of their sero-positive status alone. This ranges from 8% in Estonia to 45% in Nigeria. The results further showed that there are little differences between rural, small and big towns. In most countries, people living in rural areas were more likely to have lost employment as a result of HIV or HIV combined with another reason, however, it was alleged that this did not apply to all countries.

ML dos Santos et al. (2014) adapted The PLHIV Stigma Index and applied it to 500 PLHIV in ten HIV clinics in South Africa. The study found that 12% of the respondents indicated that they had lost their jobs in the 12 months pre-ceding the time of the study. Out of this proportion, more than half declared that their job losses were at least partially due to their sero-positive status either due to discrimination or/and being too sick to work. Also, 8% of them affirmed that they were denied employment opportunity because of their HIV status. ML dos Santos et. al. (2014) therefore concluded that the HIV status negatively affected the working life of PLHIV.

Poni-Gore et al., (2015) conducted a cross-sectional research in Juba, South Sudan from 102 PLHIV and 70 people from the public using standardized well-structured questionnaires and interviews. The study revealed that 60% of PLHIV who were employed did not disclose their HIV positive status at their work places due to fear of losing their jobs. The study also showed that 80% of PLHIV were not denied their jobs implying that about 20% of them suffered denial of employment.

In Nigeria, discrimination in the workplace manifests, most times, in the loss of employment in Nigeria. Akparanta – Emenogu (2002 cited in Nwanna, 2011) and Durojaiye (2003 cited in Nwanna, 2011) conducted qualitative studies and found independently that a naval officer was denied admission into one of the Naval Training Colleges in Rivers State, Nigeria, after being successful at the recruitment test. He was refused admission because of his sero-positive status. The respondent reported that he was admitted as a squadron leader and was later sent to Calabar, the capital of Cross River State for his assignments. An HIV test was run without his informed consent. He was later dismissed claiming that he was HIV+. Similarly, Adirieje (2003 cited in Nwanna, 2011) reported that a nurse was dismissed due to her sero-positve status. According to Adirieje (2003 cited in Nwanna, 2011), the nurse was tested for HIV without her knowledge and consent and was instantly dismissed when the laboratory result declared her sero-positive. Iwuagwu et al. (2003 cited in Nwanna, 2011) found that a Nigerian police woman living with HIV was demoted by the Nigeria Police when her sero-positive status was publicly declared by a media house without her consent.

Another study conducted by Iwuagwu et al. (2003 cited in Nwanna, 2011) showed that human rights of PLHIV have been violated in Nigeria. The study demonstrated the pattern of human rights abuse of PLWHA in Nigeria (Iwuagwu, 2001; 2003 cited in Nwanna, 2011). In this study, three states namely Lagos, Kano and Anambra were studied using focus group discussions (FGDs) that involved 53 PLWHA. The study found that an auxiliary nurse's appointment was terminated because of her sero-positive status. She had worked for five years in the hospital before she became pregnant. She developed boils which led to a laboratory test by the employer. The result of the test showed that she was HIV positive and she was instantly dismissed because the management claimed that they could not afford to put their staff and patients at risk.

From the above researches, it was observed that empirical evidences from PLHIV about their discriminatory experiences in Nigeria are scant. Most of the existing studies are qualitative. However, The Global Network of People Living with HIV (GNP+), ILO, The PLHIV Stigma Index (2012) investigated PLHIV in Nigeria among nine other countries. Nigerian results will be reviewed here. For Nigeria, 45% of respondents lost their jobs or sources of income due to HIV+ status. The study further revealed that 27% of Nigerian PLHIV lost their jobs or sources of income because of stigma while 26% lost due to stigma and poor health and another 26% due to poor health alone. About 53% lost jobs due to discrimination. Around 27% of the Nigerian respondents were denied employment or work opportunities due their HIV+ status. These findings therefore suggest that HIV-related stigma and discrimination in the workplace are causes of unemployment or a denial of work opportunity in Nigeria. Many Nigerian respondents (62%) had had their job description or nature of work changed, or had been refused promotion as a result of sero-positive status. Nigerian PLHIV respondents reported that 28% and 33% of their employers and colleagues respectively reacted discriminatorily when they became aware of respondents' HIV status (the Global Network of People Living with HIV (GNP+), ILO, The PLHIV Stigma Index, 2012).

From the above literature review, it is obvious that there is a dearth of quantitative studies on the forms of discrimination against PLHIV in the workplace therefore this chapter tends to fill this gap

Theoretical Anchorage

Discrimination is perceived to be an intergroup and interpersonal phenomenon which is related to fundamental processes associated with social categorization and the development of in-group favouritism. This chapter is anchored on social identity theory (SIT). SIT is a cognitive social psychological theory developed in Europe by Tajfel (1982 cited in Mor Barak, 2008). The theory postulates that people tend to classify themselves into social categories that have meanings for them, and this shapes the way individuals interact with others from their own identity group and from other groups. Mor Barak (2008) uses SIT to explain workplace exclusion and discrimination. According to her, social identification, categorization and comparison are very important aspects of SIT relevant to workplace exclusion and discrimination. Social identification leads to activities that are congruent with the group's collective identity, that support institutions that embody their identity, and that foster stereotypical perceptions of self and others (Mor Barak, 2008, p. 245).

Social categorization is a cognitive tool that is used to "segment, classify, and order the social environment, and thus enable the individual to undertake many forms of social actions" (Mor Barak, 2008, p. 246). After people categorize themselves within a group and identify themselves as being members of that group, they tend to compare their group (the in-group) against other groups (out-groups). To maintain their self-esteem, they and group members will compare their group favourably against other ones. This helps to explain prejudice and discrimination, since a group will tend to view members of competing groups negatively to increase self-esteem. In this chapter therefore, employers and colleagues of PLHIV will see themselves as being members of in-group while they see the PLHIV as members of the out-group thereby excluding and discriminating against them.

This SIT explains why colleagues and employers exclude and discriminate against the PLHIV from participating in some social activities and use of official facilities particularly when they do not have full knowledge of the modes of transmission and prevention of HIV infection.

MAIN FOCUS OF THE CHAPTER

Methodology

The study was conducted in two local government areas (LGAs) of Lagos State namely Epe and Lagos Mainland. Epe LGA is a rural riverine area with 95 localities and a population of 181,409 by 2006 census (Federal Government Printer [FGP], 2007). It was considered to be an urban in 2010 (Federal Ministry of Health (FMOH), 2010). The people are predominantly Ijebus (a Yoruba sub-ethnic group), farmers, polygynyous, and Muslims. The LGA was chosen because of her high HIV prevalence rate which was 6.9% in 1999 (NIMR, 2000a) although it has dropped to 2.7% by 2010 (FMOH, 2010). Factors identified as driving the HIV infection then include poverty, promiscuity, low economic status of women, early marriages that often lead to early separation, polygyny, changing of spouses, skin scarification (FHI, 2001) and fishing (Elwange & Nahamya, 2005).

Lagos Mainland LGA, an urban setting, has 17 localities with a population of 317,720 by 2006 (FGP, 2007). Lagos Mainland LGA was selected because of the presence of Nigeria Institute of Medical Research (NIMR), Yaba, one of the popular centres for the National ART Programme in Nigeria that assisted in accessing the PLHIV. Its HIV prevalence rate has not been established but it is estimated to fall within the range in Lagos metropolis i.e. between 3.3% in Ikeja LGA, the state capital and 6.3% in Lagos Island LGA (FMOH, 2010).

Sample Size

The sample size was intended to be 100 (50 from each LGA) but 80 PLHIV were accessed: 30 from Epe LGA and 50 from LM LGA. Among the 80 PLWHA surveyed, 30 (37.5%) were men while 50 (62.5%) were women.

Ethical Considerations

Research ethics were fully observed with the approval of Institutional Review Board (IRB) of Nigeria Institute of Medical Research (NIMR), Yaba, Lagos. The respondents gave their oral informed consent and were also reassured that their data would be treated with strict confidentiality.

Data Collection

Four research assistants (RAs) who were graduates of the Department of Sociology, University of Lagos, were recruited based on their possession of adequate social research skills and experience. The RAs were trained for two days to enhance the quality of the data collected. Secondary data obtained from internet sources, books, reports etc. were reviewed while the primary data were collected from September 2005 to April 2006 using structured questionnaires. Besides the background data, the questionnaire contained other questions like: if the employers and co-workers knew about the HIV positive status; their employers' and colleagues' attitudes and behaviours towards them when they got to know their status; if PLHIV were mandated to have HIV tests; whether they were deployed to other departments or units on the basis of their HIV status; If they were isolated in separate offices because of HIV status; if their movements were ever restricted to certain areas within the premises; whether they shared toilets, canteen, etc. with other workers; whether they have ever been denied access to sports/recreational facilities; Ever been denied promotion because of their HIV status; if their organisations had health insurance scheme and if they were allowed to participate in the insurance scheme if available.

Data Analysis

Data were analyzed using the Statistical Package for Social Sciences (SPSS) versions 11 and 13. Analyses were run for quantitative and comparative data using descriptive, bivariate and Chi square statistics at 0.5 level of significance.

Fieldwork Challenges

Identifying the PLHIV in Epe was a major challenge. Only 30 PLHIV out of 50 of Epe respondents were investigated. Out of these, 20 were reached in Epe General Hospital while 10 were studied at NIMR, Yaba. NIMR is one the major sites for ART in Lagos State. It was gathered from Epe General Hospital that when people tested positive, they would be referred to NIMR for confirmatory tests. It was reported that some of them never reverted to Epe General Hospital. By such, they would be lost. The probable reason for this could be that they chose to continue with NIMR for anonymity and/or to avert facing discrimination.

Findings

Table 1 presents the profile of the respondents. The ages of the PLHIV ranged from 18 to 61 years. More than two-fifths of the respondents were between 30 – 39 years with a mean age of 36.26 years. More Epe respondents (48%) than Lagos Mainland (41%) were aged 30 – 39 years category with mean ages, 36.31 years and 36.22 years respectively. This difference is not significant. Almost one-third of respondents (33%) were never married and more of these were from Lagos Mainland (34%) as against and 30.0% of the Epe LGA respondents. Among the married respondents, 50.0% were from Lagos mainland while 23% came from Epe. A significant proportion (28%) of the PLHIV was divorced, separated and widowed. There was a higher percentage of the divorced, separated and widowed PLHIV in Epe LGA (46.6%) than in Lagos Mainland LGA (16%). The difference between the two LGAs is statistically significant at $p< 0.5$.

Majority of the respondents could be said to be well educated as 44% and 36% had secondary and post-secondary education respectively. Lagos Mainland LGA had more of this category than Epe LGA. This is expected since Lagos Mainland LGA is an urban setting. However, Epe LGA had more PLHIV with primary education (30%) than those with tertiary education (27%). The difference between the two LGAs is statistically significance with X^2 of 9.386; degree of freedom (df = 3) at $p < 0.05$. Employment status indicates that 42% of the respondents were unemployed. This proportion represents 43% and 42% of Epe and Lagos Mainland respondents respectively. Around 57% were employed disaggregated into 41% of self-employed PLHIV and 16% of PLHIV in paid employment. Comparing the two LGAs shows that Epe LGA had more self-employed PLHIV (47%) than Lagos Mainland (38%). A higher proportion of Lagos Mainland respondents (20%) than Epe (10%) were engaged in paid employment. These differences between the LGAs are not statistically significant.

With respect to income, equal proportion of unemployed PLHIV (42%) was also not receiving any income at the time of the study. Moreover, a significant proportion (24%) earned less than N10, 000.00 a month. The average income of the PLHIV was N9,198.55. This is below the current national minimum wage of N18,000 therefore many of the respondents belong to the lower income group. Disaggregating the respondents into LGAs shows that 37% of Epe LGA respondents compared to 16% of Lagos Mainland LGA respondents earned less than N10,000 per month. On the other hand, more Lagos mainland respondents (26%) than Epe respondents (10%) earned more than N10,000 per month. The differences are statistically significance ($X^2 = 5.782$; df = 3; $p > 0.05$).

Forms of HIV-Related Discrimination Experienced by PLWHA in the Workplace

The study examined the different forms and levels of discrimination in the work place. Before HIV-related discrimination could be explored in the work place it was pertinent to consider if the employers and co-workers of the PLHIV knew about their sero-positive status. The respondents were asked to declare if their employers and colleagues were aware of their sero-positive status and if they were, to describe their attitudes towards the PLHIV.

The column chart in Figure 1 presents the knowledge of the respondents' HIV positive (HIV+) status by the employers and colleagues in percentages. Out of the total respondents and out of those who had worked or who were still at work at the time of the study, 58% admitted that their colleagues and employers knew about their HIV+ status. Similarly, 58% and 57% of these PLHIV were from Lagos Mainland and Epe LGA respectively. This indicates that there is no difference between the proportions of PLHIV from the rural setting, Epe LGA and those from the urban setting, Lagos Mainland LGA who affirmed so.

Column charts in Figure 2 present attitudes of employers and colleagues towards PLHIV after they (the employers and colleagues) got to know that their employees and colleagues were living with HIV respectively. About 18% of the total respondents who were involved in this analysis found their employers' attitudes unfriendly after knowing their HIV positive status. Only Lagos Mainland LGA respondents (29%) constitute this proportion. On the other hand, 36% of the respondents said their employers' attitudes were indifferent or neutral after they had learnt of their HIV positive status. More Epe respondents (50%) than Lagos Mainland ones (29%) were in this category. Meanwhile, more than two-fifths of the total respondents reported that their employers' attitudes towards them were satisfactory. Among these are one half of Epe and more than two-fifths of Lagos Mainland respondents.

Figure 1. Whether the employers and colleagues knew about the respondents' HIV+ status

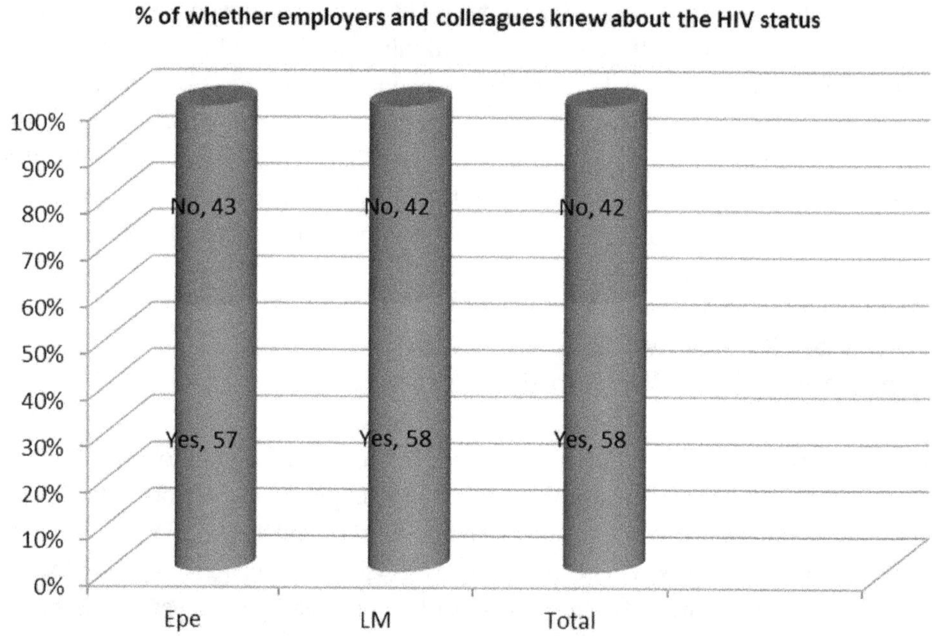

**For a more accurate representation see the electronic version.*

For colleagues, more than one half of the total PLHIV respondents reported that their colleagues' attitudes were unfriendly. It could be said that respondents' co-workers were more unfriendly than their employers because only 18% of the respondents reported that their employers were unfriendly compared with 56% of the respondents who said that their co-workers were unfriendly. About three-fifths of Lagos Mainland respondents reported that their colleagues were unfriendly while one-half of Epe respondents were so classified. More than one fifth of the respondents indicated that their colleagues' attitudes were indifferent. Similarly, the same proportion reported that their colleagues' attitudes towards them were satisfactory. Similar patterns of reporting were observed in both LGAs. One-quarter of Epe respondents reported that their co-workers were indifferent, and another one-quarter said their co-workers' attitudes were satisfactory. With respect to Lagos Mainland LGA, one-fifth of the respondents were satisfied with their colleagues' attitudes while another one-fifth said their colleagues' attitudes towards them were indifferent or neutral. The differences are not significant.

The column chart in Figure 3 presents the distributions (in percentages) of reasons why some PLHIV engaged in paid employment had stopped working. About 13% of the respondents admitted that they had stopped working. Among this percentage,

Figure 2. Attitudes of employers and co-workers

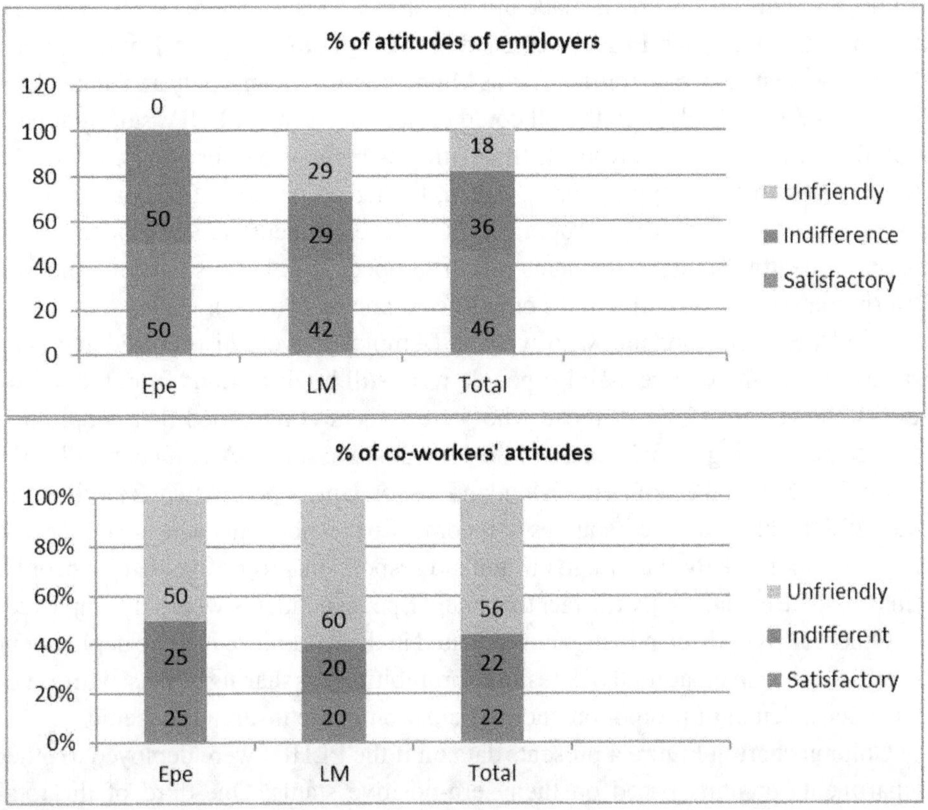

**For a more accurate representation see the electronic version.*

Figure 3. Reasons for stopping work

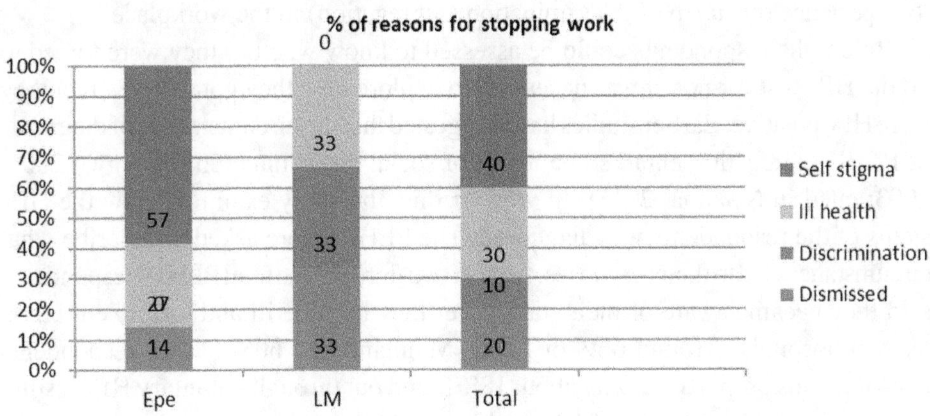

**For a more accurate representation see the electronic version.*

20% were dismissed instantly as their sero-positive status became known to the employers. This proportion is made up of 33% of Lagos Mainland and 14% of Epe respondents. One in ten PLHIV resigned because of stigma or discrimination and this is represented by one-third of Lagos Mainland respondents only and none of the Epe PLHIV was involved in this. It could be said that urban PLHIV suffered more than the rural ones in this respect. Ill health was responsible for about 30% of the total respondents in stopping work. Again, higher proportion of Lagos Mainland respondents (33%) than the proportion of Epe respondents (27%) stopped work due to ill health. Many respondents (40%) stopped work because of self-imposed discrimination and this comprises only Epe respondents (57%).

The PLHIV respondents who were self-employed were also considered. The traders among them were asked if people were still buying goods from them. The results showed that 28% of those who were traders complained that people had stopped patronizing them because of the HIV positive status. Among these PLHIV, 50% of Epe against 10% of Lagos Mainland respondents reported this. It implies that these PLHIV have lost their sources of income. Epe respondents who are traders are therefore, more likely than Lagos Mainland respondents to be avoided by people. This could be explained by the fact that many Epe respondents were self-employed.

Other forms of discrimination investigated in the workplace include deployment to other units, mandatory HIV testing, prohibition of sharing toilets with other colleagues, denial of promotion and participation in the insurance scheme.

Column chart in Figure 4 presents data on if the PLHIV were deployed to other departments or units based on their sero-positive status. One-third of the total respondents reported that they had been deployed to other departments or units. Among them are 43% of Lagos Mainland respondents and 20% of Epe respondents. In this case, a higher proportion of Lagos Mainland respondents than Epe respondents were affected. Therefore, Lagos Mainland respondents are more likely than Epe ones to experience this form of discrimination (segregation) in the workplace.

Before the respondents could be assessed to know whether they were forced to do the HIV tests or not, it was necessary to explore how they got to know that they were HIV positive. Earlier studies have suggested that the circumstances of diagnosis of PLHIV's infection entail some forms of social discrimination (Iwuagwu 2001; 2003; cited in Nwanna, 2011). In view of this, the study examined how the HIV status of the respondents was diagnosed. The PLHIV were asked to describe what circumstances led to their diagnoses. Almost two thirds of the total PLHIV respondents said they became aware of their status after they became ill and underwent blood tests in hospitals. Around 66% of Lagos Mainland and 60% of Epe respondents constitute this proportion. Only about 18% found out through voluntary HIV testing representing 17% and 14% of Epe and Lagos Mainland respectively. Six women out of 50 female PLWHA surveyed representing only 8% of the total PLWHA

Figure 4. Deployment of PLHIV respondents to other departments or units

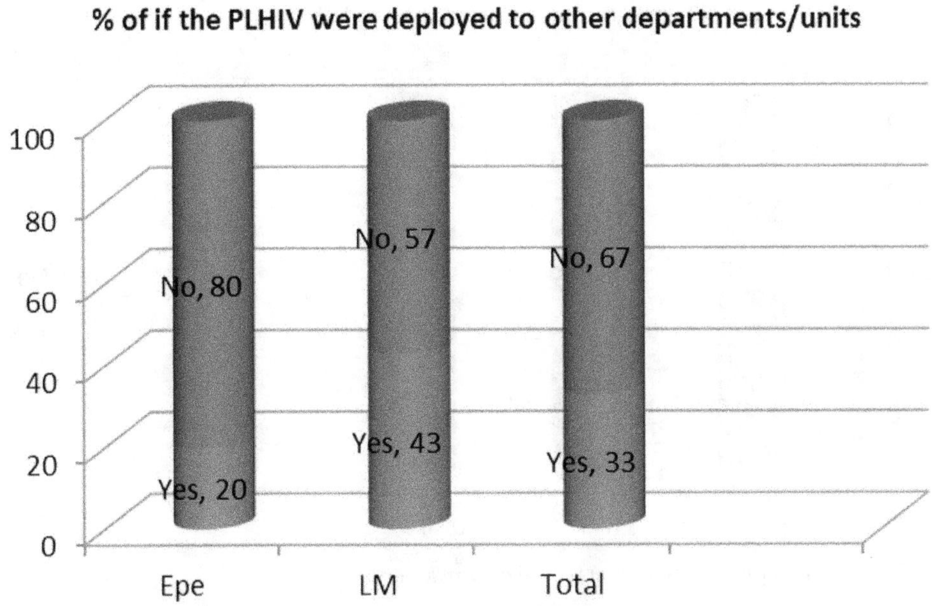

**For a more accurate representation see the electronic version.*

respondents and 12% of the female respondents; were diagnosed during antenatal care. Seven respondents (8%) were diagnosed HIV positive at pre - employment and pre -admission tests.

The column chart in Figure 5 presents percentage distribution of PLHIV respondents who were mandated to have HIV tests by the employers. About 27% of the total PLHIV had been forced by their employers to do the HIV tests. Among these are 50% of Epe and 11% of Lagos Mainland respondents. Therefore, it could be said that more Epe respondents than Lagos Mainland respondents were affected by this form of discrimination (mandatory HIV tests) in the workplace.

The column chart in Figure 6 presents the percentage distribution of PLHIV who were denied the use of same toilets with other colleagues. All the respondents who were involved in this analysis enjoyed sports facilities in their offices but 15% of the total PLHIV respondents were not allowed to share the same toilets with their co-workers. More of Epe respondents (17%) than Lagos Mainland respondents (14%) were prohibited from using the same toilets with others.

The chart in Figure 7 presents the percentage distribution of denying the PLHIV respondents promotion in the work place. About 18% of them reported being denied promotion on the basis of their sero-positive status. Only Lagos Mainland respondents (29%) were affected. Epe respondents were not affected.

Figure 5. PLHIV respondents who had been mandated to HIV tests

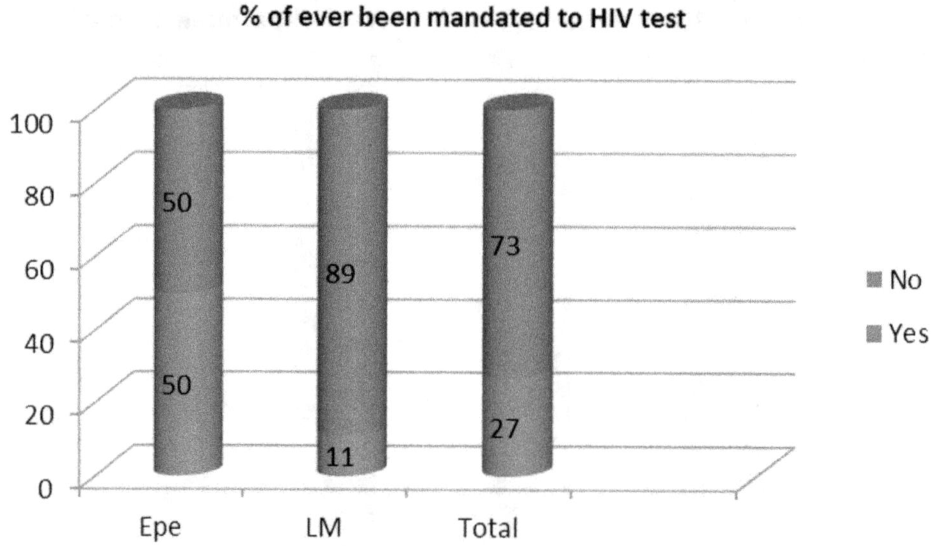

**For a more accurate representation see the electronic version.*

Figure 6. Share toilets with other workers

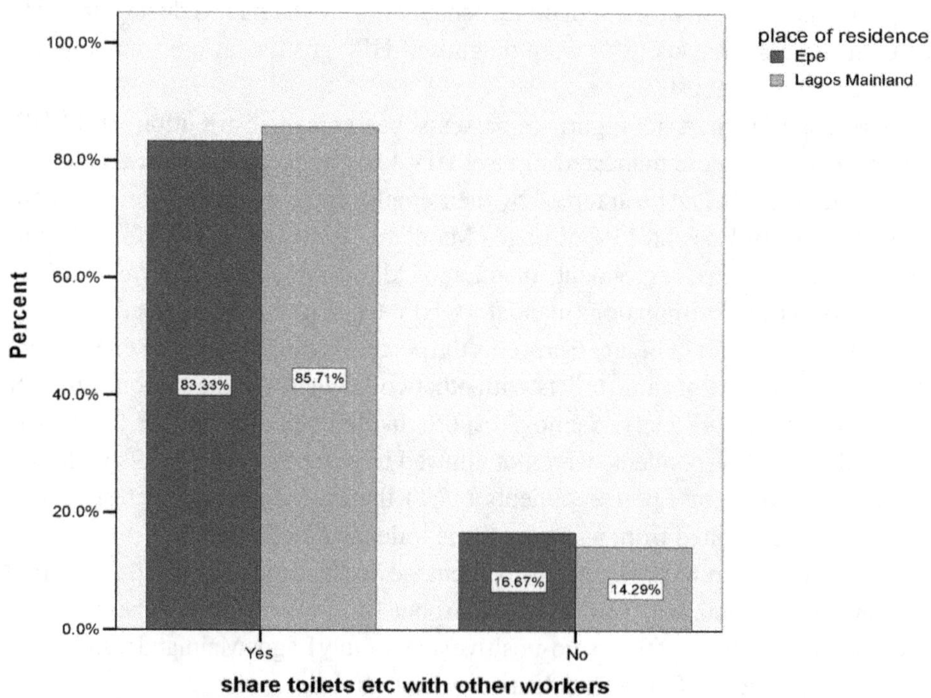

**For a more accurate representation see the electronic version.*

Figure 7. Ever been denied promotion

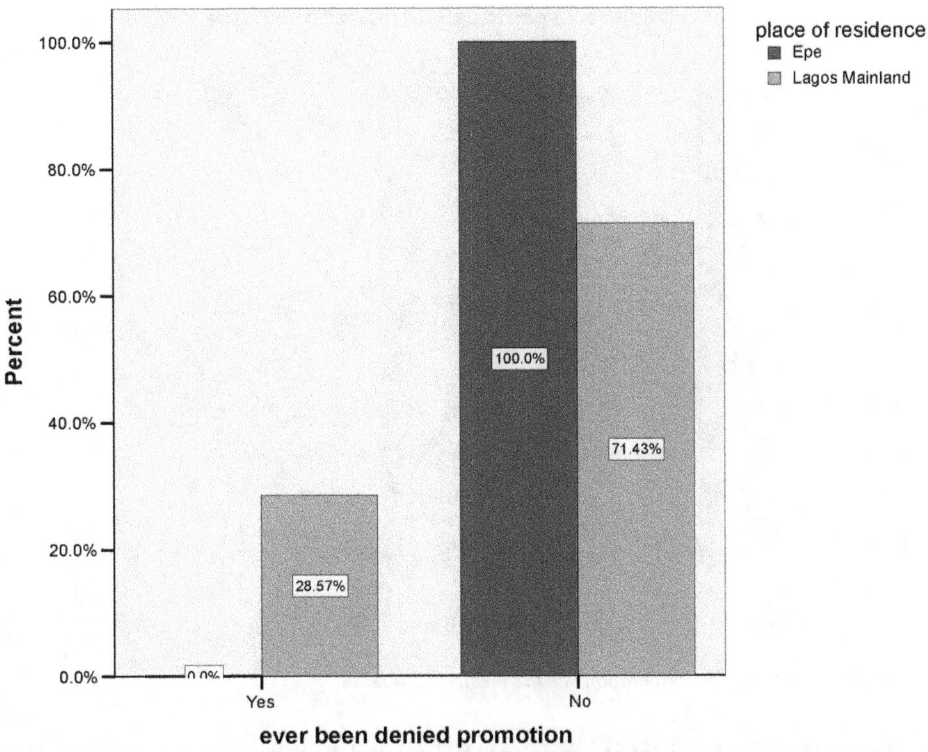

**For a more accurate representation see the electronic version.*

The respondents were asked to state if their offices were operating health insurance schemes. Among those PLHIV respondents who had worked or were working at the time of the study, 43% of them confirmed that they had health insurance schemes in their organizations. About three-fifths of the Epe respondents admitted that their organizations operated health insurance schemes against one-third of the Lagos Mainland respondents. The chart in Figure 8 presents the percentages of PLHIV who were or were not allowed to participate in insurance scheme. Although 43% of the PLHIV admitted having health insurance schemes in their offices, only 50% of this proportion were allowed to participate in the scheme. Among those who were not allowed to participate in the health insurance schemes, majority (67%) came from Lagos Mainland LGA compared to 33% of them that came from Epe LGA. More Lagos Mainland LGA respondents than Epe respondents were denied benefiting from health insurance scheme. One of the PLHIV who were provided with the health insurance cover said she was already benefiting from the scheme before her diagnosis. She therefore reiterated: "It is for all staff, irrespective of your sero-positive status. I was already benefiting from it before I was infected with the virus".

Figure 8. Allowed to participate in insurance scheme

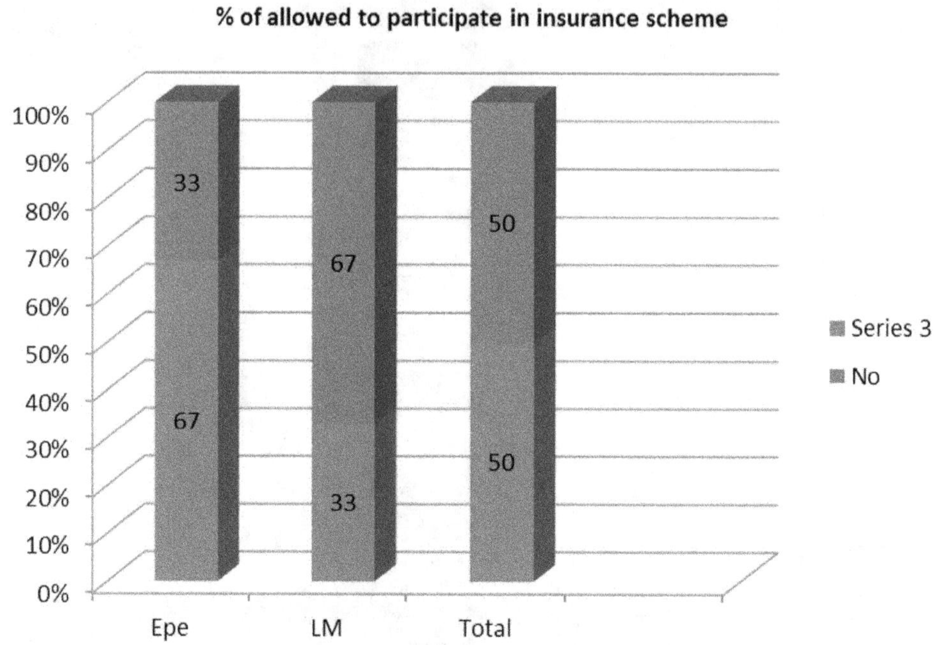

**For a more accurate representation see the electronic version.*

From the above findings, the forms of HIV-related discrimination in the workplace include mandatory HIV tests, exclusion from toilet facilities, isolation, denial of promotion and participation in the insurance scheme.

Discussion and Implications of Findings

The study revealed that more than half of the total respondents were employed and many were self-employed while the rest were in paid employment. Majority of Epe respondents were self-employed while Lagos Mainland respondents were more than Epe respondents among those in paid employment. This is probably due to the fact that Lagos Mainland respondents had higher educational level than Epe respondents. Similarly, Lagos Mainland respondents earned higher income than Epe respondents.

The results also showed that more than a half of the total respondents admitted that their colleagues and employers were aware of their sero-positive status with almost equal proportions of Lagos Mainland and Epe LGA respondents saying so. With this awareness, the study was able to assess the attitudes of the employers and co-workers towards the PLHIV. The findings revealed that almost one fifth of the employers were unfriendly towards the PLHIV and that these employers were from Lagos Mainland LGA respondents (29%) constitute this proportion. The probable explanation of this is that Lagos Mainland respondents are more likely to engaged in paid employment that those from Epe. Their employment status discussed under the respondents' profile indicated that many of the Epe respondents were self-employed and the few involved in the study might not have experienced this. The study further revealed that their colleagues' attitudes were also unfriendly. It was demonstrated that their co-workers were more unfriendly than their employers. This might be due to the closeness of co-workers to the PLHIV. A higher percentage of Lagos Mainland respondents than Epe respondents reported that their colleagues were unfriendly. This could be explained by urban factor. In urban centres individualism predominates and therefore people care less about other people while in rural settings relationships are more enveloping. These findings corroborate with that done by UNAIDS (2011) which revealed that colleagues and clients were not likely to be supportive or more likely to change their behaviours.

The results indicated that some PLHIV lost their jobs or sources of income as those who were engaged in paid employment stopped working and the self-employed PLHIV lost patronage from people respectively. It was revealed that more Epe respondents than Lagos Mainland ones lost their sources of income. This could be explained by the fact that many Epe respondents were self-employed and were traders and so were more likely to be avoided by people who knew their HIV status. Some PLHIV were dismissed instantly as soon as their employers got to know that they were living with HIV. This study confirms earlier studies by Adirieje (2003 cited in Nwanna, 2011) and Iwuagwu et al. (2003 cited in Nwanna, 2011). These studies found that some PLHIV were instantly dismissed when their sero-positive status became known to the employers. This type of treatment towards the PLHIV undermines HIV prevention and care and violates the human rights of the PLHIV.

Another reason for stopping work found in this study is stigma or discrimination. It was revealed that only Lagos Mainland respondents stopped work because of discrimination. While more urban PLHIV than the rural ones stopped work due to discrimination from other people, more rural PLHIV than urban ones stopped work because of self-imposed discrimination. In rural areas, primary relationships predominate where most people are familiar with one another. Therefore, the PLHIV would prefer to avert discrimination by stopping work. Contrary to rural relationships, urban relationships are secondary and individualistic and therefore, the PLHIV suffered more of discrimination in the work place. Another reason for stopping work is ill health. Ill health was responsible for about 30% of the total respondents in stopping work.

All these findings corroborate the results of earlier studies by UNAIDS (2011), The Global Network of People Living with HIV (GNP+), ILO, The PLHIV Stigma Index (2012) and ML dos Santos et al. (2014).

Other forms of discrimination found in this research include deployment to other units, mandatory HIV testing, prohibition of sharing toilets with other colleagues, denial of promotion and participation in the insurance scheme.

They research indicated that Lagos Mainland respondents are more likely to be deployed to other departments or units based on their sero-positive status. The finding validated the study of the Global Network of People Living with HIV (GNP+), ILO, The PLHIV Stigma Index (2012). Dismissing and deploying PLHIV to other departments or units indicate that the employers and colleagues lack full knowledge of HIV infection. Perhaps, they thought or perceived that HIV could be contracted through casual contact.

The study found that six women out of 50 female PLWHA surveyed representing only 8% of the total PLWHA respondents and 12% of the female respondents were diagnosed during antenatal care. This finding challenges the reliability of the sentinel data. The National HIV Sentinel Surveys of pregnant women visiting public antenatal clinics/hospitals provide data that are used as a representation for the general population. Therefore, the national prevalence rate may be grossly underestimated. The implication is that the Sentinel data do not accurately reflect the HIV pandemic in Nigeria.

Furthermore, seven respondents were diagnosed HIV positive at pre - employment and pre -admission tests. It is important to note that these two circumstances are among the various forms of social discrimination particularly when informed consent is not obtained. If seven out of 80 PLWHA respondents reported having gone for medical examinations for either employment or admission into schools, it is equivalent to 28,000 persons in about 3 million PLWHA in Nigeria. This is quite high.

Mandatory HIV test is another discriminatory attitude of the employers towards the PLHIV employees. It was revealed that more of Epe than of Lagos Mainland respondents were mandated to have HIV tests.

The findings indicated that PLHIV were excluded from the use of same toilets with other co-workers. It was revealed that Epe respondents were more likely than Lagos Mainland ones to be barred from sharing the same toilets with the other colleagues.

The study also showed that some PLHIV respondents were denied promotion due to their sero-positive status and this affected only the Lagos Mainland respondents. Once again, Lagos Mainland respondents are seen to be more likely to be discriminated against in the work place.

Also discovered was a significant proportion of PLHIV was not permitted to participate in health insurance scheme in their offices. One plausible reason for this is that insurance companies generally regard PLHIV as high risk insured (regarding cover) for them because it is deemed that the HIV-infection significantly increases the risk of early liability which does not augur well for their businesses which can only be mediated by increased premium payment to be borne by the prospective insured. A greater proportion of Lagos Mainland PLHIV than Epe respondents were denied participation in the health insurance scheme.

All these results demonstrate the different forms of discrimination PLHIV suffer in the workplace. The implication is that the human rights of the PLHIV are violated.

These negative attitudes of employers and co-workers towards the PLHIV could be explained with SIT. All these forms of discrimination were perpetrated by employers and co-worker because they perceived themselves as members of an in-group PLHIV as members of an out-group. The employers and colleagues of PLHIV identify, categorise and compare themselves against the PLHIV and with that perspective; they exclude and discriminate against PLHIV.

SOLUTIONS AND RECOMMENDATIONS

Identifying that using pregnant women as proxy in sentinel surveys underscores the problem of measuring HIV prevalence in Nigeria and would inform the policy decision to expand the scope of sentinel surveys. The Government should re-strategize the mode of data collection in order to include other subpopulations such as males, non-pregnant females and high-risk groups and to provide a more accurate measure of HIV prevalence in Nigeria

The rural- urban dichotomy, which shows that urban PLHIV are more likely to suffer discrimination in the work place would influence policy decisions on how to design culturally acceptable programmes that will help sensitize and enlighten the urban populace on the HIV pandemic and also protect the rights of rural PLWHA.

The identification of the different forms of discrimination should inform the policy decisions on issues related to discrimination within the workplace that should help in designing programmes that will elicit support for organisations where these PLHIV work to better handle them.

This is followed by a government's anti-discrimination policy supported by a law that will ensure the protection of the rights of PLHIV.

Identifying that using pregnant women as proxy in sentinel surveys underscores the problem of measuring HIV prevalence in Nigeria and would inform the policy decision to expand the scope of sentinel surveys. The Government should re-strategize the mode of data collection in order to include other subpopulations such as males, non-pregnant females and high-risk groups and to provide a more accurate measure of HIV prevalence in Nigeria.

Recommendations

Based on the findings the following are recommended:

- There is need to empower PLHIV through life-skill training, counselling, and education so that they can litigate when faced with discrimination.
- The PLHIV should speak out and be open about their status particularly the healthy-looking ones amongst them to demystify and dispel misinformation and generate empathy which will reduce the level of discrimination. More PLHIV should be trained extensively and engaged in public education as educators and advocates. They should also be involved as HIV policy makers at every level of decision making and engaged in equal partnerships with policy-makers.
- PLHIV who are already active in their communities should be encouraged because it will not only empower other volunteers by restoring dignity and status, but would also give a face to the epidemic and thus facilitate greater involvement of people living with HIV/AIDS.

There is need for employers to adopt and implement appropriate workplace policies.

HIV/AIDS voluntary counselling, testing and prevention/treatment services should be provided as part of regular health facilities.

Organizations should adopt legislations to prohibit mandatory-HIV testing.

- Formulate labour laws that will make organizations responsive to the challenges of HIV/AIDS and effectively guarantee to PLWHA the right to work, protection against unfair dismissal and other employment-related rights.
- Organisations should enforce the anti-discriminatory policies formulated by Lagos State and Federal governments.

FUTURE RESEARCH DIRECTIONS

This research indicates that PLHIV suffer different forms of discrimination in the work place. It will stimulate further studies in this area because it only provides the levels of the different types of discrimination. Future researches in this area should consider increasing the sample size, perhaps study different localities, and test hypotheses that may find out the categories of PLHIV who suffer these forms of discrimination since not all PLHIV are discriminated against.

CONCLUSION

This chapter investigated the people living with HIV in two local government areas of Lagos State, Nigeria, to assess the different forms of discrimination. It considered various studies done in this area and found that very few empirical researches were carried out in this area therefore this study set out to fill this gap. Secondly, it was revealed that discrimination was major factor of loss of employment or loss of sources of income, denial of promotion, change of attitudes towards PLHIV and exclusion from social activities in the work place. The chapter was premised on social identity theory of Tajfel (1982). The theory was able to explain why employers and colleagues of PLHIV could discriminate against PLHIV. Using structured questionnaires, data were collected from a purposive sample of 80 PLHIV from the two LGAs – Epe and Lagos Mainland. The results showed that the forms of HIV-related discrimination experienced by the PLWHA were instant dismissal from offices, mandatory HIV tests, alienation and exclusion from insurance scheme. The implication is that most organizations have not yet formulated HIV policy in their offices and thus do not care for their infected employees.

REFERENCES

Aggleton, P., & Parker, R. (2002). *A conceptual framework and basis for action: HIV/ADIS stigma and discrimination*. Geneva: UNAIDS.

dos Santos, M., Kruger, P., Mellors, S. E., Wolvaardt, G., & van der Ryst, E. (2014, January). An exploratory survey measuring stigma and discrimination experienced by people living with HIV/AIDS in South Africa: The People Living with HIV Stigma Index. *BioMed Central (BMC). Public Health, 27*. doi:10.1186/1471-2458-14-80

Elwange, C. B., & Nahamya, W. (2005). *Susceptibility and vulnerability among the fishing communities to HIV/AIDS in Uganda: A case of Lake Kioga*. Paper presented at the an International Conference on HIV/AIDS and Food and Nutrition Security from evidence to action, Durba, South Africa.

Family Health International (FHI). (2001). *In-depth Assessment Report*. Lagos: FHI.

Family Health International/Nigeria. (1999). HIV/AIDS: What to know and do. Lagos: FHI/Nigeria.

Federal Government Printer (FGP). (2007). Legal Notice on publication of the details of the breakdown of the national and state provisional totals 2006 census. Federal Republic of Nigeria Official Gazette, 24(94), B175 – 198.

Federal Ministry of Health (FMOH). (2010). *Technical Report: 2010 National HIV Sero-prevalence Sentinel Survey*. Abuja, Nigeria: FMOH.

Fit for Work Team. (2015). *HIV and discrimination in the workplace*. Retrieved from on 22/11/17 https://fitforwork.org/blog/hiv-and-discrimination-in-the-workplace/

Goffman, E. (1963). *Stigma: Notes on the management of spoiled identity*. Englewood Cliffs, NJ: Prentice-Hall.

Mor Barak, M. (2008). Social Psychological Perspectives of Workforce Diversity and Inclusion in National and Global Contexts. In R. Patti (Ed.), Handbook of Human Service Management. Thousand Oaks, CA: Sage Publications.

Nigerian Institute of Medical Research (NIMR). (2000a). *HIV/AIDS in Nigeria: Technical Report (Survey of Health and Laboratory Facilities) (1989-1999). In National HIV/AIDS Database Project* (1st ed.). Lagos: Federal Ministry of Science and Technology.

Nwanna, C. R. (2011). *Socio-economic status and HIV-related discrimination in Lagos, Nigeria*. LAP Lambert Academic Publishing GmbH & Co. KG.

Owolabi, R. S., Araoye, M. O., & Osagbemi, G. K. (2011). *Assessment of Stigma and Discrimination Experienced by People Living with HIV and AIDS Receiving Care/Treatment in University of Ilorin Teaching Hospital (UITH), Ilorin, Nigeria*. Retrieved November 20, 2017 from http://journals.sagepub.com/doi/abs/10.1177/1545109711399443

Poni-Gore, R., Lino, E. O., Alex, O. A., Simaya, R. J., Bion, A. J., Jette, A. J., & James, D. S. (2015). Stigma and Discrimination against People Living with HIV in Juba, South Sudan. *Journal of Community Medicine & Health Education*, *5*, 357. doi:10.4172/21610711.1000357

Population Council. (2002). Addressing HIV/AIDS Stigma and Discrimination in a Workplace Program: Emerging Findings. *Horizons*. Retrieved from http://www.popcouncil.org/uploads/pdfs/horizons/eskombslnsum.pdf

Shosanya, M. (2015). As FG enacts new law to protect PLWHA. *Daily Trust*. Retrieved from 22/11/17 https://www.dailytrust.com.ng/daily/health/49553-as-fg-enacts-new-law-to-protect-plwha

The Global Network of People Living with HIV (GNP+), ILO, The PLHIV Stigma Index. (2012). *Evidence Brief: Stigma and Discrimination at Work. Findings from the PLHIV Stigma Index*. Amsterdam: GNP+. Retrieved from https://www.gnpplus.net/assets/wbb_file_updown/4621/Stigma%20and%20Discrimination%20at%20work.pdf

UN International Labour Organization (ILO) Discrimination Convention (No. 111) 1958

UNAIDS. (2005). *HIV - Related Stigma, Discrimination and Human Rights Violations Case studies of successful programmes*. Geneva, Switzerland: UNAIDS. Retrieved November 22, 2017 from http://data.unaids.org/publications/irc-pub06/jc999-humrightsviol_en.pdf

UNAIDS. (2011). *People Living with HIV Stigma Index: Asia Pacific Regional Analysis 2011*. Retrieved from http://www.unaids.org/sites/default/files/media_asset/20110829_PLHIVStigmaIndex_en_0.pdf

UNAIDS. (2017). *UNAIDS data 2017*. Retrieved from http://www.unaids.org/en/resources/documents/2017/2017_data_book

Weiss, M. G., & Ramakrishna, J. (2001). *Interventions: Research on Reducing Stigma*. Available at http://www.stigmaconference.nih.gov/Weisspaper.htm

KEY TERMS AND DEFINITIONS

Employment Loss: A major consequence of discrimination in the workplace.

Epe General Hospital: A secondary level hospital in Epe local government area. The hospital has a screening center for HIV. Once a person's blood tests positive for HIV, the individual is referred to Nigeria Institute of Medical Research, Lagos Mainland LGA, Lagos.

Epe Local Government Area (LGA): A rural riverine area as at 2005 but is now considered an urban setting. It has a high HIV prevalence rate, which was 6.9% in 1999 but has declined to 2.7% in 2010.

Lagos Mainland Local Government Area (LGA): An urban setting located at the metropolis of Lagos State. It harbors areas that drive HIV infection. The HIV prevalence rate is not known.

Nigeria Institute of Medical Research: One of the popular centers for the National Anti-Retroviral Therapy (ART) Programme in Nigeria. The institute assisted in identifying PLHIV.

Sero-Positive Status: A state of being infected by Human Immunodeficiency Virus (HIV).

APPENDIX

Table 1. Profile of PLHIV respondents by place of residence

Characteristics	Epe		Lagos Mainland		Total	
Age	**N=30**	**%**	**N=50**	**%**	**N=80**	**%**
1. 18 – 19	2	2.6	0	0.0	2	2.6
2. 20 – 29	3	10.3	13	26.5	16	20.5
3. 30 – 39	14	48.3	20	40.8	34	43.6
4. 40 – 49	10	34.5	12	24.5	22	28.2
5. 50 and above	0	0.0	4	8.1	4	5.1
No response	1	1.3	1	2.0	2	2.0
X^2=8.951; df=4; $p>0.05$						
Marital status						
1. Never married	9	30.0	17	34.0	26	32.5
2. Married	7	23.3	25	50.0	32	40.0
3. Divorced/separated/widowed	14	46.6	8	16.0	22	27.5
X^2=9.838; df=2; $p<0.05$						
Level of education						
0 None	2	6.7	0	0.0	2	2.5
1 Primary	9	30.0	5	10.0	14	17.5
2 Secondary	11	36.6	24	48.0	35	43.8
3 Tertiary	8	26.7	21	42.0	29	36.3
X^2=9.386; df=3; $p<0.05$						
Employment status						
1 Unemployed	13	43.3	21	42.0	34	42.4
2 Self- employed	14	46.7	19	38.0	33	41.3
3 Paid employment	3	10.0	10	20.0	13	16.3
X^2=1.503; df=2; $p>0.05$						
Monthly income						
1 No income	13	43.3	22	44.0	35	42.4
2 Less than 10,000	11	36.7	8	16.0	19	23.8
3 N10,001 – 20,000	1	3.3	6	12.0	7	8.8
4 N20,001 and above	2	6.7	7	14.0	9	11.3
No response	3	10.0	7	14.0	10	13.3
X^2=5.782; df=3; $p>0.05$						

Chapter 3
The Nexus of Tamed Bureaucracy and Better Health Outcomes for Consumers in Nigeria's Health Institutions

Fatai A. Badru
University of Lagos, Nigeria

ABSTRACT

Health institution is a typology of formal organization that is designed manifestly to ensure the diagnosis, treatment, and rehabilitation of the sick and the wounded. There are three levels of health institutions in Nigeria: the primary, secondary, and the tertiary/specialist care organizations. Their clienteles range from the infants, very young, adolescents, middle-aged, and the very old afflicted with acute or chronic health conditions, contagious or non-communicable disorders. A number of healthcare workers are involved in the process of patients/clients' care and treatment. The process and the divergent human resources in the healthcare industry tend to throw up "red-tapism" and complex bottlenecks resulting from specialization, hierarchy of authority, and chains of command of bureaucracy. The chapter relying on guided participant observation, desk research, and key informants interrogated this phenomenon. The chapter concludes that if bureaucracy is tamed, there is bound to be better health outcome for health consumers in health institutions in Nigeria.

DOI: 10.4018/978-1-5225-6133-0.ch003

INTRODUCTION

Many diseases afflict human species and several attempts are deployed to seek and utilize known remedies, indigenous and foreign. Health outcome is influenced by the perception of the illness or disease, steps taken to redress the disease and the quality of services rendered by the health workers. Health Outcome is also measured by evidence-based healthcare parameters that the patients get the positive and desired goal of the healthcare intervention to the right health consumer at the right time in the most cost-effective, conducive and therapeutic environment. As Williams and Torrens (2008: 317) indicate, 'outcome reflects what happened to the patients. Quality of health care is seen in this paper as the degree to which health services for individuals, families, groups and communities, operationally tagged health consumers, increase the likelihood of desirable health outcome and consistent with current professional service. The indices of the health quality include morbidity, mortality, functional status, and other measures reflecting clinical outcomes, quality of life, patient satisfaction and related issues.

Donabedian (1966) had come up with three yardsticks of quality evaluations: the structure of care, the process of care and the outcome of care.

The Structure of care involves the environment within which the care and services are provided, organization of the building, facilities available and the personnel working therein; Location of the facility whether rural or urban, ownership, private or government; level of care, primary, secondary or tertiary are important considerations.

The Process entrenches what is done for the patient by the healthcare providers such as tests and investigations for accurate diagnosis; in this vein, mammography and a fine-needle aspiration biopsy (FNAB) may be requested by a surgeon for a patient suspected to have benign or malignant tumour of the breast and *trucut* may also be done which may not reveal any pathology different from the FNAB but the patient and his relation may bear the cost while the patient alone bears the pain. The radiographer may have issues with the test and the interpretation of the radiologist may be trenchant; Plain Chest Xray may be requested for patient suspected to have pulmonary tuberculosis beyond sputum test for microscopy, culture and sensitivity; barium meal and endoscopy may be ordered for patients with duodenal ulcer. These tests are not easy to pick for the patients. They are also not cheap.

Healthcare Outcome

Many factors are known to influence the healthcare outcome. These factors include: the number of healthcare workers available and the skill and dexterity possessed by the health workers, the specialization of the health workers, the cost of the health services, gender of the consumer, educational attainment of the patients, location of the health facilities, distance of the health facilities to where the health consumer lives, equipment available in the facilities, complexity of the healthcare organization, to mention but a few.

A health institution is a kind of facility patronized by the sick for their treatment and recovery. It is a category of formal organization that is ostensibly designed to ensure that diagnosis, treatment and rehabilitation of the sick and the wounded are professionally handled.

BACKGROUND

In Nigeria, we have two broad forms of healthcare delivery: the indigenous and the western or orthodox care. The indigenous care provisions are known to be compatible with many cultural prescriptions and in tandem with their ways of lives and cultural prescriptions and proscriptions. It is also less cumbersome to access beyond the relatively cheaper cost of the services as compared with modern medicine with avalanche of gadgets and equipment and intimidating specialized professionals that may cost health consumers a fortune to access. Tella, (1992), Oyekanmi, (1997), WHO, (1998), Badru, (2003) and Abosede, (2017) have alluded to the immense values of indigenous medicine.

But what is indigenous or traditional medicine? According to the World Health Organisation, (1998) 'traditional medicine comprises therapeutic practices that have been in existence, often for hundreds of years before the development and spread of modern scientific medicine and still in use today. These practices vary widely in keeping with the social and cultural heritage of different countries'. Abosede, (2011 cited in Abosede, 2017: 60) in a study in Nigeria, argued that there was a better health outcome of indigenous skilled birth attendance in her study. She compared and explored the factors associated with traditional maternity/herbal homes and run by traditional birth attendants. She found that infants delivered at Traditional Maternity Homes were less likely to have severe hyper-bilirubinaemia compared with infants delivered in hospitals or residential homes.

The Orthodox care is bio-medical and organic-based. Badru (2016) argued that 'western medicine' called thereafter in this chapter, orthodox medicine is the science of diagnosing and healing the sick which is rooted in biomedical science and germ theory approaches that claim that every disease has an organic root. Of course, this is debatable as some 'western' diseases are yet to be laid bare in terms of their origin and their aetiological factors are shrouded in mystery. Example is 'fever of unknown origin'.

In the orthodox training and practice, the process and the divergent human resources in the healthcare industry tend to throw up red-tapism, and complex bottlenecks resulting from specialization, hierarchy of authority and chains of command of bureaucracy. These are expected to ensure efficiency in the care, cut cost of care, allow the best professionals to come in to treat the clients, among others. However, participant observation of this researcher over the last 39 years in the healthcare industry has shown that the care rendered to clients has not most times met the expected health outcome that the clients deserve and sometimes proved counterproductive and inadvertently inimical to the treatment and recovery of patients and other health consumers.

There are iatrogenic diseases which suggest that such conditions afflict the health consumers who patronize the healthcare facility but were not the original conditions that brought them to the health institution. There are reports of client abuses, maltreatment, drug over-dosage, wrong prescriptions, negligence and physical restraint of patients with mental and behavioural disorders, among other maleficence.

Objectives of the Study

The general aim of the study is to interrogate the complexity of orthodox health care and the inherent problems that bureaucracy throws up therein. Specific objectives are: investigate the benefits of the indigenous medicine to the patients, examine the antinomies of bureaucracy in the orthodox healthcare sector, draw attention to the impact of complexity and specialization of multiple healthcare professionals in the orthodox care and draw lessons that can be learnt to lessen the burden for the clients and improve the health outcome of the patients.

Focus of the Chapter: Issues, Trends and Problems

The complexity of accessing treatment in tertiary hospitals can be excruciating. From the health record clerking, to weighing, taking of vital signs, battery of tests and investigations, waiting to see the physicians and pausing to do further tests, and purchasing the prescribed drugs.

Badru, (2003, 2010, 2016, 2017) has acerbically pointed to the fact that there are three levels of orthodox health institutions in Nigeria: primary, secondary and the tertiary/specialist care institutions.

Primary healthcare facilities are the first port of call for healthcare services and these are responsible for minor ailments and disorders such as malarial fever, immunization of children, safe maternal delivery, wellness clinics, etc. Primary Healthcare is defined as:

Essential healthcare based on practical, scientifically sound and socially acceptable methods and technology made universally accessible to individuals and families in the community and through their full participation and at a cost that the community can afford in the spirit of self reliance and self determination... It is the first level of contact with individuals, the family, and community with the national health system bringing healthcare as close as possible to where people live and work and constitutes the first element of a continuing healthcare process. (Massoud, 2008, 17; Abosede, 2017, p. 20)

Primary healthcare programme is encapsulated in nine fundamental functions:

1. Public Health education
2. Nutrition improvement
3. Adequate safe water and basic sanitation
4. Maternal and child health care, including family planning
5. Immunization
6. Prevention and control of endemic and epidemic diseases
7. Provision of essential drugs and supplies
8. Elderly and handicapped care
9. Accident and injury care

Abosede, (2017:14) asserted that the initial 'eight (later 10) components of primary care formed the basis and precursor of the current 17 Sustainable Development Goals. The other components missing from the above list include Mental health and Primary Oral Health.

Major diseases are referred to the secondary health centres such as General Hospitals and Comprehensive Health Centres for treatment and management. Surgical intervention such as caesarian sections and appendicectomy are done for elective surgeries. Specialized and major diseases like cholera, pulmonary tuberculosis, compound fractures, cancers and psychiatric disorders are referred to specialist and tertiary hospitals for treatment and management. The specialist and tertiary healthcare centres are reference hospitals. Examples of such include Mainland Hospital, Yaba, Lagos State for infectious diseases, National Orthopaedic Hospital, Igbobi, Lagos, and Dalla Orthopaedic Hospital, Kano.

In addition, we have Federal Neuro-psychiatric Hospital, Yaba, Lagos, Nigeria which was established in 1907; It is about 500-bedded Hospital that takes care of diverse behavioural and psychiatric disorders; Lagos University Teaching Hospital (LUTH) that has many clinical specialized units: Orthopaedics, Ophthalmology, Obstetrics and Gynaecology, anatomical and molecular pathology, anaesthesia, dermatology, oncology, radiotherapy, radio-diagnosis and radiology, accident and emergency, intensive care, paediatrics, nephrology, cardiology, paediatric and adult; internal medicine, neurology, haematology, surgery, among others. Basic medical units include: anatomy, biochemistry, physiology, chemical pathology, laboratory science and technology.

Badru (2010) in an edited work explores, in ten parts, the argument for the viability of indigenous healthcare system in Nigeria and the inherent benefits in accessing such healthcare services. Hitherto, 'orthodox' health care, euphemism for western-oriented healthcare system, was given and still being given undue prominence and utilized by the elites [governing and non-governing] and the non-elites in Nigeria to the detriment, undervaluing and marginalization of the indigenous health care systems. The elites covertly consult and patronize the indigenous healthcare system, yet deride it in the open. How is the so-called orthodox healthcare legitimized, constructed and perpetuated? In what ways has western medicine undermined indigenous healing system? Literature, guided observation of health industry and trends show that socialization, which passes hegemonic and western healthcare system, is contended to be partly responsible for the transmission and perpetuation of this skewed and anti-thetical health policy. This is also engendered and promoted by the imperialistic system of education in which many Nigerians at home and in the Diaspora are nurtured. The kernel of the paper is that restrained or tamed bureaucracy will undoubtedly portend a better health outcome for the health consumer.

Clarification of Key Concepts

It is apposite to clarify some striking concepts in this article. In this vein, it is germane to interrogate what constitutes an organization and bureaucracy before we delve into how the expected pristine processes encumber the practitioners and the consumers of healthcare in such institutions.

CONCEPTUAL ISSUES

Organization

An organization is defined as a coordinated unit consisting of at least two people who function to achieve a common goal or a set of goals (Gibson, Ivancevich & Donelly, 1994; see also Ifenowo, 1997). Organizations could be business in orientation, health in perspective or social in nature. Organizations are inevitable, pervasive and ubiquitous. Everyone is born in an organization (home or hospital); grew up and socialized by organization (Families); educated by organizations, (crèche, primary, secondary and tertiary schools); work and earn a living in organization,(employment); grow old and some taken care of by organizations (either assisted or independent living such as old people homes, hospices); die in organization and buried by organization. We are concerned with health organization in this piece. Organizations could also be normative, utilitarian or coercive.

The next section provides some information on these organizations.

Normative organization is a formal category of organization that sustains control through shared moral commitment. Membership in normative organizations is purely voluntary. People join because they want to or because of a strong and positive sense of obligation. Members work together to promote an important social cause. Members join voluntarily and share a positive sense of duty and purpose. Some healthcare providers volunteer their services in the normative health organization. A very good example is Red Crescent Society. Another is Red Cross Society.

Utilitarian organizations are also a formal typology that workers are engaged in and expect pecuniary rewards. Hospital or health organization is a form of utilitarian organization that renders specialized services and meet diverse needs of people as health consumers in many tasks and set goals. Health workers in utilitarian organizations are paid salaries, wages and allowances depending on their specialization and scheme of services rendered by the workers.

Coercive organization maintains control over his workers through legitimate power and authority. Individuals in such organizations do not ordinarily go in on voluntary basis but through some conscription. An example is a psychiatric hospital wherein patients with psychiatric and behavioral disorders are admitted, diagnosed and treated for mental and behavioral disorders. The patient may deny that he/she has mental disorder when he lacks insight into his condition and may be diagnosed with major psychiatric disorders such as schizophrenia and bipolar affective disorder. Another example of coercive organization is a prison. There are rigid rules, established procedures, regulations and strict chain of command. There is master-servant relationship. The warders and inmates in the prisons work in a bureaucratic setting. The inmates have time to eat, sleep and receive visitors. In hospital setting, the patients can hardly query the decision of the health providers. The words of the physician is the law!!! Patients in psychiatric hospitals are restricted, made to lose their identity by referring to them as 'bed 1' or 'bed 2'. They cannot go out without express permission of the 'exit paper' endorsed by the psychiatrist. Visitors are restrained and made to come for visits at a particular time. Foods brought for patients must be tasted by the relatives or significant others before been handed over to the patients.

Generally, organizations have two delineated morphologies: *Structure* and *processes*. The structure is the anatomy that shelters the formal pattern of how the organizations' officials are grouped and how the job specifications are laid. It is depicted by the organogram or the organizational chart. The second is tagged the processes of the organization. These are the activities that give life to the organization. These include planning, recruiting, retention and motivation of workers, effective communication within and without the organization (Lawal, 1993; Gibson, Ivancevich, & Donelly, 1994).

Healthcare Institution

According to King, (1982, p. 10.4) "...functionally, an hospital can have a floor or several floors with closely integrated central 'nucleus' supported by a shell of lesser buildings..." The healthcare institution can be privately or publicly owned. In the first, individuals and missionaries who are not directly linked with the state provide the wherewithal and recruit the personnel to man the facility. It is usually registered with the state to ensure that the benchmark equipment and human resources for health are adequate and available to the health consumers ostensibly at a profit for the proprietor. Usually the quantum of health personnel is less compared with publicly-owned facility. Unlike the first, the latter is government-owned and tends to be larger, more intricate in terms of human and material resources thus potentiating intense bureaucracy.

The healthcare institutions can be utilitarian and normative in nature as the workers get intrinsic values and professional *espirit de corps* beyond earning their wages in such organizations. Their clienteles range from the infants, very young, adolescents, middle-aged and the very old, male and females.

The conditions that make them to seek healthcare intervention could be acute, which duration of affliction is short, for instance malarial fever or chronic health conditions with prolonged duration such as pulmonary tuberculosis and malignant tumors. The conditions could also be contagious which suggests that the afflicted host can transmit the disease condition to others through interaction. Such diseases include cholera, measles, whooping cough, diphtheria, tetanus, small pox, monkey pox, chicken pox and a host of others or non-communicable disorders, which cannot be transmitted to others by interaction as typified by raised blood pressure called hypertension. Diabetes Mellitus is another non-communicable disease.

It is known there are two categories of health workers: core and ancillary or support staff. The core staffs render professional and direct clinical services to the patients. These include the doctors, dentists, nurses, pharmacists, medical social workers, physiotherapists, laboratory scientists, dieticians, radiologists, radiographers, occupational therapists, among others. The support staffs include the health service administrators, health/medical record officers, clerical officers, engineers, accountants, auditors, ambulance drivers, hospital attendants, cleaners, and a host of others.

A number of healthcare providers are involved in the process of patients/clients' care and treatment both at the indigenous and 'orthodox' layers. In the latter, the providers are many and varied: These include the medical doctors, registered nurses, trained midwives, physiotherapists, pharmacists, dieticians, medical social workers, clinical psychologists, laboratory scientists, to mention but a few. At the traditional or indigenous stratum, there are also different categories of traditional healers as espoused by Adepeju Bashua, (2016) and Badru, (2017). In this vein, among the Yoruba ethnic stock in Nigeria, there are those who utilize divination called *Babalawo* and others who resort to the use of herbs, charms and incantations called *Onisegun or Elewe Omo,* the latter is epitomized by women selling and specializing in children's herbs.

MAX WEBER'S POSTULATION ON ORGANIZATION AND BUREAUCRACY

Max Weber (1864-1920) was a great German sociologist that was concerned with increasing rationalization of human behavior in formal organizations. He wrote seven main textbooks. Weber contends that there are two major categories of domination based on authority: rational-legal structure and bureaucratic administration. This paper is concerned with the latter form of domination.

According to Weber, to be effective and efficient, as an organization, a modern organizational structure needs bureaucratic authority. Sapru (2008:81) asserted that a French man, de Gournay coined the word 'bureaucracy' but Weber, a German scholar, identified bureaucracy as the most rational and efficient form of the organization devised by man. It is rational because it involves control based on knowledge. He argued that the ideal-typical structure has clearly defined spheres of competence, operates according to analyzable rules, and has calculability in its operations (Beetham, 1974, p. 69). Weber contended further that bureaucracy is efficient because of its precision, speed, consistency, availability of records, continuity, possibility of secrecy, unity, rigorous coordination and minimization of interpersonal friction, personnel cost and material costs (Rheinstein, 1954, p. 349).

Max Weber isolated eight constitutive elements of ideal-typical bureaucracy as follows:

1. Bound by rules which ensure standardization and equality in treatment of workers.
2. Excludes the usage of personal discretion and emotions of modern society.

3. A sphere of competence with systematic division of labor and provision of the incumbent with the necessary authority to accomplish his tasks and carry out his functions.
4. This power and authority must not undermine the organizational goal.
5. Principle of hierarchy which suggests that each lower office is under the control and supervision of a higher one. The subordinates know who to report to for his actions and inactions.
6. The tasks to be done are written down unambiguously and everyone knows the breech and performance.
7. Other characteristics include need of specialized training for increasing technical rules, knowledge and skills. A fresh medical graduate needs to undergo further training to be qualified as a consultant in diverse specialities.
8. Another important element is impersonal detachment from the organization for organizational efficiency. The worker is expected to be affectively neutral and adopt collective orientation rather than self-orientation borrowing from Parsonian paradigms. The physician should not allow his feelings to color his judgment in the discharge of his duties whether the patient is a male or female, shares the same faith or not or hails from the health provider's place of residence or not, ugly or handsome. Doing otherwise will be vitiating the Hippocratic oath sworn to at professional induction. In other words, professional best practice ought to be the norm.

In sum, ideal-typical form of organization has these indices: specialization with coloration of expertise, hierarchy of authority premised on detailed and precise stratification which ought to promote discipline and coordination. Others include a system of procedures and rules which should enhance simplicity and predictability, depersonalization of relationships to ensure continuity and rationality in decision making and use of measurable reward system which illuminated promotion ladder.

PATHOLOGIES/ANTINOMIES OF BUREAUCRACY AS THEY AFFECT HEALTHCARE DELIVERY

In spite of these lofty goals of ideal-typical bureaucracy, there are issues and challenges that surround it. These include: rigidity of outlook, excessive centralization of decisions, development of impersonal rules, overzealousness of adherence to the regulations, the isolation of different levels of employees (or "strata") reinforced by group pressure and development of parallel power relationships. Selznick, Merton and Gouldner (2003) have also pointed out many other 'antinomies' and "dysfunctions", as offshoots of bureaucratic organizations as characterized by formality and lack of adaptability. Specialists tend to respond to challenges in an extremely rigid manner. What a healthcare provider can do effortlessly to make a patient comfortable may be hindered by the rigid rules that incapacitate him because of the position of the provider on the stratum of the hierarchy. Indubitably, task-shifting and task-sharing and team work are alternative strategies to nib some of these challenges in the bud.

Most critics seem to agree with the fact that whatever the justification for organizational bureaucracy, it invariably leads to stratification, inflexibility or rigidity. The organization creates a stereotyped pattern of response and ceases to be adaptable to the external environment. It leads to "dehumanized" management approach and development of "machine-models" of workers and managers. In communal jargon, bureaucracy leads to "red tape" and the building of small empires within an organization. There is an undue attachment to trivial matters and the artificial creation of work by administrators.

One of the symptoms may be resistance to technological change or other innovations; another may be inappropriate responses to changing conditions. The chances are that the bureaucratic organization will become a victim of over-routinization and lack of "enterprise". Last but not the least, bureaucracy encourages the development of minimum acceptable standard of performance by employees. Personal security, achieved partly by hiding behind the rules, at the cost of organizational effectiveness, becomes the employee's watchword in such organization. This is termed learned helplessness.

Unfortunately, most human beings are not rule-oriented and "rational" as Weber has envisaged. Over a period of time, people in these bureaucratic organizations learn to live by the rules. Rules are no longer regarded as the means to certain ends but become the end themselves. Organizations in an extreme state of bureaucracy become the embodiments of rules, regulations and self-perpetuating hierarchies and people in these organizations become robots. As indicated earlier, people quickly learn the act of hiding behind the rules and even where they could render assistance and provide services, the excuse would be on the organizational regulations which specify what to do and what should not be done. Survival and security become very important; objectives are forgotten; rules and regulations are followed for the very sake of following them; and no room is left for the use of individual's discretion and creativity.

Other 'pathologies' or negativities associated with bureaucracy include the following: bureaucracies tend to restrict the psychological growth of the individual and cause feelings of failure, frustration and conflict (Argyris, 1964). Furthermore, the two anchors of impersonal detachment and *espirit de corps* which Weber argued would accomplish administrative efficiency are incompatible. For instance, if the interface between the administrative staff is dictated by impersonal detachment, it becomes challenging how *espirit de corps* can evolve. In addition, rigid observance of principle of hierarchical relations between superiors and subordinates may give rise to mutual suspicion. To say the least, the system of promotion according to seniority and according to merit is conflicting. A worker who has stayed longer but does not improve himself is likely to be promoted before someone who came later and has not had 'cognate experience' to be considered for promotion.

Study Findings

The key highlights of the findings from the key informants are provided below:

Hospital bureaucracy in accessing healthcare:

I really don't know that the complexity of our procedures give so much trouble to our patients until a relative of mine has cause to seek for medical treatment in a specialist medical facility for oncological-related condition. Mind you, I am physician myself and I have called a colleague who facilitated my appointment and my relative to see the oncologist and radiotherapist. We were there on time by 8 am and the consultant didn't come until 10.30am. The patient was seen by the health record clerk with the referral note and searched for his appointment folder; this was taken to the nurse who performed some nursing functions such as taking of temperature, pulse, respiration and blood pressure. She also weighed the patient and measured the height. Meanwhile, the patient was very weak to go through these hurdles. After the vitals, the patient joined others to listen to the routine health education by the nurses and thereafter was arranged for physician's appointment. There were many junior doctors in training: senior residents, residents, house officers, nurses, clinical psychologists and clinical pharmacists. The patient saw the oncologist at 12.30 pm and patient was referred for chest Xray to see the level of metastases. After which the patient went to the section on Xray unit for radiography. We left the clinic at 5.30pm.

Another key informant who is a relation of a booked patient laments as follows:

I took my blood sister to the hospital after many failed appointments. I was shocked to the marrow to see that there was no light and faulty generator to power and restore light when the epileptic power went off. We had to resort to touch-light and mobile phone light to function. My sister had been referred by a General physician to a surgeon who was not available but represented by his senior resident who mistakenly prescribed 'overdosage' of drug called Taminophen. He was corrected by the consultant surgeon who was a professor of surgery. After a battery of tests: Chest Xray, and blood tests, we were requested to come after the results of the tests were ready. The tests could not be done at the facility in the teaching hospital as the equipment was said to be faulty. We went to a private facility at Oshodi, Lagos

Mainland Local Government called "Mecure' manned by the Indians. After the tests and results which cost us a fortune, we were billed for a surgery of the breast. A radical mastectomy and ancillary clearance was done. The specimen of the tissues excised were sent to the morbid anatomy for histological and cytological analyses. The patient recovered well until she came down again and became worse. She was losing weight rapidly and we were referred again to a radiotherapist who was fuming that we ought to have done chemotherapy first and the result of the test ought to have pointed out that to the attending surgeon. But the surgery had been done!!!. A dose of chemotherapeutic drugs were prescribed to be purchased. Some tests such as Electrocardiography (EEG), haematological profiles in the blood and among others were ordered again. The patient was requested to take six pints of blood at interval. It was difficult to get the blood that matches the blood group of the patient before blood grouping and cross-matching to avoid blood crisis. Thereafter, the prescribed drugs were purchased with all the infusions which were given at the out-patient clinic of the hospital. The drugs had severe unwanted effects on the patient: blackish tongues, palms and soles, gradual falling of hairs, weakness of the body, nausea and vomiting, inability of the patient to sleep at night and depression, among others. The burden of care was unbearable and unfortunately we lost the patient.

Challenges and Solutions

From the study findings it can been seen that consumers of health encounter a lot of challenges in order to access good healthcare and attain better outcome. It is worse when they are poor, live in rural areas as many health facilities are located in the urban setting, and many healthcare professionals dread going to the rural areas to work. Many low-income people are denied access to good health care and intimidated and excluded by the long wait and bottle-necks encountered in the orthodox care when there is a need to access and utilize the secondary or tertiary healthcare. Some of the suggestions to nib the problems in the bud include making available many health care facilities, integrating indigenous health care into the orthodox one, empowering the rural people, re-educating and creating awareness among the citizenry, among others. These can be pursued in further and future research and an enabling environment created for its materialization.

SUMMARY AND CONCLUSION

The central argument of the chapter is that complex organization is a formal organization and can be normative, utilitarian or coercive. The health institution is a pro-type of a complex organization. These health institutions exhibit complexities and intricacies that inadvertently impart negatively on the health outcome of the health consumers. We have three tiers of healthcare in Nigeria: Primary, secondary and the tertiary/specialist. These facilities are either privately or missionary-owned or government owned. The government institution tends to be bigger, more complex compared with private facilities. There are more specialists therein and they serve as reference hospitals for more complex health conditions. Examples of these were given in the paper. They are designed to achieve specific organizational goals.

A complex organization is made of different departments, units and sub-units and their heads that see to the smooth and proper functioning of such units/departments. Bureaucracy is expected to assist to promote meritocracy and annihilate mediocrity. There is reward for those who follow the rules and sanctions and penalties for those who flout the rules. In the hospital organization, the goal is to ensure positive health outcome and intervention for the health consumer; the patient and his significant others. It is expected that no harm is done to the consumer; that his rights are protected; his privacy is not violated and his uniqueness is respected, among others.

Using Weberian paradigm of bureaucracy, it attempts to adopt the most rational approach and process to achieve its laid down objective which can be global and local using best practices. In health institution especially in specialist and tertiary institutions, there are intricate services and processes, complex structure, varied core health providers and specialists and the cost of accessing the services are prohibitive for an average patient especially in Nigeria when health care and provisioning is accessed out of pocket rather than health insurance. Bureaucracy tends to make simple health procedure appears complex. The employers are concerned with getting things and jobs done without considering what happens especially to the welfare of employees and in the case of hospital organization, the outcome and services to the patients. The patients are at the receiving ends. The nurses form the largest crop of core health care providers; and as the odontoid process upon which the atlas of other health providers is rotated, are understaffed, overworked, overburdened, underpaid, overstressed and overstretched.

Burn-out syndrome is so prevalent among a number of nursing practitioners. Many good hands among nurses and doctors have migrated to foreign lands in search of golden fleece, constituting brain drain to Nigeria and brain gain to such countries.

The kernel of the paper is that the complexity and bureaucracy need to be tamed and constrained in the favor of the health consumers, that their rights should not be trampled upon even though they are vulnerable. Conducive and therapeutic environment should be created and sustained for their care. Services should be made affordable. Health insurance should be reinvigorated.

The paper argues that despite the lofty objectives of the ideal-typical bureaucracy as epitomized by Max Weber's postulation in ensuring rationalization of organizational goals in complex organizations such as health care industry, the established pathologies of the schema potentiate some antinomies for the health consumers and their significant others.

It is, therefore, imperative to tame these antinomies if a better outcome is achieved for the patients in the interest of the health system. The study relied on guided participant observation, perception of a range of health consumers and key informants in the health care industry. The paper submits that if the extant 'red-tapism' is tamed and, learned helplessness and other antinomies of bureaucracy taken care of, there is bound to be a better health outcome for the health consumers in the health institutions in Nigeria and thus imparting positively on healthcare delivery.

REFERENCES

Abosede, A. O. (2017). *Primary Health care in Nigeria: Gold-plating or Refining the Gold " Key to Health for All.* Lagos: University of Lagos Press and Bookshop Ltd.

Albrow, M. (1970). *Bureaucracy New York.* Praeger. doi:10.1007/978-1-349-00916-9

Argyris, C. (1964). *Integrating the Individual and the Organization New York.* Wiley.

Badru, F. A. (2003). Sociology of Health and Illness Relations. In L. Olurode & O. Soyombo (Eds.), *Sociology for Beginners* (pp. 326–355). Lagos: John West Publications.

Badru, F. A. (2004). The Role of Health Sociologists in Combating Youth Violence in Tertiary Institutions in Nigeria. In L. Olurode & O. Soyombo (Eds.), *Readings in Campus Violence* (pp. 220–236). Lagos: John West Publications Ltd.

Badru, F. A. (2006, November). Quality Assurance in Health Care Delivery: The Role of the Nurse Manager. *West African Journal of Nursing*, *17*(2), 166–173.

Badru, F. A. (2010). On the Viability of Indigenous Health Care System in Nigeria: Insights from The Yorubas. In An Interdisciplinary Discourse on the Human Condition. Lagos: Faculty of Social Sciences in Conjunction with the Department of Sociology, University of Lagos.

Badru, F. A. (2016). Western Medicine. In *Encyclopedia of the Yoruba.* Bloomington, IN: Indiana University Press.

Badru, F. A. (2017). Disease, Health Management, and Healing. In Culture and Customs of the Yoruba. Pan African University Press.

Bond, J., & Bond, S. (1993). *Sociology and Health Care.* Churchill Livingstone.

Church, D. (1982). The Architecture of Hospitals and Health Centres. In Medical Care in Developing Countries. Norfolk, UK: Oxford University Press.

Clancy, C., & Eisenberg, J. W. (1998). Outcomes Research: Measuring the End results of Healthcare. *Science*, *282*, 245–246. doi:10.1126cience.282.5387.245 PMID:9841388

Donabedian, A. (1996). Evaluating the quality of Medical care. *The Milbank Memorial Fund Quarterly*, *44*(3Suppl. Part 2), 166–206. doi:10.2307/3348969 PMID:5338568

Eneanya, A. N. (2015). 'Health Administration in Nigeria' in Theory and Practice of Public Administration Lagos. *University of Lagos Press and Bookshops Ltd Chp*, *15*, 229–254.

Eneanya, A. N. (2015). *Theory and Practice of Public Administration*. Lagos: University of Lagos Press and Bookshops Ltd.

Erinosho, O. A. (Ed.). (1989). *Health care and Health Care Services in Nigeria*. African Development Foundation.

Etzioni, A. (1975). *A Comparative Analysis of Complex Organizations*. Free Press.

Gbiri, Badru, Ladapo, & Gbiri. (2011). Socio-Economic Correlates of Relapsed Patients admitted in a Nigerian Mental Institution. *International Journal of Psychiatry in Clinical Practice, 15*(1), 19-26. Retrieved from http://informahealthcare.com/jpc

Gibson, J. L., Ivancevich, J. M., & Donelly, J. H. (1994). *Organizations, Behavior, Structure and Processes*. Irwin/McGraw Hill.

Ifenowo, D. (1997). *Elements of Public Administration*. Delinik Publishers.

Jolly, R., & King, M. (1982). The Organization of Health Services. In Medical Care in Developing Countries. Norfolk, UK: Oxford University Press.

King, M. (Ed.). (1982). *Medical Care in Developing Countries*. Norfolk, UK: Oxford University Press.

Lambo, A. (1982). The Village of Aro. In *Medical Care in Developing Countries*. Norfolk, UK: Oxford University Press.

Lewis, C. E., Fein, R., & Mechanic, D. (1976). *The Maduabum. In Introduction to Organizational Behaviour*. Concept Publications.

Massoud, O. (2008). Governance and Primary Health Care Delivery in Nigeria. In Governing Health Systems in Africa. Dakar: CODESRIA.

Oyekanmi, F.A.D (1997). *Traditional Birth Attendants: An Indispensable Partner in Health Programme in Lagos State*. Research Report.

Rashid, S. A., & Archer, M. (1983). *Organizational Behaviour*. New York: Methuen.

Rheinstein, M. (1954). *Max Weber on Law in economy and Society*. Simon and Schuster.

Sama, M., & Nguyen, V. K. (Eds.). (2008). Governing Health Systems in Africa. Dakar: CODESRIA.

Sapru, R.K. (2008). *Administrative Theories and Management Thought*. New Delhi: Prentice Hall of India Private Ltd.

Weber, M. (1947). *The Theory of Social and Economic Organization*. New York: Free Press of Glencoe.

W.H.O. (1998). *World Health Forum, 19*(1). Geneva. World Health Organization.

Williams, S. J., & Torrens, P. R. (2008). *Introduction to Health Services*. DELMAR Cengage.

Chapter 4
The Healthcare Financing and Health Outcomes in Zambia

Ali Syed
Independent Researcher, India

Urooj Afshan Jabeen
Government Degree and Postgraduate College for Women Nalgonda, India

ABSTRACT

This chapter aims to find out the sources of healthcare financing in Zambia to provide health facilities for protecting the people's right to receive healthcare and to know the health outcomes. The study revealed that significant progress is made in addressing the MDGs of health. But the achievement is less than the targets. The total health expenditure and the per capita health expenditure is less than other middle-income countries and the global average. The percent of government expenditure on healthcare to total government expenditure is also less than the target. The donor financing and out-of-pocket health expenditure are higher than the limit suggested by WHO. The private medical insurance and social insurance schemes are still in the initial stages of development. There is regional inequality in the healthcare facilities.

INTRODUCTION

The Sustainable Development Goals provide the first comprehensive blueprint for human development, within which population health plays a central role as a precondition, outcome and indicator of sustainable development (U.N., 2015). Promoting and protecting health is essential to human welfare and sustained economic

DOI: 10.4018/978-1-5225-6133-0.ch004

and social development. This was recognized more than 30 years ago by the Alma-Ata Declaration signatories, who noted that Health for All would contribute both to a better quality of life and also to global peace and security (WHO, 2010). In most countries people rate health one of their highest priorities behind only economic concerns, such as unemployment, low wages and a high cost of living (Kaiser, 2007). In 2005, the member states of World Health Organization (WHO) committed to develop their health financing systems so that all people have access to services and do not suffer financial hardship paying for them (WHO, 2005). This goal was defined as universal coverage or universal health coverage. To achieve this goal, there is need to find out the ways of financing health systems, protecting people from the financial consequences of ill-health and paying for health services and full utilization of resources. The World Health Assembly resolution 58.33 from 2005 says everyone should be able to access health services and not be subject to financial hardship in doing so (WHO, 2010). But this objective has not yet been achieved. There prevails difference in access to health services with regard to the proportion of births attended by a skilled health worker, maternal mortality, infant mortality, etc. In some countries, up to 11 percent of the population suffers financial hardship each year and up to 5 percent is forced into poverty. Globally, about 150 million people suffer financial catastrophe annually while 100 million are pushed below the poverty line. Only one in five people in the world has broad-based social security protection that also includes cover for lost wages in the event of illness and more than half the world's population lacks any type of formal social protection. Only 5-10 percent of people are covered in sub-Saharan Africa and southern Asia, while in middle-income countries, coverage rates range from 20 percent to 60 percent (WHO, 2010). Health financing is an important part of broader efforts to ensure social protection in health. WHO is joint leading agency with the International Labor Organization (ILO) in the United Nations initiative to help countries develop a comprehensive social protection which includes the type of financial risk protection and social support in the event of illness (ILO, 2010)? For achieving the universal health coverage, there is need for availability of resources, non-reliance on direct payments at the time people need care and efficient and equitable use of resources. Brazil, Chile, China, Mexico, Rwanda and Thailand made great strides on these lines. Gabon has introduced innovative ways to raise funds for health, including a levy on mobile phone use; Cambodia has introduced a health equity fund that covers the health costs of the poor and Lebanon has improved the efficiency and quality of its primary care network (WHO, 2010).

There are three broad ways to raise more money for health domestically, besides increasing Official Development Assistance (ODA). Firstly, increasing the efficiency of revenue collection, which will increase the funds that can be used to provide services, including health services. Secondly, giving priority to health sector in budget allocation. In the 2001 Abuja Declaration, African countries agreed to spend 15 percent of their government budget on health. But except Tanzania and Liberia, other countries could not fulfill this target. Thirdly, finding innovative health financing methods. The high-level Taskforce on Innovative International Financing for Health Systems included increasing taxes on air tickets, foreign exchange transactions and tobacco in its list of ways to raise an additional US10 billion annually for global health (WHO, 2010). Since many low-income countries do not have any chance to raise funds from domestic sources, there is need for global solidarity. The high-income countries should honor their commitments on ODA.

Health financing is much more than a matter of raising money for health. It is also a matter of who is asked to pay, when they pay and how the money raised is spent. There are three critical areas of health financing. They are: raising sufficient money for health; removing financial barriers to access; and reducing financial risks of illness and making better use of the available resources. Today, global annual expenditure on health is about US$ 5.3 trillion (WHO, 2010 a). It has been estimated that a high proportion of the world's 1.3 billion poor have no access to health services simply because they cannot afford to pay at the time they need them (Preker, & Carrin, 2004). Recent studies show that these out-of-pocket health payments pushed 100,000 households in both Kenya and Senegal below the poverty line in a single year. About 290,000 experienced the same fate in South Africa (ILO, 2008).

The goals of financing systems are to provide all people with access to needed health services including prevention, promotion, treatment and rehabilitation of sufficient quality to be effective and ensure that the use of these services does not expose the user to financial hardship (Carrin, James, & Evans, 2005). In 2005, The World Health Assembly unanimously adopted a resolution urging countries to develop their health financing systems to achieve these two goals which are defined as achieving universal coverage (WHO, 2005).

New priorities for health financing have now been set out in the Addis Ababa Action Agenda (2015). It is agreed that each country has the primary responsibility for its own economic and social development. The guiding principles of health financing include, for example, enhancing domestic tax administration and reducing tax avoidance to increase the overall capacity for public spending, including on health.

The primary objective of the health-financing system is to promote financial protection in health. At a global level, WHO support for monitoring financial protection is underpinned by the World Health Assembly Resolution, WHA 58.33, on sustainable health financing, universal coverage and social health insurance (WHO, 2005). Universal Health Coverage (UHC) stresses that all programs and priority interventions fall within the overall health system and are part of coverage objectives (UN, 2015). Unlike the MDG era, during which a fragmented approach to financing specific diseases or interventions was often taken, the focus now is on how to sustain increased effective coverage of priority interventions not simply specific programs. UHC brings these and other issues together under a common umbrella with a system-wide focus that is needed to tackle the challenges of sustainability (Kutzin & Sparkes, 2016).

One such important challenge is ensuring an increased emphasis on domestic public sources of revenue for the health sector. Data obtained in a number of countries demonstrate clearly that, on average, greater public spending on health is associated with a lower dependence of health systems on potentially impoverishing out-of-pocket payments (Kutzin & Sparkes, 2016). Due to the current global economic climate and as countries transition away from donor support as their economies grow, there is now a greater emphasis being placed on domestic public sources of revenue to finance the health system (WHO, 2016). This requires concerted efforts by governments to pro- vide public funding for health services derived from general taxes (Jowett & Kutzin, 2015). In particular, many countries have explicitly used general budget revenues to expand coverage of health interventions for the poor, for people in the informal sector or for the entire population. This shift requires donors and countries alike to refine the ways in which aid is targeted, while requiring governments to improve overall domestic resource-generation efforts through improved national taxation systems that are both equitable and efficient (Fryatt & Mills, 2010).

BACKGROUND

Health Sector Development in Zambia

Zambia recognized health as one of the priority sectors that contribute to the well-being Of the nation and, therefore, remains committed to providing quality health services to all its citizens. Recognizing that a healthy population is critical to improved production and productivity, Zambia will continue investing in the health sector, in order to ensure sustainability of the nation's human capital base, required for sustainable economic growth.

Zambia is a Lower Middle Income Country and since 2006, the country has been implementing the Vision 2030, which aims at transforming it into a prosperous middle-income nation by 2030. Over the past 5 years, the country recorded major improvements in macro-economic performance, with the average annual economic growth rate, above 5 percent. However, these improvements have not yet significantly impacted on the socio-economic well-being of the population, majority of whom are poor and vulnerable.

Zambia has a high burden of disease, which is mainly characterized by high prevalence and impact of communicable diseases, particularly, malaria, HIV and AIDS, STIs, and TB, and high maternal, neo-natal and child morbidities and mortalities. The country is also faced with a rapidly rising burden of non-communicable diseases, including mental health, diabetes, cardio-vesicular diseases.

Over the past five years, from 2006 to 2010, the health sector recorded significant progress in most of the key areas of health service delivery, and health support systems, leading to major improvements in most of the key health performance indicators. According to the 2007 Zambia Demographic and Health Survey (ZDHS 2007), Maternal Mortality Ratio (MMR) reduced, from 729 deaths per 100,000 live births in 2002, to 591 in 2007, Under-Five Mortality Rate (U5MR) reduced from 168 per 1000 live births in 2002, to 119 in 2007, and Infant Mortality Rate (IMR) from 95 to 70, respectively. Neo-natal Mortality Rate (NMR) reduced from 37 to 34, respectively. During the same period, HIV prevalence in adults, aged 15 to 49 years, reduced from 16.1 percent to 14.3 percent.

The malaria and TB program performance reviews conducted in 2010, and other reporting health systems, also reported major improvements in the prevention and control of malaria and TB. Malaria incidence per 1000 population dropped from 412 in 2006, to 246 in 2009. TB treatment success rate improved from 79 percent in 2005 to 86 percent in 2008.

However, despite these achievements, the sector continued to face major challenges, which include high disease burden, inadequate medical staff, weak logistics management in the supply of drugs and medical supplies, inadequate and inequitable distribution of health infrastructure, equipment and transport, and challenges related to health information systems, inadequate financing, and identified weaknesses in the health systems governance.

Zambia is not spending enough on healthcare. Public expenditure on health care stood at 11.3 percent of total government expenditure in 2014, less than the target fixed by the 2001 Abuja Declaration. Out-of-pocket payment is relatively high at about 30 percent of total health expenditure in 2014, which is above the 20 percent limit suggested by the World Health Organization.

Since 1992, Zambia has been implementing wide-ranging health sector reforms, aimed at attaining equity of access to assured cost-effective quality health services, as close to the family as possible. These reforms have been based on the National Health Policies and Strategies of 1992 (NHP&S-92) and implemented through a system of health sector plans, which includes successive five-year National Health Strategic Plans (NHSPs), three-year Medium-Term Expenditure Frameworks (MTEF), and annual action plans (AAPs) and budgets. In this respect, the country implemented the National Health Strategic Plan 2006 to 2010 and was integrated in to the Fifth National Development Plan and the National Health Strategic Plan 2010 to 2016 which was integrated in to the Sixth National Development Plan and linked to Zambia's Vision 2030 strategy. The Ministry of Health (MOH) is currently developing the National Health Strategic Plan (NHSP) 2017-21 to integrate in to the Seventh National Development Plan. The NHSP is aligned with the World Health Organization's six health system building blocks, namely service delivery, health workforce, health information systems, access to essential medicines, financing and governance. The new plan will also feature four key aspects of delivery, i.e., non-communicable diseases, communicable diseases, maternal & child health and primary health care.

Health Sector Organization and Coordination in Zambia

The health sector in Zambia is liberalized and embraced diversity in ownership.

Public health sector, which includes health facilities and programs under the MOH, and some government line ministries and departments; the private sector, including for- and not-for profit health services owned by private investors and civil society organizations (CSOs); and traditional and alternative health service providers, which however operate informally and are not regulated or monitored by MOH.

Since 1991, Zambia's approach to health sector organization has focused on decentralization of planning, management and resources, to the district level, where health services are delivered. This approach has also inevitably called for broader participation of all the key stakeholders, particularly the communities, in the governance of the health sector.

The public health system in Zambia adopts a four-level policy and implementation structure:

1. The Ministry of Health is responsible for policy, strategy, regulation, international relations, resource mobilization and standard setting
2. Provincial Health Offices are responsible for coordination of health services, technical support, dissemination of health policies and performance management at the provincial level. They also directly manage 2nd level hospitals
3. District Health Offices are responsible for management, coordination and supervision of health facilities at district level, including 1st level hospitals, health centers and health posts
4. Neighborhood Health Committees are responsible for mobilizing people in the community for health promotion activities and providing information to the district on health priorities

In addition, national units were established under the Ministry of Health to oversee specific health programs, like, the National Malaria Control Center, Child Health Unit, Reproductive Health Unit, the National Tuberculosis, the National Aids Council, etc.

Since the health expenditure and the indicators of health in Zambia are poor comparing to the world average, research on the impact of health care financing and outcomes in Zambia is relevant.

Problem Statement

Zambia made significant efforts in increasing health expenditure, especially during fifth and sixth National Development Plans, with the aim of improving health outcomes. Despite this, health outcomes have only responded marginally, raising concerns on the significance of health expenditure in improving health outcomes. Moreover, there is regional inequality in the health outcomes. Research on healthcare financing and the health outcomes in Zambia is relevant to the policy makers and the Government to find out the alternative sources of healthcare financing and to minimize the regional inequality in access to health facilities.

Objectives of the Chapter

The objectives of the Chapter are to:

- Know the healthcare expenditure during the 5th and 6th National Development Plans.
- Investigate the sources of healthcare financing, including donor funding, out of pocket payments, tax-based Government financing and medical insurance.
- Examine the regional in-equalities in health care facilities.
- Find out the health outcomes on maternal mortality, under- 5 mortality, infant mortality, HIV prevalence, malaria prevention and T.B. treatment success rate.

REVIEW OF LITERATURE

In this study, the term "Health Outcomes" is used to explain maternal mortality, under-five mortality, infant mortality, HIV prevalence, malaria prevention and T.B. mortality. In the existing literature many researchers have investigated the association between healthcare spending and health outcomes, for example, Anton, and Onofrei (2012); Or (2000); Seshamani, and Gray (2004). Some researchers examined the relationship between healthcare spending and life expectancy. Jaba et al. (2014) examined the relationship between healthcare expenditure and life expectancy (as proxy for health outcomes) for 175 countries from 1995 to 2010. Their findings revealed an association between life expectancy and healthcare expenditures. Aisa et al. (2014) found that an increase in healthcare expenditure leads to improved life expectancy. Akinci et al. (2014) researched the relationship between healthcare expenditure and health outcomes, defined as an improvement in infant, under-five, and maternal mortality, for Middle Eastern and Northern African countries, they found that increase in healthcare expenditures reduce infant, under-five and maternal mortality rates. Anyanwu and Erhijakpor (2009) investigated healthcare expenditure and health outcomes, defined as infant mortality and under-five mortality, for 47 African countries in the period between 1999 and 2004. Their results were based on econometric relationship between healthcare expenditures and health outcomes; however, the relationship was region-dependent. For sub-Saharan African countries, they documented positive relationship, yet for Northern Africa, the results indicated a negative relationship between healthcare expenditures and health outcomes. Mays and Smith (2011) measured the relationship between the increase in government healthcare expenditures and preventable deaths, particularly those related to infant mortality, cardio vascular diseases, diabetes and cancer. They empirically showed that a 10 percent increase in local public healthcare spending led to a decline in infant mortality between 1.1 and 6.9 percent and argued that the increase in public healthcare spending has a long-lasting impact on low-resource communities.

The study by Maruthappu et al. (2015) revealed that public health spending is negatively correlated with HIV mortality. Nixon and Ulmann (2006) revealed the relationship between healthcare spending and health outcomes for 15 European countries using yearly data from 1980 and 1995. Their study showed that increased healthcare expenditure reduced mortality rates, but showed limited impact on life expectancy. The study by Vavkan, et al. (2002) showed that an increase in healthcare expenditure reduced mortality and cardiovascular disease.

Eric, et al. (2017) examined the effect of health expenditure on health outcomes in the sub-Saharan African countries and found that health expenditure had a significant effect on health outcomes, reducing mortality rates and improving life expectancy at birth. Reductions in mortality rates were significantly influenced by public health expenditure, whereas, improvements in life expectancy at birth were significantly influenced by private health expenditure. Fez, et al. (2014) showed that both government and private spending on healthcare significantly improved infant, under-five, and maternal mortality in the MENA region. One percent increase in per capita government expenditure reduced the infant mortality rate by 8.6 - 9.5 deaths per 1000 live births; the under-five mortality by 10.3 - 12.1 under-five deaths per 1000 live births and maternal mortality by 26.0 – 26.3 deaths per 100,000 live births. Similarly, a percentage increase in the log per capita private expenditure reduced the infant mortality rate by 7.2 – 8.1 deaths per 1000 live births, under-five mortality rate by 9.5 – 9.8 deaths per 1000 live births and the maternal mortality rate by 25.8 – 25.9 deaths per 1000 live births.

The study by Craig, et al. (2017) revealed that healthcare spending was found to have the greatest impact on the mortality rate compared to the life expectancy. The spending elasticity for mortality was near – 0.03, whereas it was near to + 0.04 for life expectancy. David, et al. (2017) showed that there exists close relationship between user free exemption policies and improvement in healthcare quality. Murad, et al. (2017) concluded that there existed a strong positive association between total healthcare expenditures and total life expectancy. The study found that while there was a positive relationship between healthcare expenditures and female and male life expectancy, there was a negative relationship between healthcare expenditures and the number of neo-natal, infant, and under-five deaths.

This study is different from the existing literature on impact of healthcare expenditure on health outcomes. None of the above studies concentrated on Zambia. Whereas, this study reveals sources of healthcare financing in Zambia, like donor funding, out of pocket payment tax-based government financing and medical insurance. It also examines regional in-equalities in healthcare facilities and finally the relationship between healthcare financing and health outcomes on maternal mortality, under-five mortality, infant mortality, HIV prevalence, malaria prevention and T.B. mortality.

MAIN FOCUS OF THE CHAPTER: HEALTHCARE EXPENDITURE IN ZAMBIA

Healthcare Expenditure During the 5th National Development Plan in Zambia

Table 1 shows the healthcare expenditure during the Fifth National Development Plan (2006-2010):

Table 1 shows that out of total health expenditure on core health programs in the Fifth National Development Plan, 61.24 percent was from the Government of Republic of Zambia (GRZ) and 38.76 percent from Donors. It can be observed that the donors contributed more than 90 percent of expenditure on Malaria Control and Prevention, HIV/AIDs and STIs, and T.B. Control and Prevention. Whereas, the GRZ expenditure was more than 75 percent on human resources for health, essential drugs, infrastructure and medical equipment and accessories.

Healthcare Expenditure During the Sixth National Development Plan in Zambia

Table 2 shows healthcare expenditure in Sixth National Development Plan (2011-15).

Table 1.

Program	Total Expenditure (K. Billion)	GRZ (K. Billion)	Donor (K. Billion)
Human Resource for Health	2,587.4 (100)	2,482.2 (95.93)	105.2 (4.07)
Basic Healthcare Package	1,364.8 (100)	505.7 (37.05)	859.0 (62.95)
Malaria control and Prevention	402.3 (100)	30.3 (7.53)	372.0 (92.47)
HIV/AIDS and STIs	827.8 (100)	69.1 (8.34)	758.7 (91.66)
T.B. Control and Prevention	198.1 (100)	18.4 (9.28)	179.7 (90.72)
Integrated Reproductive Health	187.1 (100)	84.5 (45.16)	102.5 (54.84)
Child Health	191.1 (100)	76.4 (39.97)	114.7 (60.03)
Nutrition	36.4 (100)	18.7 (51.37)	17.7 (48.63)
Essential Drugs	727.3 (100)	547.5 (75.27)	179.8 (24.73)
Laboratory support services	119.0 (100)	65.3 (54.87)	53.7 (45.13)
Blood Transmission Services	39.9 (100)	20.5 (51.37)	19.4 (48.63)
Medical Imaging Services	50.7 (100)	20.3 (40.03)	30.4 (59.97)
Infrastructure	635.6 (100)	521.0 (81.96)	114.6 (18.04)
Medical Equipment and Accessories	338.0 (100)	271.8 (80.41)	66.2 (19.59)
Environmental Health	40.3 (100)	14.9 (36.97)	25.4 (63.03)
Mental Health	8.4 (100)	4.3 (51.19)	4.1 (48.81)
Oral Health	4.5 (100)	2.3 (51.11)	2.2 (48.89)
Helminthes and other parasitic Infestations	7.5 (100)	3.9 (52.0)	3.7 (48.0)
Other Non-Communicable Diseases	5.3 (100)	2.7 (50.94)	2.6 (49.06)
Total	7,771.3 (100)	4,759.(61.24)	3,011.6 (38.76)

Table 2 shows that the GRZ expenditure on healthcare during the Sixth National Development Plan was K 7164.4 billion. Out of which, highest percent was allocated on primary health care i.e., 21.36 percent and lowest on social health insurance, i.e., 1.5 percent. The financing on human resources for health, drugs and medical supplies and infrastructure stood at 15.59 percent, 16.94 percent and 14.25 percent, respectively.

Comparison of Healthcare Financing in Zambia With Lower Middle-Income Countries and Global

Table 3 shows healthcare financing in 2014 in Zambia (Percentage to GDP).

Table 3 shows that the percentage of total health expenditure and government expenditure to GDP and the per capita government expenditure were less than the global average. Whereas, the percentage of external sources and the out-of-pocket payments to total health expenditure were more than the benchmark set for these

Table 2.

Program	GRZ Expenditure (K' Billion)
Primary Health Care	1530.3 (21.36)
Hospital Referral Services	819.7 (11.45)
Central Support Services	1020.9 (14.25)
Social Health Insurance	108.0 (1.50)
Human Resources for Health	1116.9 (15.59)
Drugs and Medical Supplies	1214.0 (16.94)
Medical Equipment	334.1 (4.66)
Infrastructure	1020.2 (14.25)
Total	7164.4 (100)

Source: GRZ (2011): Ministry of Finance and National Planning, Sixth National Development Plan, Lusaka, p. 92. Note: Figures in parentheses are percentages.

Table 3.

Health Expenditure	Zambia	Lower Middle-Income countries	Global Average	Benchmark
Total Health Expenditure	5	5.9	6.8	Below the global average
Govt. Expenditure	11.3	10	11.8	15 percent target
Per capita Govt. Expenditure (in $)	108	162	912	Below global Average
External Sources to total health expenditure	38	14	-	Very high
Out-of-Pocket (OOP) Payments	30	-	31	20 percent limit

Source: WHO 2014: Global Benchmark of Health Expenditure

indicators. Zambia spend twice as much for out-of-pocket healthcare expenses as their counterparts in other lower middle-income countries in the region, such as Lesotho or Swaziland (UNICEF, 2016).

The percentage of total health expenditure to GDP and the per capital government expenditure in Zambia was less but the percentage of external sources to total health expenditure was higher than the lower middle-income countries.

SOURCES OF HEALTHCARE FINANCING IN ZAMBIA

The healthcare financing system is a key component of the overall healthcare system. This system raises not only sufficient funds for healthcare but also ensures efficient use of funds. Zambia has four important sources of healthcare financing system. They are: Revenue collection through taxation; Donor financing; Private Medical Insurance and Social Health Insurance.

Revenue Collection Through Taxation

It is an important source of healthcare financing in Zambia. It includes direct and indirect taxes, which made up to 48 percent and 52 percent of total taxes respectively in 2007 (Bona & Jonson, 2015). The Ministry of Health is facing competition for general taxation funds in light of other national priorities, i.e., energy, education, mining, tourism, agriculture, etc.

Donor Financing

Zambia is significantly depending on donors for health financing, i.e., 42 percent of overall healthcare revenue. The donor community consists of bilateral and multilateral agencies as well as non-governmental organizations at both domestic and international.

Private Medical Insurance (PMI)

The Private Medical Insurance (PMI) is penetrating very slowly in Zambia. The private health insurance coverage in Zambia is extremely low, with estimates ranging from 0.5 percent to 3 percent (USAID, 2016. In 2014, it accounted for only 1.6 percent of total health sector financing (WHO, 2014). Only 1.2 percent of adults in 2013 had private medical insurance. Group (corporate) health plans account for the vast majority (90 percent) of PMI premiums and employers (MNCs and larger domestic ones) offer such benefits to remain competitive in the labor market.

Social Health Insurance (SHI)

The Government of Zambia is currently developing a SHI scheme, as part of the "National Social Protection Bill". This scheme is expected to serve as an alternative and additional source of revenue for financing, decreasing the out-of-pocket burden on the population.

REGIONAL IN-EQUALITY IN HEALTHCARE FACILITIES

Province-Wise Health Facilities by Level of Care

Table 4 shows province-wise facilities in Zambia by level of care in 2010.

Table 4 reveals that there is regional in-equality in health facilities by level of care. Out of 1882 total health facilities by level of care, 14.82 percent were in Lusaka province; 13.54 percent in Southern Province; 12.48 percent in Copper belt province. But it was 7.54 percent in Luapula province; 9.24 percent in Western Province and 9.98 percent only in the Central province...

Type of Ownership and Health Facilities in Provinces

Table 5 shows Province-wise Health Facilities in Zambia by Type of Ownership (2010).

Table 4.

Province	Level 3 Hospitals	Level 2 Hospitals	Level 1 Hospitals	Urban Health centers	Rural Health Centers	Health Posts	Total
Central	0	2	6	32	113	35	188 (9.98)
Copperbelt	3	9	8	137	53	25	235 (12.48)
Eastern	0	2	8	8	156	53	227 (12.06)
Luapula	0	1	5	1	125	10	142 (7.54)
Lusaka	3	0	15	182	47	32	279 (14.82)
Northern	0	2	6	14	145	49	216 (11.47)
North-west	0	2	10	18	120	17	167 (8.87)
Southern	0	2	14	34	174	30	254 (13.54)
Western	0	1	12	10	127	24	174 (9.24)
Zambia	6 (0.34)	21 (1.11)	84 (4.46)	436 (23.16)	1060 (56.32)	275 (14.61)	1882 (100)

Source: Ministry of Health, Republic of Zambia (2010). Figures in the parentheses are percentages.

Table 5.

Province	Public	Mission	Private	Total
Central	164	10	14	188
Copperbelt	164	10	61	235
Eastern	211 (14.17)	16	0	227
Luapula	132 (8.86)	7	3	142
Lusaka	116 (7.79)	8	155	279
Northern	189	14	13	216
North-west	137 (9.20)	22	8	167
Southern	217 (14.57)	24	13	254
western	159	11	4	174
Zambia	1489 (79.12)	122 (6.48)	271 (14.40)	1882 (100)

Source: Ministry of Health, Republic of Zambia (2010) Figures in the parentheses are percentages

Table 5 reveals that out of 1882 total health facilities by type of ownership, 79.12 percent are public, 14.40 percent are private and 6.48 percent are mission health facilities. The public health facilities are more in Southern province (14.57%) and Eastern province (14.17%) but they are less in Luapula (8.86%) North-west (9.20%) and Lusaka (7.79%) provinces.

Type of Health Services Offered in Provinces

Table 6 shows the key health services offered by province in Zambia in 2012.

Table 6 reveals that there exists regional in-equality in the proportion of services offered by facilities. In some provinces they are higher than the national average. But in some other provinces they are less than the national average.

Distribution of Clinical Health Staff in Provinces

Table 7 shows regional distribution of Clinical Health Staff in 2010.

Table 7 shows that in Zambia the average clinical staff to 1,000 population is 1.24, but in provinces like Northern, Luapula and Eastern, it is less than the national average. Whereas in some provinces like Copperbelt, Lusaka, it is more than the national average.

Table 6. Key health services offered by province in Zambia in 2012 (proportion of services offered by facilities in percentage)

Province	HCT	PMC TC	MC	Delivery site	T.B. diagnostic site	EMOC site	Lab services	Dental service	X-Ray
Central	93	87	8	78	23	36	29	6	7
Copperbelt	94	81	32	63	40	17	28	11	9
Eastern	96	97	10	82	33	32	33	6	5
Luapula	96	95	8	92	14	44	17	2	4
Lusaka	74	65	17	46	16	10	17	6	6
Muchinga	67	79	9	86	15	18	20	6	6
Northern	87	75	6	90	11	10	19	12	4
North-Western	49	67	21	69	17	22	19	11	10
Southern	99	93	9	82	19	30	32	7	6
Western	93	94	6	89	41	21	33	3	5
Zambia (% total)	85	83	12	78	23	24	25	7	6

TaHCT = HIV Counseling and Testing; PMTCT=Prevention of Mother to Child transmission: MC = Male Circumcision; EMOC = Emergency Conservative Care

Source: Ministry of Health, GRZ (2013): The 2012 List of Health Facilities in Zambia, Preliminary Report, Version No. 15, April, 2013.

Table 7.

Province	Population	Clinical Health Staff	Clinical Staff to 1,000 population
Northern	1,759,600	1,191	0.68
Luapula	958,976	807	0.84
Eastern	1,707,731	1,385	0.81
Western	881,524	984	1.12
Central	1,267,803	1,442	1.14
Southern	1,606,793	2,477	1.54
North-Western	706,462	1,033	1.46
Copperbelt	1,958,623	3,260	1.66
Lusaka	2,198,996	3,648	1.66
Zambia total	13,046,508	16,227	1.24

Source: Zambia National Human Resources for Health Strategic Plan, 2011-2015.

HEALTH OUTCOMES IN ZAMBIA

The health expenditure from 2007 to 2015 and the health outcomes during this period are shown in Table 8.

Table 8 shows that total health expenditure increased by 36.91 percent during 2007 and 2015. The maternal mortality rate per 100,000 live births decreased by 32.65 percent; under-five mortality rate per 1000 live births decreased by 36.97 percent; infant mortality rate per 1000 live births decreased by 35.71 percent; HIV prevalence in adults 15-49 years reduced by 1 percent; Malaria Incidence per 1000 population dropped by 36.89 percent during the same period. The T.B treatment success rate improved by 7.0 percent during 2005 and 2010..These results confirm the results of the studies by Anton and Onafrei (2012); Akinci, et al (2014); Anyanwu and Erhijakpor (2009); Mays and Smith (2011 Maruthappu, et al. (2015); Nixon and Ulmann (2006); Vavcan, et al. (2002); Eric, et al. (2017), and; Fevzi, et al. (2014).

Table 8.

Details	2007	2015	Change	Percentage Change
Health Expenditure (in Billion Kwacha)	1349.3	1847.8	498.5	36.65
Maternal Mortality Rate (deaths per 100,000 live births)	591	398	193	32.65
Under 5 Mortality Rate (per 1000 live births)	119	75	-44	-36.97
Infant Mortality Rate (per 1000 live births)	70	45	-25	-35.71
HIV prevalence in Adults aged 15-49 years in percentage	14.3	13.3	-1.0	-1.0
Malaria incidence per 1000 population	412*	260**	152	-36.89
T.B treatment success rate	79***	86****	7.0	7.0

Source: C.S.O and 5th & 6th National Development Plans, Ministry of Finance and National Planning, Lusaka. *for the year 2006; **for the year 2012; *** for the year 2005; **** for the year 2010

SOLUTIONS AND RECOMMENDATIONS

The following solutions and recommendations are made for healthcare financing and increasing health facilities in Zambia.

- Since Zambia is depended on donors for health financing, which was indefinite, there is need to search for alternative sources of internal health financing. The health financing could be increased through health insurance, taxation, etc.,
- The main source of health financing in Zambia is revenue collected through taxes, for which, there is competition from other national priorities. Specific taxes could be imposed for health financing, like, introduction of new tax/taxes on large and profitable companies; a tax on foreign exchange transactions in the currency markets; a levy on all bank account transactions or on remittance transactions; solidarity contributions by individuals and corporations via their monthly mobile phone bill; an excise tax on tobacco products; excise tax on un-healthy food stuffs and ingredients; selling franchised products or services, where by companies are licensed to sell products and a proportion of the profits goes to health and a tourism tax could be levied on activities linked to international tourists.
- The concept of "micro-insurance" could be developed to benefit the private medical insurers. The private sector should be involved in health financing through innovative financing and health care methods. The private sector could collaborate with the Government in areas of innovation, quality control, product development, education and awareness for successful outcomes in health.
- There prevails regional in-equality in the health care facilities. Relatively more funds should be allocated to the provinces with less healthcare facilities.

FUTURE RESEARCH DIRECTIONS

Legislation can protect an individual's right to receive health care. Poor and vulnerable could be benefited from right to redress legally. Further research on the following could help in the development of health care system.

- Research on the impact of out- of- pocket payments on poor sections of society is relevant to know whether poor people have been made poorer by the need to pay for health services.

- The population could be broken down by key variables including age, sex and socio-economic status, to know the proportion of population that do not have access to needed health services because of financial barriers or other potential obstacles.
- The official health information systems should collect data for the non-government sector to obtain a full picture of the health status and usage pattern of the population.
- The strategies to attract and retain skilled health professionals.
- Research is needed to develop private medical insurance by changing the cultural norm among companies to pay the medical bills of their employees. What factors could make the business of licensed medical insurers profitable in Zambia and how the un-registered and quasi-medical insurance schemes could be stopped?
- Research is needed on funding streams for innovation in health technologies with the goal of improving access to these technologies for the protection and promotion of health.

CONCLUSION

The following conclusion is drawn from the foregoing analysis.

The total health expenditure in Zambia was less than other lower-middle-income countries and also below the global average. Zambia's government expenditure on health care was less than the target set by the Organization for African Unity's 2001 Abuja Declaration. The per capita health expenditure in Zambia was also lower than the lower-middle-income countries and the global average.

In Zambia, more than a third, i.e., 38 percent, of the total health sector expenditure was funded by the external sources, which was very high for a lower-middle-income countries' average of 14 percent. The out-of-pocket payment was higher than the limit suggested by the WHO.

The total health expenditure increased by 36.5 percent during 2007 and 2015. The maternal mortality rate decreased by 32.65 percent; under-five mortality rate reduced by 36.97 percent, the infant mortality rate decreased by 35.71 percent and the HIV prevalence in adults aged 15-49 years reduced from 14.3 percent to 13.3 percent during the same period. The malaria incidence per 1000 population was decreased by 36.89 percent during 2006 and 2012 and the T.B treatment success rate improved from 79 percent in 2005 to 86 percent in 2010.

There prevailed regional in-equality in the health care facilities, including the health staff. Some provinces like Lusaka, Southern and Copperbelt were having more health care facilities than other provinces like Luapula, Western and Central.

REFERENCES

Addis Ababa Action Agenda. (2015). *Third International Conference on financing for Development.* Addis Ababa, Ethiopia: UN.

Aisa, R., Clemente, J., & Pueyo, F. (2014). The Influence of Health Expenditure on Longevity: A Reconsideration. *International Journal of Public Health, 59*(5), 867–875. doi:10.100700038-014-0574-6 PMID:24986366

Akinci, F., Hamidi, S., Suvankuloo, F., & Akhmedjonov, A. (2014). Examining the Impact of Healthcare Expenditures on Health Outcomes in the Middle East, North Africa. *Journal of Healthcare Finance, 41*(1).

Anton, S. G., & Onofrei, M. (2012). Healthcare Performance and Health Financing Systems in Countries from Central and Eastern Europe. *Transylvanian Review of Administrative Sciences, 35*, 22–32.

Anyauwu, J. C., & Andrew, E. O. (2009). Health Expenditures and Health Outcomes in Africa. *African Development Review, 2009*(2), 400–433. doi:10.1111/j.1467-8268.2009.00215.x

Arthur, E., & Oaikhenan, H. E. (2017). The Effects of Health Expenditure on Health Outcomes in sub-Saharan Africa (SSA). *African Development Review, 29*(3), 524–536. doi:10.1111/1467-8268.12287

Carrin, G., James, C., & Evans, D.B. (2005). Achieving Universal Coverage: Developing the Health Financing system. Geneva: WHO.

Fevzi, A., Hamidi, S., Suvankulov, F., & Alisher, A. (2014). Examining the Impact of Healthcare Expenditure on Health Outcomes in the Middle East and N. Africa. *Journal of Health Care Finance, 41*(1).

Fryatt, R., & Mills, A. (2010). Taskforce on Innovative International Financing for Health Systems: Showing the way Forward. *Bulletin of the World Health Organization, 88*(6), 476–477. doi:10.2471/BLT.09.075507 PMID:20539869

Gallet, C. A., & Doucouliagos, H. (2017, April). The Impact of Healthcare Spending on Health Outcomes: A Meta-regression Analysis. *Social Science & Medicine, 179*, 9–17. doi:10.1016/j.socscimed.2017.02.024 PMID:28237460

ILO. (2008). *Social Health Protection: An ILO Strategy Towards Universal Access to Healthcare.* ILO.

ILO. (2010). *World Social Security Report, 2010/11: Providing Coverage in the Time of Crisis and Beyond.* Geneva: ILO.

Jaba, E., Balan, J. B., & Robu, E. B. (2014). The Relationship between Life Expectancy at birth and Health Expenditures Estimated by a Cross-country and Time Series Analysis. *Procedia Economics and Finance*, *15*, 108–114. doi:10.1016/S2212-5671(14)00454-7

Jowett, M., & Kutzin, J. (2015). *Rising Revenues for Health in Support of WHC: Strategic Issues for Policymakers*. Geneva: WHO.

Kaiser, H. J. (2007). *A Global Look at Public Perceptions of Health Problems, Priorities and Donors.* The Kaiser Global Health Survey.

Kutzin, J., & Sparker, S. P. (2016). Health Systems Strengthening Universal Health Coverage, Health Security and Resilience. *Bulletin of the World Health Organization*, *94*(1), 2. doi:10.2471/BLT.15.165050 PMID:26769987

Kutzin, J., Yip, W., & Cashin, C. (2016). Alterative Financing Strategies for Universal Health Coverage. In World Scientific Handbook of Global Health Economics and Public Policy. World Scientific.

Maruthappu, M., Zhou, D.C., Williams, C., Zeltner, T., & Atun, R. (2015). Unemployment, Public sector Healthcare Expenditure and HIV Mortality: An Analysis of 74 Countries, 1981-2009. *Journal of Global Health, 5*(1).

Mays, G. P., & Smith, S. A. (2011). Evidence Links Increases in Public Health Spending to Declines in Preventable Deaths. *Health Affairs*, *30*(8), 1585–1593. doi:10.1377/hlthaff.2011.0196 PMID:21778174

Murad, A. B., Unlucan, D., Olowu, G., & Kalifa, W. (2017). Healthcare Spending and Health Outcomes: Evidence from Selected East African Countries. *Journal African Health Sciences*, *17*(1), 247–254. doi:10.4314/ahs.v17i1.30 PMID:29026399

Nixon, J., & Ulmann, P. (2006). The Relationship between Healthcare expenditure and Health Outcomes. *The European Journal of Health Economics*, *7*(1), 7–18. doi:10.100710198-005-0336-8 PMID:16429295

Or, Z. (2000). Determinants of Health Outcomes in Industrial Countries: A Pooled, Cross-country, Time series Analysis. *OECD Economic Studies*, *30*, 53–78.

Preker, A., & Carrin, G. (2004). *Health Financing for Poor People: Resource Mobilization and Risk Sharing*. Washington, DC: The World Bank.

Seshamani, M., & Gray, A. (2004). Ageing and Healthcare Expenditure: A red Herring? *Health Economics*, *13*, 303–314. doi:10.1002/hec.826 PMID:15067669

UNICEF. (2016). *Zambia Health Sector Budget Brief: review of Budget Performance and 2016 Allocations*. UNICEF.

United Nations. (2015). *Transforming Our World: the 2030 Agenda for Sustainable Development.* Resolution Adopted by the General Assembly on 25 September, 2015.

USAID. (2016). Health financing Profile Zambia. USAID.

Vavken, P., Pagenstert, G., Grim, C. & Dorotka, R. (2002). Does Increased Healthcare Spending Afford better Healthcare Outcomes: Evidence from Austrian Healthcare Expenditure since the Implementation of DRGs. *Swiss Med Weekly, 142.*

WHO. (2005). Sustainable Health Financing, Universal Coverage and Social Health Insurance. Fifty Eighth World Health Assembly, Geneva, Switzerland.

WHO. (2009). *Telemedicine: Opportunities and Developments in Member States.* Report on the Second Global Survey on eHealth.

WHO. (2010a). *The World Health Report: Health Systems Financing. In The Path to Universal Coverage* (pp. ix–x). Geneva, Switzerland: WHO.

WHO. (2010b). *National Health Accounts*. Geneva: WHO.

WHO. (2014). *Global Health Expenditure data Base*. Geneva, Switzerland: WHO.

WHO. (2016). *Public Financing for Health in Africa: From Abuja to the SDGs*. Geneva: WHO.

Zombre, D., De Allegn, M., & Riddle, V. (2017). Immediate and Sustained Effects of User fee Exemption on Healthcare Utilization among Children under five in Burkana Faso: A Controlled Interrupted Time-series Analysis. *Social Science & Medicine, 179*, 27–35. doi:10.1016/j.socscimed.2017.02.027 PMID:28242542

KEY TERMS AND DEFINITIONS

Accessibility: It means the physical availability of health services to those who need them.

Clinical Health Staff: It means clinical officers, dentists, doctors, pharmacists, physiotherapists, lab-technicians, mid-wives, nurses, etc.

Communicable Diseases: The diseases which could be transmitted to others, for example, HIV and AIDS, TB, Malaria, etc.

Donor Financing: Those who donate funds for healthcare facilities are called "donors." The donor community consists of bilateral and multi-lateral agencies as well as non-governmental organizations at both domestic and international levels.

Healthcare Financing: It means raising money for healthcare. It is a matter of who is asked to pay, when they pay, and how the money raised is spent.

Non-Communicable Diseases: The diseases which cannot be transmitted to others, for example, diabetes, hypertension, cancer, cardiovascular diseases, maternal mortality, neo-natal, and child mortality.

Out-of-Pocket Payments: The amount that is paid at the time of using the healthcare facilities.

Pooling and Purchasing: Pooling means arrangement of accumulating revenues for health. Purchasing means the process of allocating the prepaid resources from the pool to the providers in exchange for service benefits.

Quality: Quality refers to the extent to which health delivery services improve health conditions or meet targeted health outcomes of individuals, families, and communities.

Social Health Insurance: A scheme initiated by the government to serve as a source of revenue for health financing to decrease the out-of-pocket burden on the people.

Chapter 5
Linking Primary Healthcare Policies With Health System for Improved Health Outcomes in Nigeria:
Issues, Controversies, Problems, and Solutions

Augustine Nduka Eneanya
University of Lagos, Nigeria

ABSTRACT

Quality healthcare is a fundamental right of all citizens of any nation. In Nigeria, there are disparities in terms of quality of healthcare provided to different groups in the rural and urban areas. It is this desire to ensure access to potential patients and the existence of a quality healthcare system in Nigeria that necessitates primary healthcare policy. The purpose of this chapter, therefore, is to investigate how primary healthcare policies affect health system performance and health outcomes in Nigeria. The chapter adopted qualitative research approach. Secondary data were collected from secondary sources, such as textbooks, journal articles, newspapers, WHO reports, government records, and internet. Content and secondary data analysis methods were adopted to analyze, interpret, and answer the research questions. Findings show that health outcomes remain poor because of weak health system as infant and maternal mortality are still high and universal access coverage still low. The chapter concludes that a strong health system would improve health outcomes.

DOI: 10.4018/978-1-5225-6133-0.ch005

INTRODUCTION

The centrality of health to national development and poverty reduction is self-evident, as improving health status and increasing life expectancy contribute to long term economic development. However, the legitimacy of any national health system depends on how best it serves the interest of the poorest and most vulnerable people, for which improvements in their health status gear towards the realization of poverty reduction goals.

Overtime, we have seen a growing commitment by Nigerian policymakers to address gaps in the health care system, including a strong focus on primary health care-the frontline of health. People turn to the primary healthcare system in their communities both to stay healthy and to get care when they fall sick. From primary health care providers, they seek prevention of disease, management of chronic conditions, access to treatment of various ailments and conditions. However, poor health outcomes persist throughout the country. No one appreciates more than we do that building a high-performing health care system, which is accessible to all in Nigeria is a great challenge.

The purpose of the chapter is to interrogate how primary healthcare policies and health systems affect health outcomes. Specifically, the chapter attempts to interrogate how primary health care policies can be linked with health system to improve health outcomes in Nigeria.

BACKGROUND

When Nigeria gained its independence in 1960, healthcare was not among the first thing government officials thought about. They focused more on the medicine that cured rather than prevented illnesses. However, in 1975, National Basic Health Services Scheme (NBHSS) was created, where primary healthcare served as the basis for the whole area. It was meant to provide medical training and healthcare facilities, although it neglected the use of new technology and community cooperation.

Following Alma Ata declaration of 1978, the Federal Government of Nigeria launched the Primary Health Care plan (PHC) in the National Health Policy of 1988 as the cornerstone of the Nigerian health system as part of efforts to improve equity in access and utilization of basic health services (Chiejina, 2014). Its objectives included among others improvement in the collection and monitoring of health data and ensuring availability of essential drugs in all areas of the country.

Another effort of evolving and sustaining community-oriented health system, which was led by late Professor Olukoye Ransome-Kuti occurred between the year 1986 and 1992. It witnessed the development of model primary health care in fifty-two (52) Local Government Areas (Abimbola, 2012). The third attempt to make PHC accessible to the grassroots was heralded by the establishment of the National Primary Healthcare Development Agency (NPHCDA) in the year 1992 (Abimbola, 2012). NPHCDA is a federal government agency with policy and over-sight roles on Primary Health Care (PHC) implementation at the state and local government levels in Nigeria. The major drawback is that a federal agency has no binding constitutional role to implement programs or policies at the state and local government levels. The government must be willing to cooperate or nothing happens and cooperation often has to come with financial commitment, which for every government are highly contested grounds (Abimbola, 2012). Another initiative of NPHCDA was the creation of Ward or Village Development Committees (WDCs and VDCs). They were designed to strengthen local communities in the hope that they can advocate for themselves. The committees were made up of influential community members who helped to enhance community participation and ownership and promote demand for quality services (Abimbola, 2012).

Another policy called Nigeria's Primary Health Care under One Roof (PHCUOR) policy was instituted in 2011 to address intractable stewardship and governance problems facing Nigeria's healthcare delivery system. The policy was designed to facilitate better management of resources by health care managers, increase patient confidence in and utilization of services, increase efficiency and coordination of health services, and reduce fragmentation (PHCUOR, 2014). To further improve primary health care performance and best practices in order to improve their own systems, a new partnership called the Primary Health Care Performance Initiative (PHCPI) was established to catalyze improvements in primary healthcare (PHCPI, 2014). Its focus was better measuring primary health care service delivery, including quality of care and the patient experiences that play a role in determining health outcomes. Thus, PHCPI was aimed to help Nigerian decision-makers identify what investments and policies deliver the best and most efficient care to meet communities' needs and improve health outcomes.

Moreover, the enactment of Nigeria's National Health Act officially recognizes Nigeria's right to health- and through the NHAct, the Basic Health Care Provision Fund provides financial resources to improve primary healthcare (NHAct, 2014). The NHAct has the potential to fuel dramatic public health improvements and rapid progress towards the attainment of Universal Health Coverage (UHC). The Act also provides that there would be improved funding of healthcare services at the grass-root so that people do not have to travel far to access medical services. Through this Act states can also participate in improving health centers through a counterpart fund that would enable them benefit from the consolidated funds. The National Health Act of 2014 provides the legal framework for National Health Policy of 2016. The overall goal of National Health Policy of 2016 is to strengthen

Nigeria's health system, particularly the Primary Health care sub-system to deliver effective, efficient, equitable, accessible, affordable, acceptable and comprehensive health care services to all Nigerians (National Health Policy, 2016)

The developments provide a critical policy base for primary health care system improvement efforts. The concept of Primary Healthcare (PHC) was formulated by 134 countries that met at the Alma-Ata Conference in Russia on September 12, 1978, which was organized by the World Health Organization (WHO, 1978). PHC is defined as the first level contact of the individual and community in the national health system and brings healthcare as close as possible to where people live and work and contribute the first element of a continuing health care process (WHO, 2000). It is a grass-root management approach and provides healthcare services to communities. The aim is meant to address the main health problems in the community by providing promotive, preventive, curative and rehabilitative services (Olise, 2007). It provides family with all health services, other than those which can only be provided in the hospital (Federal Ministry of Nigeria, FMOHN, 2004; Raids, 2008). According to WHO Report, (2008), the ultimate goal of primary healthcare is providing better health for all and identified five key elements to achieving that goal:

- Reducing exclusion and social disparities in health (universal reforms)
- Organizing health services around people's needs and expectations (Service delivery reform)
- Integrating health into all sectors (public policy reforms)
- Pursuing collaborative models of policy dialogue (leadership reforms)
- Increasing stakeholders' participation

These elements are meant to improve healthcare delivery system and represent an important complement to universal coverage and service delivery reforms.

The primary Health Care (PHC) aims at providing people of the nation with the basic health services. Primary Health Care (PHC) centers, therefore, were established uniformly throughout the 774 Local Government Areas (LGAs) in Nigeria, though PHC centers were relatively distributed in both rural and urban areas in Nigeria with the intention of equity and easy access (Nigeria Constitution, 1999). The services expected to be offered or delivered by the primary health care include among other things; education concerning prevailing health problems and the methods of preventing and controlling them, promotion of food supply and proper nutrition, maternal and child care, including family planning, immunization against the major infectious diseases, prevention, control of locally endemic and epidemic diseases and provision of essential drugs and medical supplies (Nigeria Constitution, 1999).

Unfortunately, the PHC are not fully utilized by the rural populations in Nigeria when compared with their urban counterparts. While most PHC facilities are in various state of disrepair, with equipment and infrastructure being either absent or obsolete, the referral system is almost non-existents. The goal of the National Health Care system, based on primary health care is promotive, protective, preventive, restorative and rehabilitative to all citizens within the available resources so that individuals and communities are well assured of productivity, social well-being and enjoyment of living. The primary healthcare (PHC) which forms the bedrock of the national health system is being bedeviled by underfunding, dearth of capacity at the Local Government level, which is the main implementing body. In Nigeria, three types of primary healthcare centers are recognized within the primary healthcare system. They include: the comprehensive health centers, (CHC), the primary health centers and the basic health clinic (BHC). The primary healthcare centers were placed under local government administration for the delivery of basic health services. (Obionu, 2007). The National Health policy ascribes responsibilities for primary healthcare to local governments, secondary care to states and tertiary care to the federal government level. The National Primary Healthcare Development Agency (NPHCDA) is currently engaged in primary health care services development and provisions (Abimbola, 2012). NPHCDA is charged with the responsibility of mobilizing support nationally and internationally for primary healthcare programs (FMOHN, 2004, Magawa, 2012). Although, the national policies, formulated by the Federal Ministry of Health provide some level of standardization, each level of government is largely autonomous in the financing and management of healthcare services.

The health system remains over-stretched by a burgeoning population, infrastructural dearth, paucity of skilled health professionals (brain drain) and growing medical tourism to countries like United States of America, Britain, Indian, and so on, for medical interventions such as renal transplant, open heart surgery, joint and knee replacement (Chiejina, 2014, p. 5). Health systems are complex institutions serving complex functions. The effect of healthcare system on health policy implementation matters in determining health outcomes. Health outcomes can be conceptualized as "what is actually achieved by making assessment of the stated purposes of the policy' (Eneanya, 2016, p. 216). Many factors are known to influence health outcomes. These factors include: the cost of the health services, educational attainment of the patients, location of the health facilities, distance of the health facilities to where the health consumer lives, equipment available in the facilities, complexity of the healthcare organization, the healthcare workers available, the skill and dexterity possessed by the health workers, the number and specialization of the health workers, among others (Eneanya, 2016).

However, the task of policy implementation is to establish a link that allows the goals of public policies to be realized as outcomes of activity. In other words, "... policy implementation activities can be evaluated by measuring outcomes against goals..." (Eneanya, 2016, p. 325).

In the light of this background, the study is divided into four sections. Section one examines the introduction, background and review of previous studies, and methodology. Section two discusses issues and controversies on the primary healthcare policy, health systems and health outcomes. Section three discusses the problems to Primary healthcare service in Nigeria. While, the section four concludes the chapter with solutions and recommendations for effective primary healthcare service delivery in Nigeria.

METHODOLOGY

The study adopts qualitative research approach. Data collection focused on secondary sources, such as extant literature, textbooks, journal articles, government records and reports, websites, and newspapers. Content-analysis technique was adopted to elicit key concepts, which were coded and categorized into themes. Thematic and secondary data analysis methods were utilized to analyze results, interpret and answer research questions.

LIMITATIONS

Limitation of the chapter is its reliance on secondary sources for the study. Mixed methods (quantitative and qualitative methods) would give better generalization of the research findings. However, the study has achieved its objectives based on methods adopted.

RESEARCH QUESTIONS

This following are the research questions that drive the investigation:

1. How was primary healthcare policy developed in Nigeria?
2. What are the missing links between primary healthcare policies and health system performance in Nigeria?
3. How did primary health care policies affect health systems performance in improving health outcomes in Nigeria?

4. What are the problems or challenges of primary health care service delivery in Nigeria?
5. What are the solutions to primary health care service delivery in Nigeria?

Let us examine each of these research questions:

ISSUES AND CONTROVERSIES IN PRIMARY HEALTH CARE POLICIES, HEALTH SYSTEM AND HEALTH OUTCOMES IN NIGERIA: ISSUE OF DEVELOPMENT OF PRIMARY HEALTHCARE POLICY

RQ.1: How Was Primary Healthcare Policy Developed in Nigeria?

World Health Organization (WHO) made Alma Ata declaration on Primary Health care (PHC) in 1978 to address health problems in communities by providing promotive, preventive, curative and rehabilitative services. Nigeria was among the 134 signatories to this invaluable idea. However, it is interesting to note that prior to the 1978 Alma-Ata declaration, the country had set the ball rolling with the implementation of the Basic Health Services Scheme (1975-1980), which was Nigeria's first serious attempt at the implementation of PHC. This scheme concentrated on the provision of health facilities, training of health workers and paying little attention to community participation, inter-sectoral cooperation or use of local technology (Obionu, 2007).

In 1988, the National health policy of Nigeria was launched and is seen as a collective will of the government and people of Nigeria to provide comprehensive health care system that is based on PHC. The national health policies, therefore, describe the goals, structure, strategies and direction of the healthcare delivery system in Nigeria (National Policies, 1988, 2004, 2016). In Nigeria, three types of primary health centers are recognized within the primary health care system. These include the Comprehensive Health Centers, (CHC), the Primary Health Centers and the Basic Health Clinic (BHC). For sustainability of PHC in Nigeria, the Federal Government by Decree number 29 of 1992, set up the National Primary Health Care Development Agency (NPHCDA). This body was charged with the responsibility of mobilizing, supporting national and international PHC programs (Federal Ministry of Health Organization, 2004, Raids, 2008, Magawa, 2012).

However, the burden of providing healthcare services to the grassroots was not borne by government alone. Non-governmental Organizations (NGOs) and international partners also support PHC programs with funding, capacity building, operational research and technical assistance. Prominent NGOs and international partners currently supporting PHC services in Nigeria include the Society for Family Health, United Nations Children Fund (UNICEF), Achieving Health Nigeria Initiative (AHNI), and Pathfinders international among others.

The National Health Policy (1988, 2004, 2016) also ascribed responsibilities for primary health care to local governments, secondary care to states and tertiary care to the federal level. An example of this is the National Primary Health Care Development Agency (NPHCDA) established on 2011, and which is currently engaged in primary health care services development and provisions; the latter is evidently part of its mandate. The NPHCDA is a federal government agency with policy and oversight roles on PHC implementation at the state and local government levels in Nigeria. Although national policies, formulated by the Federal Ministry of Health provide some level of standardization, each level is largely autonomous in the financing and management of services under its jurisdiction. Though, the major drawback of the NPHCDA is that it has no binding constitutional role to implement programs or policies at the state and local government levels.

Working with National Primary Health Care Development Agency (NPHCDA) in Nigeria, Health Partners International and Partners on the PRRINN-MNCH program launched the Primary Health Care Under One Roof (PHCUOR) initiative (PHCUOR, 2011). The PHCUOR aims to address key stewardship and governance issues as the most intractable problems facing Nigeria's health services delivery system and contributing to the under-performance of the overall national health sector. By creating a unitary, integrated and decentralized management structure for PHC, PHCUOR is intended to facilitate increased efficiency and coordination of health services, better management of resources by health care managers, and increased patient confidence in and utilization of services (PHCUOR, 2011).

Furthermore, Nigeria enacted National Health Act in 2014 and officially recognizes Nigerians' rights to health. The aim of the Act is to establish a framework for the Regulation, Development and Management of a National Health System, to set standards for rendering health services in the Federation and other matters concerned therewith. The Act seeks to reduce maternal and infant mortality rate by 2015. More pregnant women would have access to free delivery services while their children are assured of standard pediatric services in the nation's health (National Health Act, 2014). The Act was also mandated to provide healthcare insurance to certain class of people who are actually deprived. Currently, 28 states and the FCT and their Local Government Areas have established State Primary Health care Development Agencies in readiness for the implementation of this Act (Chiejina, 2014). The Act provides that the National Health Insurance Scheme (NHIS) would provide health coverage which will cover pregnant women, children who are under five years, the elderly and the physically challenged persons. In addition, the Act provides that part of the funds would be used to train nurses and midwives. It makes available by law financial resources for PHC through the Basic Health Care Provision Fund (NHA Act, 2014).

In 2015, Nigeria and the World Bank began a new $500 million partnership that builds on Nigeria's Saving One Million Lives (SOML) initiative to improve maternal, newborn and child health. The new Program for Results for SOML will strengthen PHC governance and link funding to results, increase accountability, improve management, and encourage public and private sector innovation (PHCPI, 2015).

National Health Policy (2016) was also established to promote health of Nigerians and accelerate socio-economic development. It came after the passage of National Health Act of 2014. The overall goal is to strengthen Nigeria's health system, particularly the Primary Health Care sub-system, to deliver effective, efficient, equitable, accessible, affordable, acceptable and comprehensive health care services to all Nigerians. The question that borders observers is: how are these health policy reforms have facilitated the health systems performance to improve health outcomes in Nigeria? Answers to this question would be demonstrated in subsequent discussions on situation analysis of health systems performance in improving health outcomes in Nigeria

ISSUE OF PRIMARY HEALTH CARE POLICIES AND HEALTH SYSTEMS PERFORMANCE

RQ2: What Are the Missing Links Between Primary Healthcare Policies and Health System Performance in Nigeria?

For past decades, Nigeria has seen great improvements in the health of populations worldwide. Yet, too many children still suffer or die from largely preventable causes, too many women still die in childbirth, too many people die from treatable chronic conditions, and too many people lack access to quality and affordable health care. Therefore, strengthening health systems-especially at the primary health care (PHC) level- is central to addressing these challenges, building on health gains, and achieving the Sustainable Development Goals, especially the goal of quality universal health coverage.

Therefore, how implemented policies affect various components of the health system and healthcare outcomes depends on whether the health system is strong or not. To answer this research questions, the World Health Organization's health system's building blocks, (WHO, 2008) were adopted as framework of analysis. The building blocks are: service delivery, health workforce, information, financing, collaboration (for medical products, vaccines and technologies), leadership and governance. Let us examine and analyze these health systems building blocks:

Service Delivery

The Nigerian government is committed to quality and accessible public health services through provision of primary health care (PHC) in rural and urban areas as well as provision of preventive and curative services (Nigerian Constitution, 1999). Primary Healthcare (PHC) is provided by local government authority through health centers and health post and they are staffed by nurses, midwives, community health officers, health technicians, community health extension workers and by physicians (doctors) especially in the southern part of the country.

Health care services at the primary level include: prevention and treatment of communicable diseases, immunization, maternal and child health services, family planning, public health education, environmental health and the collection of statistical data, health and health related events. The healthcare delivery at the local government areas is headed politically by a supervisory councilor and technically and administratively by a PHC coordinator and assisted by a deputy coordinator. The PHC coordinator reports to the supervisory councilor who in turn reports to the LGA Chairman (Adeyemo, 2005; Federal Ministry of Health, 2004). In the different components of the Local Government Area, Primary Health Centers are manned by personnel of diverse specialty.

The LGA is running her primary health care services delivery in compliance with the principles of the National Health Policy (National Health, 2014 Act). The LGA is divided into various health districts or wards, so as to enhance maximum benefit of the principle of decentralization of the health sector whereby people are involved, participate and mobilized in the PHC processes.

It is almost universally acknowledged by national and international health planners that community participation is the key to the successful implementation of primary health care (PHC).

Moreover, there has been several governmental initiatives to strengthen these institutions of community participation to improve health services (World Bank, 2003). The National Health Policy in Nigeria emphasized active community engagement in the provision of PHC services in the spirit of the Bamako Initiative of 1987. This was the meeting of Health Ministers from various African nations where resolution for promoting sustainable primary health care through community participation in financing, maintenance, and monitoring of services were adopted (Bamako Initiative, 1987).

As declared by Alma-Ata in 1978, community participation is identified as 'the process by which individuals and families assume responsibility for their own health and welfare and for those of the community, and develop the capacity to contribute to their community's development (World Health Organization, 1978). Community participation has been institutionalized through the creation of village development committees and district or ward development committees that are grassroots organizations expected to work closely with the local governments in monitoring and supporting primary health care services. The Alma Ata Declaration 1978 has not been properly implemented.

In an attempt to fix the situation, with primary healthcare in 2011, a new policy Primary Health Care Under One Roof (PHCUOR) was still not implemented due to it being fairly recent. So, there has been little change. Nigeria has about 30,000 Primary Healthcare establishments across the country and only 20 per cent of them are open (Falae, 2018). This is compounded by brain-drain syndrome, when smart, educated and capable health workers (doctors, nurses and other medical staff) migrate to other countries with better working conditions. Moreover, according to the World Health Organization (2018), Nigeria is rated 187th out of 191 countries in terms of healthcare delivery. Also, one-third of more than 700 health facilities have been destroyed in the country and about 3.7 million people are in need of health assistance (WHO, 2018).

The communities being the end-users of the services, have a stake in ensuring that services are well-provided and are also well- positioned to monitor the quality of services. With the benefit of local information, the communities can assess the specific obstacles facing facilities in providing services and they can seek to ensure that facilities have the necessary infrastructure, supplies and staff motivation to provide the services they are supposed to provide. Some of these can be done through volunteer efforts, such as donations for buying medical supplies, but most of the benefits of community participation can only be harnessed if there are specific mechanisms in place to enable them to do so.

Health Workforce

Primary Healthcare (PHC) is provided by local government authority through health centers and health post and they are staffed by nurses, midwives, community health officers, health technicians, community health extension workers and by physicians (doctors) especially in the southern part of the country. No health system can function effectively without an effective workforce. As a matter of fact, human resources form the pillar of every health system. Unfortunately, the implementation of PHC in Nigeria has met with a number of problems ranging from inadequate personnel, inequitable distribution of available personnel, inter-cadre conflicts, poor job satisfaction and paucity of accurate data on the available staff (Health Reforms Foundation of Nigeria, HERFON, 2009; Abdulraheem, 2012).

There is manpower or health workforce inadequacy. There is absence of trained medical specialist and poor working conditions. Hence, the establishment of Community Health Extension Workers (CHEW) and Community Health Officers (CHO) training in the Colleges of Health Technology. The idea was to provide low to mid-level trained health professionals with the skills to provide healthcare at the community level in response to the unwillingness of the highly trained doctors and nurses to practice in rural communities (Uzoma, 2016).

Current statistics show that there are:

...about 35,000 medical doctors currently practicing in Nigeria. By World Health Organization standard, the proportion of doctors to patients is 1:600. By this, Nigeria will need 237,000 doctors to meet the health needs of the entire population. (Uzoma, 2016, p. 11)

If Nigeria must meet this standard at the rate of production of doctors in Nigeria, it will take 100 years to meet this demand (Uzoma, 2016, p. 11). Hence, Community Health Extension Workers was established. However, due to increasing rivalry, relevance and in-fighting for supremacy among medical professionals, Community Health Extension Workers are converted to cleaners and administrative staff in tertiary and secondary hospitals (Uzoma, 2016, p. 11). With exception of programs funded by development partners targeted at the Community level where Community Health Extension Workers are employed, "most focus on utilizing other skilled health professionals" (Uzoma, 2016, p. 11). It is pertinent to review the role of this key grassroots health workforce if issues of human resources for health must be addressed. Furthermore, the problem of health workforce is compounded by lack of planning and, mismanagement of resources, such as, corruption, pilfering of drugs, project vehicles, generators, and poor maintenance of equipment to the detriment of planned programs, all these affect healthcare service delivery.

Information

The primary health care addresses several aspects of communications/health promotion linked to building awareness and achieving behavioral change. This include communication approach directed at the family and community level. To enhance the utilization of the Health Services by people, it is most important that the people recognized the need for such services. This need of course will only be felt if they start to value health as a worthwhile asset. It is for this reason that government provides adequate, relevant, scientific information and education about health, disease and hazardous environments. The information provided was expressed in simple but quantitative form, starting from simple matters, such as personal hygiene and gradually progressing towards more comprehensive health education, fostering behavioral changes and community action for health. The language for communication is also the same with greater consideration of the level of understanding of the local people. The audiovisual aids used was locally, appropriately produced, trained and experienced personnel from the locality were used to carry out the educational program. In most cases, traditional media such as drama shows and radio "giggles" in local language were made very useful tools in educating illiterate people, especially rural women, who need a rigorous campaign to utilize effectively the maternal and child health services provided at the PHC centers. Health information were made available to the public in the communication media they know and use regularly.

However, Nigeria does not have the right data. There is need to improve health information system, regular and sustainable population and health-facility-based surveys, and a functioning vital statistics and civil registration system. There is need, therefore, to strengthen evidence-linked planning for resource allocations and utilization.

Financing

The World Health Organization recommends world average of 12 per cent on budget on health and high-income country, an average of 15 per cent as increase in government expenditure is vital towards Universal Health Care and in particular to subsidizing the cost of services for poorer populations(WHO, 2015). Interestingly, Nigeria government signed several conventions and declarations in the past but too little has been done to meet the commitments made. The most significant of these declarations is the Abuja Declaration of 2001, where African countries are committed to putting down 15 per cent of their annual national budgets to their health sector. While Nigeria has through the rebasing exercise become the largest economy in Africa, the nation has not kept to Abuja declaration of allocating 15 per cent of budget to health sector even when some African countries with much less resources have reached or even surpassed this target with tangible benefits on health outcomes recorded. In Nigeria, the 2018 budget to health sector is N340.45 billion out of the N8.6 billion expenditure plan to the health sector. This represents 3.9 percent of the total budget which is a far cry from 2016 allocation of 4.23 per cent and 2017 allocation of 4.16 percent as against declared percentage of 15 per cent (Africa Healthcare Extension Services, 2018). Since 2012, Nigeria budgetary allocation to Health Sector has been at best 6 per cent (Edeh, 2016. p. 10).

The financing of public health is tied to allocation of fund from federation account. In Nigeria, health services mirror political organization. The federal government is responsible for budget on tertiary care, state governments for secondary care, and the local governments run primary care. Funds are shared between levels of government according to an allocation formula that keeps about half at the federal level, allocates a quarter to the 36 states and gives the other quarter to the local governments (Abimbola, 2012). These resources are not earmarked according to different tiers of government. The states and local governments are not constitutionally required to provide budget and expenditure reports to the federal government. This results in poor coordination and integration between levels of care, giving rise to a weak and disorganized health system in which widely varying patterns of outcomes depending on local situations (Abimbola, 2012). Thus, inadequate finance has led to overdependence of the local governments on federal, state and international agencies, such as, WHO and USAID for support.

Collaborating for Medical Products, Vaccines and Technologies

The Nigerian government is committed to quality and accessible public health services through provision of primary health care (PHC) in rural and urban areas as well as provision of preventive and curative services (Nigerian Constitution, 1999). Primary Healthcare (PHC) is provided by local government authority through health centers and health post and they are staffed by nurses, midwives, community health officers, health technicians, community health extension workers and by physicians (doctors) especially in the southern part of the country.

Health care services at the primary level include: prevention and treatment of communicable diseases, provision of vaccines, immunization, maternal and child health services, family planning, public health education, environmental health and the collection of statistical data on health and health related events.

Collaboration in PHC focuses on how to create conditions for health care providers everywhere to work together in the most effective and efficient way with the aim of producing the best health outcomes. Collaboration with other related sectors in the improvement of PHC as part of total socio-economic development is very important. It has been emphasized that no sector involved in socio-economic development especially the health sector can function properly in isolation.

Therefore, collaboration with the relevant sectors is especially important for worthwhile mutual benefits. Collaborative efforts focused on economic development and progress leads to better health. Educational institutions play an important role in the health status of the nation, especially in the field of prevention. Teachers and researchers can help in the early detection of ill-health in students. Students are used as messengers of health to the community. Literacy programs have been shown to have a great impact on equity-oriented development in rural areas. The educational status of the mother plays a pivotal role in the health of the family. As maternal education among rural and nomadic groups is relatively lack of adult educational programs has also been a great help. The mass media contributes effectively to the dissemination of health messages to the population at large. The health sector plays a leading role in health supportive public policies.

Leadership and Governance

The provision of health care at the primary healthcare level is more of the responsibility of the local government with the support of State Ministries of health within the overall national health policy (Nigeria Constitution, 1999; National Health Act, 2014, National Health Policy, 2016). The LGA is running her primary health care services delivery in compliance with the principles of the National Health Policy (Nigerian National Health Act, 2014). The LGA is divided into various health districts or wards so as to enhance maximum benefit of the principle of decentralization of the health sector whereby people are involved, participate and mobilized in the PHC processes.

The healthcare delivery at the local government areas is headed politically by a supervisory councilor and technically and administratively by a PHC coordinator and assisted by a deputy coordinator. The PHC coordinator reports to the supervisory councilor who in turn reports to the LGA Chairman (Adeyemo, 2005; Federal Ministry of Health, 2004). The different components of the LGA PHC are manned by personnel of diverse specialty.

There is also a common misconception (which sometimes is true) that politicians are not interested in health matters as there is lack of political will by leaders to implement primary healthcare services committedly. Disorganized health system, and misappropriation of allocated funds have formed negative images in peoples' heads. Lack of policy continuity is also another problem. In Nigeria, there has been no less than eight Ministers in Federal Ministry of Health. At the local government level, the headship has been very erratic. Some of the Local government councils have had their chairmen removed from office before their tenures expired because of politics. This high leadership turnover has negative influences in the implementation of PHC services (Adeyemo, 2005).

In summary, the analysis of these Health system building blocks showed that Nigerian Health's system is weak and, hence, underperforming across all building blocks. Health system governance is weak. There is inequity in access to services due to variations in socio-economic status and geographical location. For example, 11 percent of births to uneducated mothers occur in health facilities while 91 per cents of births to mothers with more than secondary education occurs in health facilities; 86 per cent of mothers in urban areas receive Ante Natal Care (ANC) from skilled providers, compared to only 48 per cent of mothers in rural areas; and ANC coverage in the North West of Nigeria is 41 per cent compared to 91 per cent in the South East (National Health Policy, 2016). Primary Health Care (PHC) is the weakest link in the health system. The Ebola epidemic both exacerbated and was partially fueled by broken PHC systems. For instance, in Nigeria, the severity of the outbreak was largely due to weak health systems, including a lack of capacity in surveillance and response (WHO Report, 2015). Because of Ebola, basic services such as treatment for common conditions, vaccinations and maternal health were at serious risk, and officials need to enact serious reforms to make things happen.

ISSUE OF LINKING PRIMARY HEALTH CARE POLICY WITH HEALTH SYSTEM TO IMPROVE HEALTH OUTCOMES IN NIGERIA

RQ.3: How Did Primary Health Care Policies Affect Health Systems Performance in Improving Health Outcomes in Nigeria?

The provisions of the National Health Act of 2014 and the new governance Primary Health Care Under One Roof (PHCUOR) renewed the hope for commitment to universal health coverage in Nigeria. However, the following are health outcomes arising from primary health care policies implemented over the years through the health systems in Nigeria:

Under-Five and Maternal Mortality Rate

Although, analyses of recent trends show that the country is making progress in cutting down infant and under-five mortality rates, the pace still remains too slow. Nigeria loses at least 2,300 under-five year olds and 145 women of child bearing age every single day (UNICEF Report, 2016). This makes the country the second largest contributor to the under-five and maternal mortality rate in the world. While Nigeria's under-five mortality rate has improved since 2000, it, nonetheless, remains very high at 109 per 1,000 live births in 2015(UNICEF, 2016).

Preventive and Communicable/Non-Communicable Diseases

Preventable or treatable infectious diseases such as malaria, pneumonia, diarrhea, measles, tuberculosis and HIV/AIDs account for more than 70 percent of the estimated one million under-five deaths (HPI, 2014). Nigeria has remained largely unchanged in the last decade; it was 22 per cent in 2000 and 20 percent in 2012. DPT3 immunization coverage of 66 percent in 2014 falls well short of the 90 per cent coverage the UN called for during its 27th Session (PHCPI, 2015). Moreover, rising disease burden including non-communicable diseases (NCDs) such as hypertension and diabetes, are creating growth prospects for pharmaceutical in Nigeria to produce drugs to address chronic conditions. This projection for pharmaceutical market within Nigeria is coming at a time when NCDs have become the leading causes of death, becoming a large public health care needs and expenditures in developed and most low and middle-income countries including Nigeria.

Inequitable Access to Quality Healthcare Delivery

Most public primary healthcare facilities in some states of the Federation are mainly health posts and dispensaries that provide only basic curative services. The huge "…out-of-pocket expenditure accounts for over 70 per cent of the estimated $10 per capita expenditure on health, thereby limiting equitable access to quality health care…" (Chiejina, 2014, p. 5). For example, health sector budget in Nigeria got N340.45 billion of the N8.6 billion expenditure plan of 2018 to the health sector. This represents 3.9 per cent of the total budget which is a far cry from 2016 allocation of 4.23 per cent and 2017 allocation of 4.16 per cent as against declared percentage of 15 per cent agreed in Abuja Declaration of 2001 (African Healthcare Extension Service, 2018). As a result of weak health system, there is lack of access to treat malaria, pneumonia and diarrhea in rural communities- three major causes of death in children under-five years old. This was evident when "Ebola struck as attention was shifted to Clinics, Quarantines and reports of cures" (Singh, 2014, p.12). About two-thirds of Nigerians who reside in both rural and urban area have the rights to be served with all the components of PHC, but these provisions are far from the Sustainable Development Goals target of universal access to reproductive health care services.

Community Perceptions of Quality of Primary Healthcare Services

Community perceptions of poor quality of service of PHC facilities determine utilization. Patients' utilization measure how health arrangements are understood by the population. Most Nigerians have a wrong perception about PHC. Such perception is the belief that PHC is meant for the rural poor which inputs the mentality that the services are meant for lower class citizens. In addition, health workers in PHC facilities, apart from being insufficient are perceived to be less qualified when compared to their counterparts in tertiary health facilities. Others include the view that PHC is an avenue for diversion and misappropriation of funds by the local government officials and that free healthcare services available in the facilities are of poor quality, all these effected community utilization of primary healthcare facilities and medication.

PROBLEMS OR CHALLENGES OF PRIMARY HEALTH CARE SERVICE DELIVERY IN NIGERIA

RQ.4: What Are the Problems or Challenges of Primary Health Care Service Delivery in Nigeria?

The essence of healthcare to the local government is to make the management of PHC services more effective and closer to the grassroots. However, in view of the level of health awareness, one begins to question the extent to which healthcare has been taken to the doorstep of the generality of the people.

Lack of Skilled Health Workers

One of the hindrances to the development of health especially in Nigeria has to do with insufficient numbers of medical personnel as well as their uneven distribution. The third Development Plan (1975-1980) for Nigeria focused on the inequity in the distribution of medical facilities and manpower/personnel. Despite the desire by the government to ensure a more equitable distribution of resources, glaring disparities are still evident.

Health Facilities/Infrastructural Decay

One can also point out the deterioration in government facilities, low salaries and poor working conditions which had resulted in a mass exodus of health professionals (Lyun, 1988). There has also been too much concentration of medical personnel at the urban to the neglect of the rural areas. Another significant problem in the effective implementation of PHC is transportation. It has been observed that in Local Government Areas, there are no sufficient vehicles for health workers to perform their tasks especially to the rural areas. Immunization outreach services are inadequately conducted. The maintenance culture of the existing vehicles is poor, while PHC vehicles are often used for purposes other than health-related activities. For example, many of the PHC vehicles donated by UNICEF in the 1980s are totally nonfunctional. According to International Finance Corporation (IFC), a total financing need for the 151 sample Primary Health Care (PHC) facilities would cost $97.5 million (IFC Report, 2014).

Based on this, the estimated bankable need at the national level is about $3 billion needed in Nigeria by pharmaceutical manufacturers, Health Maintenance Organizations (HMOs), medical equipment suppliers, hospitals, clinics, laboratories and nursing homes (IFC Report, 2014).

Inadequate Funding/Misappropriation of Funds

There is, however, financial over-dependence of the LGA on federal, state and international agencies for support as the internally generated revenue of the LGA is very small. In Nigeria, funding of healthcare activities is largely from budgetary allocations by the respective levels of government. With over-bloated personnel cost and corruption, little finance is left in the hands of the councils for other overhead costs. Most health expenditures in the grassroots are from out-of -pocket expenditures. Besides inadequate funding, misappropriation of funds, corruption and misapplication of funds are common issues.

Inadequate Community Participation

There is also a low level of community involvement. Utilization of services depends on community participation. Community participation is the hallmark of primary healthcare services delivery. The community needs to participate at village, ward, district or local government level. Community participation through the formation and creation of Village Development Committees (VDC) and Ward Development Committees (WDC) are no longer functional and used for other purposes such as politics. The expected mutual support from the community and government has broken down in recent times. Inadequate community mobilization and advocacy are part of the reasons for poor community participation.

Lack of Political Will

There are general misuse and abuse of the scarce resources by some political and administrative leadership and high leadership turnover at LGAs. Besides, most leaders do not show enough political will and commitment for the well-being of their citizens. There is great emphasis on construction of gigantic physical structures compared to the provision of good health services which in most instances are not available. In some cases, politics plays major role in primary healthcare policy implementation.

Poor Health Facilities or Infrastructure Decay

Nigerian healthcare institutions suffer from "lack of medicine, obsolete equipment, low quality of health services and many other issues. PHC facilities are in various state of disrepair, with equipment and infrastructure being either absent or obsolete, the referral system is almost non-existent" (Akinsete, 2016, p.9). With over 160,000 hospital beds as at 2015, the country suffers from a very low bed per thousand population of 0.9 (less than one) in comparison to countries as South Africa at 2.29 and Japan at 13.32 in 2013(Akinsete, 2016, p. 9).

Poor Inter-Sectoral Collaboration and Conflicts Between Local and State Governments

One of the laid down principles of PHC is inter-sectoral collaboration but we find out that this grossly missing in the Nigerian State. Inter-sectoral collaboration of other sectors are necessary in implementing PHC policy, such as agriculture, water, industry, education and so on. Besides, collaboration with other non-governmental organizations (NGOs) have often resulted in duplication of efforts because of lack of proper coordination. Poor coordination between levels of governments give rise to weak and disorganized health system and outcomes.

SOLUTIONS/RECOMMENDATIONS: LINKING PRIMARY HEALTH CARE POLICIES WITH HEALTH SYSTEM TO IMPROVE HEALTH OUTCOMES IN NIGERIA

RQ. 5: What Are the Solutions and Recommendations to Primary Health Care Service Delivery in Nigeria?

Though Nigeria has recorded some important milestones in recent years, such as the eradication of guinea worm, control of the Ebola Virus Disease Outbreak, and interruption of Wild Polio Virus transmission in the country, more efforts are required to obtain universal Health access coverage as recommended in Sustainable Development Goals Agenda of 2030. The following recommendations would assist linking primary health care policies with health system to improve health outcomes in Nigeria:

Primary Health Care Policy Reforms

Innovate and implement Primary health care policy reforms. Prioritize policy actions based on problems and potential solutions identified through rigorous measurement and analysis. Ensure PHC policies and practices reflect the experience within Nigeria and the best-available evidence on how other countries' PHC systems are succeeding. Besides, effort should made to implement PHCUOR reforms as specified in the NPHCDA's PHCUOR guidelines and the National Health Act of 2014. Advocates and Communities should be mobilized to promote awareness, ownership, and participation in the National Health Act of 2014 and utilization of health services.

Strong Primary Health Care Systems

PHC is the foundation of health system as it ensures that all people stay healthy and get care when they need it. Investing in APHC leads to high quality and cost-effective care for people and communities. Widespread access to PHC supports more equitable distribution of health. When PHC works, people and families are connected with trusted health workers and supportive systems throughout their lives, and have access to comprehensive services ranging from family planning and routine immunizations to treatment of illness and management of chronic conditions. Strengthening primary health systems is central to addressing these challenges, building on health gains, and achieving the Sustainable Development Goals, especially the goal of quality universal health coverage (PHCPI, 2014).

Adequate Funding

To improve PHC, adequate funding is critical. There is the need for the local government as well as all other levels of government to increase their allocation to the health sector. There is also the need to designate sufficient state and local funds to PHC to ensure eligibility for the Basic Health Care Provision Fund minimum 25 per cent counterpart funding (NHA Act, 2014). There is also the need to put a stop to unnecessary responsibilities being given to LGAs by the state government to shift part of their responsibilities to LGA, such as purchase of non-functioning health facilities and imposition of sponsored programs. All these are drains on the lean purse of the local governments with its attendant effects on health service delivery. Funding should be timely, and adequate to make maximum impact. This is to reduce the over-dependence on the federation account and international donor agencies in financing health programs. There is the need to strengthen the accountability mechanism for disbursing and implementing the Basic Health Care Provisions Fund established by National Health Act of 2014.

Public Education and Enlightenment

Priority should be given to improved living condition of the people beyond' the present poverty level so as to enhance better healthy living. To this end, intensive and effective health education of the public must necessarily be reinforced in other to eliminate such diseases as malaria, typhoid and other infectious diseases. There is the need for maintenance of minimum health standard, improved housing condition, adequate potable water supply, environmental sanitation and food supply for the sustenance of good health condition. Health education should be carried out at all levels by the Federal Government for a proper understanding of the real meaning of primary healthcare and the usefulness of community participation in its implementation.

Community Involvement and Participation

Community participation is the hallmark of primary healthcare services delivery. community mobilization and advocacy should be strengthened to encourage community participation in health care service delivery.

Improvement of National Health Management Information System

There is the need for the improvement of National Health Management Information System by using PHC performance initiative vital signs indicators data (HPI, 2014) to gauge aspects of the PHC system needing attention, and then develop more detailed diagnostic measures to identify the causes of problems. There is the need to have comprehensive data that will allow PHC systems pinpoint specific weaknesses, understand the casuses and strategically direct resources to the areas of greatest need. Ensure that the National Health Information Management Systems and District Health Information System contains high quality data that illuminate the components of high-performing PHC Systems. There is the need to build capacity to utilizing data and developing health information system infrastructure.

Good Leadership and Political Will

Poor leadership and political instability have been the basis for unsuccessful implementation of most government policies and programs on healthcare delivery. Therefore, good leadership and political stability are desirable to provide enabling environment for the implementation of the PHC programs. The governments of various levels should exhibit more political will and commitment towards health care service delivery in Nigeria. This will invariably reduce the problem of poor health outcomes.

Adequate Supervision, Coordination, and Collaboration Between Health Systems

Adequate supervision, coordination, and collaboration between inter-agencies should be pursued with vigor and required manpower provided to minimize conflict. The activities of some foreign donor agencies and non-governmental organizations should be properly coordinated to avoid duplication of efforts and activities. Proper coordination between levels of governments will give rise to strong and organized health system and outcomes.

Good Remunerations to Health Workers

Finally, good salary and other incentives should be provided for health workers, nurses and medical personnel involved in PHC to prevent high staff turn-over of health workers. Community mobilization and advocacy are part of the reasons for poor community participation.

FUTURE RESEARCH DIRECTIONS

Future health research on primary healthcare is required to identify community needs and their areas of strengths and weaknesses in order to appropriately deploy and utilize available resources. There is the need to adopt quantitative and qualitative research approaches to interrogate how healthcare policy would affect primary health care system and health outcomes in order to perform well and meet peoples' health needs. Concerted effort should also be made to demonstrate how ill-health and disease are closely related to illiteracy, poverty, poor sanitation and environmental conditions. The research results can then be shared among stakeholders and policymakers for quality healthcare service delivery in Nigeria.

CONCLUSION

As discussed in the chapter, PHC centers are uniformly distributed throughout Nigeria. The National Health Policy 1988 ascribed responsibilities for primary health care to local governments, secondary care to States and tertiary care to the Federal governments, respectively. National Primary Health Care Development Agency (NPHCDA) was established and they have oversight roles on PHC implementation at the State and Local government levels in Nigeria. Although national policies, formulated by the Federal Ministry of Health provide some level of standardization, each level is largely autonomous in the financing and management of services under its jurisdiction. Though, the major drawback of the NPHCDA is that it has no binding constitutional role to implement programs or policies at the state and local government levels.

Nigeria's Primary Health Care under One Roof (PHCUOR) policy reform was also established in 2011 to facilitate increased efficiency and coordination of health services, better management of resources by healthcare managers, and increased patient confidence in and utilization of services. In addition, Nigeria's National Health Act (NHAct, 2014) was established to recognize Nigerians' rights to health and make available by law financial resources for PHC through the Basic Health Care Provision Fund.

In 2015, Nigeria and the World Bank began a new $500 million partnership that builds on Nigeria's Saving one Million Lives (SOML) initiative to improve maternal, newborn and child health(HPI, 2014). The new program for Results for SOMI will strengthen PHC governance and link funding to results, increase accountability, improvement management, and encourage public and private sector innovation. All these primary health care policies were intended to fuel dramatic public health improvement and outcomes, yet, the health systems remain very weak and health outcomes have not been impactful.

Many problems to adequate primary health care outcomes abound and include among others: weak systems, lack of capacity-building, lack of orientation and public education, lack of mobilization and participation of community organization, poor information dissemination, poor remunerations for health workers, low confidence of consumers in the services provided, especially public health facilities, curative bias of health services delivered at all levels, unaffordability of services provided by the private sector to the poor and lack of political wills.

The chapter concludes by suggesting the following solutions to these problems. They include among others: cooperation and collaboration of health-related activities among inter-agencies to avoid duplication and make inter-sectoral coordination a reality, training of health workers, political will and commitment to provide adequate funding and strong health infrastructures, adequate political education and mobilization of communities on Primary Health Care delivery services.

In sum, there is great prospect of achieving impactful primary health care outcomes in Nigeria. As Federal and State governments implement the National

Health Act of 2014 and the PHCUOR policy reform 2011 guidelines for the integrated management of primary level health services, Nigeria has the potential to improve its PHC system and health outcomes. This will be critical to ensure progress toward achieving national and Sustainable Development Goals of 2030.

REFERENCES

Abdul Raheem, I. S., Olapipo, A. R., & Amodu, M. O. (2012). Primary Health Care Services in Nigeria: Critical issues and strategies for enhancing the use by the rural communities. *Journal of Public Health and Epidemiology*, *4*(1), 5–13.

Abimbola, S. (2012). *How to improve the quality of primary healthcare in Nigeria*. Abuja: National Primary Healthcare Development Agency. Retrieved on May 24, 2018 from http://nigerianstalk.org/2012/05/11/how-to-improve-thequality-of-healthcare-in-nigeria

Adeyemo, D. O. (2005). Local Government and Health Care delivery in Nigeria. *Journal of Human Ecology (Delhi, India)*, *18*(2), 149–160. doi:10.1080/09709274.2005.11905822

Akinsete, E. (2016). PPPs: The Antidote to Nigeria's Healthcare Infrastructure Deficit. *Businessday*. Retrieved on Wednesday 09, March, 2016, p.9, from www.businessdayonline.com

Appleton, S. (1995). The interaction between poverty and Gender in Human Capital Accumulation. The Case of Primary leaving Exams in Cote d'Ivoire. *Journal of African Economic, 4*(2).

Carrin, G., Evans, D., & Xu, K. (2007). Designing Health Financing Policy Towards Universal Coverage. *Bulletin of the World Health Organization*, *85*(9), 652. doi:10.2471/BLT.07.046664 PMID:18026615

Chiejina, A. (2014). Spotlight on Nigeria Health System. *Businessday*. Retrieved from www.businessdayonline.com

Dercon, S. (1996). Risk, Crop Choice and Savings: Evidence from Tanzania. *Economic Development and Cultural Change*, *44*(3), 385–514. doi:10.1086/452229

Edeh, H. (2016). Health Sector bleeds on absent of Health Act. *Businessday*. Retrieved from www.businessdayonline.com

Eneanya, A. N. (2016). *Policy Research, Analysis and Public Policymaking*. Lagos: University of Lagos Press.

Falae, V. (2018). Trace Primary Health Care in Nigeria. *Businessday*. Retrieved from https://www.naija.ng

Federal Ministry of Health. (2004). *Health Care in Nigeria*. Abuja: Annual Bulletin of the Federal Ministry of Health.

Frederick, I. (1998). *Health in Rural Tanzania. The Determinants of Health Status Healthcare Demand and Health care choice*. Discussion Paper Series. Center Paper Series DPS 98.03.

Gentham, U. G. J., Sogaard, J., Anderson, F., & Johnson, B. (1992). An Econometric Analysis of Healthcare Expenditure: A Cross-section Study of the OECD countries. *Journal of Health Economics*, *11*(1).

Grubaugh, U. G., & Santerr, R. (1994). Comparing the performance of Health Care Systems. *An Alternative Approach Southern Economic Journal*, *60*(4), 1030–1042. doi:10.2307/1060439

Health Partners International (HPI). (2014). *Bringing primary healthcare under one roof: PHCUOR Factsheets.* Available at https:resources.healthpartners-in.co.uk/resourse/

Health Reform Foundation of Nigeria (HERFON). (2009). Primary healthcare in Nigeria; 30 Years after Alma-Ata. *National Health Conference*. Abuja: HERFON.

Helmert, U., & Shea, S. (1994). Social inequalities and Health Status in Western Germany. *Public Health*, *108*(5), 341–356. doi:10.1016/S0033-3506(05)80070-8 PMID:7972675

Kaplan, G. A., Pamuk, E., Cohen, R. D., Lynch, J. W., & Balfour, J. L. (1996). Inequality in income and mortality in the United States: Analysis of Mortality and Potential Pathways. *British Medical Journal*, *312*(7037), 999–1003. doi:10.1136/bmj.312.7037.999 PMID:8616393

Lyun, F. (1988). Inequalities in health care in Ondo State. *Nigeria Health Policy and Planning*, *3*(2), 159–163. doi:10.1093/heapol/3.2.159

Magawa, R. (2012). *Primary healthcare Implementation: A brief review*. Available from: http://www.consultancyafrica.com/index

Muhammed, M. L., & Segun, T. (2015). Improving Primary health care in Nigeria: What's needed now. *Impatient Optimists* Retrieved on 24th May, 2018 from https: www.impatientoptimists.org/posts/2015/09/

Mwesiggye, F. (2002). Effects of Abolition of Cost sharing. *A Commission Study by the Uganda National NGO Forum*. Available Online at Mpra.ub.uni-muenchen.de/8558

Nigerian Constitution (1999). Section 7(1) C.

Nigerian National Health Act, 2014.

Obionu, C. N. (2007). *Primary Healthcare for Developing Countries* (2nd ed.). Enugu: Delta Publications.

Olise, P. (2007). *Primary Healthcare for Sustainable Development*. Abuja: Ozege Publications.

Raids, M. (2008). Nigeria Still Searching for right formula. *Bulletin of the World Health Organization*, *86*(9), 663–665. doi:10.2471/BLT.08.020908 PMID:18797638

Rao, S.K. Selvaraju, S., Nagpal, S. & Sakthivel, S. (2005). *Financing Health in India*. Available Online at ww.Whoindia.org/…./commission on Macroeconomic and Health Finance

Singh, P. (2014). Health in a time of Ebola. *Businessday*. Retrieved from www.businessdayonline.com

Smith, J. (1998). Healthy Bodies and Thick Wallets- the Dual Relation between Health and Economic Status. *The Journal of Economic Perspectives*, *13*(2), 145–166. doi:10.1257/jep.13.2.145 PMID:15179962

Turner, R. (1991). Better Access to Health Services in Nicaragua Lower Infant Mortality. *International Family Planning Perspective*, *17*(2).

Uzoma, C. W. (2016). Human Resource for Health: Focus on Community Health Extension Workers. *Businessday*. Retrieved from www.businessdayone.com

WHO. (2002). Report on the Study of Effect of Abolition of Cost sharing in Ugadan. In Collaboration with Ministry of Health, Kampala.

World Health Organization. (1978). *Alma –Ata Declaration: Primary Health Care*. Geneva: World Health Organization.

World Health Organization. (1991). PHS capacity-building strategies. *Public Health Report Series, Geneva*, *106*(1), 5–15.

World Health Organization. (1978). *Alma-Ata Declaration*. WHO.

World Health Organization (WHO) Report. (2015). *Sub-Saharan African lags other regions in healthcare*. Businessday. Retrieved from www.businessdayonline.com

KEY TERMS AND DEFINITIONS

Health Outcomes: Health outcomes in this chapter is measured by using these micro-indicators: objective outcomes measured by evaluating goals; subjective outcomes measured by evaluating how healthcare arrangements were understood by beneficiaries and community participation; patients' utilization of healthcare services measured by evaluating how socio-economic groups utilized healthcare services.

Health Policy: Describes the goals, structure, strategies, and policy direction of the healthcare delivery system.

Health Systems: In this chapter, health systems refer to primary health systems. There are three types of primary healthcare centers are recognized within the primary healthcare system. They include the comprehensive health centers (CHC), the primary health centers, and the basic health clinic (BHC). The primary healthcare centers were placed under local government administration for the delivery of basic health services.

Primary Healthcare: Primary healthcare is a grassroots approach towards universal and equitable healthcare for all.

Section 2

Human Rights, Public Values, and Health Policies

Chapter 6
Policy Value and Primary Healthcare Delivery in Rural Nigeria:
Issues, Challenges, and Opportunities

Akhakpe Ighodalo
Lagos State University, Nigeria

ABSTRACT

The health of a people is a major social capital to be prioritized and optimized for the growth and development of any country. Therefore, any government desirous of development should make healthcare delivery one of the cornerstones of its policy on development. In pursuance of these goals, the purpose of this chapter is to examine the dominant policy value, particularly the failure to faithfully implement government policies and achieve set goals. The method applied in the study is participant observatory method, using the basic need theory (BNT) as theoretical framework of analysis. The findings revealed that policy values frustrate the attainment of sustainable primary healthcare delivery in Nigeria. Challenges were highlighted such as improper monitoring and evaluation of policies, inadequate funding, program implementation, and lack of skilled professionals. The chapter concludes by suggesting opportunities to open primary healthcare delivery in the rural areas.

INTRODUCTION

The greatest asset of any nation is its citizens. The quality and quantity of the human resource of a nation is essential for its growth and development. There is a sense in which one can assert that a healthy nation is a wealthy nation. Good health among the population of any country is considered a pre-requisite for the society to develop

DOI: 10.4018/978-1-5225-6133-0.ch006

in the positive direction. Achieving this goal of good health for all is not always an easy task. Though with the right policies, plans and programs aimed at achieving these goals a healthy nation could be achieved if particularly, such objective is pursued with utmost commitment, dedication and integrity by all stakeholders in the health sector (Osakede & Ijimakinde, 2014).

Africa in general and Nigeria in particular, have a population that can be leveraged on to bring about the much-needed socio-economic development in this region of the world. Nigeria with a population of over 170 million people, has the potential to be one of the most developed countries in the world. However, these potentials have not been properly harnessed, invested and translated into sustainable development due perhaps to the poor healthcare system that has seen many Nigerians die from preventable and treatable diseases and ailments like malaria, Lassa fever, Zika virus, Ebola, monkey pox, polio meningitis, HIV/AIDS, among others (Idris, 2014). Also, the rate of maternal and child mortality has taken a frightening dimension due to the absence of vaccines and drugs to control and treat these ailments and diseases when they occur.

The main objective of the study, therefore, is to examine the role of policy value in primary healthcare delivery in rural Nigeria. Other specific objectives include:

1. To examine the nature of primary healthcare services;
2. To investigate the effect of policy value on primary healthcare delivery in rural areas, and;
3. To examine challenges facing the use of public policy to achieve primary healthcare.

BACKGROUND

While successive governments have demonstrated knowledge of and intentions to tackle these healthcare issues, the government policy value or lack of it has inhibited any such intention to address. While annual budgets have given some attention to these concerns albeit insufficiently, the lack of policy integrity, corruption, failure to give adequate commitment to policy implementation and the parlous state of the economy, all combine to frustrate any positive move to make the health sector efficient and effective. These challenges are mostly felt in the rural areas where health facilities are either non-existent or ill equipped and far apart. The condition of rural dwellers is made worst by the fact that majority of them are living below the poverty line, thereby making them susceptible to attack from preventable diseases. Primary Heath Care (PHC) that is targeted at this category of people, hardly meet their needs due to the incapacitation of local governments by inadequate resources.

How these issues play out in the health sector in general and Primary Health Care sub-sector in particular, are not very clear. Hence, this study aims at investigating the interface between policy value and primary healthcare delivery with a view to making them work for the growth and sustainability of primary health care in the country. To address issues raised in the study, it is organized into the following sections. The first section engaged in literature review under which it engages in conceptual and theoretical exploration. The second, interrogated the nature of policy value and primary health care in the country. Third examined the state of policy values and healthcare system. The fourth discussed some steps taken by government through policy reforms and changes to improve generally the condition of the health sector. The fifth analyzed challenges facing PHC articulation, implementation and control. The sixth charted a roadmap for the PHC sub-sector and healthcare system in general.

The Constitution of the Federal Republic of Nigeria states unequivocally that the primary responsibility of the Nigerian State is the promotion of the security and welfare of the citizens of the country. As part of its responsibility to its citizens, it has over the years come out with plans, policies and programmes to address the basic needs of Nigerians particularly, health care services. However, it would appear the policy value, that is, the premium placed on public policy has affected either positively or negatively their outcome. Also, Ayee (2008), Akhakpe (2016) and Maduabum (2014) have argued that the Neo-patrimonial nature of public policy has affected negatively the efficient delivery. While others attribute the poor state of public service delivery to failure of governments that has led to frequent strikes in the health sector (Idris, 2014). Similarly, not a few have fingered the issues of lack of political will and the decline in professionalism as causes for the poor health care delivery in the public sector particularly rural areas in Nigeria (Osakede & Ijimakinde, 2014).

However, it would seem these accounts have proved inadequate in explaining the poor primary healthcare delivery system in the rural areas of the country. It is this apparent lacuna that the chapter intends to address with a view to providing an in-depth analysis of how failure in primary healthcare delivery affects the well-being of rural dwellers in the country.

Public policy is the instrument used by government to give effects to its plans and programs for the people with a view to bringing about social changes in the society. The goal of any government is to pursue and realize the welfare and well-being of the citizenry. Henry (2007) defines public policy simply as "a course of action adopted and pursued by government". In what appear to capture the nature of public policy in developing countries, Dye (in Ikelegbe, 2005) posits that there are two schools of thoughts in the definition of the concept. The first opines that public policy is what government chooses to do or not to do. The second argues that it is not what government chooses to do but what it actually does. In the context of

Nigeria, both approaches to understanding the concept appear to converge to define how public policy evolves in the polity.

Every public policy has a goal or goals to accomplish. This goal could be universal in nature. Williams (1980) contends that the universal value of every public policy is "...to enhance the welfare of the individual through providing better educational facilities, housing, health facilities, more jobs and rising standard of living for the people as a whole". It follows therefore, that the value of welfare as the guiding premise of public policy has the virtue of overriding claims of sectional interests in any society. It offers an ideology under which all can progress and in which public objectives are taken out of political contention (William, 1980). This ostensibly is to ensure that health of the people is not compromised by competing political interests (Williams, 1980).

Healthcare can be conceived of as the process of rendering health services that meet the needs of the people. Primary Health Care (PHC) as defined by the 1978 Alma-Ata declaration (in Lambo, 2015) means:

Essential health care based on political, scientifically sound and socially acceptable methods and technology made universally accessible to individuals and families in the community through their full participation and at a cost that the community, a country can afford to maintain at every stage of their development in the spirit of self-reliance and satisfaction.

Furthermore, it notes that primary healthcare "... forms an integral part of the country's healthcare system of which it is the central function and main focus and of the whole social and economic development of the community (Alma-Nta, in Lambo, 2015). It is the first level of contact of individual, the family and the community with the national health system bringing healthcare as close as possible to where people live and work and constitutes the first element of a continuing health care process" (Alma-Ata in Lambo, 2015). From the foregoing, it can be said that PHC is focused on individuals and families in the various communities they live in and is easily accessible to them at an affordable cost. It requires the people's participation in its processes for it to be efficient and effective.

Most people in Nigeria live in rural areas. The term "rural" could be defined from economic, social, ethnic and other perspectives. To use the occupational perspective, rural areas are inhabited by people majority of whom are engaged in subsistence agriculture that is based on shifting cultivation, rudimentary mixed farming driven by irrigated cultivation and crop rotation (Olatunbosun, 1975). Over sixty (60) percent of Nigerians are said to live in the rural areas with varying degree of population density. While slightly above this figure is engaged in agriculture (Olaniyan, 2002). Central to these processes is the quest for development. No definition of development is complete without bringing to the fore increase in health status, implicit in longevity, among other ventures of development (Iwayemi, 2001).

However, to achieve the goal of increased health status for the people, healthcare delivery has to be done in an efficient and effective manner. Thus, service delivery is key to the sustainability of any healthcare system. Presently, service delivery in the public sector is being emphasized in order to give the people the best service they deserve (Maduabum & Akhakpe, 2017). To Fagbemi (2006), customer service delivery involves "a clear understanding of the specific services an organization provides and the targeted customers". The aim is for the organization and its clients to work together to realize the best of services they could render and received. People in the rural areas just as their counterparts in the urban centers, deserve qualitative services from their health provider. Unless this is done in an efficient and effective way, the goal of PHC may not be realized.

Several theoretical approaches could guide the study. Two of these theories could be useful for the purpose of this study. The Basic Need Theory (BNT) as conceptualized by the International Labor Organization (ILO) involves the availability of adequate food, clothing and shelter, education and health, basic human rights, employment as means and end and improved quality of employment (in Alemika & Olumodeji, 1998). Focusing on the Basic Needs of the rural populace particularly, their health needs, is seen as a more balanced approach to development (Ayee, 2008). However, achieving the basic needs of the people in developing countries is becoming increasingly difficult because of dwindling State capacity and resources scarcity (Fajonyomi, 2012).

The Basic Needs Theory however, tends to be silent on the role individuals, families and the community can play in achieving the basic needs of the people particularly in the light of seemingly failing state capacity. However, it focuses on the role expected of the State or government in the society which is primarily to provide for the welfare and well-being of the citizens.

Perhaps, the state is failing in meeting or providing sustainable healthcare services because of the dominance of neo-patrimonialism in the public sector (Fajonyomi, 2012). This is the use of State power and resources by public officials to gain access to socio-economic opportunities for themselves and those of close associates (Ayee, 2008). This practice has proven to be socially, economically and politically damaging to the project of development including PHC in rural communities. Under this system, focus is not on providing quality services to the people but on competition among those in power for resources of the State to serve not the general but personal interest. Under this condition, PHC is given little commitment by policy executors of PHC programs and projects. Perhaps, this practice may not be completely eradicated in any political system but can be minimized through emphasis on transparency and accountability in public affairs.

Methodology

The study employed mainly secondary sources of data consisting of archival materials such as: books, journals, magazines, newspapers and other periodicals. Content analysis of major issues in the healthcare sector was carried out. Also, participant observation method was used as the author is involved in and affected by the issue under investigation.

MAIN FOCUS OF THE CHAPTER

Basic Elements of Primary Health Care

Primary Health Care system is made up of essential tools that can lead to effective PHC delivery. These elements include:

1. Well trained and multi-disciplinary workforce
2. Properly equipped and maintained premises
3. Appropriate technology including essential drugs
4. Institutionalized systems of quality assurance
5. Sound management and governance structure
6. Sustainable funding streams that aim at universal coverage
7. Community participation in the planning and evaluation of service provided
8. Capacity to provide comprehensive proactive and curative services at the community level (Lambo, 2015)

Mechanisms for Managing PHC in Rural Communities

The tools for achieving PHC in rural communities can only be useful if certain activities are carried out. Some of these activities are highlighted below:

1. Tripartite funding system of primary health care by Federal, State and Local governments
2. Policy making that embraces an all-inclusive approach to decision making in PHC sub-sector to give community members more leverage in PHC policy initiation, formulation, implementation and evaluation
3. Continuous funding of the health care sector that will enable it to deliver its goals

4. Development of the political will to implement rather than pay lip-service to the concern with healthcare
5. More incentives for health matters to attract and retain the best hands in the sector (FGN, 2013)

The Nature of Policy Value and Primary Health Care

Every constitution the country has had since independence in 1960 commit the State and its agency government to the pursuit and realization of the security and wellbeing of the citizen of Nigeria (1999 Constitution). For this purpose, health policies, programmers and projects are embarked on by government. Their ultimate goals are to ensure increased quality and higher standard of living for the people through equitable healthcare delivery system. Annually, budgetary allocations are made to the health sector though they often fall short of the UNICEF benchmark of 17 percent of the entire budget. Constitutionally, primary healthcare fall under the jurisdiction of local government authorities in the three tier federal structure of the country. However, given the financial challenges of local governments in the country, a tripartite funding system could be more effective (Henry, 2007).

Given the fact that majority of Nigerians live in the rural areas and the skewed development pattern in the country, PHC should receive more attention from government at all levels. It would seem that successive governments have acknowledged this imperative as they have come out with policy statements and pronouncements on issues affecting healthcare delivery in the country. While several millions of Naira are allocated to constituency projects in the country's yearly budgets, most of these projects located in the rural areas are hardly implemented. Most health centers in rural communities are poorly equipped and underfunded. Some are in varying degrees of neglect due to lack of corporate governance by public officials. The reason for this is not far-fetched. As Olugbemi (in Maduabum, 2014) has rightly observed:

The civil servants ...at least the senior management cadre with responsibility for policy advancement and implementation are psychologically and socially removed from the bulk of the society that they are employed to serve... This removal and endowed, the average top Nigerian civil servant cannot appreciate the problems which confront their fellow countrymen resident in sub-urban areas..... Talk less of the vast majority in the more distant rural areas.

The phenomenon of social distance between public servants and the people they are to serve coupled with the lack of high moral order in the public sector have led to the neglect of the basic needs of the people including PHC delivery. There is a sense in which the point can be made that insofar as the interest of public servants conflict with the corporate interest of the Nigerian state insomuch, efforts at meeting the health needs of the people will be negatively affected. The material gain perspective to governance remains salient in the health sector. Public officials still see government resources as inexhaustible and its work must not be done in a hurry (Osaghae, 2002). These attitudes and behaviors of public servants are meant to punish "the rogue state" that could not cater for its citizens but was able to grant access to wealth for those in the precinct and corridors of power. These limitations notwithstanding, governments have gone ahead to make some remarkable efforts to revive and strengthen the health care system for maximum delivery of its services to the people. Some of these efforts are worthy of analysis.

Important Milestones in PHC Development

The administration of President Jonathan perhaps, made the most profound efforts to give the health sector a facelift. Some of the milestones recorded in the course of the Jonathan's administration include: the launch in 2012 of the National Strategic Health Development Plan (NSHDP), the launch of the Nigerian Health Investment Project (NSAPP), launch of SURE-P, launch of Save One Million Lives (SOML), among others (Lambo, 2015). In 2014, the National Health Bill was signed into law (National Health Act) (Ayankola, 2014). In order to give the health sector a new lease of life, the budgetary allocation to the health sector was increased from 4 percent in 2011 to 5 percent in 2012. In 2013 it was raised to 6.4 percent (Olukokun, 2013).

However, this is still a far cry from the stipulated 15 percent of annual budgets by the World Health Organization (WHO). Nigeria has not been able to meet this target in spite of enormous resources it has garnered over the years. Be that as it may, the passage into law of the National Health Act in 9th December 2014 has given the health sector a major boast for better performance (Ayankola, 2014). Under this law, some category of people, the most vulnerable in the society such as pregnant women, under five children and the elderly are to be given free healthcare services. Also, empowered by the law are: people with disabilities and accident victims who are guaranteed acceptance in public and private health institutions (Ayankola, 2014). Another cheering news is that funding for this scheme would not be an issue as it will be funded with one (1) percent deduction from the Consolidated Revenue Fund of the Federation (Ayankola, 2014). In spite of these milestones in the health sector, Primary Health Care still remains in a pitiable condition.

The State of Primary Healthcare Delivery

One area where primary healthcare has received global attention is in maternal and child mortality. Across the nations of the earth these phenomena have been witnessed of grave concern to nation-state. Records show that "sub-Saharan Africa remains the region with the highest under five mortality rate in all regions of the world with one child in two dying before his or her fifth birthday far higher than the average ratio of one in one hundred and forty seven in high income countries (UNICEF Report, 2015). The region is home to most of the highest mortality countries in the world" (UNICEF Report, 2015). The situation is so bad that "for too many babies their day of birth is also their day of death: almost one million neonatal deaths occur on the day of birth and close to two million died in the first week of life" (UNICEF Report, 2015). The leading causes of death come from infectious diseases such as pneumonia and diarrhea and neonatal complications which account for the vast majority of the under five deaths (UNICEF Report, 2015).

While globally, the number of under-five mortalities has dropped 53 (50 – 55) percent from 91 (89 – 92) deaths per 1,000 live births in 1990 to 43 (41 – 46) percent in 2015 (UNICEF Report, 2015). However, the Nigerian context continue to showcase very disturbing signals and health authorities have arduous task in their hands. Report shows that "infant mortality is very high in Nigeria, an awful national profile understood by the 2,300 under five children deaths that are recorded daily, according to UNICEF (UNICEF Report, 2015). These children are killed by preventable diseases like malaria, diarrhea, measles and HIV/AIDS. Added to this is the high rate of maternal mortality. A Demographic Health Survey in 2013 found that Nigeria contribute about 13 percent of global maternal mortality with estimated 36,000 deaths annually" (Ayankola, 2014).

These figures aptly show that all is not well with the country's health sector and healthcare delivery system were often the health authorities are not proactive enough in dealing with health issues rather they merely races to them in a poor and undedicated manner. In a country so blessed with resources, common vaccines and drugs are not available in most health centers and hospitals. This has made most of these health centers and hospitals mere consulting clinics where patients are referred to hospitals and pharmacies own and managed by doctors in public hospitals. It would seem the policy value in the country has not prioritized Primary Health Care as the foundation of healthcare services in the country.

Also, most of the funds appropriated for the health sector find their way into private pockets or diverted into other uses to the detriment of Nigerians in need of basic drugs. Poverty in the land has compounded the plight of Nigerians who increasingly are forced to purchase drugs out of pockets. As the WHO report put it:

...many as 92.2 percent of Nigeria citizens live below two hundred and fifty six naira (N256) per day and public workers earn a minimum wage of One hundred and seventy nine naira (N179.40) per day and 20 percent cannot afford the prices of medicines. The immediate effect is that they cannot access Medicare because drugs are purchased out of pockets. (Obembe, 2015)

Malaria related morbidity has not abated in spite of the Roll Back Malaria program which set a target of 75 percent reduction in its spread by 2015 – 110 million case incidences of malaria is reported per year, 30 percent of infant deaths are caused by malaria. Its occurrence stunt economic growth rate and reduces economic productivity of the nation's workforce (Obembe, 2015). All these violate the fundamental right to life and equity within the Nigerian State.

Similarly, many Nigerians particularly, children under the age of five years are unprotected and at risk of death from vaccine preventable diseases like measles, diphtheria, peruses and tuberculosis. Unfortunately, governments have not taken enough steps to redress the situation. The immunization program in the country has not gone smoothly. Report shows that:

The 2006 – 2017 National Immunization Coverage Survey indicates that only 33 percent of children between 12 and 23 months old had three doses of vaccine against the global target of 90 percent and only 23 percent were fully immunized. 40 percent do not receive any vaccine from the health system. (Ilorin, 2017)

Some of the needed vaccines are not manufactured locally while scarce resources are expended for importation of these vaccines which might not be available at the time of outbreak of some of these diseases.

From the foregoing, one can deduce that there are huge challenges confronting the health sector particularly primary healthcare in the country. In the section that follows, some of these challenges are identified for discussion. While these efforts are laudable step in the right direction, their trickle down effects on rural communities are still not pronounced due to the neglect this sub-sector is facing. At this juncture, it would be necessary to first look at challenges facing healthcare delivery globally.

CHALLENGES FACING POLICY VALUE AND PRIMARY HEALTHCARE DELIVERY

Well thought out and articulated public health policies have never been in short supply in Nigeria. The issue of concern is the ability of these policies to be translated into concrete action by anticipating and dealing with health care concerns of the people. However, this has not been the case as "quality access, efficiency and service availability of the healthcare system have stagnated and declined over the past decades" (Olukotun, 2013). Most rural dwellers often trek several kilometers to get medical services for basic health needs such as: fire burn, cuts on the body, malaria fever, neonatal and child delivery. As has been argued:

In Nigeria hospitals services are often poorly coordinated when it comes to primary healthcare services. Patients often by-pass primary care clinics to obtain treatments for minor complaints and injuries in outpatient clinic of teaching hospitals. (Iyatse, 2014)

All these developments amounts to gross violation of the right of the people to decent living and affordable healthcare system.

Funding gap in the healthcare system in general is a major handicap to efficient and effective healthcare delivery service. There has been a national outcry over poor funding of the health system in the country. In spite what would appear to be a buoyant national health budget outlay, it often does not automatically translated to quality life for the people (Iyatse, 2014). The stipulated percentage for the health sector in the national budget of nations by the World Health Organization (WHO) is 17 percent. Several countries in Africa has met this benchmark including: Rwanda and South Africa with respect to funding of the health sector. It is surprising that the country is unable to meet WHO's standard given its resources. This funding gap in the health sector has led to many public hospitals and clinics becoming mere consulting centers even the one in the presidential villa that the wife of the country's president Aisha Buhari said lack basic drugs. If the nation's seat of power lack basic drugs what happens in the primary healthcare centers in the rural areas is better imagined than described (Olukotun, 2013). This has negatively affected Nigerians majority of whom live in the rural areas.

The power elite and the rich in our society no longer have confidence in the country's healthcare system. This can be gleaned from reports of senior public officers who use public funds to travel abroad for medical treatments most times for ailments that can be treated at home here in Nigeria. For example, India is said to be making two hundred and sixty ($260) million dollars annually from Nigerian patients, while an estimated five thousand (5,000) persons travel out monthly for medical treatments many of them public officers who do so at tax payers' expense. In so far as top government officers and the rich in the society prefer foreign hospitals for medical treatments abroad than local ones insomuch the health sector in the country will continue to suffer neglect. Not only has this led to the neglect of primary healthcare centers, it has brought about more hardship and neglect of the rural poor. This is against the right to decent living.

Over the years, basic amenities for efficient and effective healthcare delivery particularly in the rural areas have not been given the attention they deserve. This is partly due to poor funding from government and lack of commitment by stakeholders to a proper management of the system. The healthcare sector like its homologue in other areas, is not devoid of corruption that inundates the whole public sector. Cases of corruption has been reported in the administration of the National Health Insurance Scheme (NHIS) where the Executive Secretary (ES) turned down the directive of the Minister of Health that the NHIS should pay the sum of One hundred and ninety seven million and seventy two Naira (N197.072) for rehabilitation works in some Federal Medical Centers (FMCs) for contracts awarded in 2016 (Ameh, 2017). His refusal to carry out the order, according to the (ES) was because there was no budgetary provision for such projects. This is just one of several cases of corruption rocking the health sector in the country. Such discrimination in favor of the rich has left the rural poor further marginalized and discriminated against by public policy and its operators.

Similarly, the working condition in the health sector has been everything but favorable. Failure of the various governments to provide the enabling environment for workers in the sector to perform their jobs has led to incessant conflict and crises in the sector. Frequent strike actions in the health sector have blighted chances of rejuvenating the sector. At the center of these crises is the issue of poor remuneration and condition of service of doctors and other workers in the sector. This has led to sacking and recall of these workers. Many competent workers in the sector have responded by travelling abroad in search for greener pasture (Idris, 2014; Ameh, 2017). Experts have "identified poor pay and harsh working environment as some of the factors that force Nigerian trained doctors to seek employment abroad" (Ameh, 2017).

Poverty and poor nutrition among inhabitants of the rural areas across Nigeria increase the risk of contracting some diseases like Lasser fever, monkey pox, polio, Ebola, chicken pox, small pox, among others. Over sixty-five (65%) percent of Nigerians live below the poverty line. Almost the same number cannot afford three square meals per day. Their conditions could grow worst with the present recession in the economy and food shortage across the country. Under these conditions, the health of the people could easily be attacked by preventable and treatable ailments. This is because their resistant level is likely to be low due to poor feeding habit and low immune system of the people. All these are possible because the rights to basic needs of the people are not promoted by state managers.

Also, the low level of literacy in most rural areas means that rural dwellers might not know how and when they should appreciate the importance of availing themselves of the modern medical facilities they might use for maintenance of their health. The rural areas in the country lack basic social amenities like educational institutions which is a violation of the social rights of the people.

POLICY VALUE AND PRIMARY HEALTHCARE DELIVERY: SOLUTIONS OR THE WAY FORWARD

In the preceding section, we identified and discussed some challenges facing primary healthcare delivery. These challenges however, are not insurmountable. In this section, how this can be done is discussed.

Policy makers should keep to the spirit and letter of primary healthcare system in the country in order to ensure their efficient and effective execution for the good of the people and fulfillment of the goal of such policies. Therefore, the integrity of any public health policy should be jealously guarded by all stakeholders in the health sector. The right to life and decent living condition of the people should be promoted at all times by policy makers and implementers.

Also, funding is key to the realization of the national, state and local government healthcare policies. As has been argued, "One of the things that have to happen is for us to reinvest in our health institutions. Many Nigerians have a lot of money but they are not spending it on healthcare (Ameh, 2017). Funding of the health sector should not be left to the government alone because even if it needs WHO's 17 percent of every annual budget, it would not still be enough. Thus, the federal, state governments, Non-Governmental Organization (NGOs) and Community Based Organizations (CBOs) should join hands to fund the primary healthcare system in particular in order to efficiently realize its laudable objectives that is, to achieve the right to life and decent living condition for all.

Proper monitoring and evaluation of primary healthcare projects should be frequently done to ensure that they conform with laid down procedures and required standards. It is not enough to make policies or budget money for the sector, they have to be monitored and evaluated frequently to ensure that performance is managed for their objectives to be achieved in the interest of the rural clients who often are discriminated against by central government policies.

Government should demonstrate the political will to ensure that the working conditions and environment of health workers are conducive to avoid incessant strikes, crises and conflicts in the sector. This will help attract competent personnel and retain them. This will halt the phenomenon of brain drain in the sector. Also, training and retraining of medical staff is indispensable to the growth and development of the sector. This is the only way the frequent strikes in the health sector and the attendant death of many Nigerians can be avoided.

All these cannot be achieved if the economy remains in crisis. The much needed funds to administer the sector efficiently and effectively can only come from a buoyant economy that will bring into government coffers the much needed foreign exchange to run this vital sector. This must not be taken lightly because only a healthy workforce can be productive. Investing in their health therefore, is needful for the people themselves and the nation at large. Therefore, avoid or address the abuse or discrimination against rural dwellers, better facilities and incentives should be given to health centers in the rural areas.

Proper and frequent enlightenment and sensitization should be carried out to bring the people of the rural areas to speed on what they need to do to enjoy a healthy life and high standard of living. Many inhabitants of the rural areas do not know that preventable and treatable diseases are at no or low cost to them. But because they are ignorant of what to do, they are tempted to patronize quacks who only assist to quicken their death. Therefore, modern and traditional channels of communication should be used to effectively communicate to the people at the grassroots on how to access healthcare services in their areas.

FUTURE RESEARCH DIRECTION

The study has done an in-depth qualitative study on the subject matter of the chapter. In view of the importance of the issues involved in the topic of investigation there might be need to carry out quantitative study of areas, regions or states in Nigeria. This will allow for theory building that could be generalized to other areas of the world.

CONCLUSION

We have analyzed Nigeria's policy value and primary healthcare delivery in rural communities, we argued that because primary healthcare is closest to the people in the communities, it should be given the attention it deserves. However, evidences in the country have shown that successive governments do not commit themselves to the values in public health policies that seek to promote the welfare and well-being of the people. Some of the reasons identified for this state of affairs in the health sector include: poor funding of the health sector, lack of adequate infrastructural facilities in the system, poor policy values of the political elite, lack of motivation of health personnel, disdain by the people for preventive medicines, just to mention few of these challenges. The study made some suggestions on how to improve primary healthcare delivery in Nigeria. These include: government commitment to public health policies, proper funding of healthcare delivery system, monitoring and evaluation of health programmers and projects and popular participation of the people of the communities in primary healthcare services where they are provided. The study concluded that once these measures are taken, healthcare delivery system will be efficient and effective.

REFERENCES

Adabayo, B. (2017, June 27). Saraki, Killwate lament high maternal deaths in Africa. *The Punch Newspaper*, p.16.

Akhakpe, I. (2017). *Local government management and democratic governance in Nigeria's fourth republic: Challenges and prospects*. Beasu – Bassin & LaunBert Academic Publishing.

Akhakpe, I. B. (2008). Food crisis, climatic change and human development in Nigeria: Challenges and the way forward. *The Nigerian Journal of Energy and Environmental Economics*, *1*(2).

Akhakpe, I. B. (2016). Public policy and sustainable national development in Nigeria's Fourth Republic: Challenges and possibilities. *International Journal of Management Perspectives*, *13*(1).

Alemika, E.E., & Olumodoji, E.O. (1998). Basic needs approach to rural development and radical skepticism: A critique. *Nigeria Journal of Social Work, 2*.

Ameh, J. (2017, July 18). Reps summon Health Minister, order him to recall NHIS Boss. *The Punch Newspaper*, p. 10.

Ayankola, M. (2014, November 19). Saving lives through National Health Act (Editorial). *The Punch Newspaper*, p. 28.

Ayankola, M. (2016, September 1). Nigeria's devastating polo eradication setback (Editorial). *The Punch Newspaper*, p. 18.

Ayee, J.R. (2008). *Reforming the African public sector: Retrospect and prospect*. Dakar: Codesria.

Deji-Folutile, O. (2012, June 27). Nigerians spend N78bn yearly on foreign medical treatments. *The Punch Newspaper*, p. 49.

Fagbemi, A. O. (2006). *Customer service delivery in public sector management*. Lagos: Concept Publication Limited.

Fajonyomi, S. O. (2012). *When the state goes to sleep of citizen and state development. LASU Inaugural Lecture Series* (46th ed.). Lagos: Lagos State University.

Federal Government of Nigeria (FGN). (2013). *Integrating primary healthcare governance in Nigeria: PHC under one roof.* Abuja: National Primary Healthcare Development Agency.

Henry, N. (2007). *Public administration and public affairs*. New Delhi: Prentice Hall of India.

Idris, A. I. (2014). Health personnel and the success of immunization in Nigeria. A study of selected local government areas in Kaduna state. *Review of Public Administration and Management, 2*(6).

Ikelegbe, A. (2006). *Public policy analysis: Concepts, issues and cases*. Lagos: Imprint Services.

Ilorin, S.N. (2017, October 24). NMA rejects FG's move to stop private practice. *The Punch Newspaper*, p. 11.

Iwayemi, P. (2001). *Nigeria's fractured development: The energy connection. An inaugural Lecture*. Ibadan: University of Ibadan.

Iyatse, G. (2014, November 12). Harvard scholars, others canvass better funding for hospitals. *The Punch Newspaper*, p. 62.

Iyoha, E. (2008). *Local government and the elusive rural development in Nigeria and constraints on local authority's capacity and the promise of decentralized participatory development.* 31st Inaugural Lecture Ekpoma Ambrose Ali University.

Lambo, E. (2015). *Primary healthcare: Realities, challenges and the way forward.* Abuja: National Primary Healthcare Agency.

Maduabum, C. P. (2014). *What has public administration got to do with it? Inaugural Lecture*. Lagos: National Open University of Nigeria.

Maduabum, C. P., & Akahkpe, I. B. (Eds.). (2017). The dynamics of public sector management: A reader. Ibadan: John Archer Publishers.

Obembe, K. (2015, April 25). Achieving community health insurance fund development goals in Nigeria. *The Punch Newspaper*, p. 53.

Ojo, J. (2016, July 27). Nigerian's disdain for preventive medicine. *The Punch Newspaper*, p. 22.

Olaniyan, A.O. (2002). *Review of the state of agricultural enterprises in Nigeria.* The 2nd LASU/CCDS Lecture Series held at the Nigerian Institute of International Affairs, Lagos, Nigeria.

Olatunbosun, D. (1975). *Nigeria's neglected rural majority.* Ibadan: Oxford University Press.

Olukotun, A. (2013, January 25). Controversy on oversees medical treatment for public officials. *The Punch Newspaper*, p. 64.

Onyekpere, E. (2016, August 1). Implementing the national health care act. *The Punch Newspaper*, p. 21.

Osaghae, E. (2002). *Crippled giant: Nigeria since independence.* Ibadan: John Archer Publishers.

Osakede, K. O., & Ijimakinde, S. O. (2014). The effects of healthcare strike on service delivery: The Nigerian experience. *Review of Journal of Public Administration and Management*, 2(6).

Public Health Policy Framework. (2016). Western Australia Department of Health.

Sapru, R. (2013). *Administrative Theories and management thoughts.* New Delhi: PHT Learning Private Limited.

UNICEF. (2015). *Level and Trends in child mortality report.* New York: UNICEF.

Williams, G. (1980). *State and society in Nigeria. Idanre.* Afrograika Publishers.

KEY TERMS AND DEFINITIONS

Basic Needs: These are essential services that should be provided by government such as food, shelter, education, healthcare, etc.

Policy Value: This refers to the ideology that drives public policy in a given context, that is, Nigeria and the rural areas of the country.

Primary Healthcare: This refers to healthcare services that relates to the basic health needs of those living in the communities.

Public Policy: The guide to action and activities of government towards its citizens.

Service Delivery: This is the provision of goods and services to the people efficiently and effectively to meet their needs for affordable and preventable healthcare.

Chapter 7
Dependents and Deviants:
The Social Construction of Mandatory HPV Policies

Leigh Nanney Hersey
University of Louisiana at Monroe, USA

ABSTRACT

Forty-two states have considered a mandatory vaccination for school-age girls, but the proposed legislation is most often met with hostility and it rarely succeeds. Using newspaper articles from Arizona, Colorado, the District of Columbia, Georgia, Texas, and Virginia during these legislative sessions, narrative analysis is used to find common themes in the debate, including a medical/clinical approach, "government to the rescue," individual cost constraint/access issues, logical narrative, sexuality/morality issues, parental rights, vaccination ethics, skepticism, and negative assumptions toward African-American girls. Using Schneider and Ingram's social construction theory, further discussion points to a better understanding of the target populations of this public policy. In reviewing this health policy debate, it is suggested that considerations go beyond the perceived health benefits of the policy and spill over into the civil and social welfare rights of the legislation.

INTRODUCTION

In June 2006, the Food and Drug Administration approved a vaccination that prevents cancer. Soon after, the Centers for Disease Control and Prevention recommended that girls between the ages of 11 and 26 receive the vaccination. This vaccination, Gardasil, is manufactured by Merck and protects women from several strains of

DOI: 10.4018/978-1-5225-6133-0.ch007

sexually transmitted cervical cancer associated with the human papillomavirus (HPV). Since this approval and subsequent recommendation, the political debate surrounding HPV vaccinations has become very heated. Since September 2006, forty-four states have considered legislation focused on HPV (National Conference of State Legislatures, 2018). The legislation has ranged from requiring insurance coverage for the vaccination (California, Hawaii) to broadly educating women about HPV (Connecticut, Illinois), to mandating vaccinations for school-aged girls (Kentucky, Maryland). While all health policy aspects of preventing cervical cancer are important, this chapter focuses on legislation mandating HPV vaccinations for school-age girls and, on the other side, legislation that prevents such requirements. These laws are analyzed in the context of social construction, with the objective of addressing the following research questions: What are the social constructions that come into play during the HPV vaccination policy debate? Are the social constructions inclusive or are some target groups neglected from the conversation? Are there underlying social constructions revolving around gender and ethnicity issues?

BACKGROUND

Human papillomavirus is a strain of viruses with more than 40 different types. Many types cause no detectable symptoms, and pass through the body with no incident. However, some varieties can lead to cervical cancer. HPV infections account for most sexually transmitted infections in the United States. Before the introduction of the vaccine, data indicated that 21.6% of women between the ages of 15 and 59 had been infected (Satterwhite, Torrone, Meites, Dunne, Mahajan, Ocfemia, & Weinstock, 2013). According to WebMD, HPV refers to a group of viruses that are the most common sexually transmitted infection in the United States (http://www.webmd.com/). By age 19, 25% of U.S. females have already been infected by the virus and several strains of the virus can lead to cervical cancer. It has been estimated that as many as 3.1 million women in the U.S. have been infected with one of the cancerous strains of HPV (Kam, n.d.). The American Cancer Society (n.d.) estimates that 13,240 cases of cervical cancer will be diagnosed in the United States in 2018 and about 4,170 women will die from cervical cancer in 2018. However, not all forms of cervical cancer are caused by HPV. The Pap test provides a screening procedure to enable early detection of cervical cancer. While this test has significantly decreased the death rate over the past 50 years, it does not prevent cancer. The administration of the HPV vaccine does aid in preventing the infection of the cancerous strains of HPV. In 2007, state legislators considered 42 specific state laws related to mandatory HPV vaccination.

POLICY DISCUSSION

A number of controversies arose during these policy discussions. Many of the controversies were based on the past inequities of healthcare in the United States. This section outlines the historical context that led to differing opinions on the approach to mandatory HPV vaccination. The primary issues revolved around women and health care, race and health care, and concerns about vaccinations in general. Understanding the context behind these issues helps understand why certain debates are prominent when discussing the policy.

Women and Health Care

Throughout American history, women have been treated differently than men in regard to health care. This disparity is particularly true when health care issues revolve around cancer of the "breast and womb," or reproductive organs. In an analysis of 20th century popular cancer education, Reagan (1997) Reagan finds that health education materials did not merely provide information, they also "produce(d) cultural meanings as they name, describe, and depict disease" (p. 1779). She describes how these materials also reinforce the gender norms of their time. Popular women's magazines of the mid-20th century focused on how cancer impacted women, teaching their readers "that cancer threatened their sex in particular" (Reagan, 1997, p. 1780). However, it was very difficult for women to make the transition to ask their doctors to check for reproductive cancers. Women of the early to mid-20th century were hindered by the cultural mores of the time. Throughout their lives, women had been taught to be "ashamed of their genitals and their sexuality, to protect their own reputations, and to 'save' themselves for their husbands" (Reagan, p. 1781). This indoctrination made it very difficult for women to visit male doctors and expose their "private parts," especially if they were not ill or in labor. Many women died from cervical cancer due to their reluctance to ask their male doctors to perform a pelvic exam. To make matters worse, many doctors were reluctant to perform such examinations. They would tell their patients that they were not the "type"' of person to get cancer, further categorizing cancer victims. Lerner (2000) argues that the radical mastectomy became an accepted practice because, in part, it reinforced "the idea that females should subjugate all concerns of appearance and sexuality to ostensibly improve their chances of permanent cure from cancer" (p. 26).

African-Americans and Health Care

Historically, African-Americans have not experienced much equity in the medical realm, often subjected to substandard treatment or experiments without informed consent. Washington (2007) states that in the antebellum south, the slave-trade was important to physicians who conducted medical research and training on slaves. Although medical care at the time was primitive for all, the slaves were more likely to suffer due to poor working conditions, malnutrition, and delayed care. (Washington, 2007). African-Americans developed a strong distrust of medical professionals based on past this past history, a sentiment that still exists in many ways today (Gamble, 1997; Corbie-Smith, Thomas, Williams, & Moody-Ayers, 1999; Washington, 2007).

The most noted medical experiment is that of the Tuskegee Syphilis Study which denied 399 Black men treatment for syphilis in order for the researchers to see how the disease progressed (Gamble, 1997). Many African-Americans believed that the Tuskegee Syphilis Study was a form of genocide, a fear that has reappeared several times since. Other medical programs that evoked the fear of genocide were the sickle cell anemia screening programs of the 1970s, birth control programs and AIDS (Gamble, 1997). A study by the Institute of Medicine (Nelson, 2002) revealed that racial disparities in health care "exist even when insurance status, income, age, and severity of conditions are comparable" (p. 666).

African-American Women

Health policy has especially discriminated against African-American women. Skloot (2009) details the story of Henrietta Lacks, a black woman who died in 1951 from cervical cancer. Her cancerous cells were used for medical testing and helped develop a number drugs for diseases including herpes, leukemia and influenza. Despite the medical advances brought about through this research, she never gave her consent, and her family did not receive compensation for generations, until her story became well-known.

Not only have they experienced the medical inequities of African-American males and Caucasian females, their sexuality has been especially exploited. Eugenics, or the promotion of refining the human race, labeled "black women as sexually indiscriminate and as bad mothers who were constrained by biology to give birth to defective children" (Washington, p. 191). From this labeling, many scientists and physicians were able to encourage increased sterilization in African-American women. In 1983, African-American women made up 12% of the population, but 43% of the mandated sterilizations (Washington, 2006). Gamble (1997) tells of an experience an African-American nursing professor had in the 1980's. She visited the emergency room because she was experiencing severe abdominal pains. While there, she was asked questions about her sexual history, associating her pains with pelvic inflammatory disease, an infection of a women's reproductive organs that is often associated with sexually transmitted diseases. As a nurse, she realized the implications of these questions and that the attending health care professionals had stereotyped her as a sexually promiscuous Black woman.

Vaccination Policy

While many of the debates focused on the disparities in health care, another narrative also comes into play – the concern over vaccinations in general. For centuries, people have opposed vaccinations based on ethical reasons. British citizens were so opposed to the mandatory smallpox vaccinations in the 1720s through the late 1800s that riots broke out (Feudtner & Marcuse, 2001). While mandatory vaccinations of children entering school have been credited with the near-eradication of many childhood diseases, concerns now are focused on side effects. Some research studies have shown that there is a causal link between autism and vaccinations containing thimerosal, including the mandatory measles, mumps, rubella (MMR) vaccination (Autism Society of America, 2004), though more research in this area is encouraged. However, other studies have found no connection between MMR and autism spectrum disorders (Jain, 2015; Uno, Uchiyama, Kurosawa, Aleksic, & Ozaki, 2015).

Medical Ethics

When deciding on policy, ethical issues also come into play. A common ethical issue is the balance of burden and benefit. Childress, et al (2002) argues that common moral considerations include fair distribution of the benefits and burdens of the public health activity. Kass (2001) suggests that "(p)ublic health interventions often are targeted to one set of individuals to protect other citizens' health" (p. 1778). Kass (2001) further acknowledges that public health initiatives also carry burdens, most commonly in the areas of risks to privacy and confidentiality, risks to liberty and self-determination, and risks to justice. In creating an ethical framework for public health, she states that "a decision must be readied about whether the expected benefits justify the identified burdens" (Kass, 2001, p. 1781).

Some of the states have proposed legislation that provides funding or mandatory insurance coverage for the HPV vaccination. This aspect is important to consider since the cost of this three-step vaccination is quite high. While many states contained exceptions to their mandatory HPV vaccination policy proposals based on religious or moral reasons, Georgia is the only state that submitted proposed legislation that allowed for an exemption for those "that cannot afford the vaccine" (NCSL, 2007). Social science studies have consistently shown a correlation between race and poverty. "It is well established in the literature that poverty rates are higher for minorities" (Rodgers & Payne, 2007, p. 7; Menifield & Dawson 2008). Therefore, it can be expected that a larger percentage of African-American children will opt out of this vaccination. Feudtner and Marcuse (2001) argue that "the benefits of immunization – namely, protection from disease – should be equitably distributed across the population" (p. 1159). If Georgia's legislation had passed, with the exemption for those that could not afford the vaccination, then there is a potential that a large number of African-American females would be excluded from protection, increasing the health care disparity in the state. During the time of this legislative debate, approximately 29.7% of Georgia's population was black (U.S. Census Bureau, 2006-2008).

Policy Agendas

Stone (2002) brings a different framework to policy analysis. While the traditional focus of policy analysis, has been on the rational model of reasoning Stone suggests that the model of reasoning is based on metaphors and analogies. Communities struggle with making policy decisions that satisfy everyone because it is difficult to incorporate different cultural communities. The differences between the cultural communities cause them to see things differently. Stone argues that "the most highly contested and passionate political fights are about membership" (p. 19) or who is included and who is not in the policy. At this point cultural communities come into play as different cultural communities are allowed in and restricted from different policies.

Stone identifies the common overarching goals in policy are centered on equality, efficiency, security and liberty. While many people support these goals, they can be at odds with each other. For example, Stone examines the trade-off between liberty and security. She describes liberty as the belief that "people should be free to do what they want unless their activity harms other people" (p. 120). Security is the "minimum requirements for biological survival" (Stone, 2002, p. 99). While this debate is often affiliated to questions surrounding terrorism defense, it can also be applied to the HPV discussion. What is the liberty of parents who do not believe in vaccinations? What is the security of those who want to vaccinate against a deadly cancer?

Additionally, Stone (2002) describes how policy problems and solutions are defined and framed. This framework can influence how people see the problem and the proposed solution. Often, political actors will often define problems and attribute cause, blame, and responsibility in calculated ways to gain support (Stone,

1989). One way to solve a policy issue may be through inducements, or "changing people's behavior with rewards and punishments or incentives and sanctions" (p. 261). Stone (2002) suggests that inducements "may have different meaning/value to target than giver intends" (p. 282). Some opposed to the HPV vaccination see the vaccination as an encouragement for young people to have sex.

When analyzing these policy agendas, Stone takes the social constructionist view (Stone 1989). Schneider and Ingram's (1993) social construction theory is used to better understand the target populations of public policy. Schneider and Ingram use the political power and social construction of target groups to develop the theory. Target groups are those groups of people that will be impacted by the policy. These groups can have either strong or weak political power and be constructed as deserving or undeserving social construction. Based on this matrix, Schneider and Ingram develop four categories – advantaged (strong political power and deserving), dependents (weak political power and deserving), deviants (weak political power and undeserving), and contenders (strong political power and undeserving).

METHODOLOGY

This research used a two-part methodology to better understand the policy debate surrounding policy concerning mandatory HPV vaccinations. First, proposed legislation from each of the states for the 2006-07, 2007-08, 2009-10, and 2011-12 legislative sessions was examined. Step one sets up an overview of the policy debate throughout the United States. Then, a content analysis of newspaper articles during the height of the debate (January 1, 2007-June 30, 2007) was conducted. The newspapers selected for this part of the study have statewide or significant regional coverage in five states - Arizona, Colorado, Georgia, Texas, and Virginia – and the District of Columbia. Each article related to HPV legislation was analyzed to create a narrative analysis that identified the dominant arguments and revealed the primary influences in the policy debate. Hence, this leads to the social construction of these influences. Additional news articles were retrieved from 2008 and 2010, but news coverage was low in the subsequent years and arguments were essentially the same. The newspapers selected for analysis include: *The Arizona Republic* (Phoenix), *The Atlanta (GA) Journal-Constitution, Austin* (TX) *American-Statesman, The Dallas (TX) Morning News, The Denver (CO) Post, Houston (TX) Chronicle, Richmond (VA) Times-Dispatch,* and *The Washington (DC) Post.* The final step of the analysis identifies common narratives between the communities throughout the policy debates.

RESULTS

As a multi-step research process, a variety of results stemmed from the analysis. This section provides the data summaries of the policy debates, the state synopsis of the policy debate, the dominant policy narratives surrounding the debate, and in conclusion, creating the social construction matrix.

Data Summaries

This section provides a brief legislative summary of each of the states included in this study. According to the National Council of State Legislatures (2018) forty-four states explored legislation concerning mandatory HPV vaccinations for school aged children. Only one state and the District of Columbia successfully passed legislation requiring the vaccine for middle school girls. Although the Texas governor enacted an executive order mandating vaccinations, it was vetoed by the state legislature. Table 1 summarizes the HPV legislation since 2006. As time passed, fewer laws were considered and less focus was on mandatory vaccination. Newer laws focused on requiring insurance companies to include the drug as a part of medical insurance and requiring the state to produce information regarding the drug to be disseminated to parents and children.

State Synopsis

The next section provides information on the six locations included in the case study analysis. It provides background on the dominant legislation as well as the media statistics for the area. The case studies include Arizona, Colorado, Georgia, Texas, Virginia and Washington, DC.

Table 1. Summary of HPV legislation

	2006 - 07	2007 - 08	2009 - 10	2011-12	2013-14	2015-16	2017-18
No. of States*	42	11	17	8	3	4	8
No. of Bills Considered	103	4	32	16	3	8	14
No. of Bills Passed	26	1	3	0	2	0	1
% Passed	25%	29%	9%	0%	67%	0%	7%
% States Considering Mandatory Vaccination	40%	9%	18%	13%	33%	25%	25%
% States Enacting Mandatory Vaccination	12%	0%	0%	0%	0%	0%	0%

*includes Washington, DC

Note: in 2015-2016, the Rhode Island Department of Health announced a HPV vaccine requirement for seventh graders starting in September, 2015. No legislative action is required to add new vaccine mandates in Rhode Island

Arizona

Public debate surrounding HPV vaccinations in Arizona was minimal. Rather than having a discussion on whether the vaccination should be mandatory or not, the state legislature included a provision in the state appropriations bill that "Immunization against the human papillomavirus is not required for school attendance" (AZ S. B. 1093, 2007). The bill was approved by a majority Republican legislature. Only one article, two editorials, and one letter to the editor was published in *The Arizona Republic* on the issue. Much of the concern surrounded morality and parental rights.

Colorado

Two bills regarding mandatory vaccination were presented to the Colorado legislature in 2007; one in each chamber. The Senate bill was sponsored by five Democrats, three of them female. A male Republican led the sponsorship of the House bill with six Democrat females co-sponsoring the bill. Public debate in Colorado was minimal with only ten stories printed in *The Denver Post* during the time period analyzed. Some concern over parental rights and morality arose during the debate. "Groups opposing government-mandated vaccines have voiced opinions, as have religious conservatives who fear that giving it to young girls will encourage promiscuity" (Auge, 2007). The Senate bill had progressed well through the legislative process, and had been seen as "destined for a fairly easy ride" (Clausing, 2007) with bipartisan support. What ultimately killed the bill was not the morality or health concerns of other states, but the question of funding the program and providing the vaccination for low-income children. At the beginning of the session, legislators established that no bills would be passed that required new funding. The mandatory vaccination bill fell under this category.

District of Columbia

The District of Columbia legislation passed through its City Council by a vote of 7 to 3. A male Independent and female Democrat sponsored the bill. Of the jurisdictions analyzed, only in the District of Columbia did the public debate take on a racial undertone, which will be expanded on in the policy narrative section.

Georgia

The bill for mandatory HPV vaccination in Georgia did not receive a lot of public debate. The bill was considered after the Texas governor had signed an executive order mandating the vaccination. Many Georgians took note of the backlash that the Texas governor received and cautioned against the bill. Of the seven articles published in *The Atlanta Journal-Constitution*, five of them were editorial pieces or letters to the editor.

Texas

The debate in Texas was the most heated of the states studied. While the common concerns of morality and parental rights again appeared, the bigger controversy surrounded the governor and his executive order mandating the bill. After Governor Perry issued the order in early February 2007, despite similar bills in both legislatives chambers already being filed, the public debate exploded. With this order, Texas became the first state to mandate the HPV vaccination for school admissions. However, "several Texas lawmakers expressed outrage at Perry for circumventing the legislative process" (Elliott, 2007a). Another round of controversy surrounded Perry when it was revealed that his former chief of staff was a lobbyist for Merck, the manufacturer of the vaccination. The Perry camp stated that his decision was based on his family's personal bout with cancer (Robison, 2007) and on discussions with his wife, a former nurse and women's health advocate (*Houston Chronicle,* 2007). In response to the order, the Texas legislature passed a bill that banned mandated HPV vaccinations. The bill passed with so much support, that the Governor did not bother to veto it. Even the author of the Senate bill that mandated HPV vaccinations signed the bill that blocked the Governor's order, stating that "she now thinks the matter should be decided by the Legislature" (Elliott, 2007b). While issues of parental rights and morality again came into play, it was Perry's "steamrolling over the democratic process (that) … crushed some of the vaccine's public support" (*Houston Chronicle,* 2007). A bill in favor of mandatory vaccination came before the house again in 2009, but saw no public debate and did not pass.

Virginia

After the Texas executive order was overridden, Virginia became the only state, along with the District of Columbia, to come through the 2007 legislative session with a bill intact that mandated HPV vaccinations for middle school girls before returning to school. The bill went into effect in October 2008. Between the two chambers, seven female Democrats sponsored the two bills that moved through the legislature relatively unopposed. The Senate voted unanimously to approve the bill and the House approved the bill 66-32 with one abstention. The Governor made recommendations to the bill which expanded the ability for parents to opt-out.

These recommendations were unanimously approved by the Senate and approved 81-17 by the House. In 2008 and 2010, legislation to remove the requirement was unsuccessfully brought to the table. Both times a male Republican sponsored the bill.

Policy Narratives

Throughout the debate in all states examined, several underlying themes reoccurred on both sides of the issue. In examining the newspaper articles during the legislative periods, those in favor of the mandated HPV vaccinations used four main themes to support their viewpoints: 1) a medical/clinical approach; 2) government to the rescue; 3) individual cost constraint/access issues, and; 4) the logical approach. In addition, those in favor of the mandated vaccination more commonly referred to HPV as a link to cervical cancer. Those opposed to mandated HPV vaccinations focused on the following framings of the issue 1) medical/clinical approach; 2) sexual issues; 3) parental rights; 4) vaccination ethics; 5) skepticism toward pharmaceutical companies, and; 6) negative assumptions toward African-American girls. In addition, those opposed to the mandated vaccination were more likely to refer to the sexually-transmitted nature of the cancer rather than the cancer itself. A further look into these viewpoints is merited.

In Support of Mandated HPV Vaccinations

Those that supported the legislation often took viewpoints supported by expertise and a concern for equitable health care options. The main narratives that developed included a medical/clinical approach, government to the rescue, cost/access issues, and a logical narrative.

Medical/Clinical Approach

Any certain kinds of policy issues, the scientific and professional values and perspectives play a large part in shaping the narrative. The intention is to create policy that is based on scientific knowledge rather than personal biases or political power. However, Schneider and Ingram (1997) call it an "illusion that policy making can become more objective by diminishing the role of politics and increasing the role of experts" (p. 151). Despite this illusion, many people turn to science as a way to validate their perspective. For the policy debate surrounding HPV vaccinations, those in favor often relied on the science that had been provided and the support of the Center of Disease Control for the vaccination. The following statements demonstrate how debaters used this expertise to argue their case.

It is important because we lead the nation in cases of cervical cancer (co-sponsor of the District of Columbia bill, David Catania) (Wilson, 2007).

Since we cannot control every future act, we should do our best to protect our young women from death due to the human papillomavirus by offering them a vaccination. (member of the board, Planned Parenthood of Georgia).

As a physician, I can truly say that the most devastating diagnosis I have to give my patients is the diagnosis of cancer (letter to the editor by an internal medicine physician, The Atlanta Journal-Constitution).

Government to the Rescue

Another common narrative in policy debates in the idea of "government to the rescue." Houck (2004) harkens this concept back to Theodore Roosevelt in his campaign against the trusts and consolidation of power in the early 20th century. He felt that government regulation was needed to protect the laborers from the men in power. In this instance, some in support of mandatory vaccination felt that is was the responsibility of the government to intervene in effort to rid the country of cancer, particularly the "daughters."

Our legislation is a small but critical component of a larger strategy of combating cancer and other illnesses that afflict our residents (in an editorial piece by District of Columbia co-sponsors Mary M. Cheh and David Catania [2007] published in The Washington Post).

... to save our daughters from the scourge of HPV (co-sponsor of the District of Columbia bill Mary M. Cheh).

Our nation's daughters are relying on it (Richmond Times-Dispatch editorial).

Perry laid blame for future cervical cancer deaths at the feet of lawmakers who supported the bill (that banned mandated vaccinations) (Austin American-Statesman).

Individual Cost Constraint/Access Issues

An important concern in social construction is how underrepresented populations may be targeted in the legislation. With this legislation, one of the most common supportive views related to how making the vaccination mandatory would increase access for girls in low-income families. It was argued that making the vaccination mandatory would encourage more health insurance companies to cover the vaccination in its policies and would make the vaccinations more regular in public health clinics.

Below are examples of quotes that support the importance of access and cost when considering mandatory vaccinations. The argument seemed to be stronger in locations where the policy was better received (District of Columbia, Texas, and Virginia).

...introducing the bill now because federal support is available for the vaccine... children receiving Medicaid benefits and others who are uninsured or underinsured can receive free HPV vaccinations (co-sponsor of the District of Columbia bill, David Catania).

If legislation passes, girls from low-income households and homes with little or no health insurance will be covered through public programs (The Washington Post).

Vaccination must be made mandatory or its use will never become widespread. Historically the only way that the government and private insurers cover the costs of vaccination and ensure public education is when vaccination is required for school attendance (Richmond Times-Dispatch editorial).

It would seem unfair if only girls with insurance and informed parents benefit from a life-saving vaccine (livestrongarmy.org, 2007).

Informed parents with resources will still learn about, and access, the vaccine for their children even if it is not mandatory. It is those in poverty, predominantly minority groups, who will continue to experience disproportionately high rates of HPV and cervical cancer (Richmond Times-Dispatch editorial).

This vaccine offers similar, if slightly less dramatic, hope to a large population of neglected Americans (The Washington Post).

...when a vaccine is mandated, it must be available for free to those who can't afford it (The Washington Post).

Even Merck argues that its lobbying efforts for mandated vaccination were aimed at improving access for all populations.

Through school requirements, you reach under-served populations, certain ethnic and socio-economic groups that wouldn't be reached otherwise.... And that's why we support state initiatives that improve immunization rates (medical director at Merck).

School requirements is one approach that has been used very successfully in the past to improve vaccine rates…a mandate tends to lead to state funding of vaccines for public health clinics, improving access for lower-income and uninsured girls (president of Merck's vaccines division).

The Dallas Morning News columnist Jacquielynn Floyd (2007) best summed up this theme with her comments after the Texas legislature overturned the Governor's executive order.

Only because, when you strip away all the huffy rhetoric about 'parental rights,' we're looking at a law that would have benefited the daughters of the least responsible parents.

It would have addressed those girls from overburdened or dysfunctional households, the ones least able or likely to take voluntary extra measures to safeguard their children's health.

Sadly and perhaps not coincidentally, girls from those very households have a greater than average likelihood of becoming sexually active at an early age and of having multiple partners – risk factors for the virus that the vaccine prevents.

Logical Narrative

The final dominant narrative was the logical one. Bardach (2005) describes this logic as "largely that of common sense" (p.36). Those that displayed this narrative felt that the policy "only makes sense."

How can anyone be against preventing cancer? (letter to the editor, The Washington Post) (Dardano, 2007).

This is good medicine and makes sense. (Catania) (Gardner, 2007).

In Opposition of Mandated HPV Vaccinations

A variety of narratives came through by those opposed to the vaccination, too. While those in favor of the vaccinations focused on the positive impacts it could have on society, those opposed spoke with fear and distrust. The medical narrative was also used by those that opposed mandatory vaccinations, but were on the cautious side rather than the proactive side. Other narratives included sexual/morality issues, parental rights, vaccination ethics, skepticism of pharmaceutical companies, and negative assumptions about African-American girls.

Medical/Clinical Approach

While those in support of the mandated vaccination policy turned to the experts to bolster their arguments, so did those in opposition to the mandate. Those that opposed the mandatory vaccination felt that the vaccination had not been tested long enough and needed further study before being mandated.

I think it's too early... This is a new vaccine. It would be wise to wait until we have additional information about the safety of the vaccine (Joseph Bocchini, chair of the American Academy of Pediatrics committee on infectious diseases).

We're not protecting the public health in the same way that we protect public health when we require measles vaccine (professor of pediatrics at ECU medical school).

Never mind that the trials may not have been long enough to show potentially dangerous side effects (letter to the editor, The Atlanta Journal-Constitution).

(The vaccine) is too new for lawmakers to declare safe (Texas state representative).

...'an experimentation' not be allowed on children (The Washington Post).

Many medical organizations support that guideline. But few have gone further, saying the drug is too new, and public understanding and financial support not well enough established, to require girls to receive it (The Washington Post).

Sexual/Morality Issues

The debate over the sexual implications of mandating that pre-teen girls be vaccinated for a sexually transmitted disease was the most frequent opposition. This narrative supports Stone's (2002) concept that inducements may have different meanings for some than the intended outcome. Although the opposition was prominent, it was rarely given more than one sentence in the articles, all very similar to each other.

Some conservatives object to the vaccine because they fear it will encourage early sexuality (Wilson, 2007).

Perhaps instead of vaccinating young people to prevent a disease transmitted by (promiscuous) sexual relations, ... the District government should promote abstinence programs, whose main side benefit would be respect for the dignity of young women (letter to the editor, The Washington Post).

Some religious organizations are lobbying against the vaccine, saying it could encourage girls to have sex and that sexual abstinence will prevent transmission of the virus (The Atlanta Journal-Constitution).

Others believe the vaccine may lower inhibitions against sexual activity, although there is no evidence that fear of HPV infection is a reason many teenagers abstain (The Washington Post).

The recommendation was that all children be given a vaccine for a carcinogenic virus whose spread is associated, in many minds, with sinful activities (The Washington Post).

Parental Rights

The issue of parental rights was another widespread area of opposition. Even those who supported mandatory vaccination in general, often felt that it should be left up to the parents to decide if the vaccination is right for their daughters. This narrative falls in line with Kass's (2001) argument that one of the ethical burdens in public health is the risk of liberty and self-determination. While it is the parents that are making the decision rather than the children themselves, it still falls in line with the idea citizens should be able to make their own decisions. As stated by Stone (2002) "(f)or many Americans, freedom is the essence of what America is about" (p. 108). The argument is a strong one for those that favor minimal government intervention.

That's really a decision between parents and doctors (co-chair of Parents United for D.C. Public Schools).

Parents should have total control over whether they vaccinate their children or not (analyst for Focus on the Family, a Colorado-based conservative group).

Some parents said the order violated their rights even though the mandate allowed parents to opt out (Austin American-Statesman).

Vaccination Reluctance

Closely tied with the medical debate and the parental right debate is the debate that questions the ethics of vaccinations. CBS News (2007) stated that the discussion of mandatory HPV vaccinations were "sparking a debate over the intersection of sex, public health and parental rights." As noted earlier, many people are concerned about the long-term health impacts of vaccination. These concerns came forward in this debate, as people opposed the vaccination based the fear of side effects.

Should citizens be injected against their will with biological agents that can injure and kill for what the state has defined as the common good? (President of the National Vaccine Information Center).

Bioethicists, who generally hold the values of patient autonomy and informed consent to be preeminent, tend to be skeptical about compulsory vaccination laws....Because HPV is not casually transmissible, they argue there is less compelling rationale for requiring protection against it than against measles or pertussis; in the absence of potential harm to a third party, such laws may be considered unacceptably paternalistic (New England Journal of Medicine).

Skepticism Toward Pharmaceutical Companies

With Merck actively lobbying in most states to encourage mandatory vaccinations, many people opposed to the vaccination policy cited concerns with how these corporate efforts impacted policy decision-making. In the case of Texas, it is this lobbying that may have thwarted public support. In mid-February 2007, Merck stopped lobbying, stating they did not want to be a distraction.

It is quite another, however, when the goal of the massive and cash-laden effort is to secure government action mandating use of the product (editorial by former congressman and U.S. Attorney Bob Barr in The Atlanta Journal-Constitution).

...interest in protecting us has been over-ridden by the influence of drug companies (letter to the editor, The Atlanta Journal-Constitution).

Legislators across the board were urged to quickly hop on the Gardasil train – one that was barreling down a track generously greased with Merck's lobbying dollars (Richmond Times-Dispatch editorial by the president of The Family Foundation).

To mandate now is to Merck's benefit, and only to Merck's benefit (lead researcher who has spent 20 years working on the HPV vaccines).

The risk of bad government becomes especially acute when private industry's drive for profit teams with government's drive to control, to create a 'perfect storm' of government control (editorial by former congressman and U.S. Attorney Bob Barr in The Atlanta Journal-Constitution).

Negative Assumptions About African-American Girls

While this viewpoint was only prominent in the debate in the District of Columbia, where an estimated 57% of the population is African-American (U.S. Census Bureau, 2007), it is one that needs mentioning. The arguments reflect the inequitable health care activities surrounding African-American women and speak to their social construction of the issue.

...your daughter is 11 and probably black, so the assumption is she'll be having unprotected sex in no time (Milloy, columnist, The Washington Post).

Let's go right at these presumed-to-be-promiscuous, 11-year-old black girls (Milloy, columnist, The Washington Post).

In addition to the debates surrounding legislative initiatives, broader public debate also occurred. At the end of a lecture about her book, *Medical Apartheid: The Dark History of Medical Experimentation on Black Americans from Colonial Times to the Present* (2006), an audience member asked Washington (2007) about the HPV vaccination. Washington, an African-American woman, noted that the "vaccine is a wonderful thing." However, she felt that the HPV vaccine was "yoked to a variety of human rights abuses.... They are taking a wonderful thing and trying to cram it down people's throats." She expressed concern that other groups that would benefit from the vaccination were being ignored, including men and adult women. She also found it very "troubling" that the case was being made that the vaccination would only benefit virgins. She questioned the money trail, and the implications that the drug manufacturer's possible role in pursuing a mandatory HPV vaccination policy. She explained that school-administered health initiatives often provide perfect research sites. There is a high pressure for 100% compliance, and making a vaccine mandatory to attend school will help push for the compliance. She noted there is a difference between the HPV vaccine and vaccines for other diseases that are communicable – when there is a need to maintain "herd immunity." Washington was particularly concerned about how mandatory HPV vaccinations played out in her host city of Baltimore, a city with a large African-American population and a "unique reproductive profile." She noted that teenage pregnancy rates in Baltimore were still very high, while they were declining around the country. She felt Baltimore could be chosen as an experimental city by researchers with a racial agenda.

Social Construction Matrix

Drawing from the narrative analysis, the final results present the social construction of the primary players during this policy process. In this analysis, 23 target groups were discovered and their social constructions are identified in Figure 1. The categorizations of these groups are based on the overall viewpoint of mainstream media from the jurisdictions analyzed. However, some groups of people may see the represented policy players differently. For example, the media generally portrayed public health experts and officials in a positive light, with high political power on this issue. However, groups that have been negatively targeted by public health policy and practice in the past, such as African-Americans, may see these experts less favorably and place them in the contenders group.

Figure 1. Social construction of target groups of HPV vaccination policy

Social Construction

Political Power

Advantaged		**Contenders**
Parents		Pharmaceutical Companies
Cervical Cancer Survivor		Government
Public Health Experts		Politicians
Cancer Survivor		Hospitals
Cancer Research Advocate		Governors (especially Perry)
Public Health Agencies		Insurance Companies
Ethics Experts		
School Districts	Doctors	
Dependents		**Deviants**
Women		
Hispanic Women		
Elderly Women	Low Income Women	
Girls	African-American Females	
(Boys)	(Gay Men)	

Drawing on Schneider and Ingram (1997), the advantaged group consists of those with more political power and considered to be deserving. The advantaged group in the HPV vaccination policy debate consists of public health experts, parents, cervical cancer survivors, doctors, cancer survivors, cancer research advocates, public health agencies, ethics experts, and school districts. As a whole, this group represents the "experts" of the debate. While many are official experts, such as public health experts and doctors, others are experts by experience, such as the cervical cancer survivors and parents. Seeing parents as experts, or advantaged, is very important in the development of the parental rights narrative that was described earlier. Doctors experience a dual role in the public debate of mandatory HPV vaccinations. Many people expressed that the decision to vaccinate should be left up to parents and their doctors putting doctors in an advantaged role. However, the debate turned to doctors' finances when the Texas Medical Association came out in opposition to the bill, because it would hurt doctors financially. This struggle over the role of doctors pushed them closer to the contender area.

Contenders are those with political power, but seen as undeserving. The contenders in the HPV policy debate include government, pharmaceutical companies, politicians, governors, insurance companies, and hospitals. Many contenders stand to make a profit through a vaccination mandate. Even nonprofit hospitals hope to remain in the black and do not want to lose money based on public policy. The pharmaceutical companies, especially Merck, are most solidly in the contender category. With Merck's lobbying efforts, it exhibited a significant amount of political power. Merck is often seen less positively due to the potentially large amount of profit they could be making off a mandated vaccination, which at the time of the 2007 legislative sessions, only Merck produced. Seeing pharmaceutical companies as contenders carried over into editorial cartoons. One cartoon depicted images of shady characters representing Merck, hiding behind trees, preying on little girls (Adams & Berger, 2007). The actions of Governor Perry (Texas) landed him firmly in the contender category as it was speculated that he would profit politically from his executive order.

Females of all types were classified as dependents of these mandated vaccination debates. Dependents are those with less political power, but seen positively. Children and mothers have historically been considered to be dependents, evoking images of being loving, sweet, blameless and helpless (Schneider & Ingram, 2007). Those in favor of the bill, wanted to protect girls and women from cervical cancer. Those in opposition of the bill, wanted to discourage girls from premarital sex. Some even argued for protection from cancer based on the premise that girls may get raped or molested, rendering them helpless. On occasion, promiscuous undertones were given to women and girls of ethnic minorities and lower socioeconomic status, shifting them closer to the deviant category. Boys and gay men are in the dependent category, but enclosed by parentheses because they are mostly forgotten. Only a few articles point out the need to vaccinate boys, too.

SOLUTIONS AND RECOMMENDATIONS

In the initial analysis, many viewpoints and social constructions were brought to light. By examining the content of the argument surrounding the access concerns, it appears that the proposed legislation aimed to increase availability for all populations, and not just those of means. However, one should be concerned about the neglect of the concerns of the African-American population, only vocalized in the District of Columbia, and the neglect of the male population. Early research indicates that the vaccination can potentially be beneficial for boys as well. When considering policy, it is important to take into consideration the different target audiences and their needs. Policy makers also need to remember the delicate balance between benefits and burdens when applying public policy, particularly when it comes to public health.

FUTURE RESEARCH

While this chapter looks specifically at one policy issue in one year of legislation, it sets forth a model that others can use to explore other controversial policies in health care. It brings to light many of the risks that Kess (2001) noted, with the risk of liberty being the most prominent. This application of the framework reflectively can help understand how the ethical question might impact the debate and ultimately the vote. Further research into the ethical considerations behind public health policy can provide insight into developing policy that truly balances the benefits and burdens.

As a continuing policy debate, the issue requires further analysis into how the narratives develop over time. Changes in policy can take years to develop and pass. Sometimes it takes a specific event that changes the tide of those making the decision. For example, legislation for the legalization of marijuana has been considered since 1998, but only in the last five years has it become a more common conversation throughout the country. Although the debate surrounding mandatory HPV vaccination has been in existence for more than ten year, there has been little traction on passing legislation. A deeper look into the legislation in each state and other influences could help determine if the debate is changing. What other influences might be swaying the conversation? What is the general political climate at the time of the legislation? Were there other funding concerns like in Colorado? Does social media play a role in the social construction of policy? A deeper understanding of these factors might help other states better address the issue in their state.

In a study of six states, Bratton and Haynie (1999) found that women legislators were more likely to introduce bills related to "women's interests" than men. Their study also found that both women and Democrats were more likely to introduce bills on health care and children issues. While vaccination can be important for both genders, the impact of the virus is most noticed in females. This policy closely aligns with "women's interests" and further research on the gender and political leaning of those in support of the vaccination could be beneficial.

CONCLUSION

To summarize, there are a number of target groups for any policy. In the process, each group has varied political power and social constructions. How they are perceived by the public can impact how policy is viewed. It is evident that policy inducements mean different things to different people. For those in support of mandatory vaccinations, it means good health and reduced chances of one type of cancer. For other, the same inducement was seen as giving young girls the permission to have sex. Understanding how these debates can influence people and policy makers can lead to improved policy decision.

Key stakeholders and leaders involved in the debate need to remember the different ways that people will be impacted by this policy, as well as other public health initiatives. As the chapter demonstrated, members of the constituency may bring a different and valid viewpoint to the conversation. It is up to those in leadership roles to make note of these viewpoints and use them to develop policy that best meets the public need. With the changing landscape of local media, it will be important for elected officials at the state and local levels to find additional ways to engage citizens in the conversation.

This analysis examined an emerging issue in health care. While the vaccination prevents one virus that causes one type of cancer, it is still a medical breakthrough leading to other discoveries of how the U.S. can reduce incidents of cancer. The policy debates surrounding the issue reflect the diversity of opinion in the country. While many people value health, how it is maintained and distributed can be hotly contested. The primary narratives of the debate pitted personal freedom against a collective good. This debate is evident in many issues and one that needs to be negotiated through carefully to create policy that is impactful.

REFERENCES

Adams, M., & Berger, D. (2007, February 7). *HPV Vaccine Texas Tyranny* (comic). Retrieved September 24, 2007, from http://www.naturalnews.com/021571.html

American Cancer Society. (n.d.). *What Are the Key Statistics About Cervical Cancer?* Retrieved July 17, 2018, from https://www.cancer.org/cancer/cervical-cancer/about/key-statistics.html

Arizona Senate Bill 1093. (2007). *Arizona Senate Bill 1093.* Retrieved November 24, 2007, from http://www.azleg.gov

Auge, K. (2007, January 17). Bill seeks proof of HPV shot or opt-out Colo. schools would require paperwork. Some say mandating the vaccine to prevent cervical cancer will encourage teen sex. Rep. May says the shot would be optional. *The Denver Post*, p. A1.

Autism Society of America. (2004). *ASA Statement on May 2004 IOM Report on Vaccines and Autism.* Retrieved October 24, 2007, from http://www.autism-society.org/site/PageServer?pagename=mmrvaccine

Bratton, K. A., & Haynie, K. L. (1999). Agenda setting and legislative success in state legislatures: The effects of gender and race. *The Journal of Politics*, *61*(3), 658–679. doi:10.2307/2647822

Catania, D. A., & Cheh, M. M. (2007, January 21). Why we believe the HPV vaccination is vital to the District's health. *The Washington Post*, p. B8.

Childress, J. F., Faden, R. R., Gaare, R. D., Gostin, L. O., Kahn, J., Bonnie, R. J., ... Nieburg, P. (2002). Public health ethics: Mapping the terrain. *The Journal of Law, Medicine & Ethics*, *30*(2), 170–178. doi:10.1111/j.1748-720X.2002.tb00384.x PMID:12066595

Clausing, J. (2007, February 25). HPV bill not immune to funding roadblocks. *The Denver Post*, p. C3.

Corbie-Smith, G., Thomas, S. B., Williams, M. V., & Moody-Ayers, S. (1999). Attitudes and beliefs of African Americans toward participation in medical research. *Journal of General Internal Medicine*, *14*(9), 537–546. doi:10.1046/j.1525-1497.1999.07048.x PMID:10491242

Dardano, B. (2007, February 1). Risk, racism, and the HPV vaccination. *The Washington Post*, p. A14.

Elliott, J. (2007a, February 6). Critics rip Perry's vaccine mandate: Governor rejects opponents' calls to reverse order. *Houston Chronicle*, p. A1.

Elliott, J. (2007b, February 8). The Legislature: Vaccination order still stoking fires. But Bell urges Democrats to back Perry for his stand on women's health. *Houston Chronicle*, p. B1.

Feudtner, C., & Marcuse, E. (2001). Ethics and immunization policy: Promoting dialogue to sustain consensus. *Pediatrics, 107*(5), 1158–1164. doi:10.1542/peds.107.5.1158 PMID:11331702

Floyd, J. (2007, March 2). HPV vaccine is a lifesaver tossed aside. *The Dallas Morning News*, p. B1.

Gamble, V. N. (1997). Under the shadow of Tuskegee: African Americans and health care. *American Journal of Public Health, 87*(11), 1773–1778. doi:10.2105/AJPH.87.11.1773 PMID:9366634

Gardner, A. (2007, February 11). Drug maker assists in pushing for mandate for HPV vaccine. *The Washington Post*, p. C5.

Houck, D. W. (2004). FDR's Commonwealth Club address: Redefining individualism, adjudicating greatness. *Rhetoric & Public Affairs, 7*(3), 259–282. doi:10.1353/rap.2005.0006

Houston Chronicle. (2007, February 8). Opting in One question should guide HPV vaccine policy: how effectively and efficiently it promotes public health. *Houston Chronicle*, p. B10.

Insinga, R. P., Perez, G., Wheeler, C. M., Koutsky, L. A., Garland, S. M., Leodolter, S., ... Brown, D. R. (2011). Incident cervical HPV infections in young women: Transition probabilities for CIN and infection clearance. *Cancer Epidemiology and Prevention Biomarkers, 20*(2), 287–296. doi:10.1158/1055-9965.EPI-10-0791 PMID:21300618

Jain, A., Marshall, J., Buikema, A., Bancroft, T., Kelly, J. P., & Newschaffer, C. J. (2015). Autism occurrence by MMR vaccine status among US children with older siblings with and without autism. *Journal of the American Medical Association, 313*(15), 1534–1540. doi:10.1001/jama.2015.3077 PMID:25898051

Kam, K. (n.d.). *What Parents Should Know About the HPV, or Cervical Cancer, Vaccine*. Retrieved September 24, 2007 from http://www.webmd.com/sex/features/what-parents-should-know-about-hpv-cervical-cancer-vaccine

Kass, N. E. (2001). An ethics framework for public health. *American Journal of Public Health, 91*(11), 1776–1782. doi:10.2105/AJPH.91.11.1776 PMID:11684600

Lerner, B. H. (2000). Inventing a curable disease: Historical perspectives on breast cancer. In *Breast Cancer* (pp. 25–49). New York: Palgrave Macmillan. doi:10.1007/978-1-137-03779-4_2

Levine, S. (2007, April 4). Council tentatively backs mandatory HPV vaccine. *The Washington Post*, p. B01.

Livestrongarmy.org. (n.d.). *Lance Armstrong on the HPV Debate*. Retrieved October 30, 2007, from www.pbs.org/now/shows/308/lance-armstrong.html

Menifield, C., & Dawson, J. (2008). Infant mortality in southern states: A bureaucratic nightmare. *Journal of Health and Human Services, 31*(3), 385–402. PMID:19209565

Milloy, C. (2007, January 10). District's HPV proposal tinged with ugly assumptions. *The Washington Post*, p. B01.

National Conference on State Legislatures. (2007, October). *HPV Vaccine*. Retrieved June 30, 2018, from http://www.ncsl.org/programs/health/HPVvaccine.htm

Nelson, A. (2002). Unequal treatment: Confronting racial and ethnic disparities in health care. *Journal of the National Medical Association, 94*(8), 666–668. PMID:12152921

Reagan, L. J. (1997). Engendering the dread disease: Women, men and cancer. *American Journal of Public Health, 87*(11), 1779–1787. doi:10.2105/AJPH.87.11.1779 PMID:9366635

Robison, C. (2007, February 16). As questions brew over his motives for vaccine, governor lays it out: Cancer runs in his family. For Perry, it's also personal. *Houston Chronicle*, p. A1.

Rodgers, H. R. Jr, & Payne, L. (2007). Child poverty in the American states: The impact of welfare reform, economics, and demographics. *Policy Studies Journal: the Journal of the Policy Studies Organization, 35*(1), 1–21. doi:10.1111/j.1541-0072.2007.00204.x

Satterwhite, C. L., Torrone, E., Meites, E., Dunne, E. F., Mahajan, R., Ocfemia, M. C. B., & Weinstock, H. (2013). Sexually transmitted infections among US women and men: Prevalence and incidence estimates, 2008. *Sexually Transmitted Diseases, 40*(3), 187–193. doi:10.1097/OLQ.0b013e318286bb53 PMID:23403598

Schneider, A., & Ingram, H. (1998). *Policy Design for Democracy*. Lawrence, KS: University Press of Kansas.

Skloot, R. (2017). *The Immortal Life of Henrietta Lacks*. New York: Broadway Books.

Stone, D. (2002). *Policy Paradox: The Art of Political Decision Making*. New York: W.W. Norton & Company.

Stone, D. A. (1989). Causal stories and the formation of policy agendas. *Political Science Quarterly*, *104*(2), 281–300. doi:10.2307/2151585

Uno, Y., Uchiyama, T., Kurosawa, M., Aleksic, B., & Ozaki, N. (2015). Early exposure to the combined measles–mumps–rubella vaccine and thimerosal-containing vaccines and risk of autism spectrum disorder. *Vaccine*, *33*(21), 2511–2516. doi:10.1016/j.vaccine.2014.12.036 PMID:25562790

U.S. Census Bureau. (2007). *District of Columbia Quick Facts*. Retrieved November 27, 2007, from http://quickfacts.census.gov/qfd/states/11000.html

U.S. Census Bureau. (2006 – 2008). *American Community Survey. Georgia Fact Sheet*. Retrieved September 30, 2010, from http://factfinder.census.gov/servlet/ACSSAFFFacts?_event=&geo_id=04000US13&_geoContext=01000US|04000US13&_street=&_county=&_cityTown=&_state=04000US13&_zip=&_lang=en&_sse=on&ActiveGeoDiv=&_useEV=&pctxt=fph&pgsl=040&_submenuId=factsheet_1&ds_name=null&_ci_nbr=null&qr_name=null&reg=null%3Anull&_keyword=&_industry=

U.S. Court of Federal Claims. (2007). *In Re: Claims for Vaccine Injuries Resulting in Autism Spectrum Disorder or a Similar Neurodevelopmental Disorder*. Retrieved October 24, 2007, from http://www.uscfc.uscourts.gov/OSM/OSMAutism.htm

Washington, H. (2006). *Medical Apartheid: The Dark History of Medical Experimentation on Black Americans from Colonial Times to the Present*. New York: Doubleday.

Washington, H. (2007, February 7). *BookTV lecture*. Retrieved September 25, 2007, from http://www.booktv.org/program.aspx?ProgramId=7904&SectionName=History&PlayMedia=Yes

WebMd. (2005 – 2013). *HPV/Genital Warts Health Center*. Retrieved July 18, 2018, from http://www.webmd.com/sexual-conditions/hpv-genital-warts/default.htm

Wilson, B. (2007, February 5). States consider requiring HPV vaccine for girls. On *All Things Considered*. National Public Radio. Retrieved October 30, 2007, from http://www.npr.org/templates/story/story.php?storyId=7190905

KEY TERMS AND DEFINITIONS

Advantaged: In social construction, a target group that has political power and is generally thought of in a positive way.

Contenders: In social construction, a target group that has political power, but is not generally thought of in a positive way.

Dependents: In social construction, a target group that has limited political power, but are generally thought of in a positive way.

Deviants: In social construction, a target group that has limited political power and are generally through of in a negative way.

Human Papillomavirus (HPV): A strain of viruses that are sexually transmitted. While most pass through the system with no effects, some lead to cervical cancer.

Social Construction: A policy design framework that examines the target populations of policy.

Chapter 8
Community Participation in the National Development Plan Through Primary Health Care:
The Case of LGBT Organizations in South Africa

Johannes Ntshilagane Mampane
University of South Africa, South Africa

ABSTRACT

The chapter explores and describes community participation in the National Development Plan through Primary Health Care by using case studies of LGBT organizations in South Africa. Post-Apartheid and democratic South Africa has endorsed community participation as one of the fundamental pillars of the public Primary Health Care approach in its governance structures. This chapter focuses on the current major health issue in South Africa, the HIV epidemic, which is one of the leading causes of death in the country. Particular attention is paid to members of the LGBT community because of their discrimination in public healthcare facilities on grounds of their sexual orientation. The chapter relies on secondary sources of data collection from extant literature, textbooks, journal articles, and internet sources. Challenges to address LGBT community discrimination in HIV testing, prevention, treatment, care, and support were identified and solutions to uphold their human rights were proffered. These solutions are based on the principles of social justice, inclusion, diversity, and equality.

DOI: 10.4018/978-1-5225-6133-0.ch008

INTRODUCTION

During the apartheid era in South Africa, the process of community participation was not encouraged due to bureaucracy and segregation policies. In post-apartheid South Africa however, this process has gained full support from the democratic government. Community participation is considered to be an empowerment tool in which local communities can take responsibility in identifying and addressing their own problems through collaboration with different stakeholders in the community, including local government. Community participation enables people to realise their rights to participate in problem-solving and decision-making processes regarding issues that affect their day-to-day life in the communities that they live in. It is regarded as the process of allowing citizens within a community to participate in the formulation of policies and proposals on issues that affect the community as a whole (Ngcaweni, 2016). In developing countries such as South Africa, community participation is generally accepted as a key component of good governance for implementing effective and efficient developmental processes. As a result, community participation is widely regarded as a catalyst for an efficacious developmental process. This has been the cornerstone of the South African National Development Plan (NDP) Vision 2030 in which communities are urged to actively participate in development issues to address problems such as poverty, inequality and health issues in society. The NDP Vision 2030 is a national strategic plan that was released in 2012 to outline South Africa's developmental goals that are to be accomplished by the year 2030. The NDP Vision 2030 has specifically identified nine key challenges that face South Africa, namely:

1. Too few people work.
2. The quality of school education for black people is poor.
3. Infrastructure is poorly located, inadequate and under-maintained.
4. Spatial divides hobble inclusive development.
5. The economy is unsustainably resource-intensive.
6. The public health system cannot meet demand or sustain quality.
7. Public services are uneven and often of poor quality.
8. Corruption levels are high.
9. South Africa remains a divided society.

Given this myriad of challenges facing South Africa, this chapter focuses on the current major health issue in South Africa, the HIV epidemic, which is one of the leading causes of death in the country. South Africa is also home to the largest number of people living with HIV and AIDS in the whole world. The South African National Strategic Plan on HIV and AIDS for 2017 – 2022 has identified the Lesbian,

Gay, Bisexual and Transgender (LGBT) community as one of the key populations at risk of HIV infection, however, members of the LGBT community have been discriminated against in public Primary Health Care (PHC) services based on their sexual orientation (Reddy, Sandfort, & Rispel, 2009). Discrimination on the basis of one's sexual orientation is a constitutional rights violation in South Africa. This is stipulated in Act No. 108 of 1996 Clause 9(3) of the Constitution of the Republic of South Africa which states that:

The state may not unfairly discriminate directly or indirectly against anyone on one or more grounds including race, gender, sex, pregnancy, marital status, ethnic or social origin, colour, sexual orientation, age, disability, religion, conscience, belief, culture, language and birth.

Against this backdrop, this chapter explores and describes community participation in the NDP through PHC by using case studies of LGBT community organisations in South Africa. The chapter is divided into four sections. Section one introduces the concept of community participation in relation to the NDP Vision 2030 in South Africa. Section two provides background on the implementation of the NDP Vision 2030 with regards to the provision of PHC to mitigate the effects of the HIV epidemic among the LGBT community. Section three describes the situation of the HIV epidemic in South Africa and the formation of LGBT civil society organisations (CSOs) to address the scourge caused by the epidemic. Section four concludes the chapter by discussing PHC efforts of LGBT CSOs in response to the epidemic through HIV/AIDS testing, prevention, treatment, care and support programmes.

BACKGROUND

The NDP Vision 2030 came up with fifteen Chapters as vision statements aimed at ameliorating the living conditions of people in the country. These Chapters and their vision statements are shown in Table 1.

Out of the fifteen NDP Vision 2030 Chapters, the discussion in this chapter will specifically focus on Chapter Ten, namely: *promoting health.* Health promotion is particularly critical to the prevention and management of major communicable diseases and epidemics of our time, including HIV and AIDS. The impact of the HIV epidemic in South Africa has resulted in a deteriorating health care system due to high HIV prevalence (number of people living with HIV) and incidence (number of new HIV infections) rates, including increasing rates of HIV-related morbidity and mortality among health care personnel who succumb to the disease. As a result, there is poor provision of HIV testing, prevention, treatment, care and

Table 1. NDP Vision 2030 Chapters and their vision statements

Chapters	Vision Statements
Chapter One	Ensuring policy making in complex environments
Chapter Two	Responding to demographic trends for equity and equality
Chapter Three	Creating economic and employment opportunities
Chapter Four	Ensuring socio-economic development
Chapter Five	Ensuring environmental sustainability and equitable transition to a low- carbon economy
Chapter Six	Ensuring an integrated and inclusive rural economy
Chapter Seven	Positioning South Africa in the world
Chapter Eight	Transforming human settlement and the national space economy
Chapter Nine	Improving education, training and innovation
Chapter Ten	Promoting health
Chapter Eleven	Ensuring social protection
Chapter Twelve	Building safer communities
Chapter Thirteen	Building a capable developmental state
Chapter Fourteen	Fighting corruption
Chapter Fifteen	Transforming society and uniting the country

(Source: NDP Vision 2030, 2012)

support services in many parts of the country. This situation is evident in high HIV transmission areas such as townships, squatter camps and informal settlements.

The first cases of HIV and AIDS in South Africa, like in the United States of America (USA), were initially diagnosed among members of the LGBT community, particularly gay men. Therefore, AIDS was initially perceived as a gay man's disease and was consequently named Gay-Related Immune Deficiency Syndrome (GRIDS). Since then, the LGBT community has been at the forefront of HIV and AIDS community activism and mobilisation worldwide (Aldrich, 2006). This has been through the formation of civil society organisations, social movement organisations or interest groups. For instance, during the early stages of the global HIV epidemic, prominent organisations such as AIDS Coalition to Unleash Power (ACT UP) in the USA and Treatment Action Campaign (TAC) in South Africa have been led by members of the LGBT community. These organisations have been advocating for the provision of HIV testing, prevention, treatment, care and support to all people living with the disease. Although the advocacy by these organisations has been at all spheres of government (local, provincial and national), the emphasis has been placed at grassroots level through the provision of PHC. This was because members of the LGBT community experienced considerable discrimination on the basis of their sexual orientation in public PHC facilities (Reddy, Sandfort,& Rispel, 2009). PHC is defined as:

...essential health care, based on practical, scientifically sound and socially accepted methods and technology made universally accessible to individuals and families in their communities through their full participation and at a cost that the community and country can afford to maintain at every stage of their development in the spirit of self-reliance and self-determination. (Kironde & Kahirimbanyi, 2002, p. 16)

Globally, PHC is recognised as a foundation for universal access, equity and community participation in health care service delivery (Ngcaweni, 2016).

In September 1978, the World Health Organisation (WHO) held an international conference on PHC in Alma Ata, Russia. At this conference, a declaration was reached to inform governments all around the world to implement the principles of community participation in the delivery of PHC services. Then in 1994, when the African National Congress (ANC) took over the South African government as the official democratic ruling party, it decided to develop the National Health Plan based on the Alma Ata principles which endorsed community participation in PHC. This plan stated that an "affordable, comprehensive health service should be developed, in which community members would have the power to decide on health issues" (ANC, 1994, p. 21). The NDP Vision 2030 argues that effective implementation of PHC in communities will increase the life expectancy of South Africans to an average age of 70 years by the year 2030. According to the NDP Vision 2030, the latter could be achieved if:

- All HIV-positive individuals are on Anti-Retroviral Therapy (ART) medication
- Consistency in condom usage is adhered to
- Effective microbicides are routinely available to all women who are 15 years of age or older
- There is universal access to Pre-Exposure Prophylaxis (PrEP) in combination with ART

THE HIV EPIDEMIC AND LGBT CIVIL SOCIETY ORGANISATION IN SOUTH AFRICA

In all sub-Saharan countries, South Africa is regarded as the epicentre of the HIV/AIDS epidemic. In 2017, Bureau of Statistics in South Africa announced that the overall HIV prevalence rate in the country was approximately 12.6 per cent, which translates to 7.06 million people living with HIV and AIDS. These shocking statistics are predicted to substantially increase because South Africa has fastest growth of HIV prevalence and incidence rates in the whole world. The scourge caused by HIV and AIDS in South Africa has been attributed to political inaction and denial respectively. According to Fourie and Meyer (2010), the apartheid government was inactive in responding to the HIV epidemic by implementing discriminatory policies in which HIV-positive persons were forced to be quarantined and secluded. There were no effective HIV surveillance mechanisms put in place to measure the severity of the epidemic. Geffen (2010) argues that the democratic government was also in denial about the severity of the epidemic by blaming HIV and AIDS on poverty. The then President Thabo Mbeki and his Minister of Health, Doctor Manto Tshabalala-Msimang refused to implement ART programmes in public health care facilities arguing that ART was rather toxic and detrimental to health and wellbeing of HIV-positive patients. Doctor Manto Tshabala-Msimang also blamed HIV and AIDS on malnutrition and publicly claimed that the disease can be cured by a mixture of garlic, olive oil, lemon and beetroot (Cullinan & Thom, 2009). Mbeki insisted that the HIV epidemic was part of a neo-colonialist conspiracy by westerners (pharmaceutical companies in particular) to exploit and dehumanise Africa and its people. Over two and a half million South Africans succumbed to HIV and AIDS during the years 1999 to 2008 when Thabo Mbeki served as the President of South Africa (Geffen, 2010).

In South Africa, like in many European countries and the USA, the LGBT community have actively lobbied for access to ART. For instance, the Treatment Action Campaign (TAC) was formed in 1998 under the leadership of openly HIV-positive LGBT activists, notably, Zackie Achmat and South African Constitutional Court Judge Edwin Cameron. The TAC was instrumental in compelling the South African government to provide ART to HIV-positive people in public health care facilities. In fact, in 2001, the TAC took the Department of Health (DoH) to the Constitutional Court in order to compel the government to provide ART to HIV-positive patients. The TAC argued that:

The largely untreated HIV and AIDS epidemic has profound implications not only for the people who are needlessly suffering and their loved ones, but also for the country as a whole...Rising levels of sickness and death place severe strain on the state, which is under growing pressure and constitutional obligation to provide adequate forms of support to families affected by HIV and AIDS. There is also an increasing burden on the public health system, as people living with HIV and AIDS require repeated treatment of opportunistic infections. (TAC, 2015)

Miraculously, in 2002 the TAC won the Constitutional Court case and the government was ordered to provide ART to patients living with HIV and AIDS. Thereafter, on the 19th of November 2003, the DoH implemented ART in public health care facilities through the Operational Plan for Comprehensive HIV and AIDS Care, Management and Treatment for South Africa. It is worth noting that in 2004 the TAC was honoured with a Nobel Prize nomination for its efforts for making ART available to people living with HIV and AIDS in South Africa. In 2008, the TAC reported that there were over 400 public health care facilities offering ART in South Africa, but only 300 000 people were able to access it, and a further 500 000 people who were in need of ART were not able to access it (TAC, 2015). Five years later in 2014, the TAC reported that there were 6 million people living with HIV and AIDS in South Africa, and only 2 million were able to access ART at public health care facilities. In October of the same year (2014), the Ministers of Health from the five countries which form BRICS (i.e. Brazil, Russia, India, China and South Africa) adopted the 90-90-90 strategy on HIV and AIDS (Ngcaweni, 2016). This strategy is in line with the South African NDP Vision 2030 and aims to achieve the following 90-90-90 objectives by the year 2030:

- 90 percent of all people living with HIV should be diagnosed
- 90 percent of people diagnosed with HIV should receive ART
- 90 percent of those on ART should have a suppressed viral load

The author argues that these objectives could only be achieved through community participation in the provision of PHC. According to Muller (2013):

...community participation is one important, yet often forgotten, fundamental principle of the primary health care approach...it is one of the key considerations if we want to build a sustainable, stable primary health care system that provides quality care for all. (p. 26)

McCoy, Hall and Ridge (2012) contend that there are factors that hinder the efficacious implementation of community participation processes in PHC in South Africa. These factors include lack of political commitment, shortage of resources, deteriorating infrastructure, limited co-operation from health care workers, inadequate capacity and skills and lack of support from government. For community participation in PHC to be efficacious, it is imperative for members of the community to be directly an actively involved in identifying and addressing health issues that affect them. According to Mchunu and Gwele (2005), community participation in PHC is defined as:

...a shift in emphasis from external agencies supplying health services, to the people of the community becoming active participants in their own health care. This means that the community members become partners in health care by generating their own ideas, assessing their needs, by involvement in decision-making processes, planning, implementing, and even evaluating the care they receive. (p. 30)

The WHO in its 1978 report on PHC defined community participation as "the process by which the individual and the families assume responsibility for their own health and welfare and for that of the community, and develop the capacity to contribute to their community's development. They come to know their own situation better and are motivated to solve their common problems. These enable them to become agents of their own development instead of passive beneficiaries of development aid."

LGBT CIVIL SOCIETY ORGANISATIONS' RESPONSE TO HIV AND AIDS THROUGH PHC IN SOUTH AFRICA

The 1980s were a crucial period in which LGBT communities across the globe formed civil society organisations (CSOs) with the aim of lobbying for their human rights. Jacobs and Call and (2002) explain that:

These popular democratic groups sought to challenge the very basis of state politics and state power, and in the process redefine the relations between state and society, between rulers and ruled. By developing alternative structures of power and government, these popular democratic organisations developed the seeds of an 'emancipatory politics', revolutionary, liberating, progressive, and fundamentally rooted in the masses of the people. (p. 5)

During the 1980s in the USA, the United Kingdom (UK), Denmark, Holland, France, Norway, Australia and South Africa, there was an increasing number of CSOs that advocated for the human rights of LGBT people. For instance, activism by CSOs in Denmark, Norway, Sweden and Holland afforded LGBT people the right to engage in same-sex marriage (Aldrich, 2006). In 2006, same-sex couples in South Africa were also afforded the right to marry, which made South Africa the only country on the African continent and the fifth in the world to allow same-sex marriages. More interestingly, South Africa is the first country in the whole world and the only country on the African continent to enshrine the rights of same-sex practising people in its Constitution.

Since the 1960s, European countries have gradually decriminalised homosexuality. Criminal laws that targeted LGBT communities have been abolished in Britain, Germany, Netherlands, France, Spain and many other European countries. At this point, there is virtually no European country where homosexuality is still a crime (Aldrich, 2006). Similarly, South Africa also followed suit and repealed its sodomy laws in the year 1999, which meant that homosexuality was decriminalised. It is worth noting that some of these homosexual liberation milestones in South Africa, are to be acknowledged and credited to the efforts made by LGBT CSOs such as the then National Coalition for Gay and Lesbian Equality and the Gays and Lesbians of the Witwatersrand. Aldrich (2006) opines that the LGBT liberation movement presented a platform for homosexual men to have freedom of sexual expression. He argued that this period appeared to have been a breeding ground for STIs including HIV as homosexual men got involved in risky sexual behaviours and practices. Supposedly, he argued that the homosexual revolutionary movement and subsequent sexual freedom of homosexuals became the reason why the world witnessed high rates of HIV and AIDS among homosexual men in the 1980s.

The first recorded cases of HIV and AIDS in South Africa were among members of the LGBT community, particularly gay men. In 1982, two gay men working for South African Airways (SAA) as air stewards died of HIV and AIDS complications. It was believed the two air stewards might have contracted the disease while travelling and working between South Africa and the USA, where the epidemic was rapidly unfolding among gay men then. Due to the fact that much was unknown about the disease at that time, passengers on SAA flights were thought to be at risk of contracting HIV supposedly because air stewards handled food and shared the same toilets with passengers. Then the SAA released a press statement that condemned homosexuality and ordered that all cabin crew be subjected to HIV tests. The statement read:

Official policy was that homosexuality should receive disapproval and nothing else...While we recognise that homosexuality is illegal in this country, there is no real way that we can establish the preferences of our staff. It is a sensitive issue and obviously we don't include sexual questions on our staff application forms. No company does. If a man is accepted for work, it's purely on his qualifications for the job, and since people keep private life apart from public, there is no real way that we have to detect homosexuality after someone joined us. It is unfortunate that the airline has been associated with the disease, but in the interests of the public's health we felt we had to let it be known that AIDS had arrived in South Africa. (Mathebe, 2005, pp. 138-139)

Later in the year 1982, 250 random blood samples were taken from homosexual men living in Johannesburg. The results revealed that starling 12.8 per cent were infected with HIV. It was also reported that between 1982 and 1984, 10 to 15 percent of 25,000 homosexual men in Johannesburg had contracted HIV. Furthermore, in 1986 surveillance data from two STI clinics in Durban and in Cape Town estimated that the HIV prevalence among homosexual men in those two cities was at 8 percent and 11 percent, respectively (Reddy, Sandfort, & Rispel, 2009). The apartheid government, under the administration of former President P.W. Botha, subsequently held a conference to address the potential threat the disease posed to the country. In 1987, regulations were issued to add HIV to the official South African list of communicable diseases. These regulations called for mandatory fourteen-day quarantine for individuals infected, or suspected to be infected with HIV. The quarantine period could be extended indefinitely if a case was confirmed to be that of AIDS. By 14 December 1988, 166 AIDS cases had been reported in South Africa, and most of the cases were found to have contracted the disease through homosexual sex (Geffen, 2010). The epidemic was characterised by a Western 'type 1' HIV pattern, which led epidemiologists to presume that the epidemic in South Africa was a result of North American and Western European infections, where sex between men was a predominant mode of transmission (Reddy, Sandfort, & Rispel, 2009).

This situation resulted in stigmatisation and discrimination of the LGBT community, particularly gay men, for spreading HIV and AIDS in the country. Many LGBT people faced human rights violations in their day-to-day life from both the government and fellow citizens. For instance, the South African National Blood Transfusion Service (SANBS) prohibited blood donations by homosexual men by stating that:

Men who have sex with other men are universally barred as blood donors because this is recognised as high risk behaviour for HIV infection and transmission...SANBS recognises that there is no local data to support the view that in South Africa, as elsewhere, men who have sex with men pose a significant risk to the blood supply. (Rispel & Metcalf, 2009, p. 136)

The media also went on to publish the names of gay men who were living with HIV and AIDS in newspapers without their consent. As a result, LGBT activists formed CSOs with the aim of protecting the human rights of LGBT people and also to respond to the HIV epidemic among members of the LGBT community. However, CSOs such as the TAC, which were initially formed by LGBT activists, responded to the HIV epidemic among all citizens of the country irrespective of sexual orientation.

ORGANISATIONS PROVIDING PHC TO LGBT PERSONS IN MAJOR SOUTH AFRICAN CITIES

Makofane, Beck and Ayala (2014) argue that there is a paucity of research on HIV prevalence among LGBT communities in Africa. This dearth of research in Africa is because homosexuality is a highly politicized issue due to its association with colonialism and Western influence. Moreover, the fact that the main mode of HIV transmission on the African continent is heterosexual, many African countries have ignored homosexual HIV transmissions (Evans, Cloete, Zungu & Simbayi, 2016; Muller, 2014; Muraguri, Temmerman & Geibel, 2012). Furthermore, Johnson (2007) contends that research on HIV prevalence among LGBT communities in Africa is scant because of the following reasons:

- The hesitancy of those who engage in same-sex practices to expose themselves to potentially judgmental researchers.
- The resistance by African research review panels to approve research on same-sex sexuality.
- A general unwillingness among otherwise rigorous scientists to address same-sex HIV-transmission due to their discomfort with homosexuality.
- Homophobic stigma faced by HIV researchers themselves when addressing issues of homosexuality.
- Denial of the frequency of same-sex behavior in Africa.

Thirty-eight out of fifty-four African countries have criminalized homosexuality (LeVasseur, Goldstein & Welles, 2014). Chikovore and Naidoo (2016) contend that the criminalisation of homosexuality in many African countries has become a major barrier for LGBT people to access and utilise PHC services such as HIV testing, prevention, treatment, care and support due to fear of being persecuted and/or prosecuted. Michel Sidibé, the Executive Director of the Joint United Nations Programme on HIV and AIDS (UNAIDS) asserted that:

The failure to respond effectively has allowed HIV to reach crisis levels in many communities...Efforts to reverse this crisis must be evidence informed, grounded in human rights and underpinned by the decriminalisation of homosexuality...We must work together to end homophobia and ensure the barriers that stop access to HIV services are removed. (Ayala, Beck, Lauer, Reynolds & Sundararaj, 2010, p. 1)

In South Africa where criminal laws against homosexuality have been repealed, LGBT people still experience stigmatisation and discrimination in public PHC facilities. In this regard, many avoid using public PHC facilities for HIV testing, prevention, treatment, care and support. The situation has resulted in many undiagnosed and increasing HIV infections among members of the LGBT community (Mampane, 2017). In a study conducted by Evans et al. (2016) in South Africa, it was discovered that members of the LGBT community avoid using public PHC facilities because:

- LGBT persons have in many instances been refused health care on grounds of their sexual orientation.
- LGBT persons have no trust in health care practitioners regarding confidentiality.
- LGBT persons in many cases conceal their sexuality to health care practitioners.
- LGBT persons often fear prejudice by health care practitioners.

These findings are consistent with the findings of the study conducted by the Human Sciences Research Council (HSRC) during the years 2012-2013 among members of the LGBT community in major South African cities (HSRC, 2014). Both the HSRC study and the study by Evans et al. revealed that LGBT people are highly vulnerable to the risk of HIV infection but they have limited access to public PHC facilities due to stigmatisation and discrimination by health care practitioners. Reddy et al. (2009) posit that:

People who engage in same-sex sexual relations are socially and culturally vulnerable to prevailing attitudes. If they are not accorded access to HIV and AIDS prevention education, treatment, care and support, they may endanger others as a result of ignorance...The government should undertake to put in place mechanisms to ensure that HIV and STI prevention, treatment, care and support can be accessed by all without discrimination, including people engaging in same-sex sexual relations. (p. 140)

Against this backdrop, many same-sex oriented South Africans, especially those who cannot afford private health care, choose to utilise LGBT-friendly services offered by LGBT organisations in major South African cities. These LGBT organisations mainly receive funds from private donors and LGBT-friendly businesses and companies in order to offer PHC services to the LGBT community, including HIV testing, prevention, treatment, care and support. These LGBT organisations are shown in Tables 2, 3 and 4.

Table 2. Pretoria (Capital city)

OUT LGBT Well-being OUT LGBT Well-being focus areas of work are direct physical and mental health services, research, mainstreaming and advocacy. The main focus of the organisation is on HIV testing, prevention, treatment, care and support. **Vision:** OUT is dedicated to the building of healthy empowered LGBT communities in South Africa by reducing heterosexist and homophobia in society. **Mission:** OUT works towards LGBT peoples' physical and mental health and related rights.

(Source: OUT LGBT Well-being, 2018)

Table 3. Cape Town

Triangle Project Triangle Project is a non-profit human rights organisation offering professional services to ensure the full realisation of constitutional and human rights for LGBT persons, their partners and families. The core services of Triangle Project centre on Health, Social Support, Community Engagement, Empowerment, Research and Advocacy. **Vision:** The development of a non-discriminatory society, where organisations such as Triangle Project are a choice and not a necessity. **Mission:** To contribute towards eradicating discrimination against and within the LGBT community, and to provide defined services to LGBT persons until they are no longer required.

(Source: Triangle Project, 2018)

Table 4. Durban

Durban Lesbian and Gay Community Health Centre The Durban Lesbian and Gay Community Health Centre is a drop-in Centre, a safe and secure space for LGBT communities in Durban and KwaZulu-Natal Province. The Centre provide HIV and AIDS Counselling and do referrals for HIV testing, prevention, treatment, care and support. **Vision:** To empower the LGBT community by providing services, support and training to enable them to claim their rights to equality, dignity and freedom within the context of transformation.

(Source: Durban Lesbian & Gay Community Health Centre, 2018)

SOLUTIONS AND RECOMMENDATIONS

Recommendation 1: Human Rights and Inclusive PHC Services

Legislators and government authorities should establish and enforce antidiscrimination laws based on human rights principles to eliminate stigmatization, discrimination and violence faced by LGBT people in order to reduce their vulnerability to the risk of HIV infection. This is because stigmatization and discrimination create barriers for LGBT people to access and utilize public PHC services such as HIV/AIDS testing, prevention, treatment, care and support. Non-discriminatory and inclusive PHC services are significant to the health and wellbeing of disenfranchised groups such as LGBT communities. Policy makers, parliamentarians and other public leaders should work together with CSOs in their efforts to confront the realities of prejudice on LGBT people and transform punitive legal and social norms towards those that are protective.

Recommendation 2: Public PHC Policy and Practice

PHC practitioners should adopt the *'Batho Pele'* (People First) principles which the South African government has implemented in its service delivery charters in all government departments. This is based on the principles of medical ethics and the basic right of access to health to all citizens of the country irrespective of differences. In this regard, PHC practitioners should be respectful of diversity and honour their professional obligations as government servants without being judgmental and by putting aside their personal views and beliefs when rendering PHC services to the LGBT community.

Recommendation 3: Public PHC Education

PHC education in South Africa has long excluded issues pertaining to the LGBT population. In this regard, universities and colleges which train health care practitioners should ensure that health issues affecting LGBT communities are integrated into the curriculum. In addition, practicing health care practitioners should attend in-service training on LGBT health issues.

FUTURE RESEARCH DIRECTIONS

The following directions are made in relation to future public PHC research:

- Community-based participatory action research approaches should be implemented in order to involve members of the LGBT community in the research processes to better gain an understanding and insight into their PHC problems and needs.
- Research on LGBT communities should not be invisible but conspicuously disseminated in publications, conferences, colloquiums, workshops and seminars to inform policy and practice in the provision of PHC services to this underserved, marginalized and minority population.

CONCLUSION

According to the Department of Health in 1997, one of the objectives of The White Paper for Transformation of the Health System in South Africa is to foster community participation in across the health sector by involving communities in various aspects of the planning and provision of health services. In this chapter, it was shown that community participation is one of the fundamental pillars of the PHC approach. In essence, the provision of PHC should be community-driven and rights-based in which people who utilise public health care facilities are directly and actively involved in identifying and addressing health issues that affect them. In other words, PHC in public health facilities should have a mission to deliver 'health for all' to ensure that every person in South Africa has access to basic health care services they need. For example, the South African National Patient's Rights Charter specifies that PHC in public health care facilities should be patient-centred and patient-friendly, and that every patient should have the right to participate in their health care service decision-making. The National Health Act 61 of 2003 in South Africa compels all public health institutions to involve members of the community in every aspect of the policy-making process. This means that community members should be involved in making decisions about how PHC services should be rendered. Participation should take place through the establishment of health committees which are comprised of members of the community. The tasks of these committees are to represent all members of the community to ensure that their needs and views are heard when consulting with management structures at public health care facilities. According to the National Health Act 61 of 2003, a functional health committee should be comprised of a local government councillor together with community representatives and PHC service managers. Through community participation, members of the community will be able to offer valuable suggestions and also lay complaints about PHC services rendered so that things can be rectified.

Communities are usually the ones who know and have experience about their health problems, in this regard, they are also the ones who are better positioned in guiding and informing PHC service providers in rendering solutions to these health problems. In this light, community members should be allowed to evaluate the effectiveness, efficiency and quality of the health service rendered in order to alert PHC service providers of the gaps that need to be addressed for a better service delivery system. For example, the South African National Patients' Rights Charter states that every patient has the right to freedom of complaining about poor quality of health care services. Although this may be in the bad light for PHC service providers, it will however alert them to be able to address the quality of health care services they provide. In a nutshell, it was shown in this chapter that effective and efficient PHC practice puts people at the heart of all activities related to their health. The aim should be that 'PHC needs to be carried out by people, and with people, rather than merely on people or to people'. This means that there should be a level of participatory mechanisms in place to ensure that PHC systems in public health care facilities run smoothly.

REFERENCES

African National Congress. (1994). *The National Health Plan*. Johannesburg: ANC.

Aldrich, R. (Ed.). (2006). *Gay life and culture: a world history*. New York: Universe Publishing.

Ayala, G., Beck, J., Lauer, K., Reynolds, R., & Sundararaj, M. (2010). *Social discrimination against men who have sex with men (MSM): implications for HIV policy and programs*. Oakland, CA: MSMGF.

Chikovore, J., & Naidoo, D. (2016). Risk from the frontlines of a hidden epidemic: sexuality, masculinity and social pressures among men who have sex with men in South Africa: An overview. *Gender & Behaviour*, *14*(3), 7609–7623.

Cullinan, K., & Thom, A. (Eds.). (2009). *The virus, vitamins and vegetables: The South African HIV/AIDS mystery*. Johannesburg: Jacana Media.

Department of Health. (1997). *The White Paper for Transformation of the Health System in South Africa*. Pretoria: Government Printers.

Durban Lesbian & Gay Community Health Centre. (n.d.). *About Us*. Retrieved June 5, 2018, from http://www.gaycentre.org.za

Evans, M., Cloete, A., Zungu, N., & Simbayi, L. (2016). HIV risk among men who have sex with men, Women who have sex with women, Lesbian, Gay, Bisexual and Transgender populations in South Africa: A mini-review. *The Open AIDS Journal*, *10*(1), 49–64. doi:10.2174/1874613601610010049 PMID:27347271

Fourie, P., & Meyer, M. (2010). *The politics of AIDS denialism: South Africa's failure to respond*. Surrey: Ashgate.

Geffen, N. (2010). *Debunking delusions: the inside story of the Treatment Action Campaign*. Auckland Park: Jacana Media.

Jacobs, S., & Calland, R. (Eds.). (2002). *Thabo Mbeki's world: myth, ideology and politics in the South African presidency*. Durban: University of Natal Press.

Johnson, C. A. (2007). *Off the Map: How HIV/AIDS programming is failing same-sex practising people in Africa*. New York: IGLHRC.

Kironde, S., & Kahirimbanyi, M. (2002). Community participation in primary health care programmes: Lessons from tuberculosis treatment delivery in South Africa. *African Health Sciences*, *2*(1), 16–23. PMID:12789110

LaVasseur, M., Goldstein, N., & Welles, S. (2014). A public health perspective on HIV/AIDS in Africa: Victories and unmet challenges. *Phatophysiology*, *21*(1), 237–256. PMID:25096828

Makofane, K., Beck, J., & Ayala, G. (2014). *MSM in sub-Saharan Africa: health, access and HIV*. Oakland, CA: MSMGF.

Mampane, J. N. (2017). *Guidelines for mitigating the risk of HIV-infection among Black men who have sex with men (MSM) in a rural community in South Africa* (Unpublished doctoral dissertation). University of South Africa, Pretoria, South Africa.

Mathebe, L. M. (2005). *The story of an immune deficiency and its representation in the South African media (1981-2000)* (Unpublished doctoral dissertation). University of South Africa, Pretoria, South Africa.

McCoy, D., Hall, J., & Ridge, M. (2012). A systematic review of literature for evidence on health facility committees in low and middle income countries. *Health Policy and Planning*, *27*(6), 449–466. doi:10.1093/heapol/czr077 PMID:22155589

Mchunu, G. G., & Gwele, N. S. (2005). The meaning of community involvement in health: The perspective of primary health care communities. *Curationis*, *28*(2), 30–37. doi:10.4102/curationis.v28i2.943 PMID:16045109

Muller, A. (2013). Community participation in health. *Nutrition Update*, *2*(1), 26–29.

Muller, A. (2014). Professionalism is key in providing services to lesbian, gay, bisexual and transgender South Africans. *South African Medical Journal*, *104*(8), 558–559. doi:10.7196/SAMJ.8447 PMID:25213846

Muraguri, N., Temmerman, M., & Geibel, S. (2012). A decade of research involving men who have sex with men in sub-Saharan Africa: current knowledge and future directions. *SAHARA-J: Journal of Social Aspects of HIV/AIDS. An Open Access Journal*, *9*(3), 137–147. PMID:23237068

National Development Plan Vision 2030. (2012). *Our future – make it work*. Pretoria: Sherino Printers.

Ngcaweni, B. (Ed.). (2016). *Sizonqoba! Outliving AIDS in Africa*. Pretoria: AISA.

OUT LGBT Well-being. (n.d.). *About Us*. Retrieved June 5, 2018, from http://www.out.org.za

Reddy, V., Sandfort, T., & Rispel, L. (Eds.). (2009). *From social silence to social science: same-sex sexuality, HIV & AIDS and gender in South Africa*. Pretoria: HSRC Press.

Rispel, L. C., & Metcalf, C. A. (2009). Breaking the silence: South African HIV policies and the needs of men who have sex with men. *Reproductive Health Matters*, *17*(33), 133–142. doi:10.1016/S0968-8080(09)33442-4 PMID:19523590

South Africa (Republic). (1996). *Constitution of the Republic of South Africa (Act 108 of 1996)*. Pretoria: Government Printers.

Treatment Action Campaign (TAC). (2015). *Access to ART in South Africa*. Retrieved October 15, 2015, from http://www.tac.org.za

Triangle Project. (n.d.). *About Us*. Retrieved June 5, 2018, from http://www.triangle.org.za

World Health Organisation. (1978). *Report on primary health care*. World Health Organisation.

KEY TERMS AND DEFINITIONS

Communities: Are usually the ones who know and have experience about their health problems. In this regard, they are also the ones who are better positioned in guiding and informing PHC service providers in rendering solutions to these health problems.

Community Participation: Is considered to be an empowerment tool in which local communities can take responsibility in identifying and addressing their own problems through collaboration with different stakeholders in the community, including local government. Community participation enables people to realize their rights to participate in problem-solving and decision-making processes regarding issues that affect their day-to-day life in the communities that they live in.

Lesbian, Gay, Bisexual, and Transgender (LGBT) Community: Is one of the key populations at risk of HIV infection; however, members of the LGBT community have been discriminated against in public Primary Health Care (PHC) services based on their sexual orientation.

South African National Development Plan (NDP) Vision 2030: Is a plan in which communities are urged to actively participate in development issues to address problems such as poverty, inequality, and health issues in society. The NDP Vision 2030 is a national strategic plan that was released in 2012 to outline South Africa's developmental goals that are to be accomplished by the year 2030.

Chapter 9
Integrating Human Rights, Equity, and Social Justice in Health Policies in America and Nigeria:
Controversies, Problems, and Way Forward

Augustine Nduka Eneanya
University of Lagos, Nigeria

ABSTRACT

Persisting absence of human rights, widening inequality, and social justice in healthcare delivery systems within and between countries present significant challenges to the focus and practice of contemporary public health. This chapter compares how cases of human rights, equity, and social justice are integrated in America's and Nigeria's healthcare policies. Qualitative research and case study design were adopted. Data were collected from secondary sources, such as reviewed literature, textbooks, journal articles, government reports, and internet. Content and critical case studies analysis methods were utilized to analyze, explain, and compare America's and Nigeria's health policies. Findings reveal absence of human rights, equity, and social justice among sub-groups in healthcare service delivery in America and Nigeria. The chapter concludes by suggesting that human rights, equity, and social justice should be integrated into health policies of America and Nigeria in order to make access to healthcare service delivery a right for citizens.

DOI: 10.4018/978-1-5225-6133-0.ch009

INTRODUCTION

One of the cardinal objectives of good government is to have effective healthcare delivery system put in place for the entire citizenry. A healthy nation is "a wealthy nation because of the absence of debilitating diseases and epidemics in such a country, which along with hunger and squalor impoverishes the citizenry" (Nwatu, 2000, p. 12). The indispensability of good healthcare system in national development underlies the government's commitment to provide adequate healthcare.

The right to the highest attainable standard of health requires a set of social criteria that is conducive to the health of all, including the availability of health services, safe working conditions, adequate housing and nutritious foods. The right to health include both freedoms and entitlements. Freedoms include the right to control one's health and body and to be free from non-consensual medical treatment and experimentation. Entitlements include the right to a system of health protection that gives everyone an equal opportunity to enjoy the highest attainable level of health. Violations or lack of attention to human rights can have serious health consequences. Overt or implicit discrimination in the delivery of health services violates fundamental human rights and social justice.

Health policies and programs have the ability to either promote or violate human rights, including the right to health, depending on the way they are designed or implemented. Taking steps to respect and protect human rights upholds the health sector' responsibility to address everyone's health. The search for value-based and ethical policy has recently gained momentum and the global literature has called for further exploration of the role of ethics (equity), human rights and social justice in public health.

The purpose of the chapter is to investigate how human rights, equity and social justice processes are integrated into national health policies of America and Nigeria.

BACKGROUND

Humans have rights to the resources necessary for health. The public code of ethics affirms by Universal Declaration of Human Rights (UDHR) states that everyone has the right to a standard of living adequate for the health and well-being of himself and his family. Health policy-making, therefore, involves complex processes where a mix of experience, politics, human right, finance, values and ethics all interweave. The failure of anyone component can be fatal to any policy.

In United States of America, from the Truman Administration to today, reform for healthcare has been seen as both progress and failure. President Truman recommended to congress a proposal for Universal Health Insurance coverage administered and paid for by National Insurance Board. Unfortunately, the American Medical Association decried it as "socialized medicine" and the Bill failed.

American healthcare policy and programs have witnessed reforms over the years. Prior to the 20th century, the involvement of the federal government in healthcare was limited to care for the military personnel and veterans. At the State level, all states had established some type of departments of public health by 1909. In 1943, the Internal Revenue Service ruled that employees did not have to pay taxes on their employers' contributions to group health benefits. This ruling made offering health benefits to recruit employee, an attraction option. The result is that the United States puts tax dollars that would have been collected by the government into employer – based health insurance.

The Kennedy administration pursued a more modest form of healthcare coverage than that of Truman. Kennedy Administration supported the King-Anderson bill, coverage would be limited to those 65 years of age and older benefits package. Kennedy in addition, created more avenues to develop the foundation of what would ultimately become Medicare. Unfortunately, Kennedy's healthcare plan was denied by congress.

A major initiative by the Clinton Administration to institute national healthcare insurance failed in 1994. However, the government enacted Health Insurance Portability and Accountability Act (HIP AA) of 1996. This provides that workers must be able to continue purchasing their health insurance if they lose their jobs or change jobs (NASW, 2003). It also prohibits insurance companies from denying coverage to people with pre-existing conditions, and it introduces Medical Savings Accounts. Medical Savings Accounts (MSA) allow people who are self-employed or working for small businesses to place their own pre-tax money in an account that can then be used to pay for routine or long-term care (NASW, 2003).

With the Bush administration, Congress passed an aggressive Medicaid expansion package called Medicare Part D – a prescription drug coverage benefit. Medicare Part D was the first successful healthcare reform in USA and laid the homework for what would eventually be the biggest, comprehensive reform package known as the Affordable Care Act (ACA) under the Obama Administration in 2010.

Under Obama's ACA, all Americans were required to have health insurance or pay a tax penalty. Companies with more than 50 employees were required to offer health insurance or pay a penalty. Obamacare also raised Medicare taxes on the wealthy and imposed new taxes on medical devices, health insurers, drug companies, investment income, tanning salons and high-end health insurance plans. Obamacare also provides for insurance for dependents under 26 years to be covered by their parents' policies. For essential benefits, Obamacare requires all insurance plans to cover certain health conditions and services, such as: emergency room visits, maternity and post-natal care, cancer treatment, annual physical examinations, prescription drug costs and mental health counselling. Obamacare prohibits insurers from denying coverage or charging more to individuals who have pre-existing medical conditions. Furthermore, Obamacare expanded Medicaid health insurance for the poor to cover more low-income individuals. Insurance companies were prohibited from charging women more than men for the same health plan and must provide core services, including maternity care and contraceptives (ACA, 2010).

In addition, insurers can charge older people no more than three times the cost for younger Americans. Finally, ACA provided refundable tax credits for low-income individuals who purchased their insurance on government – run market places and support for some out – of – pocket medical expenses (ACA, 2010).

Under President Donald Trump, reforms have been introduced to repeal and replace Obamacare. So many provisions have been repealed but replacement's provisions are still before the congress waiting to be passed into law.

On the other hand, prior to the development of National Health Policy of 2016, Nigeria had developed and implemented two National Health Policies in 1988 and 2004 respectively. National health policy was launched in 1988 aimed at achieving health for all Nigerians. This was subsequently revised in 2004, supported by National Strategic Plan of 2010 to 2015. Both policies were developed at critical stages in the evolution of the Nigeria Health system and had far-reaching impact on improving the performance of the system and development of National Health Policy of 2016. However, the National health policy of 2016 came after the enactment of National Health Act 2014 and provides the direction necessary to support the achievement of significant progress in improving the performance of the Nigerian health system. It also lays emphasis on strengthening primary health care as the bedrock of our national health system, in addition to the provision of financial risk protection to all Nigerians, particularly the poor and most vulnerable groups.

However, several studies have provided frameworks for analyzing public health programs (Kass, 2001); health policy reforms (Daniels, Bryant, Castano, Dantes, & Khan, 2000); and public health practices (Baum, Gollust, Goold, & Jacobson, 2007). Health systems are defined as all activities whose primary purpose is to promote, restore or maintain health. The health of individual depends on the health of the public. According to Mclnness and Lee (2012, p.66), health is a "fundamental right and the attainment of the highest possible level of health is a most important world-wide social goal". Davies (2010, p.67) acknowledges the grand work of Mann in situating the link between health and rights. WHO, (2000) argued that the highest attainable standard of health as a fundamental right and for health equality. Labonte and Gagnon (2010, p. 11) adds that the right to health is not fully represented in the actual international human rights Health policy, on the other hand, broadly refers to guidelines to government actions –national, state and local government- to advance public health. It is not a single action, but requires a range of legislative and regulatory efforts ranging from organization, financing and delivering of healthcare services both physical and mental health.

However, the search for the role of valued-based and ethical polices has gained momentum globally. Studies have focused on attributes of specific health policies and systems rather than the role of ethics in policy process. Ethics can be viewed as an integral component of health systems development. Crucial in this is knowledge of society and social institutions, which differs from knowledge of diseases or nature society interactions (Kass, 2001). Ethics is typically viewed as a tool to inform and constrain such decisions.

Policy processes can also be deficient in social justice when they include some perspectives at the expense of others, especially when the poor and marginalized are often excluded (Gwatkin, 2000; James, Carrin & Savedoff, 2005). Social justice, though a familiar concept is difficult to define. The difficulty in defining social justice is because of our personal perspectives on justice, equality and how we as individuals respond to the needs of others in our society. Social justice can be connected to social, religious, political, legal and health-related aspects of persons who are or have been marginalized in our society and throughout the world. Social justice may also be understood as fairness in the distribution of the benefits and burdens of social cooperation (Rawls, 1999; Gostin & Powers, 2006). The notion of social justice often play an important role in public health policy and are usually applied out of a concern for equity (O"Donnell, VanDoorslaer, Wagstaft & Lindelow, 2008). The concern for equity is to ensure that such benefits are fairly distributed within the population, reducing as much as possible the extent to which peoples' health status and lifespan are determined by morally arbitrary attributes such as race, ethnicity or socio-economic status.

Drawing from these previous studies, the chapter proposes that concepts of equity, social justice, and human rights can be studied and analyzed more broadly as integral components of health policies in USA's and Nigeria's health systems. This approach recognizes violations of rights of people to health and leaders (political, professionals and practitioners) should observe equity and social justice in health policy development and implementation. In this context, social justice, equity and human rights are organizational framework-development-oriented force that provides both methodological and motivational support to public–health practitioners and policy-makers.

Against this background, the chapter is divided into four sections. Section one examines the introduction, background, review of previous studies and analytical framework. Section two compares the case studies of health policies in America and Nigeria to determine if human rights, equity and social justice are embedded in their national health policies. Section three examines the controversies and problems associated with health policies in America's and Nigeria's health policies. Finally, section four suggests solutions and the way forward for a new national health policies for America and Nigeria.

METHODOLOGY

The study adopted qualitative case studies research approach for its investigation. Being a conceptual study, the approach will enable us to focus primarily on the kind of evidences in America and Nigeria's health systems in order to answer specific research questions. Data were, therefore, collected from secondary sources, such as: extant literature, textbooks, journal articles, government reports, records, internet, websites and newspapers. Content-analysis technique was adopted to elicit key concepts. Elicited key concepts were coded and categorized into three themes: equity, social justice, and human rights. Critical case studies analysis method was adopted to critically analyze, explain and compare human rights, equity and social justice issues in USA and Nigeria's health policies. This approach is justified because the notions of social justice, equity and human rights often play important role in public health policy development and implementation". (O' Donnel, VanDoorslaer, Wagstsaft, & Lindelow, 2008, Mann, 2006, pp. 1940 – 3).

RESEARCH QUESTIONS

This study is, therefore, driven by the following specific research questions:

1. To what extent are human rights, equity and social justice embedded in National health policies of United States of America and Nigeria?
2. What are the controversies and problems associated with human rights, equity and social justice in National health policies of United States of America and Nigeria?
3. How can human rights, equity, and social justice be integrated into National health policies of United States of America and Nigeria?

Now, let us examine the USA and Nigerian health policies:

CASE 1: NATIONAL HEALTH POLICY OF UNITED STATES OF AMERICA

RQ. 1: To What Extent Are Human Rights, Equity and Social Justice Embedded in National Health Policies of United States of America and Nigeria?

The U.S. healthcare system is driven by ideological and fiscal concerns. Primary among these is whether access to healthcare should be a right or privilege. In the United States, healthcare is rationed on a person's ability to pay. In other words, it is treated as a commodity. Healthcare has a price and people with more money get a better quality of goods or services.

Medicare was enacted in 1965 as an amendment to the nation's basic Social Security Act. Medicare provides pre-paid hospital insurance and low-cost voluntary medical insurance for the aged, directly under the federal administration. Medicare includes HI- a compulsory basic health insurance plan covering hospital costs for the aged, which is financed out of payroll taxes collected under the Social Security system and SMI-a voluntary, supplemental medical insurance program that will pay 80 percent of "allowable" charges for physicians' services and other medical expenses, financed in part by contributions from the aged and in part by general tax revenues (Dye, 1998). Healthcare is publicly supported only for people age 65 and over who are eligible for Medicare. So, those below 65 years do not qualify for publicly, supported healthcare. Although, "many citizens receive health insurance as a benefit through their places of employment, almost 16 per cent of the population had no health insurance as at 2003" (Chapin, 2007, p. 272).

Medicaid is the federal government's largest single welfare program for the poor. Its costs now exceed the costs of all other public assistance programs-including family assistance, and food stamp program. Medicaid begun in 1965. It is a combined federal and state program. The states exercise fairly broad administrative powers and carry almost half of the financial burden. Medicaid is a welfare program designed for needy persons, no prior contributions are required, monies come from general tax revenues, and most recipients are already on welfare rolls. Although, states differ in their eligibility requirements, they must cover all people receiving federally funded public assistance payments. In addition, a majority extend coverage to other "medically needy" –individuals who do not qualify for public assistance but whose incomes are low enough to qualify as needy. About half of the states extend Medicaid to families whose head is receiving unemployment compensation (Dye, 1998).

Private Health insurance is covered by either:

private or government health insurance and covers 85 per cent of the population of United States. About 15 per cent of the population as no medical insurance. Most of the uninsured are working Americans and their families- people wo are not poor enough to qualify for Medicaid nor old enough to qualify for Medicare. (Dye, 1998, p. 135)

Nursing home care begun in U.S. because of the need to accommodate those over 80 years and above not covered by Medicaid. Medicaid does not pay for long-term care or catastrophic illness. It covers only the first 60 days of hospitalization and nursing home care for 100 days only if the patient is sent there from a hospital. Medicaid assistance to the needy is paid to nursing-home patients, but middle-class people cannot qualify for Medicaid wit first "spending down" their savings. Long-term nursing home care threatens their assets and their children's inheritance. Private insurance policies covering long-term care are said to be very expensive. So, "senior citizen groups have lobbied heavily for long-term nursing-home care to be paid for by taxpayers under Medicare" (Dye, 1998, P.137).

In 2010, President Barack Obama signed the Affordable Care Act (ACA) into law with the stated goal of "ensuring all Americans have access to quality, affordable health care" (Affordable Care Act, 2010). The law though helped more people to attain health insurance coverage and prevents companies from denying those with pre-existing conditions, is still subject to debate between the Republicans and Democrats. It has been observed that ACA still contains gaps that do not cover minorities. For example, the ACA focuses its efforts on equality of healthcare, on the issue of insurance, but the issue of equity in health is currently not addressed.

Under President Donald Trump regime, health reforms have been introduced to repeal and replace Obamacare (ACA). So many provisions have been repealed but replacement's provisions are still before the congress waiting to be passed into law. The question that is begging for answer is: will the current health reform of President Donald Trump address the issue of universal health insurance coverage that makes access to health equitable and fair to Americans?

CASE 2: NATIONAL HEALTH POLICY OF NIGERIA

The National health policy and strategy to achieve health for all Nigerians was launched in 1988. It was the first comprehensive national health policy. This policy was subsequently revised in 2004. However, it became necessary to develop a new national health policy to reflect new realities and trends, such as: including the Millennium Development Goals (MDGs), the Sustainable Development Goals (SDGs) and Nigeria's commitment to universal health coverage, provision of National Act of 2014, globalization, climate change, challenges of insurgency and their impacts in the health system of Nigeria.

The National Health Policy of 2016 came to being shortly after the enactment of National Health Act of 2014. The new policy provides the direction necessary to support the achievement of significant progress in improving the performance of the Nigerian Health System. It lays emphasis on strengthening primary health care as the bedrock of our national health system, in addition to the provision of financial risk protection to all Nigerians, particularly the poor and most vulnerable groups. The overall goal is to strengthen Nigeria's health system, particularly the primary health care sub-system, to deliver effective, efficient, equitable, accessible, affordable, acceptable and comprehensive health care services to all Nigerians.

However, Nigeria has recorded some progress in performance of its system. Progress includes improvements in key indices for major communicable diseases (HIV/AIDS, tuberculosis and Malaria), as well as in maternal and child health. Nigeria in the past years has been able to halt the transmission of the wild poliovirus, eradicate the guinea-worm disease, and successfully controlled the spread of the deadly Ebola virus disease.

However, there is inequity in access to services due to variations in socio-economic status and geographical locations. Medical services are costly leading to inequity in affordability and accessibility in health care services. Majority of Nigerians-roughly, 60 per cent are poor and exist on less than $1/day. They make up the large informal sector and vulnerable groups and are presently largely excluded from National Health Insurance Scheme (NHIS, 2012a). Furthermore, National Health Insurance Scheme in Nigeria also covers health promotion activities, preventive services, family planning, curative emergency, out-and in-patient care, as well as basic dental and eye care. The benefit package exempts coverage for conditions like HIV/AIDS (PEPFAR), Tuberculosis and Leprosy, Cancers, cosmetic procedures, kidney failure, major kidney organs transplants and infertility (NHIS, 2012a).

This is also compounded with the budgetary allocation constraints to health sectors, which affect expenditure on health care service delivery and states and local governments receiving less, making it difficult for state to provide quality health facilities and infrastructures. This level of inequity in health financing between federal, state and local governments has resulted in negative health outcomes. For example, in 2018 annual budget, health sector got 3.9 per cent of total budget allocation, which is far cry from 2017 allocation to health sector of 4.16 per cent and 4.23 per cent of 2016 budget allocation. (African Healthcare Extension Service, 2018).

Besides, size and distribution of income within the country is strong determinant of health status. Studies have found direct relationship between income inequality and mortality rate (Hermert & Shea, 1994; Smith, 1998). Nigeria's population is estimated to be 182.2 million. Per cent of population living on under $1.90 per day is 52 per cent and 60 per cent of the population live in rural areas (NDHS, 2013). Inequities in health outcomes exist between rural and urban areas, between the Northern and Southern regions of the country and across income groups. Childhood mortality rates are higher in rural areas than in urban areas, and higher in the Northern zones tan in the Southern zones. Also, childhood mortality is positively correlated with the wealth quintile, as well as with te level of mothers' education. Thirty-seven per cent of children under age 5 are "staunted"; 18 per cent are wasted, and 29 per cent are underweight. The proportion of "staunted" children declined from 41 per cent in 2008 to 37 percent in 2013 (Federal Ministry of Health, 2016).

Based on this situational analysis, the National Health Policy of 2016 is aimed at providing direction necessary to support the achievement of significant progress in improving the performance of the Nigerian health system. It is also believed that successful implementation of the policy by all the stakeholders would provide universal health coverage for all Nigerians.

CRITICAL ANALYSIS OF CASE STUDIES: A COMPARATIVE PERSPECTIVE

RQ. 1: To What Extent Are Human Rights, Equity and Social Justice Embedded in National Health Policies of United States of America and Nigeria?

Issues, Controversies and Problems

The last decade has witnessed the emergence of debates about health and human rights. This is in alliance to Alma Ata Declaration which states that health is a basic right (WHO, 1978). The right to health includes access to timely, acceptable and affordable health care of appropriate quality. Three core values compete for attention in the health care arena, namely: access, quality and cost containment. Under the banner of the "Triple Aim", they simultaneously seek to enhance access to higher quality care while containing costs in order to promote universal health coverage. Universal health coverage is a means to promote the right to health. And health policies and programs have the ability to either promote or violate human rights, including the right to health, depending the way they are designed or implemented

Hybrid Health System

Analyzing cases of health policies of United States of America and Nigeria show certain similarities and differences in health system performances. The United States

America's healthcare system is unique among advance developed and developing countries. The United States of America like Nigeria does not have a uniform health system. Both Nigeria and United States of America have no universal healthcare coverage. They operate hybrid health care systems; no uniform health system. In 2014, 48 per cent of U.S. health care spending came from private funds, with 28 per cent coming from households and 20 per cent coming from private businesses. The federal government accounted for 28 per cent of spending while state and local governments accounted for 17 per cent(National Health Expenditure, 2014). Most health care, even if publicly financed is delivered privately.

Nigeria, on the other hand, also operate hybrid system. Health services in Nigeria mirror political organization. The federal government is responsible for tertiary care, state governments for secondary care and local government run primary care. The financing of (but not the responsibility for) public health is tied to the flow of funds from the federal account. Funds are shared between levels of government according to the provision of National Health Act of 2014. The basic health care provision fund shall be financed from Federal Government Annual Grant of not less than 1 per cent of its Consolidated Revenue Fund and grants by International donor partners. The funds shall be managed by three national entities such as:

1. The National Health Care Development Agency will manage 45 per cent of the fund to be disbursed through each state and the Federal Capital Territory Primary Health Care Development Board for the provision of essential drugs, vaccines and consummates;
2. The National Health Insurance Scheme (NHIS) will manage 50 percent of the fund for the basic minimum package of health facilities; and
3. The Federal Ministry of Health will manage 5 percent of the fund for the provision of basic minimum package of health facilities. The Act is also for the purpose of providing healthcare insurance for certain class of people who are actually deprived. The Act also provides that the NHIS provide health coverage that cover pregnant women, children who are under five years, the elderly and the physically challenged persons. The Act also provides that part of the funds would be used to train nurses and midwives (National Health Act, 2014).

So, both United States of America and Nigeria have no uniform health systems, no universal health care coverage, not operating a single-payer national health insurance system, or multi-payer universal health insurance fund. Both U.S. and Nigeria's health care system can best be described as a hybrid system.

Lack of Human Rights

Vulnerable and marginalized groups in societies are often less likely to enjoy the right to health. Three of the world's fatal communicable diseases –malaria, HIV/AIDS and tuberculosis- disproportionately affect world's poorest populations, placing a tremendous burden on the economies on their economies. In Nigeria, violations or lack of attention to human rights can have serious health consequences. Discrimination directed at people living with HIV and affected by AIDS has been described as a major factor limiting the successes in the fight against HIV/AIDS and impeding the effectiveness of the response to the pandemic in Nigeria. Stigmatization and discrimination are faced by people with HIV/AIDS. A large number of people do not know their HIV status because of stigma and discrimination. Discrimination limits access to drugs and service for people living with HIV/AIDS because they are ashamed or afraid of the reaction of people when seen with the drugs, and these drugs are important for living a healthy life.

Moreover, the outbreak of Ebola epidemics in Nigeria signified the maintenance of collective rights of community and elimination of individual rights. There were human rights violations during Ebola. According to UN, (2014), there were restrictions on the exercise of the right to information, the right to freedom of movement, and the rights to health and to education to infringements on the rights to life and to physical integrity through the excessive use of force. Restrictions and bans on public gatherings and places including markets, schools and places of worship were imposed without any alternatives. These restrictions impacted greatly on children's rights to education and women's rights to income generating activities.

United States of America's health system, on the other hand, the market-based insurance system in the United States has caused a human rights crisis that deprives a large number of people of the healthcare they need. The most visible problem is that about 32.9 million people are without health insurance and over half of them are African Americans (Smith & Medalia, 2015). Some indigenous communities among these Afro-Americans are exposed to greater rates of ill-health and face significant obstacles to accessing quality and affordable healthcare. This population has substantially higher mortality and morbidity rates, due to non-communicable diseases such as cancer, cardiovascular and chronic respiratory diseases. So, the health care crisis in United States of America disproportionately affects disadvantaged groups and under-resourced communities, such as people living in poverty, people of color, and undocumented immigrants. Moreover, there are barriers in access to quality health care due to burden of medical debt, shortage of primary care providers and those with employer-sponsored insurance. U.S. health system does not protect the human right to health (Smith & Medalia, 2015).

Lack of Access and Human Rights

In whatever area the debate favors, in using UN Universal Declaration of Human rights standard, American healthcare delivery falls short of human rights standards. Lack of access due to being uninsured is one of the challenges of healthcare delivery in United States of America. The tax policy is restrictive, confirming Americans to one kind of health insurance (employer-based). Because of the enormous power of the tax code government policy has tied access to health insurance almost exclusively to the workplace.

Americans now generally view access to medical care as a right. No one should be denied medical care or suffer pain or remedial illness for lack of financial resources. Medicaid is the federal government's largest single welfare program for the poor. It is a combined federal and state program. States exercise fairly broad administrative powers and carry almost half of the financial burden. Although states differ in their eligibility requirements, they must cover all people receiving federally funded public assistance payments.

Furthermore, in 2003, almost 31 per cent of people in the United States with incomes below the poverty line had no health insurance at all (U.S. Census Bureau, 2004). This rate is more than double that for people who were not poor. Health insurance coverage also varies substantially by race and ethnicity (Center on Budget and Policy Priorities, 2003). For example, "approximately 11 per cent of white, non-Hispanic Americans, 33 per cent of Hispanics or Latinos, and 19 percent of Asians. Of immigrants who are non-citizens, 45 per cent were uninsured" (Chapin, 2007, p. 274).

For Americans who remain uninsured, either they were unaware of financial subsidies or were confused by eligibility rules for Medicaid. Perhaps, they had incomes that were too high to qualify for subsidies or perhaps their employer offers health insurance, but at a cost that was not affordable. Whatever, the reason is, many Americans are still without health insurance. A report by the nonpartisan congressional Budget office issued on March 13, 2017, estimated an additional 24 million people would be uninsured by 2026 with the passage of the American Healthcare Act of 2017 (AHCA), but the bill would cut Medicaid in other significant ways. According to the Congressional Budget Office Report (2017), the AHCA "introduces the option of states turning the money into a "block grant", a lump sum rather Medicaid patient, which would cut the program still further. The block grant would ease limitation on states ability to kick people off, charge premiums and cut benefits for children, states, whether they take a block grant, could also add a work requirement for nondisabled adults, further limiting access to the program.

In Nigeria, on the other hand, there is inequity in access to services due to variations in socio-economic status and geographic location. For instance, 11 per cent of births to uneducated mothers occur in health facilities while 91 per cent of births to mothers with more than secondary education occurs in health facilities; 86 per cent of mothers in urban areas receive Ante Natal Care (ANC) from skilled providers, compared to only 48 per cent of mothers in rural areas; and ANC coverage in the North West is 41 per cent compared to 91 per cent in the South East (National Health Policy, 2016). Other inequity problems related services include: curative-bias of health services delivered at all levels; inefficiencies in the production of services; unaffordability of services provided by the private sector to the poor; low confidence of consumers in the services provided, especially in public health facilities,; absence of a minimum package of health services; lack of proper coordination between the public and private sectors; and poor referral systems (National Health Policy, 2016). However, Nigeria has recorded some important milestones in recent years, such as the eradication of guinea worm, control of the Ebola Virus Disease outbreak, and the interruption of Wild Polio Virus transmission in the country.

Lack of Equity and Social Justice in Healthcare Delivery

Majority of Nigeria's population of about 182.2 million are living on under \$1.90 per day is 53 percent (NHIS, 2012a). Majority of these poor people live in rural areas and make up the large informal and vulnerable groups excluded for National Health Insurance Scheme (NHIS, 2012a). In formal sectors, the NHIS covers health promotion activities, preventive services, family planning, curative emergency, out-and in-patient care, as well as basic dental and eye care (NHIS, 2012a). These benefits exclude coverage for conditions like HIV/AIDS, tuberculosis, leprosy, cancers, cosmetic procedures, kidney failure, major kidney organs transplants and infertility (NHIS, 2012a). Overt or implicit discrimination in the delivery of health services violates fundamental human rights.

Inequality and lack of cultural sensitivity in the provision of medical care results in disparities in health outcomes Wide disparities in the quality of care provided to different groups. If a worker is employed in large corporation with a large benefits package, the tax benefits for health coverage can be very generous. That worker will get a large chunk of tax free income. If the worker is employed in low or middle-income company, the tax breaks can be terrific. Moreover, if an employer offers no health insurance, a worker's only option would be to purchase an individual policy which may become too expensive because of administrative and marketing costs. (Barkdull, 2012, p. 160).

A new healthcare approach by President Donald Trump's Administration to reduce or cut Medicare expenses would disproportionately impact women 65 and older compared to male counterparts. Budget cuts for Medicare would put potential income strain on an already inequitably impacted minority population, women 65 and older. For this population, there are significant issues with health needs and access. Ranging from coverage for complicated chronic conditions, to financial strain due to coverage gaps for needed long term services and support. For elderly women, Medicare are likely to be living off social security and/or retirement. This monthly income is most likely to be lower for women due to the income inequality of older women live in poverty compared to 7 percent of their male peers. This then translates to higher cut of pocket costs when compared to income for women in terms of their healthcare. This results on some elderly relying on Medicare for some income and health security for elderly women (Mansfield, 2017).

It is important to take into consideration the increased impact Medicare cuts and changes will have on women 65 and older compared to their male peers. It was observed that fifty-six percent of Medicare recipients are women, and two out of three of them are 85 and older, that is approximately 80 percent of the Medicare population over 85 is women (Mansfield, 2017). This indicates that they are significant stakeholders when considering policy changes to Medicare. It has been universally accepted as a norm that women often live longer than men and do not have equitable employment benefits in terms of income. These are women who potentially have limited income security and limited access and support from non-governmental services. They are less likely to be able to adjust to add out of pocket costs as they work to maintain their health and use needed healthcare services. Sustaining the program is crucial for women as they age. However, there is financial challenges faced by this aging population (Mansfield, 2017).

Cost of Healthcare

In U.S., health care services are costly. In 2013, U.S. spent $8,713 per person or 16.4 percent of its GDP on healthcare. On a per capita basis, the U.S. spends more than double the $3,453 average of all OECD countries (Davis, Streamiskis, Squires & Schoen, 2014). Despite these investments in health care delivery services, prohibitive high cost is one of the challenges Americans face in accessing health care. Americans with below-average incomes are much more likely not to visit a physician when sick; getting a recommended test, treatment or follow-up care; filling a prescription; and seeing a dentist (Davis, Streamiskis, Squires & Schoen, 2014). Fifty-nine per cent of physicians in the U.S. acknowledge their patients have difficulty paying for care (Davis, Streamiskis, Squires, & Schoen, 2014). In 2013, 31 per cent of uninsured adults reported not getting or delaying medical care because of cost, compared to five percent of privately insured adults and 27 per cent of those on public insurance, including Medicaid and Medicare (Davis, Streamiskis, Squires & Schoen, 2014).

In Nigeria, on the other hand, health care cost is equally high. At the federal level, the total allocation from the federal budget to health rose from 3.9 per cent to 6 per cent between 2010 and 2012, but decreased again to 4 percent in 2013. In 2018 budget, health sector got 3.9 per cent of the total budget, which is a far cry from 2017 allocation of 4.16 per cent and 2016 allocation of 4.23 per cent as against 15 per cent declared by World Health Organization (National Health Policy, 2016). The overall out-of-pocket expenditure (OOPE), as a proportion of total health expenditure, remained high for the same period, ranging from 73.8 per cent in 2006 to 70 per cent in 2009 (National Health Policy, 2016). The high level in OOPE poses a barrier to accessing health services, thereby fueling the inequity in health outcomes. In formal sector, less than 5 percent of the population is currently covered by any form of prepayment schemes, such as health insurance. Only federal government workers are currently enrolled in social health insurance and civil servants from most states are yet to be enrolled. Also, the enrolled Federal Government workers have not begun to pay their employee contributions to health insurance. At the current level and trends of health financing, Nigeria will not achieve universal health coverage (National Health Policy, 2016).

Lack of Quality Health Services

In U.S., despite the relatively high level of health expenditure, there are fewer physicians per capita than in most other OECD countries. In 2013, the U.S. had 2.6 practicing physicians per 1,000 people, below the OECD average of 3.3 per cent (OECD, 2015). Moreover, there are only about 1.2 primary care physicians per 1,000 people. Projections indicate that the U.S. will need 52,000 more primary care physicians by 2025 to meet demand (AAMC, 2015). There is a significant spatial mismatch within the United States for physicians as well. While the U.S. averaged 225.6 doctors active in patient care per 100,000 people in 2014, there is a wide variance across states; Massachusetts ranks highest with 349.5 active doctors per 100,000 people, while Mississippi has only 170.3 active doctors. In 2013, infant mortality rate was 5.96 per 1,000 live birth, while the OECD median was 3.8 (National Vital Statistics Reports, 2016).

In Nigeria, on the other hand, health services are delivered through primary, secondary and tertiary health facilities by both the public and private sectors. Although primary health care is the fulcrum of the Nigerian health system, the provision, financing and management of primary health care services, as well as secondary health care services, leaves much to be desired. Many health facilities are situated far away from the people, especially in rural areas and hard-to-reach areas. The most common barriers to accessing health services by the population are the cost of services, distance to the health facility, and the attitude of health workers (NDHS, 2013). The quality of health services is generally poor and does not instill confidence in the people. This has led to some people seeking care outside Nigeria.

Furthermore, the National Health Act of 2014 provides that health facilities are required to obtain a certificate of standards, the requirements for this certificate are not specified in the Act. Regulations that would provide these requirements have also not yet been enacted (National Health Policy, 2016). Thus, quality health care services are not generally available to a large percent of the population in Nigeria.

SOLUTIONS/ RECOMMENDATIONS ON AMERICA HEALTH POLICY

Integrating human rights, equity and social justice into health policies of U.S. and Nigeria would provide strategies and solutions to address and rectify inequalities, discriminatory practices and unjust power relations which are often at the heart of inequitable health outcomes. Any of the following recommended solutions would enhance access to higher quality health care services, while containing costs:

Human Rights-Based Approach

United States of America and Nigeria should adopt human rights-based approach to design and develop health policies. Human rights-based approach has the ability to promote human rights, equity and social justice in pursuit of universal health coverage agenda of U.S. and Nigeria. The goal of this approach is that all health policies, strategies and programs are designed with the objective of progressively improving the enjoyment of all people to the right to health. For interventions to reach this objective to, there is need to adhere to World Health Organization's principles and standards (WHO, 2015) on health-related human rights:

- **Non-Discrimination Principle:** A guarantee that there is no discrimination in human rights based on race, color, sex, language, religion, social origin, marital status, gender identity, health status, economic and social situation and so on;
- **Availability:** A sufficient quantity of functioning public health and health care facilities, goods and services, as well as programs;
- **Accessibility:** Health facilities, goods and services accessible to everyone. Accessibility has four overlapping dimensions:
    - Non-discrimination
    - Physical accessibility
    - Economical accessibility (affordability)
    - Information accessibility

- **Acceptability:** All health facilities, goods and services must be respectful of medical ethics and culturally appropriate as well as sensitive to gender and life-cycle requirements;
- **Quality:** Health facilities, goods and services must be scientifically and medically appropriate and of good quality;
- **Accountability:** States and other duty-bearers are answerable for the observance of human rights;
- **Universality:** Human rights are universal and inalienable. All people everywhere in the world are entitled to them (WHO, 2015).

These principles would guide policy-makers in health policies and programs development that are responsive to the needs of the people. A human rights based-approach identifies relationships in order to empower people to claim their rights and encourage policy makers and service providers to meet their obligations in creating more responsive health systems.

Giving Tax Credit for Health Insurance

U.S. and Nigeria's need new national policies that empowers individuals to make key decisions in the healthcare sector, a system in which individuals are free to choose what kind of doctor and medical specialist they want, the type of health plan they want and the benefits they need. Using incremental approach, America and Nigeria need systems in which individuals – rather than companies, manager – care executives, or government bureaucrats, directly control the flow of dollars (Karger, Midgley & Brown, 2013). The only way to establish real patient control is to give individuals and families choice. Plans and providers, with real market competition, would then be forced to respond to patient's needs in innovative ways. Congress, National Assembly and Administrations can move the market in this direction by giving every American and Nigerian families tax credits to use toward the purchase of health insurance and to offset their healthcare costs. Likewise, Congress, National Assembly and Administrations should give refundable tax credits or direct subsidies to low-income families and individuals to mainstream them into the private healthcare system. Such tax-code changes would enable individuals to choose the plans benefits and medical treatments they want at prices they wish to pay (Karger, Midgley, & Brown, 2013). A tax credit system for health insurance would establish:

...portability, equity, human rights, social justice, consumer-based market for insurance give patients control over important and sensitive healthcare decisions and eliminate large number of uninsured. (Karger, Midgley & Brown, 2013, pp. 137-140)

National Health Insurance or Single-Payer Plans Approach

Though a rational approach, advocates for a new national healthcare policy have suggested "single – payer system as the best national health policy. National Association of social workers supports a universal right to healthcare under a single payer system (NASW, 2000, p. 153). Health policies for U.S. and Nigeria health sectors can integrate human rights, equity and social justice by using single-payer plans approach. What is a single – payer system? A single – payer means that the government pays all healthcare expenses using National Health Insurance (NHI) card. In this plan, everybody would be covered for every medically necessary service, including, doctor visits, hospital stays, prescription drugs, dental and mental health services, Nursing – home and in-home care. There would be no deductibles, no co-payments, and no out-of-pocket expenses to the consumer. All you have to do when you go to the doctor, hospital, or pharmacy is show your National Health Insurance (NHI) card. The NHI would pay hospitals, nursing homes, home health agencies, group practices and health centers a monthly hump sum. Individual physicians would be paid by the NHI on the basis of a simplified, binding fee schedule. Funds for construction, major renovation, and major equipment would be provided based on need as determined by Regional Health-Planning Boards composed of both professionals and community representatives (Karger, Midgley, & Brown, 2003). By this, social justice is seen to be in healthcare policy towards a more just society. In effect, a single-payer plan would expand Medicare, now available to only the aged, to everyone. The plan boasts of "simplicity, savings in administrative costs over multiple insurers, and direct federal control over prices to be paid for hospital and physician services and drugs (Dye, 1998). A single-payer program could pay for medical expenses as all you have to do is to show your National Health Insurance (NHI) card.

However, universal health coverage, using NHI is easier to sell than expended role of government in healthcare. However, health policy needs to address other factors in developing health policy, such as: economic, social, occupational and environmental policies that contribute to maintaining health, recognizing the relationship between these factors and quality and longevity of life (NASW, 2000, P. 152). Similarly, the American Public Health Association policy statement says, the health of the people requires not only a universal National healthcare policy, but also social and economic policies that foster the health, stability and general welfare of the population (American Public Health Association, 1997). So, these factors should be considered when integrating human rights, equity and social justice using a single-payer plans approach.

FUTURE RESEARCH DIRECTION

Though, these proposed solutions are laudable to both countries, the search for Universal National healthcare policy that makes health a right of citizens is still on-going. There is need, therefore, for future quantitative research to be directed on how to integrate human rights, equity and social justice into the development of national health policy that makes citizen's health a right, where there is equitable access to healthcare that is affordable and incorporating other variables such as: economic, social, occupational, political and environmental factors that influence the state of health and well-being.

CONCLUSION

The healthcare policies in America and Nigeria have revealed absence of human rights, equity and social justice in healthcare service delivery. For example, American healthcare policy is facing crisis with aging population and attendant increases in both acute and chronic healthcare needs. It is imperative that the government should find ways to promote wellness by allowing citizens have access to healthcare, control cost and ensure adequate healthcare across their life spans. Many health -related crises have attracted the need for government reforms on health. There is the need to determine the number and share of total population among the uninsured and under-insured; resolve problem of lack of access and high medical cost; address some moral and ethical issues pertaining to healthcare and medical services; and implement mental health policies that capture cultural settings, values and diversity of the population.

America and Nigeria need a new national health policy that would transform the health-insurance market – ruled by corporate benefit managers and regulated by government bureaucrats – into a consumer-driven, patent – oriented system based on personal choice. To do this, U.S. Congress and Nigerian National Assembly must reform the federal tax treatment of health insurance from one that gives almost exclusive tax breaks for the purchase of insurance through employment into one that give individuals and families the ability to pick and choose the plans they want at the price they wish to pay. Healthcare should be a right for citizens and government should pay for it through taxes. It is not 'socialized medicine" in which the government owns the hospitals and healthcare workers are government employees. It is much like a much-improved version of Medicare expanded to include everybody. It should be a single payer system and structured as National Health Insurance (NHI) (Physicians for National Health Program, 2001). In this plan, everybody would be covered for every medically necessary service, including, doctor visits, hospital stays, prescription drugs, Dental and mental health services, nursing – home and in-home care. There would be no deductibles, no co-payments, and no out-of-pocket expenses to the consumer. All you have to do when you go to the doctor, hospital, or pharmacy is show your NHI card. The NHI would pay hospitals, nursing homes, home health agencies, group practices and health centers a monthly hump sum. Individual physicians would be paid by the NHI on the basis of a simplified, binding fee schedule. Funds for construction, major renovation, and major equipment would be provided based on need as determined by Regional Health-Planning Boards composed of both professionals and community representatives (Karger, Midgley & Brown, 2003).

There is need, therefore, to integrate human rights, equity, and social justice into national health policies in both U.S. and Nigeria. Adopting such approach would make quality healthcare service delivery a right and accessible to all citizens with less cost.

REFERENCES

Affordable Care Act, (ACA) (2010).

African Health Care Extension Service, 2018

Asoka, T. (2011). *Ensuring Financial access to primary healthcare, the experience and challenges of the National Health Insurance – Scheme in Nigeria.* Paper presentation, National Consultation on primary healthcare, financing and National Primary Healthcare Development Agency (NPHCDA). Available at: www.carenet.inf/files/insuring_ financial_Access_to_PHC.doc

Association of American Medical Colleges. (2015). *State Physician workforce Data Book.* Available at: https://www.aamc.org/data/workforce/reports/442830/statedat-andreports.html

Barkdull, J. (2012). *Public Policy and Global change.* University Readers, Inc.

Baum, N.M., Gollust, S.E., Goold, S.D., & Jacobson, P.D. (2007). Looking ahead: addressing ethical challenges in Public health practice. *J Law Med Ethics, 35*, 657-67.

Chapin, R. (2007). *Social Policy for Effective Practice: A strength Approach.* New York: McGraw-Hill Inc.

Daniels, N, Bryant, J., Castano, R.A., Dantes, O.G., Khan, K.S., & Pannarunothai, S. (2000). Benchmarks of fairness for healthcare reform: a policy tool for developing countries. *Bull World Health Organ, 78*, 740-50.

Davis, K., Streamiskis, K., Squires, D., & Schoen, C. (2014). *"Mirror", Mirror on the wall: How the performance of the US Healthcare systems compares internationally; Update*. The Commonwealth Fund Commission on a High Performance Health System. Available at: http://www.Commonwealthfund.org/-/Media/publications/fund-report/2014/Jun/1755_davis_miror_

Dye, T. R. (1998). *Understanding Public Policy*. Prentice – Hall, Inc.

Eneanya, A. N. (2015). *Policy and Program Development, implementation and Evaluation*. Lagos: University of Lagos Press.

Eneanya, A. N. (2016). Health Policy Implementation and its Barriers: A case study of US Health System. In Social, Economic and political perspectives on Public health policy-making. Medical Information Science Reference. doi:10.4018/978-1-4666-9944-1.ch003

Gostin, L. O. (2014). Ebola: Towards an international health systems fund. *Lancet*, 61345–3. doi:10.1016/50/40-6736(14) PMID:25201591

Gwatkin, D.R. (2000). Health inequalities and the health of the poor. What do we know? What can we do? *Bull World Health Organ, 78*, 3-17.

Health Insurance Coverage in the United States. (2014). U.S. Government Printing Office.

Helmert, U. & Shea, S. (1994). Social inequalities and Health Status in Western Germany. *Public Health, 108*, 341-56. doi:10.100710728-005-2568-2

James, C., Carrin, G., Savedoff, W., & Hanvoravongchai, P. (2005). Clarifying efficiency-equity tradeoffs through explicit criteria, with a focus on developing countries. *Health Care Analysis*.

Karger, J. H., Midgley, J., & Brown, C. B. (Eds.). (2013). *Controversial Issues in Social Policy*. Boston: Pearson Education, Inc.

Kass, N.E. (2001). An ethics framework for public health. *Am J Public Health, 91*, 17776-82.

Labonte, R., & Gagnon, M. L. (2010). Framing health and foreign policy: Lesson for global health diplomacy. *Globalization and Health, 6*(1), 14. doi:10.1186/1744-8603-6-14 PMID:20727211

Mann, J. M. (2006). Health and Human Rights: If not now, when? (voices from the past). *American Journal of Public Health, 96*(11), 1940–1943. doi:10.2105/AJPH.96.11.1940 PMID:17062844

Mansfield. (2017). *Reductions in Medicare Disproportionately Impacts Women 65 and older*. Available at http://patimes.org/reductions-medicare-disproportionately-impact-w

Mclnness, C., & Lee, K. (2012). *Global Health and international relations*. Cambridge, UK: Polity.

National Association of Social Workers. (2000). *Social Work Speaks: National Association of Social Workers Policy Statements* (5th ed.). Washington, DC: NASW Press.

National Health Act, 2014.

National Health Expenditures. (2014). *Center for Medicare and Medicaid Services*. Available at: https//www.cms.gov/research-statistics-data-and–system/statistics-trends-and-reports/national health expend datat/nationalhealthaccountshistorical.html

National Health Insurance Scheme. (2012a). *Operational guidelines*. Available at: http://www.nhis.gov.ng/index. php?option=com_ content& view=article&id=92& Itemid= 77

Nwatu, R. (2000, January). Making the health system effective. *Medical Journal*.

O'Donnell, O., Van Doorslaer, E., Wagstaff, A., & Lindelow, M. (2008). *Analyzing health equity usin g household survey data*. Washington, DC: World Bank.

OECD. (2015). *Health at a Glance 2015: OECD indicators*. OECD Publishing. Available at: http://www.oecd-library.org/social-issues-migration-health/health-at-a-glance.199913112

Rawls, J. A. (1999). *A Theory of Justice* (revised edn.). Cambridge, MA: Belknap Press of Harvard University Press.

Smith, J. (1998). Healthy Bodies and Thick Wallets – the Dual Relation between Health and Economic Status. *The Journal of Economic Perspectives*, *13*(2), 145–166. doi:10.1257/jep.13.2.145 PMID:15179962

Smith, J. C., & Medalia, C. (2015). U.S. Census Bureau. *Current Population Reports. Series P-28, Special Censuses*, 5.

United Nations Organization (UNO). (2014). *A human rights perspective into the Ebola outbreak. UN. Report*. Geneva: United Nations.

WHO. (2004). *World report on knowledge for better health: Strengthening health systems*. Geneva: WHO.

WHO. (2015). Committee on Economic, Social and Cultural Rights. General Comment No. 20, Non-discrimination in economic, social and cultural rights, 2009. Available at http://www.who.int/mediacentre/fact-sheets/fs323/en/

World Health. (2000). *Health Systems: Improving Performances*. Geneva: WHO.

KEY TERMS AND DEFINITIONS

Equity: The concept of equity can be understood in terms of providing what is fair and just in order for citizens to overcome discrimination.

Health Policy: Health policy broadly refers to guidelines to government actions (national, state, and local government) to advance public health. It is not a single action but requires a range of legislative and regulatory efforts ranging from organization, financing, and delivering of healthcare services both physical and mental health.

Health System: Health system is conceptualized as consisting of all organizations, people, and actions whose primary intent is to promote, restore, or maintain health. This includes efforts to influence determinants of health as well as more direct health-improving activities including safety legislation.

Human Rights: The right to health includes access to timely, acceptable, and affordable healthcare of appropriate quality. So, there has been increasing recognition of the value of human rights approach to the understanding and practice of public health issues over the past decade.

Social Justice: Social justice is conceptualized as it relates to health-related issues. It embodies the vision of a society that is equal and in which all members are physically and psychological safe. It demands that all people have a right to human dignity with their basic needs met in healthcare equitably.

Section 3

Value-Based Leadership and Health Systems

Chapter 10
Work Leadership, Occupational Health, and Safety

Gabriel Akinbode
University of Lagos, Nigeria

ABSTRACT

Occupational health and safety (OHS) systems are designed to identify and minimize risks at the workplace. A thriving business community should seek to create jobs, wealth, good leadership, safe, and healthy working conditions that are essential for production of goods and provisions of services. Therefore, managers have a legal and moral duty to safeguard the health and safety of those who work for them, and the exercise of these duties needs to be seen as central to the role of leadership. There is a growing interest among researchers and organizational practitioners about occupational safety in recent years. The chapter provides an exhaustive discourse on the relevance of occupational health and safety systems in modern day workplaces as well as the nexus between management leadership and occupational health and safety. It highlights the guiding principles to leadership and key issues in efficient administration of OHS. The chapter concludes by recommending the role leaders should play to improve safety and health in the workplace.

INTRODUCTION

The organized workplaces across the global world has in the recent past witnessed tremendous economic, technological growth and enhanced employability except in some developing countries such as Nigeria. This growth has raised serious concerns over occupational safety in virtually all work sectors, particularly manufacturing sector, including tertiary and quaternary services. Managing Occupational Health

DOI: 10.4018/978-1-5225-6133-0.ch010

and Safety (OHS) effectively is a key element in running a successful business in today's workplace. Nowadays, work place safety is considered by World Health Organization (WHO) a priority setting for health promotion in the 21st century (Takala, 1999; WHO, 2010). Therefore, managers have a legal and moral duty to safeguard the health and safety of those who work for them, and the exercise of these duties needs to be seen as central to the role of leadership. There is a growing interest among researchers, management and organizational practitioners about occupational safety in recent years. This is probably informed by the growing incidence of workplace illness, injury and death which impose large cost on national economies and operational efficiency of organizations. International Labor Organization (ILO) and WHO reports indicated that in manufacturing industries many employees suffer from workplace injuries and property damage resulted in economic crisis (ILO, 2006; ILO, 2010; WHO, 2010). Every 15 seconds, a worker dies from a work-related accident or disease. Every 15 seconds, 153 workers have a work-related accident (Jilcha & Kitaw 2016). Every day, 6,300 people die as a result of occupational accidents or work-related diseases – more than 2.3 million deaths per year (ILO, 2010; WHO, 2010; Jilcha & Kitaw, 2016).

These costs accrue to the individual workers who suffer, their families, the businesses that employ them, and the society at large due to the costs associated with health care and treatment (Gahan, Sievewright & Evans, 2014). Economic analysis of workplace health and safety has for example, consistently shown that jobs or occupations associated with lower levels of workplace safety typically attract a wage premium (Heaney & Irish, 2007; Gahan, Sievewright & Evans, 2014)). Economists have also sought to estimate the marginal costs associated with work related death in different part of the world. For example, using Australian data, Miller, Mulvey and Norris (1997) estimate the economic cost associated with a work-related death to be between $11million and $19million only in Australia. Although estimates vary significantly from country to country, the International Labor Organization (ILO, 2006) has estimated that the cost associated with workplace death, injury and illness is approximately 4 percent of annual global domestic product. In developing countries including Nigeria, the risk of having work-related injury is almost 15 to 25 times higher than that of developed counties. This is because in developing countries (e.g. Nigeria), majority of the workforce is employed in small and medium scale industries that do not meet the minimum standards and guidelines set by the WHO and the ILO for occupational health, safety and social protection (Barling, Loghlin & Kelloway, 2002; Tadesse & Kumie, 2007). Occupational health and safety laws cover only about 10% of the population in developing countries, omitting many major hazardous industries and occupations (see LaDou, 2003; Linhard, 2005). Occupational health remains neglected in most developing countries under the pressure of devastating social, economic, and political challenges (Ahasan & Partanen, 2001; O'Neill, 2000; Christiani, durvassula, & Myers, 1990; Barling, Loghlin & Kelloway, 2003)

Occupational Health and Safety (OHS), also commonly or otherwise referred to as Occupational Safety and Health (OSH), or Workplace Health and Safety (WHS), is a multidisciplinary field concerned with the safety, health, and welfare of people at work. It is a field of healthcare concerned with enabling an individual to undertake their occupation, in the way that causes least harm to their health. As defined by the World Health Organisation (WHO) occupational health deals with all aspects of health and safety in the workplace and has a strong focus on primary prevention of hazards. While "Health" has been defined by WHO as "a state of complete physical, mental, and social well-being and not merely the absence of disease or infirmity. By implication, occupational health and safety is all about promotion of health and safety at work, which is concerned with preventing accidents, harm or injury from any incidental hazards, arising in the workplace.

In recent years however, occupational health and safety of the workers has improved and is relatively satisfactory in developed countries, whereas in developing countries, occupational health receives little attention and comes at low level in the list of national priorities (Perrow, 1984). Studies showed that there are baskets of measures providing information on a range of health and safety performances (HSE, 2001; Yusuf, Moges, & Ahmed, 2014). Nevertheless, the traditional workplace-oriented occupational health has proven to be insufficient in the developing world, and tangible progress in occupational health can be achieved only by linking occupational health to the broader context of social justice and national development (Swuste & Eijkemans, 2002; Joubert, 2002; Michaels, Barrera, & Gacharna, 1985; Mendes, 1985).

The purpose of the chapter is to examine work leadership in managing occupational health and safety issues, problems, and violations in Nigeria. It would also suggest solutions or recommendations and future research direction.

BACKGROUND

Safety and health are constituents of welfare because health is wealth. A healthy worker is a productive worker and an asset to the organization. An unhealthy worker constitutes a liability which infringes on the marginal profit of the organization, due to low productive and marginal input in the overall process of production (Machida, 2009; Onuegbu, 2010; Mokikan, 2012; Ngwama, 2016). Nigerian workers across all sectors of economy recent years, have been subjected to accidents which range from minor to fatal injuries, while some have lost their lives, some loosing vital organs and rendered permanently incapacitated (Ngwama, 2016). An estimated whooping total sum of 159 000 people in the Nigeria die each year as a result of occupational diseases and industrial accidents (ILO, 2012). Despite these entire estimated figure, unlike in the advance nations of the world, it is still very difficult to quantify the health impact of occupational diseases in the Nigeria workplace because there is no consensus on the data. The rate of the industrial accidents and the general lethargy of the employers to respond to the issues of safety and health in workplaces are becoming a growing concern in Nigeria (Bankole & Lawal, 2012; Fajana, 2012; Ahiuma-Young 2012; Ngwama, 2016).

According to Ahiuma-Young (2012) an estimated 2.3 million occupational fatalities occur annually while nothing less than 100 occupational fatalities and some billions of capital losses have been recorded in Nigeria between April 28, 2009 and April 2010 (ILO, 2012; Ngwama, 2016). Not less than 200 cases of industrial accidents occur in the workplaces in Nigeria daily with an equally high rate of fatalities. Available statistics indicates that no fewer than 400 workers have lost their lives in the power sector between 2010 and 2012 while performing their official duties. In the maritime sector, also findings show that since the concession of the ports, over 100 cases of fatal industrial accidents have occurred with over ten deaths, numerous incapacitations and innumerable serious body injuries. Fajana (2012) estimated that at least 50 million Nigerians are at risk of occupational hazards. This group he pointed out includes about 3.2 million Nigerians and children who are involved in economic activities, (even as abused participants) in the labour market.

Occupational Health as defined by the joint committee of the ILO/WHO is the promotion and maintenance of the highest degree of physical, mental and social well-being of workers in all occupation. It is further explained as the sum total of all activities and programs that are engaged upon, aiming to attain and maintain the highest level of health and safety for all people who are engaged in any type of work whatever. It involves the protection of workers' health from any hazard to which they may be exposed to in the work environment. It is a preventive and proactive approach which involves risk assessment, hazard identification, hazard mitigation, hazard elimination and treatment of work-related injuries. There is a plethora of hazards (safety and health hazards) which people are exposed to in their jobs; from the formal industries (banking, oil and gas, textile, agricultural, construction, food and beverage etc.) to the informal (logging and sawmill, roadside mechanic, carpentry, local welders, pepper grinders, market traders etc.). Exposure to these hazards occurs for fairly long hours on a daily basis as the majority of the active hours of the day is spent at work (i.e. at least 8 hours per day). These hazards include chemical, biological, physical, mechanical, psychological and ergonomic hazards. For any person affected, it could be either or a couple of the various forms of hazard.

The risk of death or injuries from fire hazards in the workplace, continue to raise concern, irrespective of the international standards to strengthening of legal and other supporting measures to improve workplace safety and health in all countries, particularly in developing countries. In Nigeria, there is lack of comprehensive data in the area of occupational/ industrial hazards and this has become a great challenge given the atrociousness of industrial accidents which is undermining workers' productive effort in the organizations (Onuegbu, 2010; Ngwama, 2016). Particularly, work-related accidents and diseases continue to be a serious problem in both developed and developing countries including Nigeria. Nigerian workers across all sectors of the economy have been subjected to workplace accidents which range from minor to fatal, as some have lost their lives right in the line of duty, while some have lost vital organs, therefore rendered permanently incapacitated. The issue of safety and health at workplace which once occupied a major place in the programmes and plans of the employers are now treated with levity (Ngwama, 2016). One such case in mind was the fire incident that razed a plastic factory in Ikorodu, Lagos State in 2002 where many workers roasted to death at night because of the negligence of the Chinese owners of the company who locked the workers in the factory without provision for emergency exit (Ngwama, 2016). There are equally other unregistered companies using the incorporation as cover, many of them have worse cases involving health and safety of their workers

The ILO estimates that 250 million workers are involved in accidents every year and out of which 300,000 are killed. There are at least 335,000 fatal injuries caused by accidents at work. Putting accidents and diseases together, the global estimate of work-related deaths amounts to 1.1 million per year, and this according to ILO is grossly underestimated probably because of lack of comprehensive statistical data from many member states (International Labor Conference 87th Session 1999:37, ILO 274th session 1999). The economic losses are enormous and, in terms of shattered families and communities, the damage is incalculable. International Labor Organization (ILO) estimates suggest that 159 000 people in the Nigeria die each year as a result of occupational diseases and industrial accidents (ILO, 2012). Despite the seeming deplorable state of occupational and safety issues in the workplace in Nigeria at present, the policy framework targeted towards reducing the rate of industrial accidents through preventive measures as well as to create awareness on the rights of victims of industrial accidents are weak and hardly enforced (Alana, 2010; Onuegbu, 2010; Fajana, 2012; Mokikan, 2012; Ngwama, 2016). More recently, the World Economic Forum (WEF, 2012) has estimated that cardiovascular diseases alone result in productivity losses of $US389 billion globally, whilst mental illnesses estimated to reduce economic output by $1.6 trillion. Other research suggests that workplace health and safety may have more far-reaching macroeconomic consequences. The ILO (2012) for example, also finds a strong correlation between national workplace fatality rates and the World Economic Forum (WEF) Global Competitive Index, suggesting that inadequate WHS practices place a heavy burden on national economic growth (Gahan, Sieve wright & Evans, 2014).

In the manufacturing sector for example, the frequency of fatal industrial accidents is very alarming. Many times, the managements collaborate with some union officials to conceal cases of industrial accidents and secretly negotiate compensation (Ahiuma-Young, 2012; Ngwama, 2016). The management simply pays out paltry sums as compensation to the families of victims in both deaths and permanent disabilities. Some of the victims who have suffered major injuries like loss of their hands or legs are often dismissed after receiving tokens that the companies give out on "compassionate" ground. The Workman Compensation Act that is supposed to address issues of industrial accidents is inconsistent and lack implementation. The alarming rate of the industrial accidents and the general lethargy of the employers to reduce the rate of industrial accidents through preventive measures demand creation of awareness on the rights of victims of industrial accidents. Ahiuma-Young (2012) observed that the incidence of industrial accidents at the workplace in Nigeria and fatality rate as well as the inherent dangers posed to the socio-economic and political development of the country constitute a serious threat. He notes that the federal government has failed in enforcing industrial safety policies at the workplace and some of the trade unions pay less attention to the safety of their members.

The employers have relegated issues of safety to the background in the country on the premise of the harsh economic environment. Most of the victims of workplace accidents preferred to suffer in silence, because they have been warned by their employers of severe consequences if they try to make any case with the organization. More often than not, most of these companies operate in secluded areas with untraceable addresses and are abound in all part of the country (Ngwama, 2016). In view of the foregoing, this chapter takes a critical look at the OHS issues, problems and trends in the workplace in Nigeria using robust descriptive qualitative analysis of extant literatures and empirical studies in Nigeria and beyond. Particularly, those critical issues threatening the lives of average workers in Nigeria and suggests recommendations that are sufficient anchored on findings from empirical studies. All stakeholders must be mobilized for concerted efforts against unpopular government policies that tend undermine occupational health and industrial safety to protect the employers at the expense of the lives of the workers.

In Nigeria today, it is no longer workers in the factory that are pruned to accidents but those in the white collar jobs are also increasingly exposed to job hazards, they may be unaware of the hazards because of the long gestation of such hazards and those in this category include workers in the financial sector, oil and gas as well as civil service (Fajana, 2012; Ngwama, 2016). However, Fajana (2012) posited that a properly-managed safety culture based on tested principles of workplace safety will produce employees who participate actively in training; these employees will be able to identify and alert one another and management to potential hazards. They develop effective control measures and feel a sense of responsibility for their safety and safety of others. These developments and its attendant fatalities therefore underscore the importance of corporate culture that place value on occupational health and safety in the 21st century Nigeria workplace.

Many definitions of 'leadership' exist in the literature (Yukl, 1989). The term "*leadership*" comes from the Anglo-Saxon word "laedan", meaning to go, and is defined as guiding, conducting, proceeding, or being foremost. Leadership has been defined in terms of individual's traits, leadership behavior, interaction patterns, role relationship, follower perception, influence over followers, influence on task goals, and influence on organizational culture. In organizational psychology it is mostly defined as a group phenomenon (including interaction between two or more people) and an intentional social exertion of influence, which aims at attaining objectives by communication processes (Steger, 2003). Leadership is more than a micro-organizational phenomenon. It goes beyond direct, dyadic relationships between leaders and subordinates; rather, it takes place at all levels of an organisation. It can occur in indirect as well as direct forms. It includes the efforts of the management to reach both short-term and long-term objectives (Gordon & Yukl, 2004). According to Goods (1959), leadership is the ability and readiness to inspire, guide or manage others. Dictionary of Behavioral Sciences (1973) defined leadership as the exercise of authority in initiating, directing, or controlling the behavior or attitude of others, and bring out their consent, those qualities of personality and training, which make the guidance, and control of others successful. According to Hemphill (1945), leadership is the initiation of a new structure or procedure for accomplishing the organizational goals and objectives for changing an organization's goals and objectives.

Tannenbaum, Weschler, and Massarik (1961) explained leadership in terms of interpersonal influence, which is defined as influencing people to co-operate towards some goals, which they come to find desirable. Halpin (1956) stated that a successful leader contributed to group objectives and to group relationship. He describes leadership behavior in two dimensions of initiating structure and consideration. Davis (1986) contended that leadership is the ability to persuade others to seek defined objectives enthusiastically. To Hersey and Blanchard (1988) leadership is a process of influencing the activities of an individual within a group in its effort towards goal achievement in given situation?

Koontz and Weihrich (1990) suggested that leadership is influence, that is, the art or process of influencing people so that they will strive willingly and enthusiastically towards the achievement of group goals. Yuki and Vanfleet (1998) stated that leadership is viewed as a process that includes influencing the task objectives and strategies of a group or organization; influencing people in the organization to implement the strategies and achieve the objectives, influencing group maintenance and identification, and influencing the culture of the organization. In line with this position, Terry (1988) concluded that leadership is, essentially, a continuous process of influencing behaviour. A leader breathes life into group and motivates it towards goals. Keys and Case (1990) defines leadership as the process of influencing and supporting others to work enthusiastically toward achieving objectives consistent with these earlier definitions Yulk (1994) defined leadership as the ability of one person to influence a group of persons toward the achievement of common goals. When comparing leadership styles, the focus typically is on the effectiveness of leaders' effectiveness. Effectiveness in turn, typically is viewed as the extent to which the leader's group or organization performs its tasks successfully or attain s its goals (Ardichivilli & Kuchinke, 2002; House & Aditya, 1997; Allio, 2009).

For several decades, researchers have investigated what constitutes effective leader behaviours, what are the pertinent personal characteristics of leaders, and what leader behaviors best suit particular contexts and conditions. Overall, effective leadership has been shown to strengthen employee commitment to the organization and to improve the work climate, enhance innovation and increase productivity (Bel, 2010; Bramming, Kristensen, & Pedersen, 2009).

A corporate culture and leadership framework that truly values health and safety as much as it values productivity, quality and profitability will generate world-class safety results. Creating a safety culture in your workplace is similar to creating a safe home and healthy habits. That is, employment relationship where leaders are seen to spend time of the "shop-floor" and ask workers relevant safety related questions, follow-up with people who are directly affected by workplace injuries to collect and review all incidents, regularly review safety management matrices, and periodically review safety culture matrices through surveying so as to hold managers and supervisors accountable for safety outcomes in the workplace. It is perhaps in consideration of occupational health and safety practices as a cornerstone of corporate social responsibility (CSR) that the full cost of occupational health and safety failure can be most appreciated (see Smallman & John, 2001; Hart, 2010; Carroll & Shabana, 2010). Smallman and John (2001, p. 231) further argued that, at a strategic level, occupational safety outcomes can be considered a "determinant of firm status, specifically corporate image and identity". In this sense, the case for investing in better occupational safety outcomes may represent strategic value to the business, rather than simply an avenue for immediate economic value.

MATERIAL AND METHODOLOGY

The study employed qualitative research method, involving collection, analyzing and interpreting qualitative data thereby integrating conclusions from those data into a cohesive whole. Qualitative method design was selected to obtain comprehensive information from extant literatures, empirical evidences and from management and employees concerning OHS practices in the Nigerian workplaces. The terms reflecting OHS included like workplace safety, safety management system, relationship between safety and quality, quality and safety, workplace health, industrial health, industrial safety, occupational safety, employee health, safety, work, health, manufacturing safety, working environment, safety committee, and workplace. More than these key terms were utilized in different approaches in line with expected methodologies that any researchers can use. The literature reviewed has attempted to identify related article with occupational safety and health hazards identification or hazards controlling mechanisms. The materials consulted were basically from electronic database and extant literatures. A comprehensive meta-analysis of more than 50 studies, reports, policies, standards and manuals were obtained from some selected databases, research and thematic papers for analysis. Depending on the relevance of the materials, the most important data considering recent publications and reading methodology and results of the papers were considered appropriate. The objective is to focus on how the workplace safety and health hazards are happening, to see current state of the art of the researches summit and to identify the drawback from previously conducted researches. The gaps that exist can be filled by the overall research works considering further research areas.

FOCUS OF THE CHAPTER: OCCUPATIONAL HEALTH AND SAFETY VIOLATIONS AND PROBLEMS IN NIGERIA

According Idubor and Oisamoje (2013) a number of conditions are responsible for the high level of violation of occupational health and safety regulations. These condionalities are identified and explained as follows:

- **Lack of Strict Judicial References:** There is a general lack of strict judicial references and strict human rights compliance is not sufficiently embedded in the national law, such as labor law, non-discrimination legislation, health and safety rights in corporations (HRIRC, 2009). Nigeria, like many other developing countries was subjected to repressive and undemocratic rule for long periods. This perhaps explains the unwillingness and inability on the part of government to enforce compliance to democratic requirements of human rights (Idubor & Oisamoje, 2013).

- **Weak Legal and National Occupational Health and Safety Standard Structures:** The legal structures and policy framework for enforcement of OHS regulations in place in Nigeria are rather very weak, particularly in terms of the interpretation and applications of the law. The standard of occupational health and safety in Nigeria is weak hence even when there is some compliance to safety and health regulations, it is regarded as excessive whereas in reality the compliance is just meeting the minimum requirements. When Corporations violate labour laws, the penalty for such violations is ridiculously liberal for these organizations (Dobro & Oisamoje, 2013). For example, under the Workmen's Compensation Act as enshrined in the 1999 constitution (section 4), the penalty for violating the requirement that an employer must insure every workman employed by him against injury or death is: "on conviction for a second or subsequent offense to a fine equivalent to the premium payable for the year in question in respect of the number of workmen employed by him or the sum of N2, 000 whichever is greater". It is only recently that the labor safety, health and welfare bill of 2012 have upwardly reviewed the rates of some violations to a fine of N500, 000 for individuals or N2m in the case of a corporate organization.
- **Corruption and Bribery:** This is perhaps the biggest problem in occupational health and safety violations in Nigeria. The Factory's act for instance clearly stipulates the criteria that are to be met by a desiring organization but most times the standards are not met yet the company has a license duly issued by the regulatory body to operate. The license presupposes that all the conditions have been met and all needed equipment and facilities provided. During yearly inspection of facilities, some companies that operate under substandard conditions are certified okay repeatedly on the payment of bribes. Another aspect of this is that most of these companies either belong to high-ranking government officials or their friends and relatives. Hence even when the inspecting officer is prepared to do his job the right way, he or she may often have "orders from above" preventing any sanction from being placed on the erring companies.
- **Lack of Corporate Responsibility and Accountability:** Many of the corporations that operate in Nigeria are multinational and they have laws that govern their operations in their parent countries. The usual practice in Nigeria is that such laws and regulations are suspended when operating in Nigeria. Such companies and corporation conveniently forget those laws and operate with a shocking lack of corporate responsibility and accountability.

The fact that certain unwholesome practices are tolerated, even accepted in Nigeria ought not to prevent these multinational companies from being socially responsible as if they were in their parent country.

- **High Rate of Unemployment and Low Educational Level of the Workforce:** Unemployment rate in Nigeria is alarming so much so that people are ready to work under dehumanizing and unsafe conditions just to have a job. As a result, more labor-intensive industries like agriculture, mining and construction have large workforces, which are mainly poorly educated. This lack of sufficient education usually prevents the workforce from fully understanding the implications of working in hazardous conditions. Even when they do, they are unable to effectively muster a force that will not only demand for but also obtain safer working conditions. More often than not people count themselves lucky for even having the job in the first place so agitating for safer working conditions is not a priority with them. Job security is a luxury for many as most of these companies hire them as contract staff or as causal workers.
- **High Cost of Doing Business in Nigeria:** The entrepreneur in Nigeria is faced with enormous problems in attempting to run a business. Most often than not, they have to provide power station (i.e. electricity) for their business at a very high cost, provide his own water plants and sometimes construct a motor able road to business place. All these tremendously increases the cost of doing business and after spending so much on infrastructure that Government is supposed to provide, therefore, entrepreneurs begins to cut corners on provision of a safe place of work for his employees.

Identifying safety and health problems in the workplace can be as easy as answering basic questions on hazards propensity at work. To determine if there are health and safety problems that need to be addressed and fixed in any workplace, the following questions requires answers:

- Do you or your co-workers have injuries or health complaints? If so, what types?
- Who has been hurt or is having symptoms of minor or major health issues?
- When do you or your co-workers feel these symptoms?
- Where in the workplace are safety or health problems occurring?
- What are the conditions that are causing the problems?

Nevertheless, the following "Caution Health Hazards" and "Caution Safety Hazards" Tables 1 and 2 provide more information to the various sources of health and safety issues at work.

Table 1.

CAUTION: Health Hazards
Common Types of Health Hazards in the Workplace are: • chemical (asbestos, solvents, chlorine) • Biological (tuberculosis, HIV, hepatitis, molds) • Physical (noise, heat and cold, radiation, vibration) • Ergonomics or Repetitive Strain Injuries (carpal tunnel syndrome, back injuries) • Psychological (stress)
How Health Hazards Enter Human Body • Breathing (inhalation) • Swallowing (ingestion) • Skin (absorption) • Cuts (injection)
Harm Caused by Health Hazards Depends on: • Strength, or potency, of the agent or reagent • amount of the agent that is present • how long you are exposed to the agent • Part of your body that is exposed
Types of Health Effects • Acute: the effect shows up right away • Chronic: problems show up after a long period of exposure and/or long after the exposure ends • Local: only the part of the body was exposed is affected • Systemic: an agent enters the body and affects other parts of the body
Cancer: • Cancer is a term for many diseases in different parts of the body • Carcinogens are agents that cause cancer • There are no totally safe level of exposure to something that causes cancer • Cancer from a workplace exposure may develop 10, 20, or more years after exposure
Sensitization: • People may become allergic or sensitive to some agents they are working with. • Sensitization can develop over time • For example, a health care worker may develop a serious allergic reaction to latex used in gloves
Reproductive Effects • both men and women can be affected by reproductive hazards at work • Reproductive hazards cause miscarriages and birth defects

Source: Safe Jobs Now: An AFSCME Guide to Health and Safety in the Workplace

SOLUTIONS AND RECOMMENDATIONS

Appropriate Legal and Policy Framework

Promotion and maintenance of highest degree of physical, mental and social well-being of workers in all occupation is majorly a function of government through appropriate OHS regulations and laws, as well as executive wills of leadership in work organizations. Government must do the needful by enacting standard and comprehensive OHS regulations with appropriate legal and policy framework

Table 2.

CAUTION: Safety Hazards
Common Types of Safety Hazards in the Workplace are: • Slips, trips and falls • Being caught in or struck by moving machinery or other objects • Fire and explosions • Transportation and vehicle-related accidents • Confined spaces • Violence
Slips, Trips and Falls • Bad house-keeping and poor drainage can make floors and other walking surfaces wet and slippery. • Electrical wires along rhea floor pose a tripping hazard • People can fall if they are not provided with fall protection equipment, guardrail, and safe ladders.
Caught in or Struck by Moving Machinery/Objects • Machinery can cause injuries in different ways: • People can get parts of their body caught in or struck by exposed moving parts of machines if they are not properly guarded, or not locked out when being repaired • People can be struck by flying objects from machines without protective guards.
Fire and Explosions • Improper labeling, handling or storage of certain materials can pose a risk of fire or explosion • Every workplace should have an evacuation plan for getting people out of a building in case of fire and an alarm or alert system to quickly inform employees of an emergency • Every worker should be trained on what to do in case of an emergency
Transportation and Vehicle-Related Accidents: • Operators of vehicles and equipment can be injured or cause injury to pedestrians if equipment is unsafe or if adequate training has not been provided • People can be seriously injured or killed after being hit by a vehicle while repairing roads of doing other work in traffic zones. This danger exists when traffic is not properly routed and/or adequate barriers are not placed between the workers and the traffic
Confined Spaces: • An area with small openings for a worker to enter or exit and is not designed for regular work. Examples of confined spaces include manholes, sewer digesters, and silos. There are many hazards in confined spaces. • Workers can become unconscious and die from a lack of oxygen • There may be too much oxygen, or other chemicals that can catch fire or explode. • Poisonous gases and vapor, such as hydrogen sulfide or carbon monoxide, may also build up in a confined space • Confined spaces can also pose physical hazards. They can be very hot or cold, very loud, or slippery and wet. • Grain, sand or gravel can bury a worker.
Violence: • Violence on the job is growing problem. • Homicides are the second leading cause of workplace fatalities. Workplace violence includes physical assault as well as near misses, verbal abuse and sexual harassment

Source: Safe Jobs Now: An AFSCME Guide to Health and Safety in the Workplace

to monitor strict compliance to occupational health and safety provisions in the country (e.g. National Occupational Health and Safety Act 85 of 1993 in South Africa; Occupational Health and Safety Administration –OSHA in Unite States of America; Health Safety Executive –HSE regulations in the UK.

Government and management of business organizations can show leadership in preventing safety and health risks at the workplace (EU-OSHA, 2012). In an attempt to seek solutions to modern workplace OHS issues, EU-OSHA (2012) has identified leadership as a key factor, hence, EU-OSHA (2012) have suggested three key underlying management principles for enhancing safety and health. These are:

1. Effective and strong leadership
2. Involving workers and their constructive engagement, and
3. Ongoing assessment and review

These three points are explored in more detail below:

1. **Effective and Strong Leadership:** Leadership is a condition for success. A preventive approach is only likely to be fruitful if it is supported by the management. A strong and visible leadership and engaged managers at all levels can provide direction and input to this preventive approach (EU-OSHA, 2012). This makes it clear to everyone that safety and health are strategic questions within the company. In practice, according to EU-OSHA (2012) this means that:
    a. Management commits itself to occupational safety and health as a core value of the organization and communicates this to the employees. That is, will "collective will" or "Political will" must be present. It is about (the government, employers and employees) wanting to and doing the right things always.
    b. Managers have an accurate picture of the risk profile of the organization, thereby engaged themselves with continuous appraisal and review of OHS regulations and standards.
    c. management leads by example and demonstrates leadership integrity, for example, by following all occupational safety and health rules at all times;
    d. Management and private businesses/agencies must commit themselves to training and development of OHS professionals in various OHS activities
    e. the roles and responsibilities of different actors in preventing and managing health and safety risks at the workplace are clearly defined and planned and
    f. Monitored proactively through active and continuous awareness OHS regulation and also making OHS certification of the criteria to be fulfilled before businesses are registered by corporate Affairs Commission (CAC) or enlisted into and retained on the Nigerian Stock Exchange (SEC).

   g. Occupational health and safety can feature in the company's sustainability and/or corporate social responsibility strategy and may be encouraged throughout the supply chain.

2. **Involving Workers and Their Constructive Engagement:** The two-way process of involving workers and their constructive engagement is important in the success of management initiatives. Employers must consult their employees about health and safety. This includes: provision of information; instruction and training; and engaging in consultation with workers and their representatives (EU-OSHA, 2012). Depending on national requirements, employers may be required to establish safety committees and the post of workers' representative. Worker participation helps to establish a culture of dialogue. Workers and their representatives are encouraged to take part in health and safety decision-making. Some employers have found benefits in going beyond these legal obligations. They encourage active health and safety involvement on a daily basis and also include workers in additional forums such as working groups on specific topics (EU-OSHA, 2012).
3. **Effective Upward Communication:** Is a recommended panacea for management intervention in health and safety at work — workers are listened to and what they say is acted upon. Equally importantly, workers accept their responsibility to follow the health and safety rules at the workplace, and are engaged with management in a constructive and helpful way (EU-OSHA, 2012). This two-way process creates a culture where relationships between employers and workers are based on collaboration, trust and joint problem-solving. And once established this culture has the potential for health and safety improvements.
4. **Ongoing Assessment and Review:** Monitoring and reporting are vital tools for enhancing workplace safety and health. Management systems which provide, for example, the company board members with specific (e.g. incident-led) and routine reports on the performance of health and safety policies can be useful in raising issues, highlighting problems and ultimately enhancing workplace safety and health (EU-OSHA, 2012). According to EU-OSHA (2012) elements of a good assessment and review system include:
   a. Procedures for reporting major health and safety failures to the company board members and owners as soon as is practical;
   b. Systems for capturing and reporting accurate and timely incident data such as accident and sickness rates;
   c. Arrangements for eliciting and incorporating worker views and experiences;
   d. Periodic reports of the impact that preventive schemes such as training and maintenance programmers have on occupational health and safety;

e. Regular audits of the effectiveness of risk controls and management;
f. Assessments of the impact that changes such as the introduction of new work processes, procedures or products have on safety and health;
g. Effective procedures for implementing new and altered legal requirements.

5. Some Recommendations for the Organizations
   a. Adequate training is needed among the workers, as most of the workforce especially the factory workers lack basic education. Pasting just information on the notice board containing information on the operating standard and procedures are not enough as many of them cannot read or write.
   b. Medical screening should be done periodically to ascertain the state of workers' health. Most of the occupational diseases gradually affect the health of the workers without them knowing, if this could be found earlier enough, a lot could be done to salvage the lives of workers.
   c. Management commitment both to better health and safety performance and participative arrangements coupled with the provision for preventive OHS are strategies for ensuring the quality and efficiency of production Support for workers' representation from trade unions in workplaces, especially in the provision of information and training, most non-unionize organizations leave the issue of occupational health exclusively to the management alone. Workers must be involved in the formulation and implementation of OHS policies.
   d. Trade unions should compel their members to comply with OHS rules, understanding its importance to their life. The issues of OHS should be a collaborative effort and a responsibility of all both the management and workers. Accidents and injuries must be reported the appropriate authority irrespective of the treat of the management.
   e. The Federal Ministry of Labor should rise to their duty for periodic inspection of the work environment and Factories in Nigeria to ensure strict compliance of the factories to factories regulations and also pay appropriate compensation to the victims of occupational hazard (Ngwama, 2016).
6. Some Recommendations for Managers
   a. **Plan:** Set the direction for effective health and safety management by setting long-term organizational improvement targets and develop positive performance indicators at both an organizational and business unit level. Add targets that drive improvements in areas of identified risk and return to work performance for the agency. Make occupational health and safety and injury management a standing item on executive meeting agendas. Consider occupational health and safety and injury management implications when developing organizational change and

human resource management strategies. Develop a strategy to address the information and training needs of the agency's managers.

b. **Monitor:** Arrange for updates to be provided to the agency's management group on emerging OSH and injury management issues relevant to the agency's business. Ensure line managers' report to executive management on workplace injuries, measures taken to prevent further injury and the rehabilitation support provided to injured employees. Allocate accountability for workers' compensation costs to a divisional level.

c. **Review:** Set baseline data so that performance improvements can be measured. Regularly review OHS and injury management systems and audit tools. Engage suitably qualified professionals to conduct impartial in-house audits or reviews, with appropriate employee and employer involvement. Incorporate the scheduling of these reviews into agency corporate governance or audit plans. Provide comprehensive report of OHS performance in the company's annual management reports. Reward excellence in OHS and injury management performance as part of organizational reward and recognition programs.

d. **Deliver:** Allocate resources to identify, assess and remedy areas of risk. Clearly specify management's OSH and injury management responsibilities in agency-wide OSH and injury management policies and procedures. Develop and then undertake an improvement program for the agency. Apply adopted work health and safety policies and measures consistently throughout your agency, whether over time or in different operational areas within the agency. Identify agency improvement priorities based on achieving targets and controlling injury risks.

FUTURE RESEARCH DIRECTION

Future research direction would be required on how health impact occupational diseases and injuries workplaces in private and public sectors in Nigeria, using qualitative and quantitative research approaches.

CONCLUSION

Health impact of occupational diseases and injuries in Nigeria workplaces is difficult to assess, because there is no consensus on the data. Despite this difficulty, International Labor Organization (ILO) estimates suggest that thousands of people die each year as a result of occupational diseases and industrial accidents. This understanding underscores the need for more awareness, education, training, advocacy for corporate commitment, legal policy framework and enforcement of occupational health and safety compliance in the country. Occupational Health and Safety systems in developed and emerging economies such as Nigeria are designed to identify and minimize risks at the workplace. Definitely there is more to gain, and nothing to lose from the implementation of OHS in Nigeria. If all the industries (government {federal and states} and private; small, medium and big scale; formal and informal) in the country embrace OHS, then one can imagine how well the health and well-being of the people will be immensely promoted and improved alongside the numerous job and employment opportunities that will be created on the overall. The relative importance of occupational health and safety in emerging economies is of utmost concern bearing in mind the unusual attendant consequences as occasioned by high rate occupational diseases, accidents, injuries and fatalities. Moreover, workplace in uniquely characterizes by large population, low cost/low knowledge workers, poor literacy rates etc. which makes industrial accidents and fatality almost inevitable. Little wonder, in today's workplaces thriving business communities are learning to seek to create jobs, wealth, good leadership, safe and healthy working conditions that are essential for production of goods and provision of services and minimize industrial accidents and fatalities. Organization that will create workplaces of the future, and sustain the blistering economic growth as well as enhancing quality of life as a whole must seek to institute enduring occupational health and safety systems, driven by appropriate leadership. However, there are many issues that need to be overcome in the areas of awareness, education, training, corporate commitment and leadership readiness, as well as legal policy framework for regulating compliance. There is need for political will, and for all the relevant stakeholders to come together in order to seek the actualization of this lofty vision in Nigeria. All these are very much possible, only if the relevant and comprehensive occupational health and safety laws are passed by the various states and national assembly because globally, the practice of occupational health and safety is mainly driven by appropriate OHS policies and legislation.

REFERENCES

Ahsan, M. R., & Partaken, T. (2001). Occupational health and safety in the least developed countries: A simple case of neglect. *Journal of Epidemiology*, *11*(2), 74–80. doi:10.2188/jea.11.74 PMID:11388496

Ahuja-Young. (2012). *Safety and health: Issues and perspectives, a conference paper delivered to Nigeria union of journalist on health and safety issues in Nigeria, Benin City, Nigeria.* Academic Press.

Allis, R. J. (2009). Leadership–the five big ideas. *Strategy and Leadership*, *37*(2), 4–12. doi:10.1108/10878570910941163

Ardichvili, A. & Kuchinke, K.P. (2002). Leadership styles and cultural values among managers and subordinates: a comparative study of four countries of the former Soviet Union, Germany and the US. *Human Resource Development International*, *5*(1), 99–117.

Bankole, R & Lawal, O.I. (2012). Percieved influence of health education on occupational health of factory workers in Lagos state, Nigeria. *British Journal of Arts and Social Sciences, 8*(1), 56-77.

Barling, J., Kelloway, E. K., & Iverson, R. D. (2003). High-quality work, job satisfaction and occupational injuries. *The Journal of Applied Psychology*, *88*(2), 276–283. doi:10.1037/0021-9010.88.2.276 PMID:12731711

Barling, J., Loghlin, C., & Kelloway, E. K. (2002). Development and test of a model linking safety-specific transformational leadership and occupational safety. *The Journal of Applied Psychology*, *87*(3), 488–496. doi:10.1037/0021-9010.87.3.488 PMID:12090606

Bel, R. (2010). Leadership and innovation: Learning from the best. *Global Business and Organizational Excellence*, *29*(2), 47–60. doi:10.1002/joe.20308

Bramming, P., Raastrup Kristensen, A., & Pedersen, M. (2009). The entry of self-leadership into work environment research. *Working Environment Challenges for the Future. Seminar Proceedings.*

Carrol, A. B., & Shabana, K. M. (2010). The business case for corporate social responsibility: A review of concepts, research and practice. *International Journal of Management Reviews*, *12*(1), 85–105. doi:10.1111/j.1468-2370.2009.00275.x

Christiani, D. C., Durvasula, R., & Myers, J. (1990). Occupational health in developing countries: Review of research needs. *American Journal of Industrial Medicine*, *17*(3), 393–401. doi:10.1002/ajim.4700170311 PMID:2407119

Davis, K. (1986). *Human Behaviour at Work.* New York: McGraw-Hill Book Company.

EU-OSHA, European Agency for Safety and Health at Work. (2010). *European survey of enterprises on new and emerging risks –managing safety and health at work.* Available at: http://osha.europa.eu/en/publications/reports/esener1_osh_management

EU-OSHA, European Agency for Safety and Health at Work. (2011). *European survey of enterprises on new and emerging risks –ESENER. Methodology.* Retrieved 26 April 2011, from: http://osha.europa.eu/en/riskobservatory/enterprise-survey/methodology-1EU-OSHA

Fajana, S. (2012). Safety at work: Issues and challenges. Paper delivered to Nigeria union of journalist on health and safety issues in Nigeria, Benin City, Nigeria.

Falana, F. (2010, November). Nigeria: Legal framework for workplace safety. Daily Independence.

Gahan, P., Sievewright, B., & Evans, P. (2014). *Workplace health and safety, business productivity and sustainability.* A report by prepared by the Centre for Workplace Leadership, University of Melbourne funded by Safe Work Australia.

Good, C. V. (1959). *Dictionary of Education* (2nd ed.). New York: McGraw Hill.

Gordon, A., & Yukl, G. (2004). The future leadership research: Challenges and opportunities. *German Journal of Human Resource Research, 18*(3), 359–365.

Halpin, A. W. (1956). *The leadership behaviour of school superintendents.* Columbus, OH: College of Education, The Ohio State University.

Hart, S. (2010). Self-regulation, corporate social responsility and the business case: Do they work in achieving workplace equality and safety? *Journal of Business Ethics, 92*(4), 585–600. doi:10.100710551-009-0174-1

Health Safety Executive. (2001). *A guide to measuring health and safety performance.* HSE. Retrieved from: http://www.hse.go.uk/opsunit/perfmeas.pdf

Heaney, R., & Irlicht, L. (2007). The impact of occupation health and safety policy on firm value. *Economic Papers, 26*(4), 308–320. doi:10.1111/j.1759-3441.2007.tb01017.x

Hemphill, J. K. (1945). *Situational factors in leadership.* Columbia, OH: Ohio State University.

Hersey, P., & Blanchard, K. H. (1988). *Management of organizational behaviour, utilizing human resources* (5th ed.). Prentice-Hall International, Inc.

Herzberg, F. (2003). One more time: How do you motivate employees? *Harvard Business Review*, 20–31. PMID:12545925

House, R. J., & Aditya, R. N. (1997). The social scientific study of leadership: Quo vadis? *Journal of Management*, *23*(3), 409–473. doi:10.1177/014920639702300306

Idubor, E. E., & Oisamoje, M. D. (2013). An exploration of health and safety management issues in nigeria's effort to industrialise. *European Scientific Journal*, *9*(12), 154–169.

Inness, M., Turner, N., Barling, J., & Stride, C. B. (2010). Transformational leadership and employee safety performance: A within-person, between -jobs design. *Journal of Occupational Health Psychology*, *15*(3), 279–290. doi:10.1037/a0019380 PMID:20604634

Internal Expert Seminar, Danish Working Environment Authority. (2009). *Partnership for European Research in Occupational Safety and Health (PEROSH)*, 53–56.

International Labor Organization. (2006). *Occupational safety and health: synergies between security and productivity*. Retrieved from http://www.ilo.org/wcmsp5/groups/public/@ed_protect/@protrav/@safework/documents/meetingdocument/wcms_110380.pdf

International Labour Organisation. (2006). *Occupational safety and health synergiesbetween security and productivity*. Retrieved from http://www.ilo.org/wcmsp5/group/public/@ed_protect@safework

International Labour Organisation. (2010). *Work related accidents and diseases take a heavy toll worldwide.* Retrieved from: http://www.scielosp.org/scielo.php

International Labour Organisation. (2012). *Safety and health at work, hopes and challenges in development cooperation development: The example of an EU-ILO joint project "Improving safety and health at work through a decent health agenda"*. Retrieved from http://www.ilo.org/wcmsp5/group/public/---ed

Jilcha, K., & Kitaw, D. (2016). A literature review on global occupational safety and health practice and accidents severity. *International Journal of Qualitative Research, 10*(2), 279–310.

Joubert, D. M. (2002). Occupational health challenges and success in developing countries: A South African perspective. *International Journal of Environment and Health*, *8*, 119–124. PMID:12019678

Keys, B., & Case, J. (1990). How to become an influential manager. *The Academy of Management Executive*, *44*, 38–51.

Koontz, H., & Weihrich, H. (1990). *Essentials of Management*. New York: McGraw-Hill.

LaDou, J. (2003). International occupational health. *International Journal of Hygiene and Environmental Health*, *206*(4-5), 303–313. doi:10.1078/1438-4639-00226 PMID:12971685

Linhard, J. B. (2005). Understanding the return on health, safety and environmental investments. *Journal of Safety Research*, *36*(3), 257–260. doi:10.1016/j.jsr.2005.06.007 PMID:16038936

Machida, S. (2009). Accident prevention – a safe workplace. *Occupational Health & Safety (Waco, Tex.)*, *19*(1), 102–112.

Mendes, R. (1985). The scope of occupational health in developing countries. *American Journal of Public Health*, *75*(5), 467–648. doi:10.2105/AJPH.75.5.467 PMID:3985233

Meswani, H. R. (2008). Safety and occupational health: Challenges and Opportunities in emerging economies. *Indian Journal of Occupational and Environmental Medicine*, *12*(1), 3–9. doi:10.4103/0019-5278.40808 PMID:20040990

Michaels, D., Barrera, C., & Gacharna, M. G. (1985). Economic development and occupational health in Latin America: New directions for public health in less developed countries. *American Journal of Public Health*, *75*(5), 536–542. doi:10.2105/AJPH.75.5.536 PMID:3985242

Miller, P., Mulvey, C., & Norris, K. (1997). Compensating differentials for risk of death in Australia. *The Economic Record*, *73*(223), 363–373. doi:10.1111/j.1475-4932.1997.tb01008.x

Mockaitis, A. I. (2005). A cross-cultural study of leadership attitudes in three Baltic Sea region countries. *International Journal of Leadership Studies*, *1*(1), 44–63.

Mokikan, N. (2012). *Realities of employee compensation in the workplace*. Paper delivered to the Nigerian union of journalist on health and safety issues in Nigeria, Benin City, Nigeria.

Ngwama, J. C. (2016). Framework for occupational health and safety in Nigeria: The implication for the trade union movement. *Journal of Economics and Sustainable Development*, *7*(11), 113–121.

O'Neill, D. (2000). Ergonomics in industrially developing countries: Does its application differ from that in industrially advanced countries? *Applied Ergonomics, 31*(6), 631–640. doi:10.1016/S0003-6870(00)00033-8 PMID:11132047

Onuegbu, C. (2010). *Emerging risks and new patterns of prevention in a changing world of work.* Paper presented at 2010 world day for safety and health at work, 28th April 2010 organised by Federal Ministry of Labor & Productivity.

Perrow, C. (1984). *Normal accidents: Living with high-risk technologies.* New York, NY: Basic Book.

Smallman, C., & John, G. (2001). British directors' perspectives on the impact of health and safety on corporate performance. *Safety Science, 38*(3), 227–39.

Steiger, T. (2003). Das Rollenkonzept der Führung. In Handbuch Angewandte Psychologie für Führungskräfte. Führungskompetenz und Führungswissen (2nd ed.). Springer.

Swuste, P., & Eijkemans, G. (2002). Occupational safety, health and hygiene in the urban informal sector of Sub-Saharan Africa: An Application of the Prevention and Control Exchange (PACE) program to the informal-sector workers in healthy city projects. *International Journal of Occupational and Environmental Health, 8*(2), 113–118. doi:10.1179/oeh.2002.8.2.113 PMID:12019677

Tadesse, T., & Kumie, A. (2007). Prevalenve and factors affecting work-related injury among workers engaged in Small and Medium-scale industries in Gondar wereda, North Gondor zone, Amhara Regional State, Ethiopia. *The Ethiopian Journal of Health Development, 21*(1). doi:10.4314/ejhd.v21i1.10028

Takala, J. (1999). International agency efforts to protect workers and the environment. *The International Journal of Occupational and Environmental Medicine, 15*(1), 30–37. doi:10.1179/oeh.1999.5.1.30 PMID:10092745

Tannenbaum, R., Weschler, I. R., & Massarik, F. (1961). *Leadership and Organization, A Behaviour Science Approach.* New York: McGraw-Hill.

Terry, G. R. (1988). *Principles of Management.* Richard D. Irwin.

World Health Organization. (2010). *The health promoting work place.* Retrieved from: http://www.cepis.org.pe/bvsast/i/full-text/whp/whp.html

Yuki, G. A., & Van-Fleet, D. D. (1998). Theory and Research on Leadership in Organizations. In Handbook of Industrial and Organizational Psychology. Mambai: Jaico Publishing House.

Yukl, G. A. (1994). *Leadership in organisations*. Englewood Cliffs, NJ: Prentice Hall.

Yusuf, S., Moges, H., & Ahmed, A. (2014). Magnitude and characteristics of occupational injury in Kombolcha textile factory, North East Ethiopia. *International Journal of Occupational Safety and Health, 3*(2). doi:10.3126/ijosh.v3i2.8381

KEY TERMS AND DEFINITIONS

Leadership: Is defined as the exercise of authority in initiating, directing, or controlling the behavior or attitude of others, and bring out their consent; those qualities of personality and training, which make the guidance and control of others successful.

Occupational Health: Is defined as the promotion and maintenance of the highest degree of physical, mental, and social wellbeing of workers in all occupation.

Workplace Health and Safety (WHS): Is a multidisciplinary field concerned with the safety, health, and welfare of people at work. It is a field of healthcare concerned with enabling an individual to undertake their occupation, in the way that causes least harm to their health.

Chapter 11
Social Organizations in Health: Public-Private Facilities Management

Paulo Oliveira Vasconcelos Filho
University of São Paulo, Brazil

ABSTRACT

The government's direct administration of public health facilities has proved to be bureaucratic and of low quality. Therefore, governments are trying new management models for some healthcare facilities using public-private partnerships (PPP). One kind of PPP is deployment of social organizations. Social organizations are nongovernmental nonprofit organizations created in Brazil, in the 1990s, engaged in such activities as teaching, research, technological development, or protection and conservation of the environment. Nonprofits enter PPPs created specifically for the purpose of running health facilities, and the state department of health monitors and evaluates contracts with them. This chapter's objective is to analyze the implementation process of the social organizations management program, focusing on the role played by factors such as administrative and financial autonomy, direction, innovative management practices, and gains in efficiency of the health facility. The chapter discusses differences between direct government management and administration by social organizations.

INTRODUCTION

Building an appropriate healthcare system that meets the needs of the population requires years of planning. Many players in healthcare systems have suggested solutions for delivering assistance programs to distinct populations. Furthermore, there is intense concern about state fiscal crises arising from the decrease in world economic growth, and the implications for the process of funding public policies.

DOI: 10.4018/978-1-5225-6133-0.ch011

In both developed and developing countries, the quality of care in public health facilities is usually perceived as inadequate or insufficient (Caballer-Tarazona & Vivas-Consuelo, 2016). Mainly in developing countries, the State is the only entity capable of building health facilities. Consequently, it inherits the facility's management. However, the State's direct administration of healthcare facilities has not been shown to adequately serve the best interest of the local community. In India, for instance, the patients treated in public hospitals are not satisfied with the attendance, due to overcrowding, poor infrastructure, and long waiting times (Baliga, Ravikiran, Rao, Coutinho, & Jain, 2016). There are many examples of misuse of resources, lack of materials or medications, and low professional satisfaction (Gerschman, 1999; Reich, 2002). People with few financial resources are kept from enjoying good treatment and good health. Thus, one fundamental aspect of these debates concerns the management of health units belonging to the State.

Furthermore, governments cannot face an increase in public spending because due to limited financing capacity (Bertucci & Alberti, 2001). State budgets face many challenges, including globalization, reduced economic growth, and monetary instability. In response, an open discussion has begun in the last three decades about the role of the State and its ability to respond to the challenges this situation poses. At the least, the debate expresses the confrontation between conceptions about the role of the State and its standards for intervention in the society. The need for State restructuring has given rise to mobilizing a great deal of energy and theoretical thinking to present possible alternatives for solving the problem (Barbosa & Elias, 2010; Bresser-Pereira, Nassif, & Feijo, 2016).

Even the World Health Organization (WHO) is following the early success of a number of high-profile partnerships South America and Africa, and increasingly working with the private for-profit sector in what is known as a Public Private Partnership (PPP). Doing so promotes a vibrant debate among public, civic, and commercial entities in society about the appropriate modes of interaction among them. The strategy is to direct the debate on issues critical to WHO and its role in the promotion and protection of public health (Buse & Waxman, 2001; Widdus, 2001).

Different modalities of public-private partnership (PPP) for provision of such public services as healthcare have proliferated (La Forgia & Harding, 2009; Roehrich, Lewis, & George, 2014; Alonso, Clifton, & Diaz-Fuentes, 2016). The private responsibility varies from full privatization to merely issuing a management contract. One management model for some healthcare facilities or hospitals is the deployment of Social Organizations (SO). Created, in Brazil, specifically for running public health facilities, they are engaged in management contracts monitored and evaluated by the Regional Health Department (RHD) (Seixas, 2003; Barbosa & Elias, 2010). Some local research studies on the experience of the SO management model point to its competitive advantage, as compared to State Direct Administration Units

(SDAU) (Ibañez, Bittar, Sá, Yamamoto, Almeida, & Castro, 2001; Ferreira, 2002; Seixas, 2003). However, until now, the studies conducted by academic programs or RHDs have not referred to elements influencing the efficiency of the units under SO models, compared to the units under direct state administration.

This chapter's objective is to analyze the implementation process of SO management, focusing on the role of factors such as administrative and financial autonomy, direction and use of instruments, and innovative management practices. These factors are conditional for the gain in health facility efficiency, and the chapter discusses the differences between government direct management and social organization management in healthcare facility administration.

BACKGROUND

United Nations General Comment 14 of the Committee on Economic, Social, and Cultural Rights (2011) (Article 12), created by a committee of independent experts responsible for overseeing adherence to the covenant, defines the right to health. The right includes the following core components: availability (i.e., the need for a sufficient quantity of functioning public health and healthcare facilities, goods and services, and programs for all); accessibility (i.e., health facilities, goods, and services accessible to everyone); acceptability (i.e., attending to the specific needs of diverse population groups); and quality.

According to the WHO Constitution (2006), "the highest attainable standard of health as a fundamental right of every human being" is a State's obligation, including maximizing resources in health policy and programs that prioritize the needs of population health in an equal way. No matter what the level of resources at their disposal, progressive governments must take immediate steps within their means toward the fulfillment of these rights. Regardless of resource capacity, they must act to eliminate discrimination and improve the legal and judicial systems, with immediate effect.

Over the last thirty years, a series of measures has been implemented that aim to adapt the State and its policies to changes in the dynamics of population growth and capitalist accumulation in the world. The emergence of a new stage in the process of internationalization of the economy, known as globalization, with ramifications for other fields of human activity such as healthcare, has marked the proposed agenda for confronting these changes (Elias, 2004).

The power of the State to drive these macroeconomic adjustments is part of a debate around how much size and presence the State must have to serve the society. This question arises between two major concepts—opposition to liberal views (minimal State), and social democracy (welfare state)—on a continuum that passes through various hues. The neoliberal project represents the response of governments aligned with the strategy of reducing the role of the State, transferring the provision and financing of goods and public services to a laissez-faire free-market economy (Bresser-Pereira, Nassif, & Feijo, 2016). The views that give rise to the debate point to the growth of the State manifesting as interventions in the social order on one hand, and on the other the crisis resulting from State growth. What should the effort to streamline and reorganize State social policies look like? The conflict between increasing costs and containing the deficit in the public sector is political and ideological in nature, marked by the end of the experience of real socialism and the consequent strengthening of belief in the power of the market. However, the economic crisis of 2008 resulted in a financial State budget plunge, despite all the growth the economy had shown in the beginning of the last decade. The rate of economic activity was below expected growth in the decade's latter years (Villarreal, 2010).

The development of health programs shows a profound transformation in assistance delivery, a marked incorporation of technology, and trends in population aging. These transformations, objectives related to epidemiological (chronic degenerative diseases prevalence) and demographic (increased life expectancy) aspects of the debate, strongly impacted public policies, notably in health and social security (Barbosa & Elias, 2010). The rise in the economic health index, as a reflection of the age dependency ratio and health costs, displays all the difficulties that health systems face. Administrative actions are necessary to overcome low economic growth and its impacts on public-policy funding.

In this scenario, the management model gains strength over political interests in the approach that public administrators adopt. The management model is based on the development of a new economy characterized by decline of the power of the unions, weakening autonomy of professionals, growth of an elite of public leaders and the fight against rent-seeking[1] and new forms of responsibility. There is greater participation of society in activities previously developed by the State, through privatization, decentralization, and outsourcing (Reich, 2002; Nigenda-López, Juárez-Ramirez, Ruiz-Larios, Herrera, & Ramirez, 2003). The management model has some common principles that include actions to counter time and production waste, performance incentives, and focus on efficiency. The most substantial change in the emergence of this new paradigm relates to the formation of new markets, more employment, and changes in organizational behavior (Boyne, 2002).

The central idea is to stimulate the introduction of market mechanisms into public service, to include the competition among medical-supply providers. Contracts made between suppliers and executors of management contracts, with the purpose of rewarding efficiency in services rendered, utilize the logic of spending the resource only if the user needs it (Buse & Walt, 2000).

PPP models within the public health system boomed during the period of economic crisis. One of the reasons behind this choice is that the private sector has greater capacity to handle the investment in hospitals, freeing the public sector from considerable investment (Barlow, Roehrich & Wright 2013). Nongovernment organizations (NGOs) can execute activities related to the health system, and the government role becomes setting the major guidelines for social development, formulating macroeconomic policies, inducing formation of markets, guiding the priorities for the protection of vulnerable groups, and stimulating citizen co-responsibility in the management of public policies (Buse & Waxman, 2001).

Certain principles and guidelines that converge toward decentralization and the search for efficiency steered the implementation of reforms. Decentralization consisted of the privatization of a number of economic activities the State had carried out, resulting in NGOs incorporating those tasks and actions, and leading to the emergence of social organizations (SO).

Earlier Studies

The last decade saw a proliferation of different modalities of public-private partnership (PPP) for public service in health. This section reviews earlier studies on the subject.

In 2009, La Forgia and Harding analyzed a PPP in a public hospital's performance in São Paulo, Brazil. The PPP model gave facility managers latitude to manage human resources, a critical factor for success. Given the prevalence of direct management of public hospitals in developing countries, São Paulo's experience has implications for policymakers seeking to improve hospital performance through innovation in public-hospital management, and offers a model for other developing countries struggling with the same set of problems.

Giraldes (2007) evaluated hospital quality by comparing public business entities (PBEs) and the public administrative sector (PAS) using quality indicators. She reported that comparing PBE and PAS hospitals with the same characteristics, classified under the same group and conveniently homogenized, showed that PBE hospitals had better results in terms of efficiency.

Another study conducted by Nikjoo, Beyrami, Jannati, and Jaafarabadi (2012) in Iran verified that in the field of public hospitals, expert evidence showed that selections from among the most common PPP options determine the appropriateness of PPP for public hospitals, and the effect of private-sector presence in a public hospital can be readily distinguished.

Corroborating the above findings, Baliga et al. (2016) did an interesting study addressing the perceived quality of care among parents of children admitted to two government district hospitals in India. The satisfaction and perception ratings of responders provided evidence that the perceived quality of hospital care was better in the PPP-model hospital. The study concluded that developing countries could emulate the model to draw patients of lower socioeconomic classes to less expensive tertiary-care public hospitals.

Caballer-Tarazona and Vivas-Consuelo (2016) evaluated the efficiency of the PPP experience in five hospitals in Spain, to identify the influence of private management on the results, by comparing performance, cost, and quality indicators of public and PPP hospitals. The performance and efficiency analysis shows that the PPP group obtains good results, above the average but not always better than those of directly managed hospitals. The paper ends by pointing out the necessity of new studies with a greater number of PPP hospitals to obtain conclusive results.

These studies show a varied range of PPP models with different degrees of responsibility, from simple public-sector contracts with the private provider, to the complete privatization of the service. The involvement of the private sector started with just infrastructure, and now embraces the development, financing, and provision of public infrastructures and delivery services. This provision of public infrastructure or services by the private sector bears significant risk and management responsibility.

MAIN FOCUS OF THE CHAPTER

As mentioned, different models involve diverse forms of risk management, incentive, financing, and payment. One argument in defense of the PPP model maintains that the public sector also has greater incentives for undertaking construction investment leading to operational-cost reduction (Caballer-Tarazona & Vivas-Consuelo, 2016).

The PPP models are classified in categories based on design and build, operation, management, service delivery, ownership, and payment mechanism criteria. Using characteristics discussed in the literature, this chapter compares characteristics of SDAU and SO health facilities. Social organizations are nongovernmental nonprofit organizations created in Brazil in the late 1990s (Ibañez, Bittar, Sá, Yamamoto, Almeida, & Castro, 2001). They are legal entities of interest and public benefit, engaged with activities of teaching, research, technological development, and protection and conservation of the environment. Created specifically for running public health facilities, these organizations are engaged in management contracts with the State.

This chapter has as its objective to observe the implementation process of SO management, focusing on the role of factors such as administrative and financial autonomy, direction and use of instruments, and innovative management practices; and then to compare that with correlates identified in SDAU management. These factors are conditional for the gains in efficiency of health facilities.

Administrative and Financial Autonomy

The administrative and financial autonomy granted to an SO allows it to set limits for acquisition of goods and services, recruitment of human resources, and budgeting all institutional arrangements to ensure the best possible use of resources. The acquisition of goods and services is subject to compliance with established regulations for buying medical products (Buse & Harmer, 2007). This management scheme simplifies the process of goods acquisition, and allows the health service to buy goods at smaller intervals. Simplified procedures require a small number of workstations. The focus is on the needs for a period of consumption, with less use of equipment and a greater turnover in stock. In addition, agility in the execution of the task tends to make it less expensive (Savas, 1990).

The environment found in the SO contrasts with the SDAUs being subject to a set of external rules and bureaucratic rituals that lead to slower and less efficient purchasing of goods and services (Ibañez, Bittar, Sá, Yamamoto, Almeida, & Castro, 2001). The purchasing process in the SDAU has many steps and lasts over long time intervals. Even with scheduled supplier delivery, a purchase generates a large amount of stock and high costs. The same process in the SO has only three steps (request, supplier selection, and stockroom). The possibility of organizing flows of goods and services in an un-bureaucratic way allows the negotiation of payment terms and favorable material replacement for the organization (Barbosa & Elias, 2010).

Another aspect is the model for structuring the decision-making process for acquiring goods and services. In the SDAU, there is a higher level of tension between bureaucrats and health professionals, related to responsibility for defining criteria for specifying the process. In the SO, the tension has moderated toward negotiated solutions. Health professionals rely on just the proof of the effectiveness of materials and supplies listed for purchase, followed by examination in the context of the budget and SO financial capacity (Barbosa & Elias, 2010).

Management Contract

The role of the management contract is to establish targets, goals, and performance indicators for use in the evaluation of these organizations, and then to establish contracted responsibilities as commitments accepted, and to transfer financial resources and technical cooperation needed to achieve the desired results (Ferreira, 2002).

The definition of targets and indicators directs the work processes implemented in the organization. Unified goals among various departments, including the human resources department, guide the results that must be sought by the departmental sectors and professionals. The contracting agency and the hired unit agree upon these targets and indicators, based on the capacity and the unit's historical production records (Barbosa & Elias, 2010).

The managerial capacity of top management in any organization drives the levels of efficiency and effectiveness that the organization reaches. In the case of the SO, the fulfillment of the goals set out in the management contract satisfies the contract (Ferreira, 2002).

Management contracts are fundamental to the discipline in the public-private relationship, but also in interactions with other public entities or between agencies and linkage mediators. The contract establishes the directionality of the work processes for all parties, defining the objectives and goals and the conditions that have to be achieved by the contracting organization. The scope of the management contract, as an efficiency-inducing tool or as an instrument of adjustment between the public and private sectors, enables the management of new units that would be impossible for the State to install directly. In the case of the SO, fulfilling the agreement maintains the contractual linkage. In this sense, observance of the agreed-upon standards guides every management process and organizational effort, focusing on the productive capacity of the units (Barbosa & Elias, 2010).

However, there is a problem with this kind of contract. For long periods, the system of targets and the quest for results can alter the real scope of the organization, and results reflected in the population-health indicators can suffer declines where responsibilities for executing the contract reside.

Instruments and Innovative Managerial Practices

Technologies applied to the organization, its controls, and the evaluations of activities developed to reach defined objectives enable the implementation of instruments and management practices. This process implies the ability to optimize the use of resources available in the organization, and to articulate internal negotiation that aims to reach consensus among the various existing interests (Broom, Turner, Schwab, & Pesely, 2017).

The State Department of Health has the assignment of managing all units' work plans, taking into consideration the objectives and targets agreed upon with the leadership of the unit, and incorporated into the management contract in the case of the SO. In the case of a direct administration unit, the Board or management must report the results. In both cases, the goal adopted is predominantly the evaluation of an historical series of procedures, and the evolution of indicators of quantity and quality of services (Elias, 2004).

In general, any unit's structures and working practices guide the decision-making process and support management. The sectors identified as strategic for this purpose include information systems, cost systems, the Ombudsman's Office, and beyond to management personnel themselves. Information systems fulfill the role of signaling the critical areas regarding established goals, and pointing out what indicators require improvement. Cost systems identify the level of efficiency, taking into consideration the relationship between spending and the number of procedures performed, by sector. The Ombudsman has the function of identifying the level of satisfaction/dissatisfaction with the quality of the service provided (Bittar, 1996).

There is great convergence of methods in the use of these systems in the two kinds of units. An integrated system accessible from several points throughout the units accomplishes monitoring indicators of capacity utilization. This system also informs staff of inventory levels of material and supplies, updated with each request.

Cost systems deployed in the units are also structured using the same methodology (absorption costing) and must operate under the same methodological logic in both the SO and the SDAU. External companies deploy and develop the SO system in order to homogenize the systems applied to these units, and from that principle they establish conditions of comparability among units under this form of management. In the SDAU, the organization's technicians develop the cost of the system, aiming to meet the need of establishing forms of management control over spending, regardless of any external demands (Barbosa & Elias, 2010).

Human Resources

Human resources (HR) management comprises multiple elements (e.g., recruitment, selection, performance incentives, penalties, and administrative costs). In health units operating under the management of a direct administration model, it is possible to verify a low-autonomy situation, over which HR control prevails. A combination of regulatory capacity requirements and the control of personnel costs results from obedience to fiscal responsibility and a centralized HR management policy (André, Ciampone, & Santelle, 2013).

In the SDAU facilities, laws set limits for deployment and implementation of HR policy. Federal legal instruments establish, regulate, and condition institutional public spending. There are limits for spending and for hiring people, and regulation that defines the form of entrance and permanence in public service (Barbosa & Elias, 2010).

The main gateway to working in SDAU units is public searches. The literature reports that around 70-80% of the health professionals who work in health facilities come from public searches (Ibañez, Bittar, Sá, Yamamoto, Almeida, & Castro, 2001; Ferreira, 2002; Seixas, 2003; André, Ciampone, & Santelle, 2013). This form of recruitment depends on the economic-area authorization. Furthermore, besides the limited legal spending for personnel, the criteria for allocation of resources almost never takes into account the importance of the health sector and the development of a region, state, or county, but only the expenses involved in service provision.

The staff allocation follows technical parameters based on professional/capacity ratio (professionals per bed), which set the quantity that comprises the staff framework of assistance units (Zucchi, 1998). However, very often the technocratic logic of allocation does not incorporate the changes in demographics and the epidemiological profile of the regions where these health facilities are located.

Usually, an SDAU's professionals work in the institution for years. The creation of new services demands the hiring of professionals that are not part of this situation. The newly hired staff submits to a temporary contract with few supports in labor law. This aspect is a clear disadvantage of SDAU units, compared to SO units. In the units under direct administration, the limitations on managing work relations also are highlighted in aspects related to control over the resignation processes and functional progress. These have implications for the levels of efficiency of these organizations, considering the over-bureaucratized way of dealing with these issues (André, Ciampone, & Santelle, 2013).

With regard to job access in the SO, a segmentation of responsibilities guides the hiring selection process. It occurs in three major sectors: medical, nursing, and administration. The first two are responsible for the selection of their peers. The latter is selected by the HR Department. Admission is by selection process, anchored mainly in CV analysis and interviews, which aim to identify the profile of the candidate. The definition of ways of hiring people respects what was defined with unions, and respects the budget limit for spending on personnel (Carneiro, 2002).

In any health facility, it is difficult to discover any plan for promotions, salaries, and career development. The functional progression is implemented with a strong informal component, based on employee performance, with the evaluation conducted by immediate supervisors. The problems described above have an impact on organizational performance, influencing production capacity (André, Ciampone, & Santelle, 2013).

The existence of a system of targets allows for better sector performance assessment and HR's assessment of personnel in the healthcare unit, in addition to indicating the criteria for the efficiency with which they operate. Among the indicators for evaluating productivity of hospital units, one of the most frequently employed refers to the relationship of employees to beds. Despite the tendency to decrease the number of health-unit beds by transferring several procedures to an outpatient network, stimulating patient deinstitutionalization for some health problems (especially mental health), or even the institution of homecare services, the available data on this indicator demonstrate an increase in this ratio, probably influenced by the process of incorporating technology in the health sector (Zucchi, 1998).

The data available indicate better capacity utilization of HR by the SO. This can be explained by the limited spending on HR imposed by contract management, combined with the need to achieve the goals set in the contract agreement within budgetary limits. There is a discrete tendency to increase the ratio of employees/beds in SO units (the easiest process of hiring) in contrast to SDAU units, due to the difficulty of recruiting qualified personnel to fill the needs.

Turnover Rates and Remuneration

The turnover rate measures the relationship between entrance and exit of employees during the period evaluated, expressed in the form of a percentage (the net of hires and layoffs, divided by the average employees in a given period, multiplied by 100) (Bittar, 1997).

In the SO units, the adoption of market mechanisms for hiring staff can assure a job position replacement faster than can occur in general public service. This pattern allows better utilization of job recruitment and HR departments, and it seems to be more connected to the needs of the user population, even though the appeal to the market feature leads to greater instability in the staff, characterized by high rates of turnover. Before the beginning of the SO system, the expectation was that the payment of higher wages on average would be an advantage for working in distant areas. However, it has not been a factor in employment maintenance. High turnover rate can be attributed to the location of the unit, or problems with access to distant parts of cities, which usually does not happen in central areas (Barbosa & Elias, 2010).

In the direct administration units, the job position is more stable, with low turnover rates. This fact occurs for basically two reasons. The first is the greater flexibility in the exercise of activities. The second is due to the conditions for access to get the job, in most cases, after an approval a public tender. This process makes it difficult changing an employee.

The effect of a high turnover rate relates to the risk of discontinuity in development of activities, as well as to the workload for those who remain in the unit until the replacement arrives, and functional adaptation of new staff occurs. The effect on institutional development projects will depend on the expertise of the professional who left the organization.

The main issue related to replacement of human resources remains the low wages. Remuneration levels in SDAU and SO units remain low when compared to the private sector. The difficulties of facing the problem of ranking working conditions, particularly as regards remuneration levels, leave room for the adoption of measures that aim to compensate for lags in value between the public and private sectors, such as the institution of various types of bonus (e.g., for attendance, productivity, transportation to the workplace) (Bittar, 1997; André, Ciampone, & Santelle, 2013).

ISSUES, CONTROVERSIES, PROBLEMS

Any model of public-private partnership must ensure equity and its maintenance. Disparities that exist between rich and poor, in terms of access to healthcare and purchasing-power parity, must be prosecuted. One of the concerns with regard to the PPP is private-sector profit. Profit maximization disadvantages the poorer segment of the society with respect to receiving care and accessing services, since the poor cannot afford such services by other means (Thadani, 2014).

Quality is another issue that must be consistent over time. Public health services have been observed to be of inferior quality. Over the years, efforts have been made to revamp, improvise, and make necessary changes, but still there have always been certain drawbacks. In the case of PPP, it is imperative to ensure maintenance of quality. Certain restraints such as accountability and environmental regulation must be enforced. Access to healthcare is not a complete goal if the quality is diluted. The cost of providing access to healthcare is another challenge that must be worked out. It is evident that the cost of providing health services is too high and it is impossible for any nation to provide all health-related activities. Therefore, one must prioritize and conduct a proper cost-benefit analysis to provide universal access to healthcare (Mitchell, 2014).

The management stage of PPP entails transparency, extensive communication, and participatory decision-making among partner organizations. It is possible to find in the literature the difficulties, challenges, and effective responses during the partnering process (Anyaehie, Nwakoby, Chikwendu, Dim, Uguru, Oluka, & Ogugua, 2014; Baht, 2001). In particular, the emerging legal figure of the SO, an establishment of new institutional arrangements in the relationship between the public and the private health sectors, put the healthcare system to the challenge of creating new forms of labor relations that fit the diverse forms of selection, hiring, and remuneration, and link with the management mode that already existed, as well as applying equality mechanisms between the professionals in the sector (Medhekar, 2014).

In 2016, Alonso et al. analyzed whether privatization affects employment. Their findings illustrate that clinical-staff employment levels seem to be substantially lower in public-private partnership hospitals than in directly managed public hospitals, particularly as regards nursing staff, and in those types of hospitals where the private sector manages both clinical and nonclinical staff.

Frequently, the government's direct administration of public health facilities has been shown to be bureaucratic and of low quality (Camposa, Normana, & Jadada, 2001). However, a critical challenge will be to convince public-sector workers, who are the anticipated partners, to accept and support private-sector participation.

The SO in healthcare delivery is feasible with massive awareness, elaborate stakeholder engagements, and well-structured policy before implementation. It is fundamental that governments clarify their policy toward the private sector and ensure that public spending on health does not decline. It may also determine a structure of subsidies and incentives for such partnership.

The SO might fill gaps left by health systems because of their inability to provide public goods on their own, due to lack of resources or competing priorities, among other issues (Meredith & Ziemba, 2007). In other health fields, SOs have emerged with the intention to strengthen health services, improve coordination and product quality or regulation, and provide public education (Wheeler & Berkley, 2001). Table 1 displays the main differences observed between health facilities run direct by the State and those run by Social Organizations.

FUTURE RESEARCH DIRECTIONS

In spite of the scale and scope of public-private partnerships, there remain important gaps in scholarly and practitioner understanding of how the concept has been applied

Table 1. Differences between health facilities run direct by the State or by Social Organizations

Health Facility	State Direct Administrative	Social Organization
Administrative	• Bureaucratic • Led the purchasing of goods and services slower and inefficient	• Autonomy • Simplifies the process of goods acquisitions
Finances	• Difficult to audit • External approval of resources for goods acquisition	• Audited • Set limits for goods acquisition.
Stock	• Large stocks • Low turnover • Expensive to maintain	• Fast turnover • Small number of workstation • Less use of equipment
Decision power	Higher level of tension between bureaucrats and health professionals	Negotiated solutions
Managerial Practices	Must operate under the same methodological logic.	
	Reported by the Board of Directors.	Incorporated into the management contract.
Human Resources Department	Low autonomy	Performance assessment methods of evaluation
Turnover	• Low • More stable jobs	• High • Loss of task continuity
Remuneration compared with private sector	Still lower than private sector, however the workers have some types of bonus (e.g., for attendance, productivity, transportation to the workplace)	Still lower than private sector, despite the efforts of social organizations to equate the wages.

(Roehrich, Lewis, & George, 2014). Examining the foundations of the PPP for health facilities in literature, the complex architecture of a healthcare system, associated with the difficulty of implementation in such diverse contexts of population, requires experienced new management models and services able to generate organizational learning necessary for the development of the system.

Further studies could explore this matter and advance the field toward practical recommendations and potential guidelines for developing and managing public health facilities. Any model of collaboration may offer a way to advance population health at present, while creating streams of innovation that can yield future social and financial dividends in enhancing the public's health more widely.

CONCLUSION

The administrative and financial autonomy in acquisition of goods and services and personnel administration has interfered with the performance of different health units. The ability to decide on the organization services and infrastructure is consistent with criteria of efficiency and effectiveness in such an unbureaucratic setting, enabling the SO units to better allocate time and prioritize agendas.

With the greater level of autonomy granted to the SO, the health units can be quickly audited and evaluated. From these results, it is possible to create new concepts or tools that can focus on performance, rather than general unspecific control over procedures. The integration between resources and goals allows a structured work process focused on pursuit of efficiency. The role played by management contracts serves as the parameter for setting internal allocation of resources, and costs of procedures and services delivered. In addition, the management contracts establish control over the performance of contracted units. From the systematic analysis and synthesis of PPP studies, conclusions can emerge for public and private healthcare actors in particular, and for the management field in general.

Best management practices seem to provide significant improvements in service assistance and practices, strengthening the principles that underlie basic attention to health. Without the understanding of identified scenarios and tendencies in management, it would not be possible to specify competencies necessary to better prepare local managers.

It was difficult to find any effect of institutional arrangements on the development and management aspects of the two kinds of administration. Emerging trends in administration can be adopted in any model. The possibilities and limits of the management innovation experiences should indicate the key elements that must constitute the structuring of public administration. The results of experiments and the possibility of incorporation into the public management process can be decisive for the design of a new form of administrative organization for any sector in search of efficiency, effectiveness, and dedication to preserving the public interest.

REFERENCES

Alonso, J. M., Clifton, J., & Díaz-Fuentes, D. (2016). Public private partnerships for hospitals: Does privatization affect employment? *Journal of Strategic Contracting and Negotiation*, *2*(4), 313–325. doi:10.1177/2055563617710619

André, A. M., Ciampone, M. T. H., & Santelle, O. (2013). Health care units and human resources management trends. *Revista de Saude Publica*, *47*(1), 158–163. doi:10.1590/S0034-89102013000100020 PMID:23703142

Anyaehie, U. S. B., Nwakoby, B. A. N., Chikwendu, C., Dim, C. C., Uguru, N., Oluka, C. P. I., & Ogugua, C. (2014). Constraints, challenges and prospects of public-private partnership in health-care delivery in a developing economy. *Annals of Medical and Health Sciences Research*, *4*(1), 61–66. doi:10.4103/2141-9248.126615 PMID:24669333

Baliga, B. S., Ravikiran, S. R., Rao, S. S., Coutinho, A., & Jain, A. (2016). Public–private partnership in health care: A comparative cross-sectional study of perceived quality of care among parents of children admitted in two government district-hospitals, southern India. *Journal of Clinical and Diagnostic Research: JCDR*, *10*(2), SC05–SC09. doi:10.7860/JCDR/2016/17124.7250 PMID:27042545

Barbosa, N. B., & Elias, P. E. M. (2010). Health social organizations as a way of public/private management. *Ciencia & Saude Coletiva*, *15*(5), 2483–2495. doi:10.1590/S1413-81232010000500023 PMID:20802881

Barlow, J., Roehrich, J., & Wright, S. (2013). Europe sees mixed results from public-private partnerships for building and managing health care facilities and services. *Health Affairs*, *32*(1), 146–154. doi:10.1377/hlthaff.2011.1223 PMID:23297282

Bertucci, G., & Alberti, A. (2001). *Globalization and the role of the state: Challenges and perspectives*. Retrieved October 20, 2017, from: https://pdfs.semanticscholar.org/9edd/97224bb2978453e6ff5c08afc56dd9e6064e.pdf

Bhat, R. (2001). Issues in health: Public-private partnership. *Economic and Political Weekly*, *35*(52/53), 4706–4716.

Bittar, O. J. N. V. (1996). Productivity in hospitals according to some indicators. *Revista de Saude Publica, 30*(1), 53–60. doi:10.1590/S0034-89101996000100007 PMID:9008922

Bittar, O. J. N. V. (1997). Distribution of human resources in eight general hospitals in São Paulo. *Revista Panamericana de Salud Pública/Pan American, 2*(31), 37-43. Retrieved October 15, 2017, from http://www.scielosp.org/scielo.php?script=sci_arttext&pid=S1020-49891997000700007&lng=pt&nrm=iso

Boyne, G. A. (2002). Public and private management: What's the difference? *Journal of Management Studies, 39*(1), 97–122. doi:10.1111/1467-6486.00284

Bresser-Pereira, L. C., Nassif, A., & Feijo, C. (2016). The reconstruction of the Brazilian industry: The connection between the macroeconomic regime and the industrial policy. *Brazilian Journal of Political Economy, 36*(3), 493–513. doi:10.1590/0101-31572015v36n03a03

Broom, K. D., Turner, J. S., Schwab, S. D., & Pesely, M. P. (2015). Does quality matter? A study of stock price reactions and the implications for healthcare organizations. *Journal of Health Care Finance, 42*(2). Retrieved from http://healthfinancejournal.com/index.php/johcf/article/view/40

Buse, K., & Harmer, A. (2007). Seven habits of highly effective global public-private health partnerships: Practice and potential. *Social Science & Medicine, 64*(2), 259–271. doi:10.1016/j.socscimed.2006.09.001 PMID:17055633

Buse, K., & Walt, G. (2000). Global public-private partnerships: Part I—what are the health issues for global governance? *Bulletin of the World Health Organization, 78*(5), 699–709. PMID:10859865

Buse, K., & Waxman, A. (2001). Public-private health partnerships: A strategy for World Health Organization. *Bulletin of the World Health Organization, 79*(8), 748–754. PMID:11545332

Caballer-Tarazona, M., & Vivas-Consuelo, D. (2016). A cost and performance comparison of public private partnership and public hospitals in Spain. *Health Economics Review, 6*(1), 1–7. doi:10.118613561-016-0095-5 PMID:26743635

Camposa, K. D. P., Normana, C. D., & Jadada, A. R. (2011). Product development public-private partnerships for public health: A systematic review using qualitative data. *Social Science & Medicine, 73*(7), 986–994. doi:10.1016/j.socscimed.2011.06.059 PMID:21839562

Carneiro, N., Jr. (2002). *The public non-State sector: social organizations as possibilities and limits on public health management* (Unpublished doctoral dissertation). University of São Paulo, São Paulo, SP, Brazil.

Committee on Economic, Social, and Cultural Rights (CESCR), Office of the High Commissioner for Human Rights. (2011). *General Comment No. 14: The Right to the Highest Attainable Standard of Health (Art. 12). Guiding principles for business and human rights, Implementing the United Nations "Protect, Respect and Remedy" Framework*. Retrieved October 18, 2017, from http://www.refworld.org/pdfid/4538838d0.pdf

Elias, P. E. M. (2004). State and health: The challenges of contemporary brazil. *São Paulo em Perspectiva, 18*(3), 41–46. doi:10.1590/S0102-88392004000300005

Ferreira, W. C., Jr. (2002). São Paulo state hospitals management through social health organizations. *Revista de Admininstração Pública, 37*(2), 243-264. Retrieved October 14, 2017, from http://bibliotecadigital.fgv.br/ojs/index.php/rap/article/view/6486 (in Portuguese)

Gerschman, S. (1999). Public sector and social and health policy reforms: An inventory on the eve of the new millennium. *Cadernos de Saude Publica, 2*(15), 293–302. doi:10.1590/S0102-311X1999000200014 PMID:10409782

Giraldes, M. R. (2007). Evaluation of efficiency and quality in public business and government hospitals. *Acta Medica Portuguesa, 20*(5), 471–490. PMID:18282447

Ibañez, N., Bittar, O. J. N. V., Sá, E. N. C., Yamamoto, E. K., Almeida, M. F., & Castro, C. G. J. (2001). Social health organizations: The São Paulo State model. *Ciencia & Saude Coletiva, 6*(2), 391–404. doi:10.1590/S1413-81232001000200009

La Forgia, G. M., & Harding, A. (2009). Public-private partnerships and public hospital performance in São Paulo, Brazil. *Health Affairs, 28*(4), 1114–1126. doi:10.1377/hlthaff.28.4.1114 PMID:19597211

Medhekar, A. (2014). Public-private partnerships for inclusive development: Role of private corporate sector in provision of healthcare services. *Procedia: Social and Behavioral Sciences, 157*, 33–44. doi:10.1016/j.sbspro.2014.11.007

Meredith, S., & Ziemba, E. (2007). *A new landscape of partnerships. Global forum update on research for health: Equitable access: Research challenges for health in developing countries.* Geneva, Switzerland: Global Forum for Health Research.

Mitchell, M. (2014). *An overview of public private partnerships in health.* Retrieved from https://wiki.unece.org/download/attachments/23759108/overview%20of%20PPP%20in%20health.pdf?version=1&modificationDate=1410288914634&api=v2

Nigenda-López, G. H., Juárez-Ramírez, C., Ruiz-Larios, J. A., Herrera, C. M., & Ramírez, C. J. (2013). Social participation and quality of health care: The experience of citizens' health representatives in Mexico. *Revista de Saude Publica, 47*(1), 44–51. doi:10.1590/S0034-89102013000100007 PMID:23703129

Nikjoo, R. G., Beyrami, H. J., Jannati, A., & Jaafarabadi, M. A. (2012). Prioritizing public-private partnership models for public hospitals of Iran based on performance indicators. *Health Promotion Perspectives, 2*(2), 251–264. PMID:24688942

Reich, M. R. (Ed.). (2002). *Public-private partnerships for public health.* Cambridge, MA: Harvard Center for Population and Development Studies.

Roehrich, J. K., Lewis, M. A., & George, G. (2014). Are public-private partnerships a healthy option? A systematic literature review. *Social Science & Medicine, 113*, 110–119. doi:10.1016/j.socscimed.2014.03.037 PMID:24861412

Savas, E. S. (1990). A taxonomy of privatization strategies. *Policy Studies Journal: the Journal of the Policy Studies Organization, 18*(2), 343–355. doi:10.1111/j.1541-0072.1989.tb00837.x

Scharfstein, D. S., & Stein, J. C. (2000). The dark side of internal capital markets: Divisional rent-seeking and inefficient investment. *The Journal of Finance, 55*(6), 2537–2564. doi:10.1111/0022-1082.00299

Seixas, P. H. D. (2003). *Social health organizations in São Paulo: 1998-2002* (Unpublished Master's thesis). Getúlio Vargas Foundation, São Paulo, SP, Brazil.

Thadani, K. B. (2014). Public private partnership in the health sector: Boon or bane. *Procedia: Social and Behavioral Sciences, 157*, 307–316. doi:10.1016/j.sbspro.2014.11.033

Villarreal, M. A. (2010). The Mexican economy after the global financial crisis. *Congressional Research Service Report.* Retrieved October 19, 2017, from http://www.dtic.mil/get-tr-doc/pdf?AD=ADA529130

Wheeler, C., & Berkley, S. (2001). Initial lessons from public-private partnerships in drug and vaccine development. *Bulletin of the World Health Organization, 79*(8), 728–734. PMID:11545329

WHO Constitution. (2006). (14th ed.). World Health Organization. Retrieved from http://www.who.int/governance/eb/who_constitution_en.pdf

Widdus, R. (2001). Public-private partnerships for health: Their main targets, their diversity, and their future directions. *Bulletin of the World Health Organization, 79*(8), 713–720. PMID:11545327

Zucchi, P. (1998). Employees per bed: A study in some public and private hospitals. *Revista de Admininstração Publica, 32*(3), 65-76. Retrieved October 15, 2017, from http://bibliotecadigital.fgv.br/ojs/index.php/rap/article/view/7734

KEY TERMS AND DEFINITIONS

Decentralization: Transferring the competence and administrative and financial responsibilities to the level of local authorities.

Economic Growth: An increase in real gross domestic product, which means an increase in the value of national output/national expenditure. Economic growth is an important macroeconomic objective because it enables increased living standards and improved tax revenues, and helps to create new jobs.

Globalization: The worldwide movement toward economic, financial, trade, and communications integration. Countries interdepend with free transfer of capital, goods, and services across national frontiers.

Management Contract: An arrangement under which operational control of an enterprise is vested by contract in a separate enterprise that performs the necessary managerial functions in return for a fee.

Minimal State: A state with the least possible amount of powers. It is a term used in political philosophy where the state's duties are so minimal that they cannot be reduced much further.

Population Aging: A shift in the distribution of a country's population toward older ages.

Rent-Seeking: A practice of appropriation of public assets for private interests, whether by bureaucracy, nepotism, or corrupting private agents.

Turnover: The act of replacing an employee with a new employee.

Turnover Rate: A calculation of the number of employees who have left the company, expressed as a percentage of the total number of employees. Although turnover rate is usually calculated and reported as a percentage per year, it can be for different periods.

Welfare State: A social system based on the assumption by a political state of primary responsibility for the individual and social welfare of its citizens.

Chapter 12
Sustainable Development Goal 3 and Maternal Health in Nigeria:
Any Hope of Meeting the Target by 2030?

Idongesit Eshiet
University of Lagos, Nigeria

ABSTRACT

This chapter addresses the feasibility of Nigeria achieving Target 3.1 of Sustainable Development Goal 3, which aims at reducing maternal deaths to less than 70 per 100,000 live births by 2030. Maternal deaths occur due to lack of access to maternal healthcare, which encompasses the healthcare dimensions of family planning, preconception, prenatal, and postnatal care for women. Nigeria is presently the second largest contributor to maternal deaths globally, having a maternal mortality ratio of 814 per 100,000 live births. Will Nigeria achieve this goal by 2030? This chapter assesses the maternal health landscape of Nigeria and the measures taken by the government to address maternal health from the perspective of the feasibility of achieving SDG 3, Target 3.1 by 2030.

INTRODUCTION

Maternal morbidity and mortality have remained an endemic health issue for women through the ages. However, to stem the tide of maternal mortality, the United Nations had as its fifth Millennium Development Goal - a commitment to improve maternal health. The goal targeted a reduction in maternal mortality ratio by three-quarters

DOI: 10.4018/978-1-5225-6133-0.ch012

between 1990 and 2015, as well as the achievement of universal access to reproductive health by the same year (United Nations (UN), 2005). Subsequently, the goal spurred up commitments by various national governments to maternal healthcare. This led to a reduction in maternal deaths. Thus, maternal mortality ratio declined globally by about 44 per cent - from 385 deaths to 216 deaths per 100,000 live births. Similarly, the approximate global lifetime risk of maternal death fell considerably from 1 in 73 in 1990 to 1 in 180 in 2015 (WHO, 2015). Statistically, this meant a 2.3 per cent annual rate reduction - a remarkable progress, but it unfortunately failed to meet the estimated 5.5 per cent annual rate reduction that was needed to achieve the targeted three-quarters reduction in 2015 (WHO, 2015).

This progress in stemming maternal deaths is however, unevenly distributed among the different regions of the world. While the developed world has been freed from the shackles of maternal deaths, the developing world is still grappling with the challenge. A majority of the deaths still occurs in the developing world. For example, the developing world accounted for approximately 99% (302,000) of the deaths in 2015, and had a maternal mortality ratio of 239. This was 20 times higher than the 12 deaths per 100,000 live births that occurred in the developed world. Similarly, the estimated lifetime risk of maternal death in the developing world stands at 1 in 3,300, as compared with 1 in 41in the developing world (WHO, 2015).

Regionally, sub-Saharan Africa has the highest maternal mortality ratio. It accounted for about 66% (201,000) of the deaths in 2015 with a maternal mortality ratio of 546. Equally, a woman's life time risk of dying during or following a pregnancy in sub-Saharan Africa, is estimated at 1 in 36 as compared to 1 in 4,900 for the developed world (WHO, 2015). At the country level, Nigeria and India are estimated to account for over one third of all maternal deaths globally. Nigeria accounted for 19% (58,000) with a maternal mortality ratio of 814 in 2015, while India accounted for 15% (45,000) of the deaths (WHO, 2015).

The Millennium Development Goal 5 has been rested, as the target year (2015) for its achievement had come and gone. Although, its targets of reducing maternal mortality ratio by three-quarters and the achievement of a universal access to reproductive health were not achieved, nevertheless, the progress made as a result of the goal is quite remarkable. Field findings reveal that all regions of the world that implemented the Millennium Development Goals have experienced considerable reductions in maternal mortality rate (UN, 2015). In view of this, the Sustainable Development Goals (SDGs) (which replaced the Millennium Development Goals), have established a transformative new agenda for maternal health, towards ending preventable maternal mortality. Thus, Target 3.1 of SDG 3 (Ensure Healthy Lives and Promote well-being for all at all Ages), aims at reducing the global Maternal Mortality Ratio (MMR) to less than 70 per 100,000 live births by 2030 (UN, 2016).

Will Nigeria achieve this target with a current maternal mortality ratio of 814 deaths per 100,000 live births? What policies and actions has the Nigerian state taken to address the problem of high maternal mortality ratio, in line with the World Health Organization's advice to countries to identify and address the barriers that limit access to quality maternal healthcare? These are some of the contending issues that this chapter interrogates.

BACKGROUND

Maternal health refers to the health of women during pregnancy, childbirth and the postpartum period. It encompasses the health care dimensions of family planning, preconception, prenatal and postnatal care, which aims at reducing maternal morbidity and mortality (World Health Organization (WHO), 2012[a]).

- **Family Planning:** Refers to a conscious effort by a couple to limit their family size or space their children through the use of contraceptives. According to the World Health Organization (WHO), a vital issue in tackling maternal morbidity and mortality is the prevention of unwanted and too-early pregnancies. Thus, the Organization observes that satisfying the unmet need for family planning of women alone could reduce the number of maternal deaths by almost a third (WHO, 2012[b]). The Organization therefore, advocates that all women including adolescents should be given access to family planning (WHO, 2012[a]).
- **Antenatal Care (ANC):** Refers to the medical care of a woman during pregnancy. The major objective of antenatal care is to ensure optimal health outcomes for the mother and child. Antenatal care from a trained healthcare provider helps to monitor the pregnancy and reduce morbidity risks for mother and child during pregnancy and delivery. It has been observed that ANC provides the following benefits for mother and child:

(a) it enables early detection of complications and prompt treatment (for example, detection and treatment of sexually transmitted infections, malaria, high blood pressure, etc.) (b) it enables the prevention of diseases through immunization and micronutrient supplementation (c) it enables birth preparedness and complication readiness and (d) it enables health promotion and disease prevention through health messages and counselling. (National Population Commission & ICF International, 2014, p. 128)

The World Health Organization recommends a minimum of four ANC visits for every pregnant woman who has no complications. The first visit should occur by the end of 16 weeks of pregnancy, the second visit should be between 24 and 28 weeks of pregnancy, while the third visit should be by 32 weeks and the fourth visit by 36 weeks. However, women with complications, special needs or conditions beyond the scope of basic care may require additional visits (National Population Commission & ICF International, 2014). Nigeria's ANC policy aligns with that of the WHO.

- **Delivery Care:** Entails delivery in a health facility and by a skilled attendant – skilled attendance at delivery encompasses the presence of health professionals such as doctors, midwives, and nurses as well as an enabling environment, where the equipment, drugs and other resources required for effective and efficient management of complications are available. Evidence from the developed world shows that delivery in health facility and by a skilled attendant are the factors that have aided the drastic reduction in maternal deaths (Adamu, 2011; Kruk, Galea, Prescott, & Freedman, 2007).
- **Postnatal Care (PNC):** The postnatal period is the time from immediately after birth up to 40 days. The postpartum period is particularly important for women, because during this period, they may develop serious life-threatening complications, especially in the interval immediately after delivery. Evidence shows that a large proportion of maternal and neonatal deaths occur during the first 48 hours after delivery (National Population Commission & ICF International, 2014; Adamu, 2011). Thus, receiving postnatal care is critical in making a difference between life and death for mother and child (WHO, 2012[a]). Postnatal care visits also provide opportunity to learn and acquire information on issues such as family planning, maternal and child nutrition, immunization, hygiene and sanitation, etc. (USAID, 2009). WHO recommends that all women receive a health check within three days of giving birth.

Factors Influencing Uptake of Maternal Healthcare

Healthcare solutions to prevent or manage maternal health issues are well known, according to the World Health Organization (WHO, 2012[a]). Thus, all that a woman needs is to have access to antenatal care in pregnancy, skilled care during childbirth, and care and support in the weeks after childbirth, in order to escape an unnecessary death (WHO, 2012[a]). However, there are certain factors that may impede access to maternal healthcare. These factors include socio-economic, demographic, cultural and geographical factors.

Studies reveal mother's age at child birth as influencing utilization of maternal healthcare, although there are contradictory findings with regard to the direction of the effect of mother's age and utilization of maternal healthcare services. While some studies show a lack of association between mother's age and utilization of maternal healthcare services (Magadi et al., 2007; Celik & Hotchkiss, 2000), some others show higher utilization for younger women than older women (Abou-Zahr & Wardlaw, 2001), yet some others show a higher utilization for older women than younger women (Tsawe, Moto, Netshivhera, Ralesego, Nyathi, & Susuman, 2015; Reynolds, Wong, & Tucker, 2006).

Similarly, birth order is shown as a predictor of maternal healthcare services utilization. Evidence shows that women who have more than three living children are more confident about their ability to handle their maternal health issues and so do utilize maternal health services less frequently than those who have had less than three children (Tsawe, Moto, Netshivhera, Ralesego, Nyathi, & Susuman, 2015; Raj Baral, Lyons, Skinner, & van Teijlingen, 2012; Simkhada, Teijlingen, Porter, & Simkhada, 2008). Maternal education is also shown as a factor influencing the utilization of maternal healthcare services. Studies reveal that the higher a woman's level of education, the more likely she is to access and use maternal healthcare services (Tsawe, Moto, Netshivhera, Ralesego, Nyathi, & Susuman, 2015; Ononokpono & Odimegwu, 2014: Ayele, Belayihun, Teji, & Ayana, 2014). However, some other studies do question the independent effect of education on maternal health utilization, arguing that some other factors such as husband's educational level, socio-economic environment do mediate on the association between education and utilization of maternal healthcare services (Gage & Calixte, 2006; Raghupathy, 1996).

Studies similarly show a relationship between women's employment status and access to and utilization of maternal healthcare services. While it could be assumed that working women who earn income would have more autonomy and the financial wherewithal to seek maternal healthcare services, in reality this is not always so, as the context in which women are employed does impact on their access to maternal healthcare services. Thus, the contextual differences in women's employment have given rise to different findings on the association between employment and access to and utilization of maternal health services. Studies reveal a positive relationship between a woman's formal employment and utilization of maternal healthcare services as such healthcare provisioning are part of the official employment benefits (Ononokpono & Odimegwu, 2014; Dalal, Shabnam, Andrews-Chavez, Mårtensson & Timpka, 2012). However, in context where women have no control over their earnings and where women do not earn money for the work they do or where employment is poverty-induced, employment is found not to be associated with maternal healthcare services utilization (Lowe, Chen, & Huang, 2016; Furuta & Salway, 2006; Addai, 2000; Nwakoby 1994).

The place of residence similarly plays a significant role in access to and utilization of maternal healthcare services. Studies show that women who reside in urban areas are more likely to have access to and utilize maternal healthcare services than those who reside in the rural areas (Muchabaiwa, Mazambani, Chigusiwa, Bindu, & Mudavanhu, 2012; Dagne, 2010; Babalola & Fatusi, 2009). This may be attributed to the lopsided healthcare provisioning in developing countries in which sophisticated health facilities are often situated in the urban areas (Peltzer, Skinner, Mfecane, Shisana, Nqeketo, & Mosala, 2005). Thus, issues of accessibility and affordability have been critical factors in determining maternal healthcare utilization as rural women often have to travel long distances before accessing the nearest heath facility (Tsawe & Susuman, 2014; Silal, Penn-Kekana, Harris, Birch, & McIntyre, 2012; Ensor & Cooper, 2004).

Household wealth quintile is also associated with the use of maternal healthcare services. This is however, not surprising, as the use of maternal healthcare services entails some monetary costs such as cost of transportation, medication, user fees, etc. Thus, women from rich families are more likely to utilize maternal healthcare services than women from poor families (Gabrysh & Campbell, 2009). Likewise, the use of maternal healthcare also increases with the wealth quintile of women themselves, thus women from the rich quintile use maternal healthcare services more than those from the poor quintile (Fotso, Ezeh, Madise, Ziraba & Ogollah, 2009).

Religion also mediates access to and utilization of maternal healthcare services. For example, studies reveal a higher use of maternal healthcare services by non-Muslim women, and a lower rate of use by Muslim women (Babalola & Fatusi, 2009; Ethiopian Society of Population Studies, 2008; Addai, 2000). Similarly, cultural factors such as the traditional gender division of labour, patriarchy, which denies women autonomy in decision making, etc. are associated with non-utilization of maternal healthcare services (Lowe, Chen, & Huang, 2016; Ayele, Belayihun, Teji, & Ayana, 2014).

The World Health Organization however, advises countries to identify and address these barriers that limit access to quality maternal healthcare, in order to improve maternal health of their women (WHO, 2012a).

THEORECTICAL FRAMEWORK

The chapter situates its analysis within the functionalist perspective in Sociology. The functionalist perspective derives its analysis from the works of Sociologists such as

Herbert Spencer, Emile Durkheim, Talcott Parsons and Robert Merton (Haralambos & Holborn, 2013). Functionalists argue that the society could be viewed as a unified system that is made up of differentiated but interrelated parts that work together for the effective functioning of the whole. These parts are the social institutions such as the family, government, economy, education, health, religion, media, etc., which provide different functions to the society. Since the parts work together for the effective functioning of the whole society, a dysfunction in any of these parts, affects the effective functioning of the whole society.

From this vein, the family institution is one of the component parts of the society that ensures societal continuity by reproducing its members, while the health institution ensures system maintenance by taking care of the sick and health needs of societal members. The family adequately reproduces her members through a functional healthcare system. Therefore, a dysfunctional health institution affects the family's reproductive role and this in turn disrupts the societal functioning.

Maternal death therefore, goes beyond being an individual problem to a societal problem. High maternal deaths such as that, which occur in Nigeria, impede human and societal development. And these deaths cannot be curbed unless the health system and the other institutions of the society are functioning effectively. Empirical evidence shows an association between the level of a country's development and maternal mortality rate (World Economic Forum, 2017a). Thus, in a context of poverty, patriarchy, poor healthcare delivery, poor education, ineffective transportation system and a general atmosphere of underdevelopment, maternal deaths will be high. This explains the difference between the developed and developing world where maternal mortality ratio is 12 and 239 per 100,000 live births respectively and the estimated lifetime risk of maternal death is 1 in 3,300 and 1 in 41for the developed and developing world respectively (UN, 2015). Therefore, from the functionalist perspective, achieving Sustainable Development Goal 3, Target 3.1, in Nigeria requires having a viable healthcare system, as well as a general development of the society that is the effective functioning of all the other social institutions.

METHODOLOGY

The study utilises secondary sources for its analysis. Extant literature in textbooks, journals, government's reports and records as it pertains to the research topic serve as the source materials for the chapter.

MAIN FOCUS OF THE CHAPTER

Maternal Health Landscape in Nigeria

The indicators measuring the different components of maternal health in Nigeria reveal a rather gloomy picture. Findings of the National Demographic and Health Survey (NDHS) 2013 reveal that contraceptive prevalence among Nigerian women stands at 16%, while only 15% of married women use a contraceptive and 16% has an unmet need for family planning. This poor access to family planning has resulted in a high fertility rate, which stands at 5.6 children per woman. With regards to antenatal visits, the survey reveals that only 51% of pregnant women have four antenatal visits while 34% have no antennal care. In terms of delivery care, only 38% of births are delivered by a skilled health provider (midwife, doctor or nurse) and only 36% of them are delivered in a health facility while 63% are delivered at home. For postnatal care, about 58% of women do not have postnatal check-up. Similarly, there is a high prevalence (23%) of teenage (15-19 years) pregnancy, which is a major health concern due to its association with higher morbidity and mortality for both mother and child (National Population Commission & ICF International, 2014).

These statistics reveal a poor maternal health landscape in Nigeria, hence Nigeria's present status as the second largest contributor to maternal deaths globally, accounting for 19 per cent (58,000) of the overall deaths with a Maternal Mortality Ratio (MMR) of 814 (WHO, 2015).

In view of this high maternal mortality rate, what steps has Nigeria taken (as a signatory to the Millennium Development Goals and now Sustainable Development Goals) to stem the tide of maternal deaths?

Measures Taken to Address Maternal, Newborn and Child Health Since the Adoption of Millennium Development Goals 4 and 5 by the Nigerian Government

Nigeria was one of the signatories to the Millennium Development Goals (MDGs) in 2000. Thus, it adopted the Goals as a strategy for achieving sustainable human development by the target year 2015. In view of this, Goals 4 and 5 were adopted to address Maternal, Newborn and Child Health (MNCH). Goal 4 aimed at reducing under-five mortality to 71 per 1,000 live births while Goal 5 aimed at reducing maternal mortality ratio by three-quarters between 1990 and 2015. Nigeria's efforts yielded a positive result as there was a consistent decrease in child and maternal mortality ratio from 1990 to 2015.

A key strategy adopted by the federal government towards the implementation of MDGs 4 and 5 was the Integrated Management of Newborn, Infant, and Childhood

Health (IMNCH) strategy - an all-encompassing evidence-based approach, which incorporates all aspects of maternal and child healthcare system, including material and human resources, health governance, health information, strengthening of clinical services and community engagement (Findley, Uwemedimo, Doctor, Green, Adamu, & Afenyadu, 2013). The strategy was adopted under the auspices of the Federal Ministry of Health in 2007 (Federal Ministry of Health, 2007).

The implementation of the IMNCH strategy led to the following actions by the federal government:

- **Institutionalization of a Bi-Annual Maternal, Newborn and Child Health Week (MNCHW):** This is a week celebrated twice yearly in all states of the federation. MNCHW was introduced in 2010 as a strategic action to accelerate the reduction of child mortality and improve maternal health through improved access to maternal and child healthcare services. During the week, integrated high-impact and no-cost package of protective and preventive services are rendered to the whole family by taking services to the communities (UNICEF, 2016). The Week's interventions complement routine health services by ensuring that basic maternal and child healthcare reaches all mothers and children.
- **Strengthening Institutional Capacity and Infrastructure:** This led to the building of more Primary Health Centers (PHCs). In fact, PHCs are located in every local government in order to enable an extended coverage of maternal and child healthcare interventions (UNICEF, 2013). Equally, tertiary health facilities were refurbished and provided with equipment for emergency obstetric and newborn care, while supplies of Reproductive, Maternal, Newborn and Child Health (RMNCH) commodities such as midwifery kits, magnesium sulphate, treated mosquito nets, contraceptives, anti-retroviral (ARV) drugs, etc. was strengthened (and this is continuous and on-going) (Onyebuchi Chukwu, 2015).
- **Midwives Service Scheme (MSS):** Similarly, to improve and increase the number of personnel at the PHCs, the Midwives Service Scheme (MSS) was introduced in 2009. The MSS focuses on ensuring the availability of skilled attendance at birth in order to reduce maternal, infant and child mortality through increased recruitment and training (National Primary Healthcare Development Agency, 2010). Equally, capacity building of the existing health workers was carried out (this is continuous and on-going). Thus, midwives and nurses were trained in Life Saving Skills (LSS) and in Integrated Management of Child Illness (IMCI) strategy. This was done in order to equip them with the requisite skills needed to save lives (National Primary Healthcare Development Agency (NPHDA), 2010).

- **Improved Health Financing:** This has been done through various measures such as the MDGs (now SDGs) conditional grant scheme, which is a scheme in which States and Local Governments are availed the opportunity to access funds annually from the Federal Government through counterpart contribution for the execution of projects, in line with the objectives of MDGs (SDGs) (Federal Republic of Nigeria, 2012). Also, health financing is made available through the Community Based Social Health Insurance Programme (CBSHIP), which is a programme under the auspices of the National Health Insurance Scheme (NHIS). The CBSHIP is targeted at the informal sector groups, which comprise a substantial proportion of the Nigerian population. The aim of CBSHIP is to address the critical problem of financial and geographical access to healthcare services by the informal groups. The CBSHIP has been implemented in some selected states. Similarly, to increase health financing, the budgetary allocation to the health sector was increased. For example, from 5% in 2006 to 7% in 2011 (Onyebuchi Chukwu, 2015). However, in recent times, the budgetary allocation has been decreasing, from 5.78% in 2015 to 4.23% in 2016 and further down to 4.17% in 2017 (Ifijeh, 2017).
- **Development and Review of Reproductive, Maternal, Newborn and Child Health (RMNCH) Policy Guidelines:** The various policies regulating RMNCH in Nigeria were reviewed. In 2010, the *National Reproductive Health (RH) Policy,* which was formulated in 2001 was reviewed in line with the objectives of the IMNCH strategy. The Reproductive Health Policy is a comprehensive framework, designed to address the reproductive health needs of Nigerians by designing and implementing appropriate programmes that would result in a well-functioning healthcare delivery system that guarantees access to affordable good quality care at all levels (Federal Ministry of Health, 2001).

Similarly, in 2010, *Training Manuals (Trainer and Trainee's versions) on the Use of Magnesium Sulphate in the Management of Severe Pre-Eclampsia and Eclampsia* was developed for the training of health workers. The manuals provide hands-on, detailed, descriptive and practical instructions and tips necessary to respond to obstetric emergencies (pre-eclampsia and eclampsia), the avoidable cause of maternal and child deaths (Federal Ministry of Health, 2010a; 2010b).

Also, the *National Family Planning/Reproductive Health Service Protocols* formulated in 2004 was reviewed in 2010. The National Family Planning/Reproductive Health Service Protocols is a framework for facilitating the provision of reproductive health services and quality care at service delivery points (Federal Ministry. of

Health, 2010c). The review was done in response to new global trends in family planning and reproductive health practices.

Equally, the World Health Organization's Integrated Management of Childhood Illness (IMCI) strategy was adopted and this led to the development of the *Integrated Management of Childhood Illness Health Facility and Community Guidelines and Protocols* in 2011. The IMCI strategy is designed to reduce child mortality and morbidity in developing countries. The approach focuses on the major causes of death in children through improving case management skills of health workers, strengthening the health system and addressing family and community practices (Ketsela, Habimana, Martines, Mbewe, Williams, & Sabiiti, 2012).

- **Tapping into the Support of Multi and Bilateral Agencies, Non-Governmental Organizations (NGOs) and the Private Sector:** Through partnerships with multi and bilateral agencies as well as with NGOs and the private sector, a lot of interventions were carried out (this is continuous and on-going) in the health sector (Onyebuchi Chukwu, 2015). Such partners include UNICEF, DFID, Pathfinder, etc.
- **Enactment of the National Health Act (2014):** Which is a comprehensive framework for the development and management of a national health system in Nigeria. The Act provides free basic healthcare services for children under-age five, and pregnant women. This would grant more pregnant women access to maternal healthcare services, especially delivery services. However, regrettably, three years down the line, the Act is yet to be translated from law into reality. The Act is yet to be implemented.
- **Actions by State Governments:** Taking a cue from the steps taken by the Federal Government to address MCNH, some State Governments (Lagos, Akwa Ibom, etc.) became more sensitive to maternal and child health issues. This resulted in increased budgetary allocations to the health sector, as well as the abolition of user fees for rendering of basic health services to mother and child.

These steps culminated in a downward trend in MMR from 1350 per 100,000 live births in 1990 to 814 per 100,000 live births in 2015, as depicted in Table 1.

In terms of the annual rate of reduction, statistics in Table 2 reveal that there was a 2% reduction between 1990 – 2015. Similarly, there was a 1.4% reduction between 1990 – 2000 while there was 1.5% reduction between 2000 – 2015. These statistics reveal that the progress has not only been slow but retrogressing in recent times.

The progress made by Nigeria in reducing maternal deaths, as depicted in Tables 1 and 2 was not significant to meet the target of MDG 5. Thus, MDG 5 was a missed

Table 1. Trend of maternal deaths in Nigeria (1990 to 2015)

Year	Maternal Mortality Ratio (MMR) per 100, 000 live births	Number of Deaths
1990	1350	57,000
1995	1250	59,000
2000	1170	62,000
2005	946	56,000
2010	867	57,000
2015	814	58,000

Source: World Health Organization, 2015

Table 2. Annual rate of reduction of maternal deaths in Nigeria

Years	%
1990 – 2015	2
1990 – 2000	1.4
2000 – 2015	1.5

Source: World Health Organization, 2015

goal for Nigeria, just as it was globally. Till date, a lot of women still die during pregnancy or due to complications associated with child birth. Hence, Nigeria still remains the second largest contributor to maternal death globally. So is Nigeria poised to achieve SDG 3 Target 3.1 by 2030?

BARRIERS TO ACHIEVING SDG 3 IN NIGERIA AND SOLUTIONS

Although the achievement of MDG 5 was a missed goal for Nigeria, the most worrisome part is that Nigeria still remains the second and third largest contributor to maternal and child deaths respectively globally. This raises some salient questions – 'why is Nigeria still the second and third largest contributor to maternal and child deaths respectively, despite the implementation of an Integrated Management of Newborn, Infant, and Childhood Health (IMNCH) strategy?' 'Will Nigeria achieve Sustainable Development Goal 3, Target 3.1, by the year 2030?' This section of the chapter attempts to answer these questions by identifying the barriers to achieving SDG 3, Target 3.1 and proffering solutions.

A critical factor influencing maternal health is the level of a country's development. Evidence shows an association between the level of a country's development and maternal mortality rate (World Economic Forum, 2017a). For example, the global reduction in maternal deaths by about 44 per cent (from 385 deaths in 1990 to 216 deaths in 2015 per 100,000 live births) as a result of commitments by national governments to achieving MDG 5, was not evenly distributed between the developed and developing countries. While maternal deaths have reduced significantly in the developed world, a high number of maternal deaths still occur in the developing countries. In 2015, an approximately 99% (302,000) of the global maternal deaths took place in developing countries. Similarly, the maternal mortality ratio of 239 per 100,000 live births for the developing world is 20 times higher than the 12 deaths per 100,000 live births for the developed world. Equally, the estimated lifetime risk of maternal death in the developing world is 1 in 3,300, as compared to1 in 41in the developing world (WHO, 2015). These statistics clearly show that there is a relationship between the level of a country's development and maternal mortality rate. A core reason accountable for this differential in maternal mortality rate is the disparity in the healthcare systems of both climes. While the developed world has a viable healthcare and referral system in which pregnant women can receive emergency obstetric care when needed, this is absent in most of the developing world.

It must however, be noted that the burden of maternal deaths is also not evenly borne by developing countries. Evidence shows that among the developing countries, progress in stemming maternal and infant deaths in response to the then MDGs 4 and 5 did vary widely. Thus, some Low and Middle Income Countries (LMICs) did make significant progress more than others (World Health Organization & United Nations Children's Fund, 2014). Some had fast-track progress, while others had slow progress. Thus, to ascertain the causes of this differential in progress, a consortium of development agencies (World Health Organization, World Bank, Partnership for Maternal, Newborn and Child Health and Alliance for Health Policy and Systems) undertook some studies in 144 Low and Middle Income Countries. The objective was to ascertain the success factors responsible for the fast-track progress of some LMICs (Kuruvilla, Schweitzer, Bishai, Chowdhury, Caramani, & Frost, 2014). Findings reveal that the key to progress is the improvement across a range of health determinants, both within and beyond the health sector. Thus, apart from reforms within the health sector, factors such as good governance, improved levels of education, women's political and socio-economic participation, environmental management (access to clean water, sanitation, etc.), reduced levels of fertility and poverty among others, were some of the identified success factors. In essence, countries that made fast-track progress were those who addressed a range of factors within and beyond the health sector.

Good governance, especially the control of corruption (as measured by the World Bank's World Governance Indicators (World Bank, 2017) and women's political and socio-economic empowerment were found to be key critical success factors. Thus, ensuring value for money in project interventions (a key indicator of good governance) was a key success factor. Therefore, countries with fast-track progress have improved health outcomes, despite having relatively low levels of investment and an environment of political and economic challenges. This finding confirmed the finding of an earlier study, which reveals that health can be achieved with relatively low resources, if the resources are used efficiently and strategically (Balabanova, Mills, Conteh, Akkazieva, Banteyerga, & Dash, 2013).

In terms of women's political and socio-economic empowerment, findings of the studies also affirmed findings of earlier studies (World Economic Forum, 2017[b]; Bishai, Cohen, Alfonso, Adam, Kuruvilla, & Schweitzer, 2014; Caramani & Eugster, 2014; PMNCH WHO, World Bank, & AHPSR, 2014; Options Consultancy Services/ Evidence for Adam & Franz-Vasdeki, 2012). The studies unravel the relationships between education, protection of women's rights, women's political empowerment, women's participation in socio-economic activities and improved maternal and child health. Countries with fast-track progress were those who recognized and addressed these factors. Such countries have a significant number of women in their parliaments and labour force (WHO, 2014; World Bank, 2017; Asian Development Bank and World Bank, 2012).

Nigeria's readiness to meet SDG 3 Target 3.1 is assessed in this chapter in the light of these success factors. Nigeria is categorized among the Low Human Development Countries (LHDC) with a Human Development Index (HDI) of 0.527, ranking 152 out of the 188 countries in the Index (UNDP, 2016). Nigeria has 50.9% of her population being multi-dimensionally poor, while 18.4% live near multi-dimensional poverty. (Multidimensional poverty refers to multiple overlapping deprivations suffered by individuals in three dimensions of - education, health and living standards) (UNDP, 2016). Nigeria does not have a viable healthcare system. The ratio of doctors per 10,000 population is 4.0, while that of nurses and midwives is 16.1. Similarly, the number of hospital beds per 10,000 population is 5. These are far below the World Health Organization's standards, which prescribes for example, one doctor to 600 patients (WHO, 2016).

In terms of literacy, Nigeria has a literacy rate of 59.6%. Gender disparity of literacy level reveals that 69.2% males are literate as compared to 49.7% females (Central Intelligence Agency, 2017). The unemployment rate in Nigeria is high. The National Bureau of Statistics reports that 18.8% of Nigerians are unemployed, while 40.0% are both unemployed and underemployed. Among the unemployed, females constitute 21.2%, while males constitute 16.5%. Similarly, 24.2% of females are underemployed while 17.9% of males are similarly underemployed. In terms of rural/urban dichotomy, 16.4% of rural dwellers are unemployed while 23.4% of urban dwellers are similarly unemployed (National Bureau of Statistics, 2017). The NBS also reports that Nigeria has a poverty rate of 60.9% with 61.8% of urban dwellers being poor, while 73.2% of rural dwellers are similarly poor (NBS, 2012). According to UNICEF (2017) about 70 million Nigerians lack access to safe drinking water, and over 110 million lacked access to improved sanitation in 2013. Similarly, open defecation rate at 28.5%, poses grave public health risks. UNICEF estimates the economic impact of poor sanitation and hygiene, as costing the Nigerian economy about 1.3 per cent of her Gross Domestic Product (GDP).

Nigeria is plagued with bad governance. Corruption is at its peak. Transparency International Corruption Perceptions Index (2016) ranks Nigeria 136 out of 176 countries with a score of 28%. Nigeria has been ranked in this position consecutively for the past four years. In terms of political participation, women have a marginal representation of 5.6% in parliament as compared to 94.4% for men. Similarly, only 12.0% women are in ministerial positions as compared to 28.9% for men. In terms of out of school children, Nigeria has 10.5 million out-of-school children with 40.0% being females, while 28.9% are males. On the overall, Nigeria ranks 122 out of 144 countries in the Global Gender Gap Index (World Economic Forum, 2017[b]).

These indicators show that Nigeria has not done much to address maternal health determinants both in the health sector and beyond the health sector. As the evidence of the success factors has shown, tackling maternal health challenges involves much more than addressing issues within the health sector. It entails a commitment to address a range of factors both within and beyond the health sector.

SOLUTIONS AND RECCOMMENDATIONS

To achieve SDG 3, Target 3.1 by 2030, there is a need for a total overhauling of the Nigerian State. However, this cannot be done with the present crop of political leadership, but with a new set of visionary and purpose driven leadership who are committed to using the common wealth of Nigeria to improve the well-being of all Nigerians. Such leaders should be elected through free and fair elections. This also calls for an overhauling of the electoral process, to allow for free and fair elections devoid of violence and rigging, which currently characterise the Nigerian electoral landscape. Such visionary leaders when instituted to power should carry out reforms that address the following issues both within and beyond the health sector.

Beyond the Health Sector

- Practice good governance. This should be done based on the yard sticks of good governance as measured by the World Bank (2017).
- Control of corruption. This leadership should control corruption by a demonstration of the political will to legislate, prosecute and punish offenders to serve as a deterrent to others.
- Gender parity in political and socio-economic participation. They should take deliberate steps to increase the enrolment of women in education, especially higher education. Also, the political space and labour force should be opened to more women to be involved in decision-making. A start up point can be through deliberate policies in line with the thirty-five percent prescription of the Beijing Platform of Action (1995).
- Intensive environmental management through the provision of access to clean water, sanitation, adequate housing, etc.
- Reduction of the level of poverty through provision of direct employment and employment opportunities such as trainings, micro credit, business tools, etc.
- Provision of critical infrastructures such as electricity, security, transportation, etc.

Within the Health Sector

- Immediate implementation of the National Health Act (2014), which is yet to be implemented since its promulgation in 2014.
- Ensuring value for money in project interventions. This should be done through laid down procedures that enable transparency and accountability in projects' execution.
- Reduction in fertility rate through targeted campaigns, using diverse means (drama, songs, jingles, bill boards, fliers, door to door, etc.) to create awareness on the dangers of high fertility.
- Provision of free contraceptives and family planning to poor women and adolescents who are actively engaged in sex.

FUTURE RESEARCH DIRECTION

The diverse factors associated with the achievement of quality maternal and infant health as unravelled by this study calls for the conduct of more studies, especially empirical studies that will address a range of factors within and beyond the health sector that impact on maternal health in Nigeria. Such studies should focus on issues such as poverty, women socio-economic and political empowerment, governance, corruption, cultural practices, environmental management, health expenditure, etc.

CONCLUSION

In response to the then MDG 4 and 5, the Nigerian government took deliberate steps to stem maternal and infant mortality. The Integrated Maternal, Newborn and Child Heath (IMNCH) strategy was adopted as a radical measure to curb the very high rate of maternal and infant mortality. This led to a revitalization of the then weak and moribund primary healthcare system characterized by - insufficient health centres, insufficient, unskilled and poorly motivated staff, none or outdated equipment, lack of drugs, etc. The introduction of the strategy led to the building of more primary health centres, improved supply management, enhanced capacity of health personnel and support of high impact intervention packages by development partners. These actions led to a consistent reduction in maternal deaths from 1350 per 100,000 live births in 1990 to 814 per 100,000 live births in 2015. However, the progress made was painfully slow. The rate of reduction was a far cry from the stipulated 5.5% reduction target for MDG 5 by 2015.

Evidence shows that the failure of Nigeria to make fast-track progress was due to her failure to address other health determinants beyond the health sector. Health sector reforms were not accompanied by reforms or fundamental changes in other sectors, such as governance, education, women's political and socio-economic empowerment, environmental management, poverty alleviation, etc.

Millennium Development Goal 5 was rested in 2015 (its target year). However, the goal has been replaced by another transformative agenda for maternal health - Sustainable Development Goal 3 (Target 3.1). Nigeria has also adopted this goal, but an observation of the health and related landscape shows that Nigeria has done nothing radically different with a view to meet the target of this goal by 2030. Health financing is still very low and in fact depreciating over the years. For example, budgetary allocation to the health sector has been decreasing from 5.8% in 2015 to 4.2% in 2016 and further down to 4.1% in 2017. These figures are far below the 13% allocation recommended by the World Health Organization or the 15% recommended by the Abuja Declaration of the African Union. Furthermore, in a socio-political context characterized by bad governance and high level of corruption, the situation is even worse, as the money may not be spent for value in project interventions but may end up in the private pockets of government officials, leaving the health sector worst for it.

Similarly, poverty, a key determinant of health including maternal health is on the increase. The unemployment rate is rising on a daily basis. Many are losing their jobs, while only few new jobs are created. At the same time, those in employment go without salaries for months. In the midst of high rate of poverty, people will hold unto traditional values such as depriving the girl child of education and giving her out in an early marriage. Women will prefer to patronize the nearby community traditional birth attendant rather than expend scarce resource to travel to a primary health centre located far from the community. Also, pregnant women will have no access to the required nutrition due to lack of income, etc. In sum, the current development indicators of Nigeria, as highlighted in this study, tell it all. Therefore, if Nigeria does not take radical steps to address a range of health determinants, both within and beyond the health sector as recommended by this study, SDG 3 Target 3.1 will remain a missed goal by 2030 just like MDG 5.

REFERENCES

AbouZahr, C., & Wardlaw, T. (2001). Maternal Mortality at the End of the Decade: What Signs of Progress? *Bulletin of the World Health Organization, 79*(6), 561–573. PMID:11436479

Adam, T., & Franz-Vasdeki, J. (2012). *Success Factors for Women's and Children's Health.* Background Paper. A Quantitative Mapping of Trends in Reductions of Maternal and Child Mortality in the High Mortality-Burden countdown to 2015 Countries. Alliance for Health Policy and Systems Research and the Partnership for Maternal, Newborn & Child Health. Retrieved on July 8, 2017 from http://www.who.int/pmnch/knowledge/publications/adam.pdf

Adamu, H. A. (2011). *Utilization of Maternal Health Care Services in Nigeria: An Analysis of Regional differences in the Patterns and Determinants of Maternal Health Care Use* (Master of Public Health Dissertation). University of Liverpool.

Addai, I. (2000). Determinants of Use of Maternal-Child Health Services in Rural Ghana. *Journal of Biosocial Science, 32*(1), 1–15. PMID:10676056

Asian Development Bank and World Bank. (2012). *Country Gender Assessment for Lao People's Democratic Republic: Reducing Vulnerability and Increasing Opportunity.* Asian Development Bank and World Bank.

Ayele, D. Z., Belayihun, B., Teji, K., & Ayana, D. A. (2014). Factors Affecting Utilization of Maternal Health Care Services in Kombolcha District, Eastern Harare Zone, Oromia Regional State, Eastern Ethiopia. *International Scholarly Research Notices*. Retrieved from https://www.hindawi.com/journals/isrn/2014/917058/

Babalola, S., & Fatusi, A. (2009). Determinants of Use of Maternal Health Services in Nigeria - Looking Beyond Individual and Household Factors. *BMC Pregnancy and Childbirth*, *9*(43), 1–13. PMID:19754941

Balabanova, D., Mills, A., Conteh, L., Akkazieva, B., Banteyerga, H., Dash, U., ... McKee, M. (2013). Good Health at Low Cost 25 years on: Lessons for the Future of Health Systems Strengthening. *Lancet*, *381*(9883), 2118–2133. doi:10.1016/S0140-6736(12)62000-5 PMID:23574803

Bishai, D. M., Cohen, R., Alfonso, Y. N., Adam, T., Kuruvilla, S., & Schweitzer, J. (2016). Factors Contributing to Maternal and Child Mortality Reductions in 146 Low- and Middle-Income Countries between 1990 and 2010. *PLoS One*, *11*(1), e0144908. doi:10.1371/journal.pone.0144908 PMID:26783759

Caramani, D., & Eugster, B. (2014). *Which Factors are necessary and/or Sufficient for Accelerated Reduction of Maternal and Child Mortality in Low and Middle Income Countries? Results from a Boolean, Qualitative Comparative Analysis (QCA)*. Partnership for Maternal, Newborn & Child Health and Partners Technical Paper. Geneva: World Health Organization. Retrieved on October 3, 2017 from http://www.who.int/pmnch/knowledge/publications/success_factors.pdf

Celik, Y., & Hotchkiss, D. R. (2000). The Socio-Economic Determinants of Maternal Healthcare Utilization in Turkey. *Social Science & Medicine*, *50*(12), 1797–1806. doi:10.1016/S0277-9536(99)00418-9 PMID:10798333

Central Intelligence Agency. (2017). *World Fact Book*. Retrieved on November, 2017 from https://www.cia.gov/library/publications/the-world-factbook/geos/ni.html

Dagne, E. (2010). *Role of Socio-Demographic Factors on Utilization of Maternal Healthcare Services in Ethiopia*. UMEA University Dissertation.

Dalal, K., Shabnam, J., Andrews-Chavez, J., Mårtensson, L. B., & Timpka, T. (2012). Economic Empowerment of Women and Utilization of Maternal Delivery Care in Bangladesh. *International Journal of Preventive Medicine*, *3*(9), 628–636. PMID:23024852

Ensor, T., & Cooper, S. (2004). Overcoming Barriers to Health Service Access: Influencing the Demand Side. *Health Policy and Planning*, *19*(2), 69–79. doi:10.1093/heapol/czh009 PMID:14982885

Ethiopian Society of Population Studies. (2008). *Maternal Healthcare seeking Behavior in Ethiopia: Findings from EDHS 2005*. Retrieved from http://ethopia.unfpa.org/drive/Maternal Health.pdf

Federal Government of Nigeria (2012). *MDGs Conditional Grants Scheme: Implementation Manual (Revised)*. Abuja, Nigeria: Office of the Senior Special Assistant to the President on MDGs.

Federal Ministry of Health. (2001). *National Reproductive Health Policy and Strategy to Achieve Quality Reproductive and Sexual Health for all Nigerians*. Abuja, Nigeria: Federal Government of Nigeria.

Federal Ministry of Health. (2007). *Integrated Maternal, Newborn and Child Health Strategy Nigeria*. Abuja, Nigeria: Federal Ministry of Health.

Federal Ministry of Health. (2010a). Training Manuals (Trainee's Version) on the use of Magnesium Sulphate in the Management of severe Pre-Eclampsia and Eclampsia. Abuja, Nigeria: Federal Government of Nigeria, Population Council & MacAurthur Foundation.

Federal Ministry of Health. (2010b). Training Manuals (Trainer's Version) on the use of Magnesium Sulphate in the Management of severe Pre-Eclampsia and Eclampsia. Abuja, Nigeria: Federal Government of Nigeria, Population Council & MacAurthur Foundation.

Federal Ministry of Health. (2010c). National Family Planning/Reproductive Health Service Protocols. Abuja, Nigeria: Federal Government of Nigeria.

Federal Ministry of Health. (2014). *National Health Act*. Abuja, Nigeria: Federal Government of Nigeria.

Findley, S. E., Uwemedimo, O. T., Doctor, H. V., Green, C., Adamu, F., & Afenyadu, G. (2013). Early Results of an Integrated Maternal, Newborn and Child Health Program, Northern Nigeria, 2009 to 2011. *BMC Public Health, 13*(1), 1034. doi:10.1186/1471-2458-13-1034 PMID:24175944

Fotso, J. C., Ezeh, A., Madise, N., Ziraba, A., & Ogollah, R. (2009). What does Access to Maternal Care Mean among the Urban Poor? Factors Associated with Use of Appropriate Maternal Health Services in the Slum Settlements of Nairobi, Kenya. *Maternal and Child Health Journal, 13*(1), 130–137. doi:10.100710995-008-0326-4 PMID:18297380

Furuta, M., & Salway, S. (2006). Women's Position within the Household as a Determinant of Maternal Health Care Use in Nepal. *International Family Planning Perspectives*, *32*(1), 17–27. doi:10.1363/3201706 PMID:16723298

Gabrysch, S., & Campbell, O. M. (2009). Still too Far to Walk: Literature Review of the Determinants of Delivery Service Use. *BMC Pregnancy and Childbirth*, *9*(1), 34. doi:10.1186/1471-2393-9-34 PMID:19671156

Gage, A. J., & Calixte, M. G. (2006). Effects of Physical Accessibility of Maternal Health Services on their Use in Rural Haiti. *Population Studies*, *60*(3), 271–288. doi:10.1080/00324720600895934 PMID:17060054

Haralambos & Holborn. (2013). Sociology Themes and Perspectives (8th ed.). London: Harper Collins Publishers limited.

Ifijeh, M. (2017, February 9). Nigeria's Grossly Inadequate 2017 Health Budget. *This Day Newspaper*. Retrieved on November 12, 2017 from https://www.thisdaylive.com/index.php/2017/02/09/nigerias-grossly-inadequate-2017-health-budget/

Ketsela, T., Habimana, P., Martines, J., Mbewe, A., Williams, A., & Sabiiti, J. N. (2012). *Integrated Management of Childhood Illness (IMCI)*. Retrieved on August 3, 2017 from http://www.who.int/pmnch/media/publications/aonsectionIII_5.pdf

Kruk, M. E., Galea, S., Prescott, M. R., & Freedman, L. P. (2007). Healthcare Financing and Utilization of Maternal Health Services in Developing Countries. *Health Policy and Planning*, *22*(5), 303–310. doi:10.1093/heapol/czm027 PMID:17681975

Kuruvilla, S., Schweitzer, J., Bishai, D., Chowdhury, S., Caramani, D., … Frost, L. (2014). Success factors for reducing maternal and child mortality. *Bulletin of the World Health Organization*, *92*, 533-544. Retrieved on November 29, 2017 from http://www.who.int/bulletin/volumes/92/7/14-138131/en/

Lowe, M., Chen, D. R., & Huang, S. L. (2016). Social and Cultural Factors Affecting Maternal Health in Rural Gambia: An Exploratory Qualitative Study. *PLoS One*, *11*(9), e0163653. doi:10.1371/journal.pone.0163653 PMID:27661617

Magadi, M. A., Agwanda, A. O., & Obare, F. O. (2007). A Comparative Analysis of the Use of Maternal Health Services between Teenagers and Older Mothers in sub-Saharan Africa: Evidence from Demographic Health Surveys. *Social Science & Medicine*, *64*(6), 1311–1325. doi:10.1016/j.socscimed.2006.11.004 PMID:17174017

Muchabaiwa, L., Mazambani, D., Chigusiwa, L., Bindu, S., & Mudavanhu, V. (2012). Determinants of Maternal Healthcare Utilization in Zimbabwe. *International Journal of Economic Science Application Res.*, *5*(2), 145–162.

National Bureau of Statistics (NBS). (2012). *Nigeria Poverty Profile 2010*. Abuja, Nigeria: Federal Government of Nigeria.

National Bureau of Statistics (NBS). (2017). *Unemployment/Underemployment Report. Q4 2016*. Abuja, Nigeria: Federal Government of Nigeria.

National Population Commission & ICF International. (2014). *Nigeria Demographic and Health Survey 2013*. Abuja, Nigeria: NPC & ICF International.

National Primary Healthcare Development Agency (NPHCDA). (2010). *Midwives Service Scheme*. Retrieved on August 10, 2017 from https://www.nphcda.org/programmes/midwives-service-scheme/

Nwakoby, B. N. (1994). Use of Obsteric Services in Rural Nigeria. *Journal of the Royal Society of Health, 114*(3), 132–136. doi:10.1177/146642409411400304 PMID:7932482

Ononokpono, D. N., & Odimegwu, C. O. (2014). Determinants of Maternal Health Care Utilization in Nigeria: A Multilevel Approach. *The Pan African Medical Journal, 17*(1), 2. Retrieved from http://www.panafrican-med-journal.com/content/series/17/1/2/full on 6/7/2017 PMID:24643545

Onyebuchi Chukwu, C. O. (2015). *Maternal, Newborn and child Health in Nigeria: Where are we now?* Presentation by the Honorable Minister of Health, Nigeria. Retrieved on October 26, 2017 from http://www.who.int/pmnch/about/steering_committee/B11_11_02_nigeriapresentation.pdf

Options Consultancy Services/Evidence for Action, Cambridge Economic Policy Associates, & the Partnership for Maternal, Newborn and Child Health. (2013). *Success Factors for Women's and Children's Health: Country Specific Review of Data and Literature on 10 Fast-Track Countries' Progress Towards MDGs 4 and 5*. Retrieved on July 10, 2017 from http://www.who.int/pmnch/knowledge/publications/country_data_review.pdf

Peltzer, K., Skinner, D., Mfecane, S., Shisana, O., Nqeketo, A., & Mosala, T. (2005). Factors Influencing the Utilization of Prevention of Mother-to-Child-Transmission Services by Pregnant Women in the Eastern Cape, South Africa. *Health SA Gesondheid, 10*(1), 26–40. doi:10.4102/hsag.v10i1.186

PMNCH, WHO, World Bank, & AHPSR. (2014). Success Factors for Women's and Children's Health: Policy and Programme Highlights from 10 Fast-Track Countries. Geneva: Authors.

Raghupathy, S. (1996). Education and the Use of Maternal Health Care in Thailand. *Social Science & Medicine*, *43*(4), 459–471. doi:10.1016/0277-9536(95)00411-4 PMID:8844947

Raj Baral, Lyons, & Skinner, & van Teijlingen. (2012). Maternal Health Services Utilization in Nepal: Progress in the New Millennium? *Health Science Journal*, *6*(4), 618–633.

Reynolds, H. W., Wong, E. L., & Tucker, H. (2006). Adolescents Use of Maternal and Child Health Services in Developing Countries. *International Family Planning Perspectives*, *32*(1), 6–16. doi:10.1363/3200606 PMID:16723297

Silal, S., Penn-Kekana, L., Harris, B., Birch, S., & McIntyre, D. (2012). Exploring Inequalities in Access to and Use of Maternal Health Services in South Africa. *BMC Health Services Research*, *12*(1), 120. doi:10.1186/1472-6963-12-120 PMID:22613037

Simkhada, B., Teijlingen, E. R., Porter, M., & Simkhada, P. (2008). Factors Affecting the Utilization of Antenatal Care in Developing Countries: Systematic Review of the Literature. *Journal of Advanced Nursing*, *61*(3), 244–260. doi:10.1111/j.1365-2648.2007.04532.x PMID:18197860

Tsawe, M., Moto, A., Netshivhera, T., Ralesego, L., Nyathi, C., & Susuman, A. S. (2015). Factors Influencing the Use of Maternal Healthcare Services and Childhood Immunization in Swaziland. *International Journal For Equity in Health*. Retrieved from https://www.ncbi.nlm.nih.gov/pmc/articles/PMC4391603/

Tsawe, M., & Susuman, A. S. (2014). Determinants of Access to and Use of Maternal Health Care Services in the Eastern Cape, South Africa: A Quantitative and Qualitative Investigation. *BioMed Central Research Notes, 7*, 723. Retrieved from https://www.ncbi.nlm.nih.gov/pmc/articles/PMC4203863/

United Nations. (2005). *The Millennium Development Goals Report 2005*. New York: United Nations.

United Nations. (2016). *Transforming Our World: The 2030 Agenda for Sustainable Development. ARES/70/1*. Retrieved on August 2, 2017 from sustainabledevelopment.org

United Nations Children's Fund (UNICEF). (2013). *Maternal and Child Mortality*. Retrieved on May 1, 2013 from http://www.unicef.org/nigeria/children_1926.html

United Nations Children's Fund (UNICEF). (2016). *Evaluation of the Maternal, Newborn and Child Health Week in Nigeria*. Abuja, Nigeria: UNICEF Nigeria Country Office.

United Nations Children's Fund (UNICEF). (2017). *Water Sanitation and Hygiene*. Retrieved on November 29, 2017 from https://www.unicef.org/nigeria/wes.html

United Nations Development Programme. (2016). *Human Development Report*. Washington, DC: United Nations Development Programme.

USAID. (2009). *Maternal and Child Health*. Retrieved on August,2, 2017 from http://www.usaid.gov/our_work/global_health/mch/mh/techareas/post.html

World Bank. (2014). *The Worldwide Governance Indicators (WGI) project*. Washington, DC: World Bank. Retrieved on October 4, 2017 from http://info.worldbank.org/governance/wgi/index.aspx

World Bank. (2017). *World Governance Indicators*. Retrieved on November 29, 2017 from https://data.worldbank.org/data-catalog/worldwide-governance-indicators

World Economic Forum. (2017a). *The Global Competitiveness Report*. Geneva, Switzerland: World Economic Forum.

World Economic Forum. (2017b). *The Global Gender Gap Report*. Geneva, Switzerland: World Economic Forum.

World Health Organization. (2012a). Trends in Maternal Mortality: 1990-2010. WHO, UNICEF, UNFPA, World Bank Estimates. Geneva: World Health Organization.

World Health Organization. (2012b). *MDG 5: Improve Maternal Health*. Retrieved on May 31, 2013 from http://www.who.int/topics/maternal_health/en/

World Health Organization. (2014). *Success Factors for Women's and Children's Health: Country Multistakeholder Policy Reviews*. Geneva: World Health Organization. Retrieved on September18, 2017 from http://www.who.int/pmnch/knowledge/publications/successfactors/en/index2.html

World Health Organization. (2014). *Success Factors for Women's and Children's Health: Multisector Pathways to Progress*. Geneva: World Health Organization.

World Health Organization. (2015). *Trends in Maternal Mortality: 1990-2015. WHO, UNICEF, UNFPA, World Bank Estimates*. Geneva, Switzerland: World Health Organization.

World Health Organization. (2016). *Global Health Workforce Statistics*. Retrieved on November 29, 2017 from http://www.who.int/hrh/statistics/hwfstats/

World Health Organization & United Nations Children's Fund. (2014). *Countdown to 2015 and beyond: Fulfilling the Health Agenda for Women and Children*. Geneva: World Health Organization & United Nations Children's Fund.

KEY TERMS AND DEFINITIONS

Antenatal: Healthcare given to a pregnant woman before childbirth.

Child: A person who is under five years.

Childbirth: The act of bringing to the world a new life (person).

Death: The end of the existence of an individual in the world.

Family Planning: The act of preventing unwanted pregnancies.

Federal Ministry of Health, Nigeria: The institutional framework that regulates healthcare in Nigeria.

Mortality: The ratio of deaths per certain number of population.

Pregnancy: The act of conception of a new life in the womb by a woman.

Postnatal: Healthcare given to a woman immediately after childbirth and within 40 days of delivery.

Postpartum: The period immediately after childbirth and health issues that occur during this period.

World Health Organization: The international body that provides regulatory guide for healthcare practices globally.

Compilation of References

Abdul Raheem, I. S., Olapipo, A. R., & Amodu, M. O. (2012). Primary Health Care Services in Nigeria: Critical issues and strategies for enhancing the use by the rural communities. *Journal of Public Health and Epidemiology*, *4*(1), 5–13.

Abimbola, S. (2012). *How to improve the quality of primary healthcare in Nigeria*. Abuja: National Primary Healthcare Development Agency. Retrieved on May 24, 2018 from http://nigerianstalk.org/2012/05/11/how-to-improve-thequality-of-healthcare-in-nigeria

Abosede, A. O. (2017). *Primary Health care in Nigeria: Gold-plating or Refining the Gold " Key to Health for All*. Lagos: University of Lagos Press and Bookshop Ltd.

AbouZahr, C., & Wardlaw, T. (2001). Maternal Mortality at the End of the Decade: What Signs of Progress? *Bulletin of the World Health Organization*, *79*(6), 561–573. PMID:11436479

Adabayo, B. (2017, June 27). Saraki, Killwate lament high maternal deaths in Africa. *The Punch Newspaper*, p.16.

Adam, T., & Franz-Vasdeki, J. (2012). *Success Factors for Women's and Children's Health*. Background Paper. A Quantitative Mapping of Trends in Reductions of Maternal and Child Mortality in the High Mortality-Burden countdown to 2015 Countries. Alliance for Health Policy and Systems Research and the Partnership for Maternal, Newborn & Child Health. Retrieved on July 8, 2017 from http://www.who.int/pmnch/knowledge/publications/adam.pdf

Adams, M., & Berger, D. (2007, February 7). *HPV Vaccine Texas Tyranny* (comic). Retrieved September 24, 2007, from http://www.naturalnews.com/021571.html

Adamu, H. A. (2011). *Utilization of Maternal Health Care Services in Nigeria: An Analysis of Regional differences in the Patterns and Determinants of Maternal Health Care Use* (Master of Public Health Dissertation). University of Liverpool.

Addai, I. (2000). Determinants of Use of Maternal-Child Health Services in Rural Ghana. *Journal of Biosocial Science*, *32*(1), 1–15. PMID:10676056

Addis Ababa Action Agenda. (2015). *Third International Conference on financing for Development*. Addis Ababa, Ethiopia: UN.

Adeyemo, D. O. (2005). Local Government and Health Care delivery in Nigeria. *Journal of Human Ecology (Delhi, India), 18*(2), 149–160. doi:10.1080/09709274.2005.11905822

Affordable Care Act, (ACA) (2010).

African Health Care Extension Service, 2018

African National Congress. (1994). *The National Health Plan*. Johannesburg: ANC.

Aggleton, P., & Parker, R. (2002). *A conceptual framework and basis for action: HIV/ADIS stigma and discrimination*. Geneva: UNAIDS.

Ahsan, M. R., & Partaken, T. (2001). Occupational health and safety in the least developed countries: A simple case of neglect. *Journal of Epidemiology, 11*(2), 74–80. doi:10.2188/jea.11.74 PMID:11388496

Ahuja-Young. (2012). *Safety and health: Issues and perspectives, a conference paper delivered to Nigeria union of journalist on health and safety issues in Nigeria, Benin City, Nigeria*. Academic Press.

Aisa, R., Clemente, J., & Pueyo, F. (2014). The Influence of Health Expenditure on Longevity: A Reconsideration. *International Journal of Public Health, 59*(5), 867–875. doi:10.100700038-014-0574-6 PMID:24986366

Akhakpe, I. (2017). *Local government management and democratic governance in Nigeria's fourth republic: Challenges and prospects*. Beasu – Bassin & LaunBert Academic Publishing.

Akhakpe, I. B. (2008). Food crisis, climatic change and human development in Nigeria: Challenges and the way forward. *The Nigerian Journal of Energy and Environmental Economics, 1*(2).

Akhakpe, I. B. (2016). Public policy and sustainable national development in Nigeria's Fourth Republic: Challenges and possibilities. *International Journal of Management Perspectives, 13*(1).

Akinci, F., Hamidi, S., Suvankuloo, F., & Akhmedjonov, A. (2014). Examining the Impact of Healthcare Expenditures on Health Outcomes in the Middle East, North Africa. *Journal of Healthcare Finance, 41*(1).

Akinsete, E. (2016). PPPs: The Antidote to Nigeria's Healthcare Infrastructure Deficit. *Businessday*. Retrieved on Wednesday 09, March, 2016, p.9, from www.businessdayonline.com

Albrow, M. (1970). *Bureaucracy New York*. Praeger. doi:10.1007/978-1-349-00916-9

Aldrich, R. (Ed.). (2006). *Gay life and culture: a world history*. New York: Universe Publishing.

Alemika, E.E., & Olumodoji, E.O. (1998). Basic needs approach to rural development and radical skepticism: A critique. *Nigeria Journal of Social Work, 2*.

Allis, R. J. (2009). Leadership–the five big ideas. *Strategy and Leadership, 37*(2), 4–12. doi:10.1108/10878570910941163

Alonso, J. M., Clifton, J., & Díaz-Fuentes, D. (2016). Public private partnerships for hospitals: Does privatization affect employment? *Journal of Strategic Contracting and Negotiation*, *2*(4), 313–325. doi:10.1177/2055563617710619

Amaya, A., Rollet, V., & Kingah, S. (2015). What's in a word? The framing of health at the regional level: ASEAN, EU, SADC and UNASUR. *Global Social Policy*, *15*(3), 229–260. doi:10.1177/1468018115599816 PMID:26635496

Ameh, J. (2017, July 18). Reps summon Health Minister, order him to recall NHIS Boss. *The Punch Newspaper*, p. 10.

American Cancer Society. (n.d.). *What Are the Key Statistics About Cervical Cancer?* Retrieved July 17, 2018, from https://www.cancer.org/cancer/cervical-cancer/about/key-statistics.html

André, A. M., Ciampone, M. T. H., & Santelle, O. (2013). Health care units and human resources management trends. *Revista de Saude Publica*, *47*(1), 158–163. doi:10.1590/S0034-89102013000100020 PMID:23703142

Anton, S. G., & Onofrei, M. (2012). Healthcare Performance and Health Financing Systems in Countries from Central and Eastern Europe. *Transylvanian Review of Administrative Sciences*, *35*, 22–32.

Anyaehie, U. S. B., Nwakoby, B. A. N., Chikwendu, C., Dim, C. C., Uguru, N., Oluka, C. P. I., & Ogugua, C. (2014). Constraints, challenges and prospects of public-private partnership in health-care delivery in a developing economy. *Annals of Medical and Health Sciences Research*, *4*(1), 61–66. doi:10.4103/2141-9248.126615 PMID:24669333

Anyauwu, J. C., & Andrew, E. O. (2009). Health Expenditures and Health Outcomes in Africa. *African Development Review*, *2009*(2), 400–433. doi:10.1111/j.1467-8268.2009.00215.x

Appleton, S. (1995). The interaction between poverty and Gender in Human Capital Accumulation. The Case of Primary leaving Exams in Cote d'Ivoire. *Journal of African Economic, 4*(2).

Ardichvili, A. & Kuchinke, K.P. (2002). Leadership styles and cultural values among managers and subordinates: a comparative study of four countries of the former Soviet Union, Germany and the US. *Human Resource Development International*, *5*(1), 99–117.

Argyris, C. (1964). *Integrating the Individual and the Organization New York.* Wiley.

Arizona Senate Bill 1093. (2007). *Arizona Senate Bill 1093.* Retrieved November 24, 2007, from http://www.azleg.gov

Arthur, E., & Oaikhenan, H. E. (2017). The Effects of Health Expenditure on Health Outcomes in sub-Saharan Africa (SSA). *African Development Review*, *29*(3), 524–536. doi:10.1111/1467-8268.12287

Asian Development Bank and World Bank. (2012). *Country Gender Assessment for Lao People's Democratic Republic: Reducing Vulnerability and Increasing Opportunity.* Asian Development Bank and World Bank.

Asoka, T. (2011). *Ensuring Financial access to primary healthcare, the experience and challenges of the National Health Insurance – Scheme in Nigeria*. Paper presentation, National Consultation on primary healthcare, financing and National Primary Healthcare Development Agency (NPHCDA). Available at: www.carenet.inf/files/insuring_ financial_Access_to_PHC.doc

Association of American Medical Colleges. (2015). *State Physician workforce Data Book*. Available at: https://www.aamc.org/data/workforce/reports/442830/statedat-andreports.html

Auge, K. (2007, January 17). Bill seeks proof of HPV shot or opt-out Colo. schools would require paperwork. Some say mandating the vaccine to prevent cervical cancer will encourage teen sex. Rep. May says the shot would be optional. *The Denver Post*, p. A1.

Autism Society of America. (2004). *ASA Statement on May 2004 IOM Report on Vaccines and Autism*. Retrieved October 24, 2007, from http://www.autism-society.org/site/PageServer?pagename=mmrvaccine

Ayala, G., Beck, J., Lauer, K., Reynolds, R., & Sundararaj, M. (2010). *Social discrimination against men who have sex with men (MSM): implications for HIV policy and programs*. Oakland, CA: MSMGF.

Ayankola, M. (2014, November 19). Saving lives through National Health Act (Editorial). *The Punch Newspaper*, p. 28.

Ayankola, M. (2016, September 1). Nigeria's devastating polo eradication setback (Editorial). *The Punch Newspaper*, p. 18.

Ayee, J.R. (2008). *Reforming the African public sector: Retrospect and prospect*. Dakar: Codesria.

Ayele, D. Z., Belayihun, B., Teji, K., & Ayana, D. A. (2014). Factors Affecting Utilization of Maternal Health Care Services in Kombolcha District, Eastern Harare Zone, Oromia Regional State, Eastern Ethiopia. *International Scholarly Research Notices*. Retrieved from https://www.hindawi.com/journals/isrn/2014/917058/

Babalola, S., & Fatusi, A. (2009). Determinants of Use of Maternal Health Services in Nigeria - Looking Beyond Individual and Household Factors. *BMC Pregnancy and Childbirth*, *9*(43), 1–13. PMID:19754941

Badru, F. A. (2010). On the Viability of Indigenous Health Care System in Nigeria: Insights from The Yorubas. In An Interdisciplinary Discourse on the Human Condition. Lagos: Faculty of Social Sciences in Conjunction with the Department of Sociology, University of Lagos.

Badru, F. A. (2017). Disease, Health Management, and Healing. In Culture and Customs of the Yoruba. Pan African University Press.

Badru, F. A. (2003). Sociology of Health and Illness Relations. In L. Olurode & O. Soyombo (Eds.), *Sociology for Beginners* (pp. 326–355). Lagos: John West Publications.

Badru, F. A. (2004). The Role of Health Sociologists in Combating Youth Violence in Tertiary Institutions in Nigeria. In L. Olurode & O. Soyombo (Eds.), *Readings in Campus Violence* (pp. 220–236). Lagos: John West Publications Ltd.

Badru, F. A. (2006, November). Quality Assurance in Health Care Delivery: The Role of the Nurse Manager. *West African Journal of Nursing*, *17*(2), 166–173.

Badru, F. A. (2016). Western Medicine. In *Encyclopedia of the Yoruba*. Bloomington, IN: Indiana University Press.

Balabanova, D., Mills, A., Conteh, L., Akkazieva, B., Banteyerga, H., Dash, U., ... McKee, M. (2013). Good Health at Low Cost 25 years on: Lessons for the Future of Health Systems Strengthening. *Lancet*, *381*(9883), 2118–2133. doi:10.1016/S0140-6736(12)62000-5 PMID:23574803

Baliga, B. S., Ravikiran, S. R., Rao, S. S., Coutinho, A., & Jain, A. (2016). Public–private partnership in health care: A comparative cross-sectional study of perceived quality of care among parents of children admitted in two government district-hospitals, southern India. *Journal of Clinical and Diagnostic Research: JCDR*, *10*(2), SC05–SC09. doi:10.7860/JCDR/2016/17124.7250 PMID:27042545

Bankole, R & Lawal, O.I. (2012). Percieved influence of health education on occupational health of factory workers in Lagos state, Nigeria. *British Journal of Arts and Social Sciences, 8*(1), 56-77.

Barbosa, N. B., & Elias, P. E. M. (2010). Health social organizations as a way of public/private management. *Ciencia & Saude Coletiva*, *15*(5), 2483–2495. doi:10.1590/S1413-81232010000500023 PMID:20802881

Barkdull, J. (2012). *Public Policy and Global change*. University Readers, Inc.

Barling, J., Kelloway, E. K., & Iverson, R. D. (2003). High-quality work, job satisfaction and occupational injuries. *The Journal of Applied Psychology*, *88*(2), 276–283. doi:10.1037/0021-9010.88.2.276 PMID:12731711

Barling, J., Loghlin, C., & Kelloway, E. K. (2002). Development and test of a model linking safety-specific transformational leadership and occupational safety. *The Journal of Applied Psychology*, *87*(3), 488–496. doi:10.1037/0021-9010.87.3.488 PMID:12090606

Barlow, J., Roehrich, J., & Wright, S. (2013). Europe sees mixed results from public-private partnerships for building and managing health care facilities and services. *Health Affairs*, *32*(1), 146–154. doi:10.1377/hlthaff.2011.1223 PMID:23297282

Baum, N.M., Gollust, S.E., Goold, S.D., & Jacobson, P.D. (2007). Looking ahead: addressing ethical challenges in Public health practice. *J Law Med Ethics*, *35*, 657-67.

Bel, R. (2010). Leadership and innovation: Learning from the best. *Global Business and Organizational Excellence*, *29*(2), 47–60. doi:10.1002/joe.20308

Bertucci, G., & Alberti, A. (2001). *Globalization and the role of the state: Challenges and perspectives*. Retrieved October 20, 2017, from: https://pdfs.semanticscholar.org/9edd/97224bb2978453e6ff5c08afc56dd9e6064e.pdf

Bhat, R. (2001). Issues in health: Public-private partnership. *Economic and Political Weekly, 35*(52/53), 4706–4716.

Bishai, D. M., Cohen, R., Alfonso, Y. N., Adam, T., Kuruvilla, S., & Schweitzer, J. (2016). Factors Contributing to Maternal and Child Mortality Reductions in 146 Low- and Middle-Income Countries between 1990 and 2010. *PLoS One, 11*(1), e0144908. doi:10.1371/journal.pone.0144908 PMID:26783759

Bittar, O. J. N. V. (1997). Distribution of human resources in eight general hospitals in São Paulo. *Revista Panamericana de Salud Pública/Pan American, 2*(31), 37-43. Retrieved October 15, 2017, from http://www.scielosp.org/scielo.php?script=sci_arttext&pid=S1020-49891997000700007&lng=pt&nrm=iso

Bittar, O. J. N. V. (1996). Productivity in hospitals according to some indicators. *Revista de Saude Publica, 30*(1), 53–60. doi:10.1590/S0034-89101996000100007 PMID:9008922

Bond, J., & Bond, S. (1993). *Sociology and Health Care*. Churchill Livingstone.

Bortel. (2016). Psychosocial effects of an Ebola outbreak at individual, community and international levels. *Bulletin of the World Health Organization, 94*(3), 210–214. doi:10.2471/BLT.15.158543 PMID:26966332

Boyne, G. A. (2002). Public and private management: What's the difference? *Journal of Management Studies, 39*(1), 97–122. doi:10.1111/1467-6486.00284

Bramming, P., Raastrup Kristensen, A., & Pedersen, M. (2009). The entry of self-leadership into work environment research. *Working Environment Challenges for the Future. Seminar Proceedings.*

Bratton, K. A., & Haynie, K. L. (1999). Agenda setting and legislative success in state legislatures: The effects of gender and race. *The Journal of Politics, 61*(3), 658–679. doi:10.2307/2647822

Bresser-Pereira, L. C., Nassif, A., & Feijo, C. (2016). The reconstruction of the Brazilian industry: The connection between the macroeconomic regime and the industrial policy. *Brazilian Journal of Political Economy, 36*(3), 493–513. doi:10.1590/0101-31572015v36n03a03

Brolin Ribacke, K. J., Saulnier, D. D., Eriksson, A., & von Schreeb, J. (2016). Effects of the West Africa Ebola Virus Disease on Health-Care Utilization – A Systematic Review. *Frontiers in Public Health, 4*, 222. doi:10.3389/fpubh.2016.00222 PMID:27777926

Broom, K. D., Turner, J. S., Schwab, S. D., & Pesely, M. P. (2015). Does quality matter? A study of stock price reactions and the implications for healthcare organizations. *Journal of Health Care Finance, 42*(2). Retrieved from http://healthfinancejournal.com/index.php/johcf/article/view/40

Brundtland, G. (1999). The Globalization of Disease. *New Perspectives Quarterly, 16*(5), 17–17. doi:10.1111/j.1540-5842.1999.tb00008.x

Buse, K., & Harmer, A. (2007). Seven habits of highly effective global public-private health partnerships: Practice and potential. *Social Science & Medicine*, *64*(2), 259–271. doi:10.1016/j.socscimed.2006.09.001 PMID:17055633

Buse, K., & Walt, G. (2000). Global public-private partnerships: Part I—what are the health issues for global governance? *Bulletin of the World Health Organization*, *78*(5), 699–709. PMID:10859865

Buse, K., & Waxman, A. (2001). Public-private health partnerships: A strategy for World Health Organization. *Bulletin of the World Health Organization*, *79*(8), 748–754. PMID:11545332

Caballer-Tarazona, M., & Vivas-Consuelo, D. (2016). A cost and performance comparison of public private partnership and public hospitals in Spain. *Health Economics Review*, *6*(1), 1–7. doi:10.118613561-016-0095-5 PMID:26743635

Callan, P. (2014). *Ebola quarantine is perfectly legal.* Retrieved from http://edition.cnn.com/2014/10/06/justice/callan-law-on-quarantine/index.html

Camposa, K. D. P., Normana, C. D., & Jadada, A. R. (2011). Product development public-private partnerships for public health: A systematic review using qualitative data. *Social Science & Medicine*, *73*(7), 986–994. doi:10.1016/j.socscimed.2011.06.059 PMID:21839562

Caramani, D., & Eugster, B. (2014). *Which Factors are necessary and/or Sufficient for Accelerated Reduction of Maternal and Child Mortality in Low and Middle Income Countries? Results from a Boolean, Qualitative Comparative Analysis (QCA).* Partnership for Maternal, Newborn & Child Health and Partners Technical Paper. Geneva: World Health Organization. Retrieved on October 3, 2017 from http://www.who.int/pmnch/knowledge/publications/success_factors.pdf

Carneiro, N., Jr. (2002). *The public non-State sector: social organizations as possibilities and limits on public health management* (Unpublished doctoral dissertation). University of São Paulo, São Paulo, SP, Brazil.

Carrin, G., James, C., & Evans, D.B. (2005). Achieving Universal Coverage: Developing the Health Financing system. Geneva: WHO.

Carrin, G., Evans, D., & Xu, K. (2007). Designing Health Financing Policy Towards Universal Coverage. *Bulletin of the World Health Organization*, *85*(9), 652. doi:10.2471/BLT.07.046664 PMID:18026615

Carrol, A. B., & Shabana, K. M. (2010). The business case for corporate social responsibility: A review of concepts, research and practice. *International Journal of Management Reviews*, *12*(1), 85–105. doi:10.1111/j.1468-2370.2009.00275.x

Catania, D. A., & Cheh, M. M. (2007, January 21). Why we believe the HPV vaccination is vital to the District's health. *The Washington Post*, p. B8.

Celik, Y., & Hotchkiss, D. R. (2000). The Socio-Economic Determinants of Maternal Healthcare Utilization in Turkey. *Social Science & Medicine*, *50*(12), 1797–1806. doi:10.1016/S0277-9536(99)00418-9 PMID:10798333

Centers of Disease Control and Prevention. (2016). *About Ebola Virus Disease*. Retrieved from https://www.cdc.gov/vhf/ebola/about.html

Central Intelligence Agency. (2017). *World Fact Book*. Retrieved on November, 2017 from https://www.cia.gov/library/publications/the-world-factbook/geos/ni.html

Chapin, R. (2007). *Social Policy for Effective Practice: A strength Approach*. New York: McGraw-Hill Inc.

Chiejina, A. (2014). Spotlight on Nigeria Health System. *Businessday*. Retrieved from www.businessdayonline.com

Chikovore, J., & Naidoo, D. (2016). Risk from the frontlines of a hidden epidemic: sexuality, masculinity and social pressures among men who have sex with men in South Africa: An overview. *Gender & Behaviour, 14*(3), 7609–7623.

Childress, J. F., Faden, R. R., Gaare, R. D., Gostin, L. O., Kahn, J., Bonnie, R. J., ... Nieburg, P. (2002). Public health ethics: Mapping the terrain. *The Journal of Law, Medicine & Ethics, 30*(2), 170–178. doi:10.1111/j.1748-720X.2002.tb00384.x PMID:12066595

Christiani, D. C., Durvasula, R., & Myers, J. (1990). Occupational health in developing countries: Review of research needs. *American Journal of Industrial Medicine, 17*(3), 393–401. doi:10.1002/ajim.4700170311 PMID:2407119

Church, D. (1982). The Architecture of Hospitals and Health Centres. In Medical Care in Developing Countries. Norfolk, UK: Oxford University Press.

Clancy, C., & Eisenberg, J. W. (1998). Outcomes Research: Measuring the End results of Healthcare. *Science, 282*, 245–246. doi:10.1126cience.282.5387.245 PMID:9841388

Clausing, J. (2007, February 25). HPV bill not immune to funding roadblocks. *The Denver Post*, p. C3.

Committee on Economic, Social, and Cultural Rights (CESCR), Office of the High Commissioner for Human Rights. (2011). *General Comment No. 14: The Right to the Highest Attainable Standard of Health (Art. 12). Guiding principles for business and human rights, Implementing the United Nations "Protect, Respect and Remedy" Framework*. Retrieved October 18, 2017, from http://www.refworld.org/pdfid/4538838d0.pdf

Corbie-Smith, G., Thomas, S. B., Williams, M. V., & Moody-Ayers, S. (1999). Attitudes and beliefs of African Americans toward participation in medical research. *Journal of General Internal Medicine, 14*(9), 537–546. doi:10.1046/j.1525-1497.1999.07048.x PMID:10491242

Cullinan, K., & Thom, A. (Eds.). (2009). *The virus, vitamins and vegetables: The South African HIV/AIDS mystery*. Johannesburg: Jacana Media.

Dagne, E. (2010). *Role of Socio-Demographic Factors on Utilization of Maternal Healthcare Services in Ethiopia*. UMEA University Dissertation.

Dalal, K., Shabnam, J., Andrews-Chavez, J., Mårtensson, L. B., & Timpka, T. (2012). Economic Empowerment of Women and Utilization of Maternal Delivery Care in Bangladesh. *International Journal of Preventive Medicine*, *3*(9), 628–636. PMID:23024852

Daniels, N, Bryant, J., Castano, R.A., Dantes, O.G., Khan, K.S., & Pannarunothai, S. (2000). Benchmarks of fairness for healthcare reform: a policy tool for developing countries. *Bull World Health Organ, 78*, 740-50.

Dardano, B. (2007, February 1). Risk, racism, and the HPV vaccination. *The Washington Post*, p. A14.

Davies, S. (2010). Global politics of health. *Polity*.

Davis, K., Streamiskis, K., Squires, D., & Schoen, C. (2014). *"Mirror", Mirror on the wall: How the performance of the US Healthcare systems compares internationally; Update*. The Commonwealth Fund Commission on a High Performance Health System. Available at: http://www.Commonwealthfund.org/-/Media/publications/fund-report/2014/Jun/1755_davis_miror_

Davis, K. (1986). *Human Behaviour at Work*. New York: McGraw-Hill Book Company.

Deji-Folutile, O. (2012, June 27). Nigerians spend N78bn yearly on foreign medical treatments. *The Punch Newspaper*, p. 49.

Delamou, A., Delvaux, T., El Ayadi, A. M., Beavogui, A. H., Okumura, J., Van Damme, W., & De Brouwere, V. (2017, March). Public health impact of the 2014–2015 Ebola outbreak in West Africa: Seizing opportunities for the future. *BMJ Global Health*, *2*(2), e000202. doi:10.1136/bmjgh-2016-000202 PMID:28589018

Department of Health. (1997). *The White Paper for Transformation of the Health System in South Africa.* Pretoria: Government Printers.

Dercon, S. (1996). Risk, Crop Choice and Savings: Evidence from Tanzania. *Economic Development and Cultural Change*, *44*(3), 385–514. doi:10.1086/452229

Donabedian, A. (1996). Evaluating the quality of Medical care. *The Milbank Memorial Fund Quarterly*, *44*(3Suppl. Part 2), 166–206. doi:10.2307/3348969 PMID:5338568

dos Santos, M., Kruger, P., Mellors, S. E., Wolvaardt, G., & van der Ryst, E. (2014, January). An exploratory survey measuring stigma and discrimination experienced by people living with HIV/AIDS in South Africa: The People Living with HIV Stigma Index. *BioMed Central (BMC). Public Health*, *27*. doi:10.1186/1471-2458-14-80

Durban Lesbian & Gay Community Health Centre. (n.d.). *About Us*. Retrieved June 5, 2018, from http://www.gaycentre.org.za

Dye, C. (2014). After 2015: Infectious diseases in a new era of health and development. *Philosophical Transactions of the Royal Society of London. Series B, Biological Sciences*, *369*(1645), 20130426. doi:10.1098/rstb.2013.0426 PMID:24821913

Dye, T. R. (1998). *Understanding Public Policy*. Prentice – Hall, Inc.

Eba, P. (2014). Ebola and human rights in West Africa. *Lancet*, *384*(9960), 2091–2093. doi:10.1016/S0140-6736(14)61412-4 PMID:25245179

Edeh, H. (2016). Health Sector bleeds on absent of Health Act. *Businessday*. Retrieved from www.businessdayonline.com

Edeh, H. (2016). Sector bleeds on absent Health Act. *Businessday*. Retrieved on May 26, 2016 from www.businessdayonline.com

Elias, P. E. M. (2004). State and health: The challenges of contemporary brazil. *São Paulo em Perspectiva*, *18*(3), 41–46. doi:10.1590/S0102-88392004000300005

Elliott, J. (2007a, February 6). Critics rip Perry's vaccine mandate: Governor rejects opponents' calls to reverse order. *Houston Chronicle*, p. A1.

Elliott, J. (2007b, February 8). The Legislature: Vaccination order still stoking fires. But Bell urges Democrats to back Perry for his stand on women's health. *Houston Chronicle*, p. B1.

Elwange, C. B., & Nahamya, W. (2005). *Susceptibility and vulnerability among the fishing communities to HIV/AIDS in Uganda: A case of Lake Kioga*. Paper presented at the an International Conference on HIV/AIDS and Food and Nutrition Security from evidence to action, Durba, South Africa.

Eneanya, A. N. (2016). Health Policy Implementation and its Barriers: A case study of US Health System. In Social, Economic and political perspectives on Public health policy-making. Medical Information Science Reference. doi:10.4018/978-1-4666-9944-1.ch003

Eneanya, A. N. (2015). 'Health Administration in Nigeria' in Theory and Practice of Public Administration Lagos. *University of Lagos Press and Bookshops Ltd Chp*, *15*, 229–254.

Eneanya, A. N. (2015). *Policy and Program Development, implementation and Evaluation*. Lagos: University of Lagos Press.

Eneanya, A. N. (2015). *Theory and Practice of Public Administration*. Lagos: University of Lagos Press and Bookshops Ltd.

Eneanya, A. N. (2016). *Policy Research, Analysis and Public Policymaking*. Lagos: University of Lagos Press.

Ensor, T., & Cooper, S. (2004). Overcoming Barriers to Health Service Access: Influencing the Demand Side. *Health Policy and Planning*, *19*(2), 69–79. doi:10.1093/heapol/czh009 PMID:14982885

Erinosho, O. A. (Ed.). (1989). *Health care and Health Care Services in Nigeria*. African Development Foundation.

Ethiopian Society of Population Studies. (2008). *Maternal Healthcare seeking Behavior in Ethiopia: Findings from EDHS 2005*. Retrieved from http://ethopia.unfpa.org/drive/Maternal Health.pdf

Etzioni, A. (1975). *A Comparative Analysis of Complex Organizations*. Free Press.

EU-OSHA, European Agency for Safety and Health at Work. (2010). *European survey of enterprises on new and emerging risks –managing safety and health at work*. Available at: http://osha.europa.eu/en/publications/reports/esener1_osh_management

EU-OSHA, European Agency for Safety and Health at Work. (2011). *European survey of enterprises on new and emerging risks –ESENER. Methodology*. Retrieved 26 April 2011, from: http://osha.europa.eu/en/riskobservatory/enterprise-survey/methodology-1EU-OSHA

Evans, M., Cloete, A., Zungu, N., & Simbayi, L. (2016). HIV risk among men who have sex with men, Women who have sex with women, Lesbian, Gay, Bisexual and Transgender populations in South Africa: A mini-review. *The Open AIDS Journal*, *10*(1), 49–64. doi:10.2174/1874613601610010049 PMID:27347271

Fagbemi, A. O. (2006). *Customer service delivery in public sector management*. Lagos: Concept Publication Limited.

Fajana, S. (2012). Safety at work: Issues and challenges. Paper delivered to Nigeria union of journalist on health and safety issues in Nigeria, Benin City, Nigeria.

Fajonyomi, S. O. (2012). *When the state goes to sleep of citizen and state development. LASU Inaugural Lecture Series* (46th ed.). Lagos: Lagos State University.

Falae, V. (2018). Trace Primary Health Care in Nigeria. *Businessday*. Retrieved from https://www.naija.ng

Falana, F. (2010, November). Nigeria: Legal framework for workplace safety. Daily Independence.

Family Health International (FHI). (2001). *In-depth Assessment Report*. Lagos: FHI.

Family Health International/Nigeria. (1999). HIV/AIDS: What to know and do. Lagos: FHI/Nigeria.

Farmer, P. (1999). Pathologies of power: Rethinking health and human rights. *American Journal of Public Health*, *89*(10), 1486–1496. doi:10.2105/AJPH.89.10.1486 PMID:10511828

Federal Government of Nigeria (2012). *MDGs Conditional Grants Scheme: Implementation Manual (Revised)*. Abuja, Nigeria: Office of the Senior Special Assistant to the President on MDGs.

Federal Government of Nigeria (FGN). (2013). *Integrating primary healthcare governance in Nigeria: PHC under one roof*. Abuja: National Primary Healthcare Development Agency.

Federal Government Printer (FGP). (2007). Legal Notice on publication of the details of the breakdown of the national and state provisional totals 2006 census. Federal Republic of Nigeria Official Gazette, 24(94), B175 – 198.

Federal Ministry of Health (FMOH). (2010). *Technical Report: 2010 National HIV Sero-prevalence Sentinel Survey*. Abuja, Nigeria: FMOH.

Federal Ministry of Health. (2001). *National Reproductive Health Policy and Strategy to Achieve Quality Reproductive and Sexual Health for all Nigerians*. Abuja, Nigeria: Federal Government of Nigeria.

Federal Ministry of Health. (2004). *Health Care in Nigeria*. Abuja: Annual Bulletin of the Federal Ministry of Health.

Federal Ministry of Health. (2007). *Integrated Maternal, Newborn and Child Health Strategy Nigeria*. Abuja, Nigeria: Federal Ministry of Health.

Federal Ministry of Health. (2010a). Training Manuals (Trainee's Version) on the use of Magnesium Sulphate in the Management of severe Pre-Eclampsia and Eclampsia. Abuja, Nigeria: Federal Government of Nigeria, Population Council & MacAurthur Foundation.

Federal Ministry of Health. (2010b). Training Manuals (Trainer's Version) on the use of Magnesium Sulphate in the Management of severe Pre-Eclampsia and Eclampsia. Abuja, Nigeria: Federal Government of Nigeria, Population Council & MacAurthur Foundation.

Federal Ministry of Health. (2010c). National Family Planning/Reproductive Health Service Protocols. Abuja, Nigeria: Federal Government of Nigeria.

Federal Ministry of Health. (2014). *National Health Act*. Abuja, Nigeria: Federal Government of Nigeria.

Ferreira, W. C., Jr. (2002). São Paulo state hospitals management through social health organizations. *Revista de Admininstração Pública, 37*(2), 243-264. Retrieved October 14, 2017, from http://bibliotecadigital.fgv.br/ojs/index.php/rap/article/view/6486 (in Portuguese)

Feudtner, C., & Marcuse, E. (2001). Ethics and immunization policy: Promoting dialogue to sustain consensus. *Pediatrics, 107*(5), 1158–1164. doi:10.1542/peds.107.5.1158 PMID:11331702

Fevzi, A., Hamidi, S., Suvankulov, F., & Alisher, A. (2014). Examining the Impact of Healthcare Expenditure on Health Outcomes in the Middle East and N. Africa. *Journal of Health Care Finance, 41*(1).

Fidler, D. (2005). Health, globalization and governance: an introduction to public health's new world order. *Global Change and Health*, 161-177.

Fidler, D. (2001). The globalization of public health: 100 years of international health diplomacy. *Bullentin of the WHO, 79*, 842–849. PMID:11584732

Findley, S. E., Uwemedimo, O. T., Doctor, H. V., Green, C., Adamu, F., & Afenyadu, G. (2013). Early Results of an Integrated Maternal, Newborn and Child Health Program, Northern Nigeria, 2009 to 2011. *BMC Public Health, 13*(1), 1034. doi:10.1186/1471-2458-13-1034 PMID:24175944

Fit for Work Team. (2015). *HIV and discrimination in the workplace*. Retrieved from on 22/11/17 https://fitforwork.org/blog/hiv-and-discrimination-in-the-workplace/

Floyd, J. (2007, March 2). HPV vaccine is a lifesaver tossed aside. *The Dallas Morning News*, p. B1.

Fotso, J. C., Ezeh, A., Madise, N., Ziraba, A., & Ogollah, R. (2009). What does Access to Maternal Care Mean among the Urban Poor? Factors Associated with Use of Appropriate Maternal Health Services in the Slum Settlements of Nairobi, Kenya. *Maternal and Child Health Journal, 13*(1), 130–137. doi:10.100710995-008-0326-4 PMID:18297380

Fourie, P., & Meyer, M. (2010). *The politics of AIDS denialism: South Africa's failure to respond.* Surrey: Ashgate.

Frederick, I. (1998). *Health in Rural Tanzania. The Determinants of Health Status Healthcare Demand and Health care choice.* Discussion Paper Series. Center Paper Series DPS 98.03.

Fryatt, R., & Mills, A. (2010). Taskforce on Innovative International Financing for Health Systems: Showing the way Forward. *Bulletin of the World Health Organization, 88*(6), 476–477. doi:10.2471/BLT.09.075507 PMID:20539869

Furuta, M., & Salway, S. (2006). Women's Position within the Household as a Determinant of Maternal Health Care Use in Nepal. *International Family Planning Perspectives, 32*(1), 17–27. doi:10.1363/3201706 PMID:16723298

Gabrysch, S., & Campbell, O. M. (2009). Still too Far to Walk: Literature Review of the Determinants of Delivery Service Use. *BMC Pregnancy and Childbirth, 9*(1), 34. doi:10.1186/1471-2393-9-34 PMID:19671156

Gage, A. J., & Calixte, M. G. (2006). Effects of Physical Accessibility of Maternal Health Services on their Use in Rural Haiti. *Population Studies, 60*(3), 271–288. doi:10.1080/00324720600895934 PMID:17060054

Gahan, P., Sievewright, B., & Evans, P. (2014). *Workplace health and safety, business productivity and sustainability.* A report by prepared by the Centre for Workplace Leadership, University of Melbourne funded by Safe Work Australia.

Gallet, C. A., & Doucouliagos, H. (2017, April). The Impact of Healthcare Spending on Health Outcomes: A Meta-regression Analysis. *Social Science & Medicine, 179*, 9–17. doi:10.1016/j.socscimed.2017.02.024 PMID:28237460

Gamble, V. N. (1997). Under the shadow of Tuskegee: African Americans and health care. *American Journal of Public Health, 87*(11), 1773–1778. doi:10.2105/AJPH.87.11.1773 PMID:9366634

Gardner, A. (2007, February 11). Drug maker assists in pushing for mandate for HPV vaccine. *The Washington Post*, p. C5.

Gbiri, Badru, Ladapo, & Gbiri. (2011). Socio-Economic Correlates of Relapsed Patients admitted in a Nigerian Mental Institution. *International Journal of Psychiatry in Clinical Practice, 15*(1), 19-26. Retrieved from http://informahealthcare.com/jpc

Geffen, N. (2010). *Debunking delusions: the inside story of the Treatment Action Campaign.* Auckland Park: Jacana Media.

Gentham, U. G. J., Sogaard, J., Anderson, F., & Johnson, B. (1992). An Econometric Analysis of Healthcare Expenditure: A Cross-section Study of the OECD countries. *Journal of Health Economics*, *11*(1).

Gerschman, S. (1999). Public sector and social and health policy reforms: An inventory on the eve of the new millennium. *Cadernos de Saude Publica*, *2*(15), 293–302. doi:10.1590/S0102-311X1999000200014 PMID:10409782

Gibson, J. L., Ivancevich, J. M., & Donelly, J. H. (1994). *Organizations, Behavior, Structure and Processes*. Irwin/McGraw Hill.

Giraldes, M. R. (2007). Evaluation of efficiency and quality in public business and government hospitals. *Acta Medica Portuguesa*, *20*(5), 471–490. PMID:18282447

Goffman, E. (1963). *Stigma: Notes on the management of spoiled identity*. Englewood Cliffs, NJ: Prentice-Hall.

Good, C. V. (1959). *Dictionary of Education* (2nd ed.). New York: McGraw Hill.

Gordon, A., & Yukl, G. (2004). The future leadership research: Challenges and opportunities. *German Journal of Human Resource Research*, *18*(3), 359–365.

Gostin, L. (2014). Ebola: Towards an international health systems fund. *Lancet*, *384*(9951), e49–e51. doi:10.1016/S0140-6736(14)61345-3 PMID:25201591

Gostin, L. O., & Friedman, E. A. (2015). A retrospective and prospective analysis of the west African Ebola virus disease epidemic: Robust national health systems at the foundation and an empowered WHO at the apex. *Lancet*, *385*(9980), 1902–1909. doi:10.1016/S0140-6736(15)60644-4 PMID:25987158

Grubaugh, U. G., & Santerr, R. (1994). Comparing the performance of Health Care Systems. *An Alternative Approach Southern Economic Journal*, *60*(4), 1030–1042. doi:10.2307/1060439

Gwatkin, D.R. (2000). Health inequalities and the health of the poor. What do we know? What can we do? *Bull World Health Organ, 78*, 3-17.

Halpin, A. W. (1956). *The leadership behaviour of school superintendents*. Columbus, OH: College of Education, The Ohio State University.

Haralambos & Holborn. (2013). Sociology Themes and Perspectives (8th ed.). London: Harper Collins Publishers limited.

Hart, S. (2010). Self-regulation, corporate social responsility and the business case: Do they work in achieving workplace equality and safety? *Journal of Business Ethics*, *92*(4), 585–600. doi:10.100710551-009-0174-1

Health Insurance Coverage in the United States. (2014). U.S. Government Printing Office.

Health Partners International (HPI). (2014). *Bringing primary healthcare under one roof: PHCUOR Factsheets.* Available at https:resources.healthpartners-in.co.uk/resourse/

Health Reform Foundation of Nigeria (HERFON). (2009). Primary healthcare in Nigeria; 30 Years after Alma-Ata. *National Health Conference*. Abuja: HERFON.

Health Safety Executive. (2001). *A guide to measuring health and safety performance*. HSE. Retrieved from: http://www.hse.go.uk/opsunit/perfmeas.pdf

Heaney, R., & Irlicht, L. (2007). The impact of occupation health and safety policy on firm value. *Economic Papers*, *26*(4), 308–320. doi:10.1111/j.1759-3441.2007.tb01017.x

Helmert, U. & Shea, S. (1994). Social inequalities and Health Status in Western Germany. *Public Health, 108*, 341-56. doi:10.100710728-005-2568-2

Helmert, U., & Shea, S. (1994). Social inequalities and Health Status in Western Germany. *Public Health*, *108*(5), 341–356. doi:10.1016/S0033-3506(05)80070-8 PMID:7972675

Hemphill, J. K. (1945). *Situational factors in leadership*. Columbia, OH: Ohio State University.

Henry, N. (2007). *Public administration and public affairs*. New Delhi: Prentice Hall of India.

Hersey, P., & Blanchard, K. H. (1988). *Management of organizational behaviour, utilizing human resources* (5th ed.). Prentice-Hall International, Inc.

Herzberg, F. (2003). One more time: How do you motivate employees? *Harvard Business Review*, 20–31. PMID:12545925

Hoffman, S. J., Cole, C. B., & Pearcey, M. (2015). *Mapping Global Health Architecture to Inform the Future*. Chatham House.

Houck, D. W. (2004). FDR's Commonwealth Club address: Redefining individualism, adjudicating greatness. *Rhetoric & Public Affairs*, *7*(3), 259–282. doi:10.1353/rap.2005.0006

House, R. J., & Aditya, R. N. (1997). The social scientific study of leadership: Quo vadis? *Journal of Management*, *23*(3), 409–473. doi:10.1177/014920639702300306

Houston Chronicle. (2007, February 8). Opting in One question should guide HPV vaccine policy: how effectively and efficiently it promotes public health. *Houston Chronicle*, p. B10.

Hwenda, L., Mahlathi, P., & Maphanga, T. (2011). Why African Countries Need to Participate in Global Health Security Discourse. *Global Health Governance*, *4*(2), 1–24. PMID:24729828

Ibañez, N., Bittar, O. J. N. V., Sá, E. N. C., Yamamoto, E. K., Almeida, M. F., & Castro, C. G. J. (2001). Social health organizations: The São Paulo State model. *Ciencia & Saude Coletiva*, *6*(2), 391–404. doi:10.1590/S1413-81232001000200009

Idris, A. I. (2014). Health personnel and the success of immunization in Nigeria. A study of selected local government areas in Kaduna state. *Review of Public Administration and Management*, *2*(6).

Idubor, E. E., & Oisamoje, M. D. (2013). An exploration of health and safety management issues in nigeria's effort to industrialise. *European Scientific Journal*, *9*(12), 154–169.

Ifenowo, D. (1997). *Elements of Public Administration*. Delinik Publishers.

Ifijeh, M. (2017, February 9). Nigeria's Grossly Inadequate 2017 Health Budget. *This Day Newspaper*. Retrieved on November 12, 2017 from https://www.thisdaylive.com/index.php/2017/02/09/nigerias-grossly-inadequate-2017-health-budget/

Ikelegbe, A. (2006). *Public policy analysis: Concepts, issues and cases*. Lagos: Imprint Services.

ILO. (2008). *Social Health Protection: An ILO Strategy Towards Universal Access to Healthcare*. ILO.

ILO. (2010). *World Social Security Report, 2010/11: Providing Coverage in the Time of Crisis and Beyond*. Geneva: ILO.

Ilorin, S.N. (2017, October 24). NMA rejects FG's move to stop private practice. *The Punch Newspaper*, p. 11.

Inness, M., Turner, N., Barling, J., & Stride, C. B. (2010). Transformational leadership and employee safety performance: A within-person, between -jobs design. *Journal of Occupational Health Psychology*, *15*(3), 279–290. doi:10.1037/a0019380 PMID:20604634

Insinga, R. P., Perez, G., Wheeler, C. M., Koutsky, L. A., Garland, S. M., Leodolter, S., ... Brown, D. R. (2011). Incident cervical HPV infections in young women: Transition probabilities for CIN and infection clearance. *Cancer Epidemiology and Prevention Biomarkers*, *20*(2), 287–296. doi:10.1158/1055-9965.EPI-10-0791 PMID:21300618

Internal Expert Seminar, Danish Working Environment Authority. (2009). *Partnership for European Research in Occupational Safety and Health (PEROSH)*, 53–56.

International Labor Organization. (2006). *Occupational safety and health: synergies between security and productivity*. Retrieved from http://www.ilo.org/wcmsp5/groups/public/@ed_protect/@protrav/@safework/documents/meetingdocument/wcms_110380.pdf

International Labour Organisation. (2006). *Occupational safety and health synergiesbetween securityandproductivity*. Retrievedfromhttp://www.ilo.org/wcmsp5/group/public/@ed_protect@safework

International Labour Organisation. (2010). *Work related accidents and diseases take a heavy toll worldwide*. Retrieved from: http://www.scielosp.org/scielo.php

International Labour Organisation. (2012). *Safety and health at work, hopes and challenges in development cooperation development: The example of an EU-ILO joint project "Improving safety and health at work through a decent health agenda"*. Retrieved from http://www.ilo.org/wcmsp5/group/public/---ed

Iwayemi, P. (2001). *Nigeria's fractured development: The energy connection. An inaugural Lecture*. Ibadan: University of Ibadan.

Iyatse, G. (2014, November 12). Harvard scholars, others canvass better funding for hospitals. *The Punch Newspaper*, p. 62.

Iyoha, E. (2008). *Local government and the elusive rural development in Nigeria and constraints on local authority's capacity and the promise of decentralized participatory development.* 31st Inaugural Lecture Ekpoma Ambrose Ali University.

Jaba, E., Balan, J. B., & Robu, E. B. (2014). The Relationship between Life Expectancy at birth and Health Expenditures Estimated by a Cross-country and Time Series Analysis. *Procedia Economics and Finance, 15*, 108–114. doi:10.1016/S2212-5671(14)00454-7

Jacobs, S., & Calland, R. (Eds.). (2002). *Thabo Mbeki's world: myth, ideology and politics in the South African presidency*. Durban: University of Natal Press.

Jain, A., Marshall, J., Buikema, A., Bancroft, T., Kelly, J. P., & Newschaffer, C. J. (2015). Autism occurrence by MMR vaccine status among US children with older siblings with and without autism. *Journal of the American Medical Association, 313*(15), 1534–1540. doi:10.1001/jama.2015.3077 PMID:25898051

James, C., Carrin, G., Savedoff, W., & Hanvoravongchai, P. (2005). Clarifying efficiency-equity tradeoffs through explicit criteria, with a focus on developing countries. *Health Care Analysis*.

Jilcha, K., & Kitaw, D. (2016). A literature review on global occupational safety and health practice and accidents severity. *International Journal of Qualitative Research, 10*(2), 279–310.

Jimoh, O. (2015). Managing epidemic: The british approach to 1918–1919 influenza in Lagos. *Journal of Asian and African Studies*. doi:10.1177/0021909615587367

Johnson, C. A. (2007). *Off the Map: How HIV/AIDS programming is failing same-sex practising people in Africa*. New York: IGLHRC.

Jolly, R., & King, M. (1982). The Organization of Health Services. In Medical Care in Developing Countries. Norfolk, UK: Oxford University Press.

Joubert, D. M. (2002). Occupational health challenges and success in developing countries: A South African perspective. *International Journal of Environment and Health, 8*, 119–124. PMID:12019678

Jowett, M., & Kutzin, J. (2015). *Rising Revenues for Health in Support of WHC: Strategic Issues for Policymakers*. Geneva: WHO.

Kabia, J. (2014). *The human rights dimension of West Africa's Ebola outbreak*. Retrieved from http://globalhumanrights.org/the-human-rights-dimension-of-west-africas-ebola-outbreak

Kaiser, H. J. (2007). *A Global Look at Public Perceptions of Health Problems, Priorities and Donors*. The Kaiser Global Health Survey.

Kam, K. (n.d.). *What Parents Should Know About the HPV, or Cervical Cancer, Vaccine*. Retrieved September 24, 2007 from http://www.webmd.com/sex/features/what-parents-should-know-about-hpv-cervical-cancer-vaccine

Kaplan, G. A., Pamuk, E., Cohen, R. D., Lynch, J. W., & Balfour, J. L. (1996). Inequality in income and mortality in the United States: Analysis of Mortality and Potential Pathways. *British Medical Journal, 312*(7037), 999–1003. doi:10.1136/bmj.312.7037.999 PMID:8616393

Karger, J. H., Midgley, J., & Brown, C. B. (Eds.). (2013). *Controversial Issues in Social Policy*. Boston: Pearson Education, Inc.

Kass, N.E. (2001). An ethics framework for public health. *Am J Public Health, 91*, 17776-82.

Kass, N. E. (2001). An ethics framework for public health. *American Journal of Public Health, 91*(11), 1776–1782. doi:10.2105/AJPH.91.11.1776 PMID:11684600

Ketsela, T., Habimana, P., Martines, J., Mbewe, A., Williams, A., & Sabiiti, J. N. (2012). *Integrated Management of Childhood Illness (IMCI)*. Retrieved on August 3, 2017 from http://www.who.int/pmnch/media/publications/aonsectionIII_5.pdf

Keys, B., & Case, J. (1990). How to become an influential manager. *The Academy of Management Executive, 44*, 38–51.

King, M. (Ed.). (1982). *Medical Care in Developing Countries*. Norfolk, UK: Oxford University Press.

Kironde, S., & Kahirimbanyi, M. (2002). Community participation in primary health care programmes: Lessons from tuberculosis treatment delivery in South Africa. *African Health Sciences, 2*(1), 16–23. PMID:12789110

Koontz, H., & Weihrich, H. (1990). *Essentials of Management*. New York: McGraw-Hill.

Kruk, M. E., Galea, S., Prescott, M. R., & Freedman, L. P. (2007). Healthcare Financing and Utilization of Maternal Health Services in Developing Countries. *Health Policy and Planning, 22*(5), 303–310. doi:10.1093/heapol/czm027 PMID:17681975

Kuruvilla, S., Schweitzer, J., Bishai, D., Chowdhury, S., Caramani, D., … Frost, L. (2014). Success factors for reducing maternal and child mortality. *Bulletin of the World Health Organization, 92*, 533-544. Retrieved on November 29, 2017 from http://www.who.int/bulletin/volumes/92/7/14-138131/en/

Kutzin, J., Yip, W., & Cashin, C. (2016). Alterative Financing Strategies for Universal Health Coverage. In World Scientific Handbook of Global Health Economics and Public Policy. World Scientific.

Kutzin, J., & Sparker, S. P. (2016). Health Systems Strengthening Universal Health Coverage, Health Security and Resilience. *Bulletin of the World Health Organization, 94*(1), 2. doi:10.2471/BLT.15.165050 PMID:26769987

La Forgia, G. M., & Harding, A. (2009). Public-private partnerships and public hospital performance in São Paulo, Brazil. *Health Affairs, 28*(4), 1114–1126. doi:10.1377/hlthaff.28.4.1114 PMID:19597211

Labonté, R., & Gagnon, M. L. (2010). Framing health and foreign policy: Lessons for global health diplomacy. *Globalization and Health*, *6*(1), 14. doi:10.1186/1744-8603-6-14 PMID:20727211

LaDou, J. (2003). International occupational health. *International Journal of Hygiene and Environmental Health*, *206*(4-5), 303–313. doi:10.1078/1438-4639-00226 PMID:12971685

Lakoff, A., & Collier, S. J. (Eds.). (2008). *Biosecurity interventions: global health & security in question*. Columbia University Press. doi:10.7312/lako14606

Lambo, A. (1982). The Village of Aro. In *Medical Care in Developing Countries*. Norfolk, UK: Oxford University Press.

Lambo, E. (2015). *Primary healthcare: Realities, challenges and the way forward*. Abuja: National Primary Healthcare Agency.

Lamy, M., & Phua, K. H. (2012). Southeast Asian cooperation in health: A comparative perspective on regional health governance in ASEAN and the EU. *Asia Europe Journal*, *10*(4), 233–250. doi:10.100710308-012-0335-1

LaVasseur, M., Goldstein, N., & Welles, S. (2014). A public health perspective on HIV/AIDS in Africa: Victories and unmet challenges. *Phatophysiology*, *21*(1), 237–256. PMID:25096828

Leary, V. (1994). The right to health in international human rights law. *Health and Human Rights*, *1*(1), 24. doi:10.2307/4065261 PMID:10395710

Lerner, B. H. (2000). Inventing a curable disease: Historical perspectives on breast cancer. In *Breast Cancer* (pp. 25–49). New York: Palgrave Macmillan. doi:10.1007/978-1-137-03779-4_2

Levine, S. (2007, April 4). Council tentatively backs mandatory HPV vaccine. *The Washington Post*, p. B01.

Lewis, C. E., Fein, R., & Mechanic, D. (1976). *The Maduabum. In Introduction to Organizational Behaviour*. Concept Publications.

Linhard, J. B. (2005). Understanding the return on health, safety and environmental investments. *Journal of Safety Research*, *36*(3), 257–260. doi:10.1016/j.jsr.2005.06.007 PMID:16038936

Livestrongarmy.org. (n.d.). *Lance Armstrong on the HPV Debate*. Retrieved October 30, 2007, from www.pbs.org/now/shows/308/lance-armstrong.html

Lowe, M., Chen, D. R., & Huang, S. L. (2016). Social and Cultural Factors Affecting Maternal Health in Rural Gambia: An Exploratory Qualitative Study. *PLoS One*, *11*(9), e0163653. doi:10.1371/journal.pone.0163653 PMID:27661617

Lyun, F. (1988). Inequalities in health care in Ondo State. *Nigeria Health Policy and Planning*, *3*(2), 159–163. doi:10.1093/heapol/3.2.159

Machida, S. (2009). Accident prevention – a safe workplace. *Occupational Health & Safety (Waco, Tex.)*, *19*(1), 102–112.

Maduabum, C. P., & Akahkpe, I. B. (Eds.). (2017). The dynamics of public sector management: A reader. Ibadan: John Archer Publishers.

Maduabum, C. P. (2014). *What has public administration got to do with it? Inaugural Lecture.* Lagos: National Open University of Nigeria.

Magadi, M. A., Agwanda, A. O., & Obare, F. O. (2007). A Comparative Analysis of the Use of Maternal Health Services between Teenagers and Older Mothers in sub-Saharan Africa: Evidence from Demographic Health Surveys. *Social Science & Medicine*, *64*(6), 1311–1325. doi:10.1016/j.socscimed.2006.11.004 PMID:17174017

Magawa, R. (2012). *Primary healthcare Implementation: A brief review*. Available from: http://www.consultancyafrica.com/index

Makofane, K., Beck, J., & Ayala, G. (2014). *MSM in sub-Saharan Africa: health, access and HIV*. Oakland, CA: MSMGF.

Mampane, J. N. (2017). *Guidelines for mitigating the risk of HIV-infection among Black men who have sex with men (MSM) in a rural community in South Africa* (Unpublished doctoral dissertation). University of South Africa, Pretoria, South Africa.

Mann, J. M. (2006). Health and Human Rights: If not now, when? (voices from the past). *American Journal of Public Health*, *96*(11), 1940–1943. doi:10.2105/AJPH.96.11.1940 PMID:17062844

Mansfield. (2017). *Reductions in Medicare Disproportionately Impacts Women 65 and older*. Available at http://patimes.org/reductions-medicare-disproportionately-impact-w

Maruthappu, M., Zhou, D.C., Williams, C., Zeltner, T., & Atun, R. (2015). Un-employment, Public sector Healthcare Expenditure and HIV Mortality: An Analysis of 74 Countries, 1981-2009. *Journal of Global Health*, *5*(1).

Massoud, O. (2008). Governance and Primary Health Care Delivery in Nigeria. In Governing Health Systems in Africa. Dakar: CODESRIA.

Mathebe, L. M. (2005). *The story of an immune deficiency and its representation in the South African media (1981-2000)* (Unpublished doctoral dissertation). University of South Africa, Pretoria, South Africa.

Mays, G. P., & Smith, S. A. (2011). Evidence Links Increases in Public Health Spending to Declines in Preventable Deaths. *Health Affairs*, *30*(8), 1585–1593. doi:10.1377/hlthaff.2011.0196 PMID:21778174

McCoy, D., Hall, J., & Ridge, M. (2012). A systematic review of literature for evidence on health facility committees in low and middle income countries. *Health Policy and Planning*, *27*(6), 449–466. doi:10.1093/heapol/czr077 PMID:22155589

Mchunu, G. G., & Gwele, N. S. (2005). The meaning of community involvement in health: The perspective of primary health care communities. *Curationis*, *28*(2), 30–37. doi:10.4102/curationis.v28i2.943 PMID:16045109

McInnes, C., & Lee, K. (2012). *Global health and international relations*. Cambridge, UK: Polity.

McInnes, C., & Lee, K. (2012). Global health and international relations. *Polity*.

McInness, C., & Lee, K. (2012). *Global Health and international relations*. Cambridge, UK: Polity.

Medhekar, A. (2014). Public-private partnerships for inclusive development: Role of private corporate sector in provision of healthcare services. *Procedia: Social and Behavioral Sciences*, *157*, 33–44. doi:10.1016/j.sbspro.2014.11.007

Mendes, R. (1985). The scope of occupational health in developing countries. *American Journal of Public Health*, *75*(5), 467–648. doi:10.2105/AJPH.75.5.467 PMID:3985233

Menifield, C., & Dawson, J. (2008). Infant mortality in southern states: A bureaucratic nightmare. *Journal of Health and Human Services*, *31*(3), 385–402. PMID:19209565

Meredith, S., & Ziemba, E. (2007). *A new landscape of partnerships. Global forum update on research for health: Equitable access: Research challenges for health in developing countries.* Geneva, Switzerland: Global Forum for Health Research.

Meswani, H. R. (2008). Safety and occupational health: Challenges and Opportunities in emerging economies. *Indian Journal of Occupational and Environmental Medicine*, *12*(1), 3–9. doi:10.4103/0019-5278.40808 PMID:20040990

Michaels, D., Barrera, C., & Gacharna, M. G. (1985). Economic development and occupational health in Latin America: New directions for public health in less developed countries. *American Journal of Public Health*, *75*(5), 536–542. doi:10.2105/AJPH.75.5.536 PMID:3985242

Miller, P., Mulvey, C., & Norris, K. (1997). Compensating differentials for risk of death in Australia. *The Economic Record*, *73*(223), 363–373. doi:10.1111/j.1475-4932.1997.tb01008.x

Milloy, C. (2007, January 10). District's HPV proposal tinged with ugly assumptions. *The Washington Post*, p. B01.

Mitchell, M. (2014). *An overview of public private partnerships in health.* Retrieved from https://wiki.unece.org/download/attachments/23759108/overview%20of%20PPP%20in%20health.pdf?version=1&modificationDate=1410288914634&api=v2

Mockaitis, A. I. (2005). A cross-cultural study of leadership attitudes in three Baltic Sea region countries. *International Journal of Leadership Studies*, *1*(1), 44–63.

Mokikan, N. (2012). *Realities of employee compensation in the workplace*. Paper delivered to the Nigerian union of journalist on health and safety issues in Nigeria, Benin City, Nigeria.

Mor Barak, M. (2008). Social Psychological Perspectives of Workforce Diversity and Inclusion in National and Global Contexts. In R. Patti (Ed.), Handbook of Human Service Management. Thousand Oaks, CA: Sage Publications.

Muchabaiwa, L., Mazambani, D., Chigusiwa, L., Bindu, S., & Mudavanhu, V. (2012). Determinants of Maternal Healthcare Utilization in Zimbabwe. *International Journal of Economic Science Application Res.*, *5*(2), 145–162.

Muhammed, M. L., & Segun, T. (2015). Improving Primary health care in Nigeria: What's needed now. *Impatient Optimists* Retrieved on 24th May, 2018 from https: www.impatientoptimists.org/posts/2015/09/

Muller, A. (2013). Community participation in health. *Nutrition Update*, *2*(1), 26–29.

Muller, A. (2014). Professionalism is key in providing services to lesbian, gay, bisexual and transgender South Africans. *South African Medical Journal*, *104*(8), 558–559. doi:10.7196/SAMJ.8447 PMID:25213846

Murad, A. B., Unlucan, D., Olowu, G., & Kalifa, W. (2017). Healthcare Spending and Health Outcomes: Evidence from Selected East African Countries. *Journal African Health Sciences*, *17*(1), 247–254. doi:10.4314/ahs.v17i1.30 PMID:29026399

Muraguri, N., Temmerman, M., & Geibel, S. (2012). A decade of research involving men who have sex with men in sub-Saharan Africa: current knowledge and future directions. *SAHARA-J: Journal of Social Aspects of HIV/AIDS. An Open Access Journal*, *9*(3), 137–147. PMID:23237068

Mwesiggye, F. (2002). Effects of Abolition of Cost sharing. *A Commission Study by the Uganda National NGO Forum*. Available Online at Mpra.ub.uni-muenchen.de/8558

National Association of Social Workers. (2000). *Social Work Speaks: National Association of Social Workers Policy Statements* (5th ed.). Washington, DC: NASW Press.

National Bureau of Statistics (NBS). (2012). *Nigeria Poverty Profile 2010*. Abuja, Nigeria: Federal Government of Nigeria.

National Bureau of Statistics (NBS). (2017). *Unemployment/Underemployment Report. Q4 2016*. Abuja, Nigeria: Federal Government of Nigeria.

National Conference on State Legislatures. (2007, October). *HPV Vaccine*. Retrieved June 30, 2018, from http://www.ncsl.org/programs/health/HPVvaccine.htm

National Development Plan Vision 2030. (2012). *Our future – make it work*. Pretoria: Sherino Printers.

National Economic & Social Rights Initiative (NESRI). (2018). *Health Care in the United States*. Retrieved on May 24, 2018 from https://www.nesri.org/programs/healt-care-in-the-united-states

National Health Act, 2014.

National Health Expenditures. (2014). *Center for Medicare and Medicaid Services*. Available at: https//www.cms.gov/research-statistics-data-and–system/statistics-trends-and-reports/national health expend datat/nationalhealthaccountshistorical.html

National Health Insurance Scheme. (2012a). *Operational guidelines.* Available at: http://www.nhis.gov.ng/index. php?option=com_ content& view=article&id=92& Itemid= 77

National Health Policy Act. (2016). Abuja: Federal Government Printing Press.

National Population Commission & ICF International. (2014). *Nigeria Demographic and Health Survey 2013.* Abuja, Nigeria: NPC & ICF International.

National Primary Healthcare Development Agency (NPHCDA). (2010). *Midwives Service Scheme.* Retrieved on August 10, 2017 from https://www.nphcda.org/programmes/midwives-service-scheme/

Negin, J., Morgan, C., & Condon, R. (2012). Regional Health Meetings in the Pacific and their Impact on Health Governance. *Global Health Governance, 5*(2).

Nelson, A. (2002). Unequal treatment: Confronting racial and ethnic disparities in health care. *Journal of the National Medical Association, 94*(8), 666–668. PMID:12152921

Ngcaweni, B. (Ed.). (2016). *Sizonqoba! Outliving AIDS in Africa.* Pretoria: AISA.

Ngwama, J. C. (2016). Framework for occupational health and safety in Nigeria: The implication for the trade union movement. *Journal of Economics and Sustainable Development, 7*(11), 113–121.

Nigenda-López, G. H., Juárez-Ramírez, C., Ruiz-Larios, J. A., Herrera, C. M., & Ramírez, C. J. (2013). Social participation and quality of health care: The experience of citizens' health representatives in Mexico. *Revista de Saude Publica, 47*(1), 44–51. doi:10.1590/S0034-89102013000100007 PMID:23703129

Nigerian Constitution (1999). Section 7(1) C.

Nigerian Institute of Medical Research (NIMR). (2000a). *HIV/AIDS in Nigeria: Technical Report (Survey of Health and Laboratory Facilities) (1989-1999). In National HIV/AIDS Database Project* (1st ed.). Lagos: Federal Ministry of Science and Technology.

Nigerian National Health Act, 2014.

Nikjoo, R. G., Beyrami, H. J., Jannati, A., & Jaafarabadi, M. A. (2012). Prioritizing public-private partnership models for public hospitals of Iran based on performance indicators. *Health Promotion Perspectives, 2*(2), 251–264. PMID:24688942

Nixon, J., & Ulmann, P. (2006). The Relationship between Healthcare expenditure and Health Outcomes. *The European Journal of Health Economics, 7*(1), 7–18. doi:10.100710198-005-0336-8 PMID:16429295

Nwakoby, B. N. (1994). Use of Obsteric Services in Rural Nigeria. *Journal of the Royal Society of Health, 114*(3), 132–136. doi:10.1177/146642409411400304 PMID:7932482

Nwanna, C. R. (2011). *Socio-economic status and HIV-related discrimination in Lagos, Nigeria.* LAP Lambert Academic Publishing GmbH & Co. KG.

Nwatu, R. (2000, January). Making the health system effective. *Medical Journal.*

O'Donnell, O., Van Doorslaer, E., Wagstaff, A., & Lindelow, M. (2008). *Analyzing health equity usin g household survey data.* Washington, DC: World Bank.

O'Neill, D. (2000). Ergonomics in industrially developing countries: Does its application differ from that in industrially advanced countries? *Applied Ergonomics, 31*(6), 631–640. doi:10.1016/S0003-6870(00)00033-8 PMID:11132047

Obembe, K. (2015, April 25). Achieving community health insurance fund development goals in Nigeria. *The Punch Newspaper*, p. 53.

Obionu, C. N. (2007). *Primary Healthcare for Developing Countries* (2nd ed.). Enugu: Delta Publications.

OECD. (2015). *Health at a Glance 2015: OECD indicators*. OECD Publishing. Available at: http://www.oecd-library.org/social-issues-migration-health/health-at-a-glance.199913112

Ojo, J. (2016, July 27). Nigerian's disdain for preventive medicine. *The Punch Newspaper*, p. 22.

Olaniyan, A.O. (2002). *Review of the state of agricultural enterprises in Nigeria.* The 2nd LASU/CCDS Lecture Series held at the Nigerian Institute of International Affairs, Lagos, Nigeria.

Olatunbosun, D. (1975). *Nigeria's neglected rural majority*. Ibadan: Oxford University Press.

Olise, P. (2007). *Primary Healthcare for Sustainable Development*. Abuja: Ozege Publications.

Olukotun, A. (2013, January 25). Controversy on oversees medical treatment for public officials. *The Punch Newspaper*, p. 64.

Ononokpono, D. N., & Odimegwu, C. O. (2014). Determinants of Maternal Health Care Utilization in Nigeria: A Multilevel Approach. *The Pan African Medical Journal, 17*(1), 2. Retrieved from http://www.panafrican-med-journal.com/content/series/17/1/2/full on 6/7/2017 PMID:24643545

Onuegbu, C. (2010). *Emerging risks and new patterns of prevention in a changing world of work.* Paper presented at 2010 world day for safety and health at work, 28th April 2010 organised by Federal Ministry of Labor & Productivity.

Onyebuchi Chukwu, C. O. (2015). *Maternal, Newborn and child Health in Nigeria: Where are we now?* Presentation by the Honorable Minister of Health, Nigeria. Retrieved on October 26, 2017 from http://www.who.int/pmnch/about/steering_committee/B11_11_02_nigeriapresentation.pdf

Onyekpere, E. (2016, August 1). Implementing the national health care act. *The Punch Newspaper*, p. 21.

Options Consultancy Services/Evidence for Action, Cambridge Economic Policy Associates, & the Partnership for Maternal, Newborn and Child Health. (2013). *Success Factors for Women's and Children's Health: Country Specific Review of Data and Literature on 10 Fast-Track Countries' Progress Towards MDGs 4 and 5.* Retrieved on July 10, 2017 from http://www.who.int/pmnch/knowledge/publications/country_data_review.pdf

Or, Z. (2000). Determinants of Health Outcomes in Industrial Countries: A Pooled, Cross-country, Time series Analysis. *OECD Economic Studies*, *30*, 53–78.

Osaghae, E. (2002). *Crippled giant: Nigeria since independence*. Ibadan: John Archer Publishers.

Osakede, K. O., & Ijimakinde, S. O. (2014). The effects of healthcare strike on service delivery: The Nigerian experience. *Review of Journal of Public Administration and Management*, *2*(6).

OUT LGBT Well-being. (n.d.). *About Us*. Retrieved June 5, 2018, from http://www.out.org.za

Owolabi, R. S., Araoye, M. O., & Osagbemi, G. K. (2011). *Assessment of Stigma and Discrimination Experienced by People Living with HIV and AIDS Receiving Care/Treatment in University of Ilorin Teaching Hospital (UITH), Ilorin, Nigeria*. Retrieved November 20, 2017 from http://journals.sagepub.com/doi/abs/10.1177/1545109711399443

Oxfam. (2015). *Quarantines in Sierra Leone: Putting people first in the Ebola crisis*. Oxfam Report.

Oyekanmi, F.A.D (1997). *Traditional Birth Attendants: An Indispensable Partner in Health Programme in Lagos State*. Research Report.

Peltzer, K., Skinner, D., Mfecane, S., Shisana, O., Nqeketo, A., & Mosala, T. (2005). Factors Influencing the Utilization of Prevention of Mother-to-Child-Transmission Services by Pregnant Women in the Eastern Cape, South Africa. *Health SA Gesondheid*, *10*(1), 26–40. doi:10.4102/hsag.v10i1.186

Perrow, C. (1984). *Normal accidents: Living with high-risk technologies*. New York, NY: Basic Book.

PMNCH, WHO, World Bank, & AHPSR. (2014). Success Factors for Women's and Children's Health: Policy and Programme Highlights from 10 Fast-Track Countries. Geneva: Authors.

Poni-Gore, R., Lino, E. O., Alex, O. A., Simaya, R. J., Bion, A. J., Jette, A. J., & James, D. S. (2015). Stigma and Discrimination against People Living with HIV in Juba, South Sudan. *Journal of Community Medicine & Health Education*, *5*, 357. doi:10.4172/21610711.1000357

Population Council. (2002). Addressing HIV/AIDS Stigma and Discrimination in a Workplace Program: Emerging Findings. *Horizons*. Retrieved from http://www.popcouncil.org/uploads/pdfs/horizons/eskombslnsum.pdf

Preker, A., & Carrin, G. (2004). *Health Financing for Poor People: Resource Mobilization and Risk Sharing*. Washington, DC: The World Bank.

Public Health Policy Framework. (2016). Western Australia Department of Health.

Raghupathy, S. (1996). Education and the Use of Maternal Health Care in Thailand. *Social Science & Medicine*, *43*(4), 459–471. doi:10.1016/0277-9536(95)00411-4 PMID:8844947

Raids, M. (2008). Nigeria Still Searching for right formula. *Bulletin of the World Health Organization*, *86*(9), 663–665. doi:10.2471/BLT.08.020908 PMID:18797638

Raj Baral, Lyons, & Skinner, & van Teijlingen. (2012). Maternal Health Services Utilization in Nepal: Progress in the New Millennium? *Health Science Journal*, *6*(4), 618–633.

Rao, S.K. Selvaraju, S., Nagpal, S. & Sakthivel, S. (2005). *Financing Health in India*. Available Online at ww.Whoindia.org/…./commission on Macroeconomic and Health Finance

Rashid, S. A., & Archer, M. (1983). *Organizational Behaviour*. New York: Methuen.

Rawls, J. A. (1999). *A Theory of Justice* (revised edn.). Cambridge, MA: Belknap Press of Harvard University Press.

Reagan, L. J. (1997). Engendering the dread disease: Women, men and cancer. *American Journal of Public Health*, *87*(11), 1779–1787. doi:10.2105/AJPH.87.11.1779 PMID:9366635

Reddy, V., Sandfort, T., & Rispel, L. (Eds.). (2009). *From social silence to social science: same-sex sexuality, HIV & AIDS and gender in South Africa*. Pretoria: HSRC Press.

Reich, M. R. (Ed.). (2002). *Public-private partnerships for public health*. Cambridge, MA: Harvard Center for Population and Development Studies.

Reynolds, H. W., Wong, E. L., & Tucker, H. (2006). Adolescents Use of Maternal and Child Health Services in Developing Countries. *International Family Planning Perspectives*, *32*(1), 6–16. doi:10.1363/3200606 PMID:16723297

Rheinstein, M. (1954). *Max Weber on Law in economy and Society*. Simon and Schuster.

Rispel, L. C., & Metcalf, C. A. (2009). Breaking the silence: South African HIV policies and the needs of men who have sex with men. *Reproductive Health Matters*, *17*(33), 133–142. doi:10.1016/S0968-8080(09)33442-4 PMID:19523590

Robison, C. (2007, February 16). As questions brew over his motives for vaccine, governor lays it out: Cancer runs in his family. For Perry, it's also personal. *Houston Chronicle*, p. A1.

Rodgers, H. R. Jr, & Payne, L. (2007). Child poverty in the American states: The impact of welfare reform, economics, and demographics. *Policy Studies Journal: the Journal of the Policy Studies Organization*, *35*(1), 1–21. doi:10.1111/j.1541-0072.2007.00204.x

Roehrich, J. K., Lewis, M. A., & George, G. (2014). Are public-private partnerships a healthy option? A systematic literature review. *Social Science & Medicine*, *113*, 110–119. doi:10.1016/j.socscimed.2014.03.037 PMID:24861412

Rollinson, R. (2015). *Public health and human rights in an era of epidemics*. Academic Press.

Sama, M., & Nguyen, V. K. (Eds.). (2008). Governing Health Systems in Africa. Dakar: CODESRIA.

Sapru, R.K. (2008). *Administrative Theories and Management Thought*. New Delhi: Prentice Hall of India Private Ltd.

Sapru, R. (2013). *Administrative Theories and management thoughts*. New Delhi: PHT Learning Private Limited.

Satterwhite, C. L., Torrone, E., Meites, E., Dunne, E. F., Mahajan, R., Ocfemia, M. C. B., & Weinstock, H. (2013). Sexually transmitted infections among US women and men: Prevalence and incidence estimates, 2008. *Sexually Transmitted Diseases*, *40*(3), 187–193. doi:10.1097/OLQ.0b013e318286bb53 PMID:23403598

Savas, E. S. (1990). A taxonomy of privatization strategies. *Policy Studies Journal: the Journal of the Policy Studies Organization*, *18*(2), 343–355. doi:10.1111/j.1541-0072.1989.tb00837.x

Scharfstein, D. S., & Stein, J. C. (2000). The dark side of internal capital markets: Divisional rent-seeking and inefficient investment. *The Journal of Finance*, *55*(6), 2537–2564. doi:10.1111/0022-1082.00299

Schneider, A., & Ingram, H. (1998). *Policy Design for Democracy*. Lawrence, KS: University Press of Kansas.

Seixas, P. H. D. (2003). *Social health organizations in São Paulo: 1998-2002* (Unpublished Master's thesis). Getúlio Vargas Foundation, São Paulo, SP, Brazil.

Seshamani, M., & Gray, A. (2004). Ageing and Healthcare Expenditure: A red Herring? *Health Economics*, *13*, 303–314. doi:10.1002/hec.826 PMID:15067669

Shosanya, M. (2015). As FG enacts new law to protect PLWHA. *Daily Trust*. Retrieved from 22/11/17 https://www.dailytrust.com.ng/daily/health/49553-as-fg-enacts-new-law-to-protect-plwha

Silal, S., Penn-Kekana, L., Harris, B., Birch, S., & McIntyre, D. (2012). Exploring Inequalities in Access to and Use of Maternal Health Services in South Africa. *BMC Health Services Research*, *12*(1), 120. doi:10.1186/1472-6963-12-120 PMID:22613037

Simkhada, B., Teijlingen, E. R., Porter, M., & Simkhada, P. (2008). Factors Affecting the Utilization of Antenatal Care in Developing Countries: Systematic Review of the Literature. *Journal of Advanced Nursing*, *61*(3), 244–260. doi:10.1111/j.1365-2648.2007.04532.x PMID:18197860

Singh, P. (2014). Health in a time of Ebola. *Businessday*. Retrieved from www.businessdayonline.com

Skloot, R. (2017). *The Immortal Life of Henrietta Lacks*. New York: Broadway Books.

Smallman, C., & John, G. (2001). British directors' perspectives on the impact of health and safety on corporate performance. *Safety Science, 38*(3), 227–39.

Smith, J. C., & Medalia, C. (2014). U.S. Census current population Reports, Health Insurance coverage in the United States. Washington, DC: U.S. Government Printing Office.

Smith, J. (1998). Healthy Bodies and Thick Wallets- the Dual Relation between Health and Economic Status. *The Journal of Economic Perspectives*, *13*(2), 145–166. doi:10.1257/jep.13.2.145 PMID:15179962

Smith, J. C., & Medalia, C. (2015). U.S. Census Bureau. *Current Population Reports. Series P-28, Special Censuses*, 5.

South Africa (Republic). (1996). *Constitution of the Republic of South Africa (Act 108 of 1996)*. Pretoria: Government Printers.

Steiger, T. (2003). Das Rollenkonzept der Führung. In Handbuch Angewandte Psychologie für Führungskräfte. Führungskompetenz und Führungswissen (2nd ed.). Springer.

Stone, D. (2002). *Policy Paradox: The Art of Political Decision Making*. New York: W.W. Norton & Company.

Stone, D. A. (1989). Causal stories and the formation of policy agendas. *Political Science Quarterly*, *104*(2), 281–300. doi:10.2307/2151585

Swuste, P., & Eijkemans, G. (2002). Occupational safety, health and hygiene in the urban informal sector of Sub-Saharan Africa: An Application of the Prevention and Control Exchange (PACE) program to the informal-sector workers in healthy city projects. *International Journal of Occupational and Environmental Health*, *8*(2), 113–118. doi:10.1179/oeh.2002.8.2.113 PMID:12019677

Tadesse, T., & Kumie, A. (2007). Prevalenve and factors affecting work-related injury among workers engaged in Small and Medium-scale industries in Gondar wereda, North Gondor zone, Amhara Regional State, Ethiopia. *The Ethiopian Journal of Health Development*, *21*(1). doi:10.4314/ejhd.v21i1.10028

Takala, J. (1999). International agency efforts to protect workers and the environment. *The International Journal of Occupational and Environmental Medicine*, *15*(1), 30–37. doi:10.1179/oeh.1999.5.1.30 PMID:10092745

Tannenbaum, R., Weschler, I. R., & Massarik, F. (1961). *Leadership and Organization, A Behaviour Science Approach*. New York: McGraw-Hill.

Terry, G. R. (1988). *Principles of Management*. Richard D. Irwin.

Thadani, K. B. (2014). Public private partnership in the health sector: Boon or bane. *Procedia: Social and Behavioral Sciences*, *157*, 307–316. doi:10.1016/j.sbspro.2014.11.033

The Global Network of People Living with HIV (GNP+), ILO, The PLHIV Stigma Index. (2012). *Evidence Brief: Stigma and Discrimination at Work. Findings from the PLHIV Stigma Index*. Amsterdam: GNP+. Retrieved from https://www.gnpplus.net/assets/wbb_file_updown/4621/Stigma%20and%20Discrimination%20at%20work.pdf

Treatment Action Campaign (TAC). (2015). *Access to ART in South Africa*. Retrieved October 15, 2015, from http://www.tac.org.za

Triangle Project. (n.d.). *About Us*. Retrieved June 5, 2018, from http://www.triangle.org.za

Tsawe, M., & Susuman, A. S. (2014). Determinants of Access to and Use of Maternal Health Care Services in the Eastern Cape, South Africa: A Quantitative and Qualitative Investigation. *BioMed Central Research Notes, 7*, 723. Retrieved from https://www.ncbi.nlm.nih.gov/pmc/articles/PMC4203863/

Tsawe, M., Moto, A., Netshivhera, T., Ralesego, L., Nyathi, C., & Susuman, A. S. (2015). Factors Influencing the Use of Maternal Healthcare Services and Childhood Immunization in Swaziland. *International Journal For Equity in Health*. Retrieved from https://www.ncbi.nlm.nih.gov/pmc/articles/PMC4391603/

Turner, R. (1991). Better Access to Health Services in Nicaragua Lower Infant Mortality. *International Family Planning Perspective*, *17*(2).

U.S. Census Bureau. (2006 – 2008). *American Community Survey. Georgia Fact Sheet.* Retrieved September 30, 2010, from http://factfinder.census.gov/servlet/ACSSAFFFacts?_event=&geo_id=04000US13&_geoContext=01000US|04000US13&_street=&_county=&_cityTown=&_state=04000US13&_zip=&_lang=en&_sse=on&ActiveGeoDiv=&_useEV=&pctxt=fph&pgsl=040&_submenuId=factsheet_1&ds_name=null&_ci_nbr=null&qr_name=null&reg=null%3Anull&_keyword=&_industry=

U.S. Census Bureau. (2007). *District of Columbia Quick Facts*. Retrieved November 27, 2007, from http://quickfacts.census.gov/qfd/states/11000.html

U.S. Court of Federal Claims. (2007). *In Re: Claims for Vaccine Injuries Resulting in Autism Spectrum Disorder or a Similar Neurodevelopmental Disorder.* Retrieved October 24, 2007, from http://www.uscfc.uscourts.gov/OSM/OSMAutism.htm

UN High-Level panel. (2004). *Panel on Threats, Challenges, and Change. A more secure world: our shared responsibility*. New York: Author.

UN International Labour Organization (ILO) Discrimination Convention (No. 111) 1958

UN. (2014). *A human rights perspective into the Ebola outbreak. UN report*. Geneva: United Nations.

UNAIDS. (2005). *HIV - Related Stigma, Discrimination and Human Rights Violations Case studies of successful programmes.* Geneva, Switzerland: UNAIDS. Retrieved November 22, 2017 from http://data.unaids.org/publications/irc-pub06/jc999-humrightsviol_en.pdf

UNAIDS. (2011). *People Living with HIV Stigma Index: Asia Pacific Regional Analysis 2011*. Retrieved from http://www.unaids.org/sites/default/files/media_asset/20110829_PLHIVStigmaIndex_en_0.pdf

UNAIDS. (2017). *UNAIDS data 2017*. Retrieved from http://www.unaids.org/en/resources/documents/2017/2017_data_book

UNFPA. (2014). *Liberia's Ebola outbreak leaves pregnant women stranded.* Retrieved from www.unfpa.org/news/liberias-ebola-outbreak-leaves-pregnant-womenstranded#sthash.zdvmnjF2.dpuf

UNICEF. (2015). *Level and Trends in child mortality report*. New York: UNICEF.

UNICEF. (2016). *Zambia Health Sector Budget Brief: review of Budget Performance and 2016 Allocations*. UNICEF.

United Nations Children's Fund (UNICEF). (2013). *Maternal and Child Mortality*. Retrieved on May 1, 2013 from http://www.unicef.org/nigeria/children_1926.html

United Nations Children's Fund (UNICEF). (2016). *Evaluation of the Maternal, Newborn and Child Health Week in Nigeria*. Abuja, Nigeria: UNICEF Nigeria Country Office.

United Nations Children's Fund (UNICEF). (2017). *Water Sanitation and Hygiene*. Retrieved on November 29, 2017 from https://www.unicef.org/nigeria/wes.html

United Nations Development Group. (2015). *Socio-economic impact of Ebola Virus Disease (United Nations Development Programme report). Western and central Africa*. Author.

United Nations Development Programme. (2016). *Human Development Report*. Washington, DC: United Nations Development Programme.

United Nations Organization (UNO). (2014). *A human rights perspective into the Ebola outbreak. UN. Report*. Geneva: United Nations.

United Nations. (2005). *The Millennium Development Goals Report 2005*. New York: United Nations.

United Nations. (2015). *Transforming Our World: the 2030 Agenda for Sustainable Development*. Resolution Adopted by the General Assembly on 25 September, 2015.

United Nations. (2016). *Transforming Our World: The 2030 Agenda for Sustainable Development. ARES/70/1*. Retrieved on August 2, 2017 from sustainabledevelopment.org

Uno, Y., Uchiyama, T., Kurosawa, M., Aleksic, B., & Ozaki, N. (2015). Early exposure to the combined measles–mumps–rubella vaccine and thimerosal-containing vaccines and risk of autism spectrum disorder. *Vaccine*, *33*(21), 2511–2516. doi:10.1016/j.vaccine.2014.12.036 PMID:25562790

USAID. (2009). *Maternal and Child Health*. Retrieved on August,2, 2017 from http://www.usaid.gov/our_work/global_health/mch/mh/techareas/post.html

USAID. (2016). Health financing Profile Zambia. USAID.

Uzoma, C. W. (2016). Human Resource for Health: Focus on Community Health Extension Workers. *Businessday*. Retrieved from www.businessdayone.com

Vavken, P., Pagenstert, G., Grim, C. & Dorotka, R. (2002). Does Increased Healthcare Spending Afford better Healthcare Outcomes: Evidence from Austrian Healthcare Expenditure since the Implementation of DRGs. *Swiss Med Weekly, 142*.

Villarreal, M. A. (2010). The Mexican economy after the global financial crisis. *Congressional Research Service Report.* Retrieved October 19, 2017, from http://www.dtic.mil/get-tr-doc/pdf?AD=ADA529130

W.H.O. (1998). *World Health Forum, 19*(1). Geneva. World Health Organization.

Washington, H. (2007, February 7). *BookTV lecture*. Retrieved September 25, 2007, from http://www.booktv.org/program.aspx?ProgramId=7904&SectionName=History&PlayMedia=Yes

Washington, H. (2006). *Medical Apartheid: The Dark History of Medical Experimentation on Black Americans from Colonial Times to the Present*. New York: Doubleday.

Weber, M. (1947). *The Theory of Social and Economic Organization*. New York: Free Press of Glencoe.

WebMd. (2005 – 2013). *HPV/Genital Warts Health Center*. Retrieved July 18, 2018, from http://www.webmd.com/sexual-conditions/hpv-genital-warts/default.htm

Weiss, M. G., & Ramakrishna, J. (2001). *Interventions: Research on Reducing Stigma*. Available at http://www.stigmaconference.nih.gov/Weisspaper.htm

Wheeler, C., & Berkley, S. (2001). Initial lessons from public-private partnerships in drug and vaccine development. *Bulletin of the World Health Organization, 79*(8), 728–734. PMID:11545329

WHO Constitution. (2006). (14th ed.). World Health Organization. Retrieved from http://www.who.int/governance/eb/who_constitution_en.pdf

WHO. (2002). Report on the Study of Effect of Abolition of Cost sharing in Ugadan. In Collaboration with Ministry of Health, Kampala.

WHO. (2004). *World report on knowledge for better health: Strengthening health systems.* Geneva: WHO.

WHO. (2005). Sustainable Health Financing, Universal Coverage and Social Health Insurance. Fifty Eighth World Health Assembly, Geneva, Switzerland.

WHO. (2009). *Telemedicine: Opportunities and Developments in Member States.* Report on the Second Global Survey on eHealth.

WHO. (2010a). *The World Health Report: Health Systems Financing. In The Path to Universal Coverage* (pp. ix–x). Geneva, Switzerland: WHO.

WHO. (2010b). *National Health Accounts*. Geneva: WHO.

WHO. (2014). *Global Health Expenditure data Base*. Geneva, Switzerland: WHO.

WHO. (2015). Committee on Economic, Social and Cultural Rights. General Comment No. 20, Non-discrimination in economic, social and cultural rights, 2009. Available at http://www.who.int/mediacentre/fact-sheets/fs323/en/

WHO. (2016). *Public Financing for Health in Africa: From Abuja to the SDGs*. Geneva: WHO.

Widdus, R. (2001). Public-private partnerships for health: Their main targets, their diversity, and their future directions. *Bulletin of the World Health Organization*, *79*(8), 713–720. PMID:11545327

Williams, G. (1980). *State and society in Nigeria. Idanre*. Afrograika Publishers.

Williams, S. J., & Torrens, P. R. (2008). *Introduction to Health Services*. DELMAR Cengage.

Wilson, B. (2007, February 5). States consider requiring HPV vaccine for girls. On *All Things Considered*. National Public Radio. Retrieved October 30, 2007, from http://www.npr.org/templates/story/story.php?storyId=7190905

World Bank. (2014). *The Worldwide Governance Indicators (WGI) project*. Washington, DC: World Bank. Retrieved on October 4, 2017 from http://info.worldbank.org/governance/wgi/index.aspx

World Bank. (2016). *2014-2015 West African Ebola crisis: Impact update (World Bank report)*. Geneva, Switzerland: Author.

World Bank. (2017). *World Governance Indicators*. Retrieved on November 29, 2017 from https://data.worldbank.org/data-catalog/worldwide-governance-indicators

World Economic Forum. (2017a). *The Global Competitiveness Report*. Geneva, Switzerland: World Economic Forum.

World Economic Forum. (2017b). *The Global Gender Gap Report*. Geneva, Switzerland: World Economic Forum.

World Health Organisation. (1978). *Report on primary health care*. World Health Organisation.

World Health Organisation. (2007). *Working together for health (World Health Organisation report)*. Geneva, Switzerland: Author.

World Health Organization & United Nations Children's Fund. (2014). *Countdown to 2015 and beyond: Fulfilling the Health Agenda for Women and Children*. Geneva: World Health Organization & United Nations Children's Fund.

World Health Organization (WHO) Report. (2015). *Sub-Saharan African lags other regions in healthcare*. Businessday. Retrieved from www.businessdayonline.com

World Health Organization (WHO). (2015). Sub-Saharan African Lags other Regions in health care. *Businessday*. Retrieved on September 29, 2015 from www.businessdayonline.com

World Health Organization. (1978). *Alma –Ata Declaration: Primary Health Care*. Geneva: World Health Organization.

World Health Organization. (1978). *Alma-Ata Declaration*. WHO.

World Health Organization. (1991). PHS capacity-building strategies. *Public Health Report Series, Geneva*, *106*(1), 5–15.

World Health Organization. (2010). *The health promoting work place*. Retrieved from: http://www.cepis.org.pe/bvsast/i/full-text/whp/whp.html

World Health Organization. (2012a). Trends in Maternal Mortality: 1990-2010. WHO, UNICEF, UNFPA, World Bank Estimates. Geneva: World Health Organization.

World Health Organization. (2012b). *MDG 5: Improve Maternal Health*. Retrieved on May 31, 2013 from http://www.who.int/topics/maternal_health/en/

World Health Organization. (2014). *Success Factors for Women's and Children's Health: Multisector Pathways to Progress*. Geneva: World Health Organization.

World Health Organization. (2014). *Success Factors for Women's and Children's Health: Country Multistakeholder Policy Reviews*. Geneva: World Health Organization. Retrieved on September18, 2017 from http://www.who.int/pmnch/knowledge/publications/successfactors/en/index2.html

World Health Organization. (2015). *Trends in Maternal Mortality: 1990-2015. WHO, UNICEF, UNFPA, World Bank Estimates*. Geneva, Switzerland: World Health Organization.

World Health Organization. (2016). *Global Health Workforce Statistics*. Retrieved on November 29, 2017 from http://www.who.int/hrh/statistics/hwfstats/

World Health. (2000). *Health Systems: Improving Performances*. Geneva: WHO.

Yamin, A. (2014). Ebola, human rights, and poverty – making the links. *openDemocracy*. Available at https://www.opendemocracy.net/openglobalrights-blog/alicia-ely-yamin/ebola-human-rights-and-poverty-%E2%80%93-making-links

Yoon, S. (2015). *The Role of Epistemic Communities in the Global Response to Severe Acute Respiratory Syndrome: Implications for Global Health Governance* (Doctoral dissertation). London School of Hygiene & Tropical Medicine.

Youde, J. (2012). *Global health governance*. Cambridge, UK: Polity.

Yuki, G. A., & Van-Fleet, D. D. (1998). Theory and Research on Leadership in Organizations. In Handbook of Industrial and Organizational Psychology. Mambai: Jaico Publishing House.

Yukl, G. A. (1994). *Leadership in organisations*. Englewood Cliffs, NJ: Prentice Hall.

Yusuf, S., Moges, H., & Ahmed, A. (2014). Magnitude and characteristics of occupational injury in Kombolcha textile factory, North East Ethiopia. *International Journal of Occupational Safety and Health, 3*(2). doi:10.3126/ijosh.v3i2.8381

Zombre, D., De Allegn, M., & Riddle, V. (2017). Immediate and Sustained Effects of User fee Exemption on Healthcare Utilization among Children under five in Burkana Faso: A Controlled Interrupted Time-series Analysis. *Social Science & Medicine, 179*, 27–35. doi:10.1016/j.socscimed.2017.02.027 PMID:28242542

Zucchi, P. (1998). Employees per bed: A study in some public and private hospitals. *Revista de Admininstração Publica, 32*(3), 65-76. Retrieved October 15, 2017, from http://bibliotecadigital.fgv.br/ojs/index.php/rap/article/view/7734

About the Contributors

Augustine Nduka Eneanya is a Senior Lecturer in the Department of Political Science, University of Lagos, Akoka, Yaba, Lagos, Nigeria. He specializes in Public Policy and Administration. He has worked in Public Sector for 16 years and private sector for 12 years and advanced to the post of General Manager. He also worked as the Managing Consultant of a Human Resources Consulting Firm in Lagos, Nigeria. He is a member of many professional associations, among which are America Society for Public Administration (ASPA), Chartered Institute of Personnel Management (CIPM), Nigerian Institute of Management (NIM) and Nigerian Institute of Management Consultants. He is the author of several books, among which are: Theory and Practice of Public Administration; Policy Research, Analysis and Policy making; Comparative Public Administration and Public Policy; Managing Personnel in Public Sector; Program development, implementation and evaluation; Local government Administration; Research Methods in Political Science and Public Administration. He has published widely in scholarly papers in local and international journals. He was awarded "Distinguished Scholarship Award" by Zambia Society of Public Administration on December 2, 2016. He also an edited international book, published by IGI Global, titled: Environmental Policies for Emergency Management and Public Safety.

* * *

Ighodalo Akhakpe holds a Ph.D in Political Science with interest in Policy and development studies. He has written widely in national and international journal. Also, he has contributed chapters in edited books and has several authored books to his credit. These books include: Leading issues in Political Thoughts, Public Policy Making and Policy Analysis, Administration and Management of Public Enterprise and Bureaucracy and Good Governance. He is currently an Associate Professor in the Department of Public Administration, Lagos State University, Ojo Lagos.

Gabriel A. Akinbode is a Senior Lecturer in the Department of Psychology, University of Lagos, where he has obtained his first degree, Master Degrees and Ph.D in Industrial/Organizational and work Psychology. Research interest is in the area of Work Psychology: Leadership and supervision, Industrial Psychometrics, Occupational Health and Safety Psychology, Forensic and Environmental Psychology, Human Psychological Functioning and Dysfunctional behaviors (i.e. Territoriality, Violence, Terrorism and Aggression), Psychology and Public Policy.

Syed Ali, PhD, is a Professor of Economics Mulungushi University, Kabwe, Zambia.

Fatai A. Badru had five academic certificates at the University of Lagos, Akoka Nigeria and between 2013-2014, he was visiting and Faculty Scholar at the University of North Texas (UNT), USA for post-doc. Specialist certificate in applied gerontology. He had specialized training at Stanford University, USA for self- management of chronic health conditions and nutrition. Prof. Badru has *bio-psycho-socio-educational* training and skills. He is multi-skilled, dogged, resilient and diligent. He is a registered general and psychiatric nurse. He is a *Fellow*, West African College of Nursing (FWACN) (2005) - Faculty of Mental Health and Psychiatric Nursing. He is a certified and registered teacher with *Teachers Registration Council of Nigeria;* a trained Journalist, certified marketer from Cheshire, England; Social Work Educator and registered Medical Social Worker. He is a *Fellow*, Institute of Policy Management Development (*FIPMD*)-(2017). Professor Badru was in August 2017 conferred with the highest honour by the Nigerian Institute of Management (Chartered), as a *Fellow* (FNIM). Fatai Badru is a peer reviewer of many journals: UNILAG Journal of Humanities; UNILAG Sociological Review, (USR); The Journal of Private and Property Law; International and Comparative Journal of Peace and Environment; LAUTEC Journal of Nursing, Ogbomosho; Yoruba Studies Review (YSR) based in University of Florida, among others. He is a member of Editorial Board, Journal of Business and Social Sciences, a faculty journal of Social Sciences, UNILAG. He is the 'Managing Officer', *Journal of Society, Development and Public Health (JSDPH)*, an academic and institutional-based double-blind peer-reviewed journal. He is a member of several professional organisations. These include: International Sociological Association (ISA); African Sociological and Anthropological Association; Nigerian Sociological and Anthropological Association; International Women's Health Coalition Based in New York; Nigeria Association of Social Workers (NASoW); Nigerian Association of Social Work Educators (NASWE); Association of Medical Social Workers of Nigeria (AMSWON), among others.

Idongesit Eshiet is a Senior Lecturer with the Department of Sociology, University of Lagos, Lagos, Nigeria. She holds a Doctor of Philosophy (PhD) degree in Sociology with specialization on Gender and Development Studies. Idongesit Eshiet is passionate about issues that affect women. From this vein she has conducted and published extensively both empirical and theoretical papers on Gender and Development issues both nationally and internationally. Idongesit Eshiet believes that women's empowerment is a panacea to Africa's underdevelopment, as well as a catalyst to sustainable development. She holds membership in various local and international academic and professional bodies.

Sheriff F. Folarin (PhD) is a Professor of International Relations at Covenant University, Ota, Ogun State, Nigeria.

Leigh Nanney Hersey is an assistant professor and MPA Coordinator at the University of Louisiana at Monroe. She brings more than a dozen years of fundraising experience. She continues building on this experience through her research on philanthropy and volunteerism. Dr. Hersey earned her bachelor's degree in journalism from the University of Georgia and an M.Ed. in Athletic Administration from Temple University. Her Ph.D. in Public Administration is from Arizona State University with a graduate certificate in Nonprofit Leadership & Management.

Urooj Jabeen works as Assistant Professor of Economics, Department of Economics, Government Degree and Postgraduate College for Women, Nalgonda. Having 5 years of teaching and research experience. Holding PhD in Economics.

Johannes Mampane, PhD, is a Senior Lecturer and Researcher in the Department of Adult Education and Youth Development at the University of South Africa. His research interests lie in the fields of Gender, Health and Sexuality Studies. He advocates for social justice, inclusivity, equality and diversity issues concerning disenfranchised, vulnerable and minority populations in society.

Oluwatobi Njoaguani is a Lecturer in the Department of Political Science and International Relations, Covenant University, Ota, Ogun State, Nigeria.

Chinwe R. Nwanna (PhD) is an Associate Professor in the Department of Social Work, University of Lagos, Nigeria. Her areas of interest cover reproductive health including HIV and AIDS, child protection and juvenile justice system, Urbanization and labour migration. She has published widely both in national and international reputable peer-reviewed journals and books. She is also a recipient of many grants and awards for academic and research excellence and affiliated to numerous professional associations.

Index

G

H

I

L

M

N

O

P

Q

R

S

T

U

V

W

www.ingramcontent.com/pod-product-compliance
Lightning Source LLC
LaVergne TN
LVHW061547290926
849162LV00004B/939